Contemporary Issues in Database Design and Information Systems Development

Keng Siau,
University of Nebraska – Lincoln, USA

IGI PUBLISHING

Hershey • New York

Acquisition Editor: Kristin Klinger
Senior Managing Editor: Jennifer Neidig
Managing Editor: Sara Reed
Assistant Managing Editor: Sharon Berger
Development Editor: Kristin Roth
Copy Editor: Jillian Kozak
Typesetter: Michael Brehm
Cover Design: Lisa Tosheff
Printed at: Yurchak Printing Inc.

Published in the United States of America by
        IGI Publishing (an imprint of IGI Global)
        701 E. Chocolate Avenue
        Hershey PA 17033
        Tel: 717-533-8845
        Fax: 717-533-8661
        E-mail: cust@igi-pub.com
        Web site: http://www.igi-pub.com

and in the United Kingdom by
        IGI Publishing (an imprint of IGI Global)
        3 Henrietta Street
        Covent Garden
        London WC2E 8LU
        Tel: 44 20 7240 0856
        Fax: 44 20 7379 0609
        Web site: http://www.eurospanonline.com

Library of Congress Cataloging-in-Publication Data

Contemporary issues in database design and information systems development / Keng Siau, editor.
       p. cm.
  Summary: "This book presents the latest research ideas and topics on databases and software development. It provides a representation of top notch research in all areas of database and information systems development"--Provided by publisher.
  Includes bibliographical references and index.
  ISBN 978-1-59904-289-3 (hardcover) -- ISBN 978-1-59904-291-6 (ebook)
  1. Database design. 2. System design. I. Siau, Keng, 1964-
  QA76.9.D3C67135 2007
  005.74--dc22
                          2006039748

British Cataloguing in Publication Data
A Cataloguing in Publication record for this book is available from the British Library.

Advances in Database Research Series

ISSN: 1537-9299

The Advances in Database Research (ADR) Book Series publishes original research publications on all aspects of database management, systems analysis and design, and software engineering. The primary mission of ADR is to be instrumental in the improvement and development of theory and practice related to information technology and management of information resources. The book series is targeted at both academic researchers and practicing IT professionals.

Contemporary Issues in Database Design and Information Systems Development
Copyright 2007 * ISBN 978-1-59904-289-3 (hardcover)

Research Issues in Systems Analysis and Design, Databases and Software Development
Copyright 2007 * ISBN 978-1-59904-927-4 (hardcover)

Advanced Topics in Database Research, Volume 5
Copyright 2006 * ISBN 1-59140-935-7 (hardcover)

Advanced Topics in Database Research, Volume 4
Copyright 2005 * ISBN 1-59140-471-1 (hardcover)

Advanced Topics in Database Research, Volume 3
Copyright 2004 * ISBN 1-59140-471-1 (hardcover)

Advanced Topics in Database Research, Volume 2
Copyright 2003 * ISBN 1-59140-255-7 (hardcover)

Advanced Topics in Database Research, Volume 1
Copyright 2002 * ISBN 1-93078-41-6 (hardcover)

Order online at www.igi-pub.com or call 717-533-8845 x10 –
Mon-Fri 8:30 am - 5:00 pm (est) or fax 24 hours a day 717-533-8661

Contemporary Issues in Database Design and Information Systems Development

Table of Contents

Preface

Considering today's business environment that emphasizes data, information, and knowledge as essential components of an organization's resource, database management has quickly become an integral part of many business applications. Information systems development activities enable many organizations to effectively compete and innovate. New database and information systems applications are constantly being developed. Examples of new applications include data warehousing, data mining, OLAP, data visualization, visual query languages, and many more.

Similar to previous advances in database research volumes, we are once again proud to present a compilation of excellent cutting-edge research, conducted by experts from all around the world. This volume, *Contemporary Issues in Database Design and Information Systems Development*, is a collection of the latest research-focused chapters on database design, database management, and information systems development for researchers and academicians. It is also designed to serve technical professionals in the industry with hopes in enhancing professional understanding of the capabilities and features of new database and information systems applications, and forthcoming technologies.

The following are short descriptions of each chapter:

Chapter I, "Towards an Ontology for Information Systems Development: A Contextual Approach," presents an ISD ontology that aims to provide an integrated conceptualization of ISD through anchoring it on a contextual approach. The authors believe that the ISD ontology can promote the achievement of a shared understanding of contextual aspects in ISD.

Chapter II, "Ontological Analysis of KAOS Using Separation of References," applies a structured approach to describe a well-known goal-oriented language, KAOS, by mapping it onto a philosophically grounded ontology. The structured approach facilitates language interoperability because when other languages are described using the same approach, they become mapped onto the same ontology.

Chapter III, "Applying UML for Modeling the Physical Design of Data Warehouses," presents modeling techniques for physical design of data warehouses using component diagrams and deployment diagrams of UML. The authors illustrate the techniques with a case study.

Chapter IV, "Supporting the Full BPM Life-Cycle Using Process Mining and Intelligent Redesign," shows that techniques for process mining and intelligent redesign can be used to offer better support for the redesign and diagnosis phases, and thus close the BPM life-cycle. It also briefly reports on the work done in the context of the ProM tool, which is used as framework to experiment with such techniques.

Chapter V, "Efficient Placement and Processing in Shared-Nothing Data Warehouses," discusses the basic system architecture and the design of data placement and processing strategy. This chapter compares the shortcomings of a basic horizontal partitioning for the environment with a simple design that produces efficient placements. The discussion and results provide important information on how low-cost efficient data warehouse systems can be built.

Chapter VI, "Factors Affecting Design Decisions for Customer Relationship Management Data Warehouses," presents a robust multidimensional starter model that supports CRM analyses. This chapter also introduces two new measures, percent success ratio and CRM suitability ratio by which CRM models can be evaluated, and identification of and classification of CRM queries can be performed. A preliminary heuristic for designing data warehouses to support CRM analyses is also reported in the chapter.

Chapter VII, "Effective Processing of XML-Extended OLAP Queries Based on a Physical Algebra," extends previous work on the logical federation of OLAP and XML data sources by presenting simplified query semantics, a physical query algebra, and a robust OLAP-XML query engine as well as the query evaluation techniques.

Chapter VIII, "Is There a Difference Between the Theoretical and Practical Complexity of UML?" offers the idea that the complexity metrics previously developed and used to analyze UML can be differentiated into theoretical and practical complexities. The chapter also discusses better ways of learning and using UML.

Chapter IX, "Data Quality: An Assessment," presents results from a large-scale survey of Australian CPA members regarding data quality. The research investigates and reports major stakeholders' opinions on the importance of critical success factors affecting data quality and the actual performance on each of those factors.

Chapter X, "Cover Stories for Key Attributes: Expanded Database Access Control," extends the multi-level secure (MLS) data model to include non-key related cover stories so that key attributes can have different values at different security levels. This chapter presents the necessary model changes and modifications to the relational algebra that are required to implement cover stories for key.

The ten chapters in this volume provide a snapshot of top notch research in all areas of the database and information systems development. We are confident that this volume will provide insightful and valuable resources for scholars and practitioners alike.

Professor Keng Siau, PhD, University of Nebraska – Lincoln
E.J. Faulkner Professor of Management Information Systems
Editor-in-Chief, Advances in Database Research Book Series
Editor-in-Chief, Journal of Database Management

Chapter I

Towards an Ontology for Information Systems Development:
A Contextual Approach

Mauri Leppänen, University of Jyväskylä, Finland

Abstract

This chapter presents an ISD ontology, which aims to provide an integrated conceptualization of ISD through anchoring it upon a contextual approach. The ISD ontology is composed of concepts, relationships, and constraints referring to purposes, actors, actions, and objects of ISD. It is presented as a vocabulary with explicit definitions and in meta models in a UML-based ontology representation language. We believe that although not complete the ISD ontology can promote the achievement of a shared understanding of contextual aspects in ISD. It can be used to analyze and compare existing frameworks and meta models and as a groundwork for engineering new ISD methods, and parts thereof.

Introduction

To advance the understanding, management, and improvement of an information system development (ISD) process, a large number of frameworks, meta models, and reference models, in short ISD artifacts, have been suggested for ISD and ISD methods. Most of these artifacts view ISD from perspectives that are based on some specific approaches, such as a transformation approach (e.g., Moynihan, 1993; Saeki, Iguchi, Wen-yin, & Shinokara, 1993; Song, & Osterweil, 1992), a decision-making approach (e.g., Grozs et al., 1997; Jarke, Jeusfeld, & Rose, 1990; NATURE Team, 1996; Rolland, Souveyet, & Moreno, 1995), a problem-solving approach (e.g., Bodard et al., 1983; Jayaratna, 1994; Sol, 1992), or a learning approach (e.g., Iivari, 1990). In consequence of this, ranges of concepts and constructs in these artifacts are rather narrow. To enable a more comprehensive view on ISD, ISD should be conceived as a context with all its meaningful facets, distinguishing purposes, actors, actions, objects, facilities, locations, and time aspects.

The purpose of this study is to present an ISD ontology that is based on a contextual approach. An ontology is a kind of framework unifying different viewpoints, thus functioning in a way like a lingua-franga (Chandrasekaran, Josephson, & Benjamins, 1999). More specifically, an ontology is an explicit specification of a conceptualization of some part of reality that is of interest (Gruber, 1993). The *ISD ontology* provides a conceptualization of contextual aspects of ISD through a vocabulary with explicit definitions. To enhance the clarity and preciseness of the ontology, we deploy a UML-based ontology representation language to describe the ISD ontology in meta models.

The ISD ontology is intended for descriptive, analytical, and constructive use. For the descriptive purposes, the ontology offers concepts and a vocabulary for conceiving, understanding, structuring, and presenting contextual aspects of ISD. In the analytical sense, the ontology can be used to analyze and compare existing ISD artifacts. In the constructive sense, the ontology is to support the engineering of new ISD artifacts, such as ISD models, techniques and methods, by providing a coherent and consistent groundwork for them. The ISD ontology is not yet a complete ontology. It should be enhanced with more specialized concepts and constructs and assessed for validity and applicability by empirical tests.

The rest of the chapter is structured as follows. In the next section, we define the notions of context and contextual approach and apply them to define the ISD ontology. Moreover, we discuss the process of engineering the ISD ontology. In the next five sections, we specify four main ISD domains (i.e., ISD purpose domain, ISD actor domain, ISD action domain, and ISD object domain) and inter-relationships between them. After that, we make a comparative analysis of current ISD artifacts to find out how comprehensive they are in terms of contextual features and demonstrate the usability of the ISD ontology as an analytical means. The chapter concludes with discussions and implications to research and practice.

Contextual Approach and Engineering of the ISD Ontology

Based on a large literature review on the notion of context in several disciplines, such as knowledge representation and reasoning (e.g., Brezillon, Pomerol, & Saker, 1998; Sowa, 2000), pragmatics (e.g., Levinson, 1983), computational linguistics (e.g., Clark & Carlson, 1981), sociolinguistics (e.g., Halliday, 1978), organizational theory (e.g., Weick, 1995), and information systems (e.g., Kyng & Mathiassen, 1997), we came to the following generic conclusion: *context* denotes a whole that is composed of things connected to one another with contextual relationships. A thing captures its meaning through the relationships it has to the other things in that context. To recognize a proper set of contextual concepts and relationships, we drew upon relevant meaning theories. Based on the three topmost layers in the semiotic ladder (Stamper, 1975), we identified semantics (especially case grammar by Fillmore (1968)), pragmatics (Levinson, 1983), and the activity theory (Engeström, 1987) to be such theories. They concern sentence context, conversation context, and action context, correspondingly.

In the case grammar (Fillmore, 1968), the sentence in its basic structure consists of a verb and one or more noun phrases, each associated with the verb in a particular case relationship. The notion of case is a language element that is more stable than surface-level grammatical terms. Cases identify "certain types of judgments human beings are capable of making about the events which are going on around them, judgments about such matters as who did, who it happened to, and what got changed," (Fillmore, 1968, p. 24). Pragmatics is "the study of the ability of language users to pair sentences with the contexts in which they would be appropriate," (Levinson, 1983, p. 23). In such a study, one of the most essential issues deals with deixis. Deixis concern the ways in which "languages encode or grammaticalize features of the context of expressions or speech events," (Levinson, 1983, p. 54). Traditional categories of deixis are person, place, and time deixis. The activity theory presents highly general propositions of the nature of human activity, incorporating several psychological, educational, cultural, and developmental approaches (Leont'ev, 1978). According to the theory, there exists a fundamental type of context called activity. Activity is a minimal meaningful context for individual actions. The systemic structure of human activity (Engeström, 1987; Engeström, 1999), built upon the activity theory, is composed of seven fundamental concepts: subject, object, tool, rules, community, division of labor, and outcome from the activity. The concepts are interrelated in terms of mediating; for instance, the relationship between subject and object is mediated by tools.

Based on this groundwork, we define seven domains which serve concepts for specifying and interpreting contextual phenomena. These contextual domains are: purpose, actor, action, object, facility, location, and time (Figure 1). To structure

Figure 1. Contextual framework

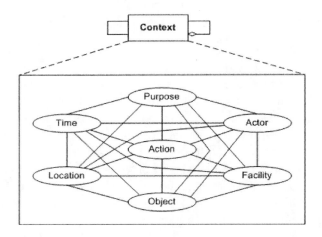

the concepts within and between these domains, we specify the Seven S's scheme: *For Some* purpose, *Somebody* does *Something* for *Someone,* with *Some* means, *Sometimes* and *Somewhere*.

Implied from the above, we define the *contextual approach* to be the approach according to which individual things in reality are seen to play specific roles in a certain context, and/or to be contexts themselves. The contexts can be decomposed into more elementary ones and related to one another through inter-context relationships (see Figure 1). As far as we know, there is no approach or framework similar to our contextual framework. The closest is the so-called "5Ws and H" scheme, which is based on six interrogatives ("Why," "Who," "What," "Where," "When," and "How"). This scheme is used for many purposes (see Couger, Higgins, & McIntyre, 1993; Curtis, Kellner, & Over, 1992; Krogstie & Sölvberg, 1996; Short, 1991; Sowa & Zachman, 1992; Söderström, Anderson, Johannesson, Perjons, & Wangler, 2002; Zachman, 1987; Zultner, 1993). However, no theoretical grounds have been presented for the scheme, and it addresses only part of the contextual aspects that our framework does.

We have previously applied the contextual approach to enterprise ontologies (Leppänen, 2005b), method engineering (Leppänen, 2005c), and method integration (Leppänen, 2006). Here, we apply it to ISD. Based on the contextual approach, we see *information system development* as a context in which ISD actors carry out ISD actions to produce ISD deliverables contributing to a renewed or a new IS, by means of ISD facilities, in a certain organizational and spatio-temporal context, in order to satisfy ISD stakeholders' goals. The notion provides an extensive view on contextual aspects of ISD. ISD work is guided by ISD requirements and goals which, through elicitations and negotiations, become more complete, shared, and formal

(Pohl, 1993). ISD work is carried out by ISD actors with different motives, skills, and expertise, acting in different roles in organizational units that are situationally established. ISD work is composed of various ISD actions, structured in concordance with the selected ISD approaches and ISD methods, and customized according to conventions in the organization. The final outcome of ISD is a new or improved information system composed of interacting social arrangements and technical components. ISD work consumes resources (e.g., money and time) and is supported by computer-aided tools (e.g., CASE tools). ISD actors, ISD deliverables, and ISD facilities are situated in certain locations, and are present in certain times.

Based on the aforementioned, we define the ISD ontology as follows: the *ISD ontology* provides concepts and constructs for conceiving, understanding, structuring, and representing contextual phenomena in ISD. The concepts and constructs in the ISD ontology have been defined in a deductive and inductive manner, as described below. Following an iterative procedure, derived from the works of Uschold and King (1995), Fernandez-Lopez, Gomez-Perez, Pazos-Sierra, and Pazos-Sierra (1999), and Staab, Schnurr, Studer, and Sure (2001), we first determined the purpose, domain, and scope of the ontology. Second, we searched for disciplines and theories that address social and organizational contexts and derived the basic categorization of concepts into contextual domains from them. Third, we analyzed current ISD artifacts to find out whether they include parts that could be reused and integrated, as such or refined, into our ontology. Fourth, we defined the basic concepts and constructs for each contextual domain, and when possible, adapted and integrated those concepts of other artifacts that were found suitable. We also closely examined empirical studies on ISD practice (e.g., Sabherwal & Robey, 1993) to test the relevance of our concepts. Our aim was to establish a common core from which concepts and constructs for specific ISD approaches could be specialized. Results from this gradually evolving conceptualization were presented in a graphical form. The last step of the ontology engineering procedure was evaluation. We applied a set of quality criteria for ontologies (e.g., Burton-Jones, Storey, Sugumaran, & Ahluwalia, 2005; Gruber, 1995; Uschold, 1996; Weinberger, Te'eni, & Frank, 2003) to evaluate the ISD ontology in several stages.

In the following, we define four of the ISD domains, namely the ISD purpose domain, the ISD actor domain, the ISD action domain, and the ISD object domain. The other three ISD domains are excluded due to the page limit. For each domain, we define basic concepts, relationships, and constraints. After that, we delineate relationships between the domains. A more profound discussion about the ISD domains and the inter-domain relationships is given in Leppänen (2005a).

ISD Purpose Domain

The *ISD purpose domain* embraces all those concepts and constructs that refer to goals, motives, or intentions of someone or something in the ISD context (Figure 2). The concepts show a direction in which to proceed, a state to be attained or avoided, and reasons for them. Reasons, expressed in terms of requirements, problems, and so forth, are used to indicate why certain goals have been or should be set up. The ISD purpose domain is highly important as, only through its concepts, it is possible to demonstrate "Why" an ISD effort, an ISD action, or an ISD deliverable is necessary.

An *ISD goal* expresses a desired state or event with qualities and quantities, related to the ISD context as a whole, or to some parts thereof. *Hard ISD goals* have pre-specified criteria for the assessment of the fulfillment of ISD goals, while *soft ISD goals* have not (Lin & Ho, 1999; Mylopoulos, Chung, Liao, & Wang, 2001). An *ISD requirement* is some quality or performance demanded in and for the ISD context. It is a statement about the future (NATURE Team, 1996). ISD requirements can be classified along three orthogonal dimensions (Pohl, 1993): specification, representation, and agreement. In the specification dimension, the requirements range from opaque to complete. The representation dimension categorizes requirements into informal, semi-formal, and formal requirements. The agreement dimension reflects the fact that ISD requirements are initially personal views which are negotiated and agreed on to achieve a shared view. ISD requirements become goals in the ISD context after agreement has been reached. All the requirements cannot be accepted as goals, since their fulfillment may, for instance, go beyond the resources available. An *ISD problem* is the distance or mismatch between the prevailing ISD state and the state

Figure 2. Meta model of the ISD purpose domain

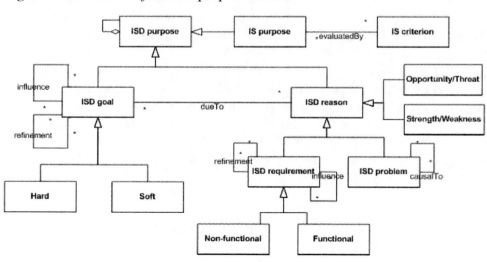

reflected by the ISD goals (cf. Goldkuhl, & Röstling, 1988; Jayaratna, 1994). ISD problems can be structured, semi-structured, or non-structured.

Strength signifies something in which one is good, something that is regarded as an advantage and thus increases the possibility of gaining something better. *Weakness* means something in which one is poor, something that could or should be improved or avoided. The "one" can refer to any contextual element of the ISD, the current IS, the business system deploying the IS, or the environment. *Opportunity* is a situation or condition favorable for attainment of a goal (Webster, 1989). *Threat* is a situation or condition that is a risk for attainment of a goal.

Some of the ISD purposes directly concern an IS. They are called *IS purposes*, and they are sub-divided into IS goals and IS reasons, and further into IS requirements, IS opportunities/IS threats, and IS strengths/IS weaknesses. IS goals are specified to guide the ISD actors in the selection and implementation of IS requirements. A large variety of IS criteria are available for the evaluation and comparison of IS designs, implementation, and use. An *IS criterion* is a standard of judgment presented as an established rule or principle for evaluating some feature(s) of an IS in terms of IS purposes. Next, we consider the IS requirements more closely. An *IS requirement* stands for a condition or capability of the IS needed by an IS client or an IS worker to solve a problem or achieve a goal (cf. IEEE, 1990). The IS requirements are divided into functional requirements and non-functional requirements. A *functional IS requirement* specifies what the IS should do and for whom (cf. Pohl, 1993). A *non-functional IS requirement* sets some quality attributes upon the services or functions offered by the IS (Cysneiros, Leite, & Neto, 2001; Pohl, 1994). It can be expressed in terms of performance, safety, quality, maintainability, portability, usability, reliability, confidentiality, security, accuracy, and so forth (Chung, Nixon, Yu, & Mylopoulos, 2000, Cysneiros et al., 2001).

The ISD goals, as well as the ISD requirements, are related to one another through refinement relationships and influence relationships. A *refinement relationship* means that an ISD goal can be reached when certain ISD goals, also known as satisfying or argumentation goals (Cysneiros et al., 2001), below it in the ISD goal hierarchy are fulfilled (Rolland, Souveyet, & Ben Achour, 1998). An *influence relationship* means that an ISD goal impacts the achievement of another ISD goal (Kavakli, & Loucopoulos, 1999; Loucopoulos et al. 1998,). The influence can be either positive or negative. The ISD goals with negative interrelationships are referred to as conflicting requirements (Chung et al., 2000, Lee, Xue, & Kuo, 2001). A *causalTo relationship* between two ISD problems means that the appearance of one ISD problem (e.g., lack of human resources) is at least a partial reason for the occurrence of another ISD problem (e.g., delays in the delivery of project outcomes).

ISD Actor Domain

The *ISD actor domain* consists of all those concepts and constructs that refer to the human and active part of the ISD context (Figure 3). Actors own, communicate, transform, design, interpret, and code objects in the ISD context. They are responsible for or responsive to triggering and causing changes in the states of objects. They are also aware of their own intentions and capable, at least to some degree, of reacting to fulfill their goals.

An *ISD actor* is an ISD human actor or an ISD administrative actor who is, one way or another, involved in the ISD context. An *ISD human actor* means an individual person or a group of persons contributing to ISD work. An *ISD administrative actor* is an ISD position or a composition of ISD positions. An *ISD position* is a post of employment occupied by an ISD human actor in the ISD context (e.g., a database administrator). It is identified with a title, composed of the defined ISD roles, and equipped with a set of skill or capability characterizations (i.e., expertise profile). A capability denotes a skill or attribute of the personal behavior, according to which action-oriented behavior can be logically classified (Acuna & Juristo, 2004). An *ISD role* is a collection of ISD responsibilities and authorities, stipulated in terms of ISD actions (e.g., a member of a project team, a database expert). Some ISD roles may not be included in any ISD position but are nonetheless played by one or more persons.

Figure 3. Meta model of the ISD actor domain

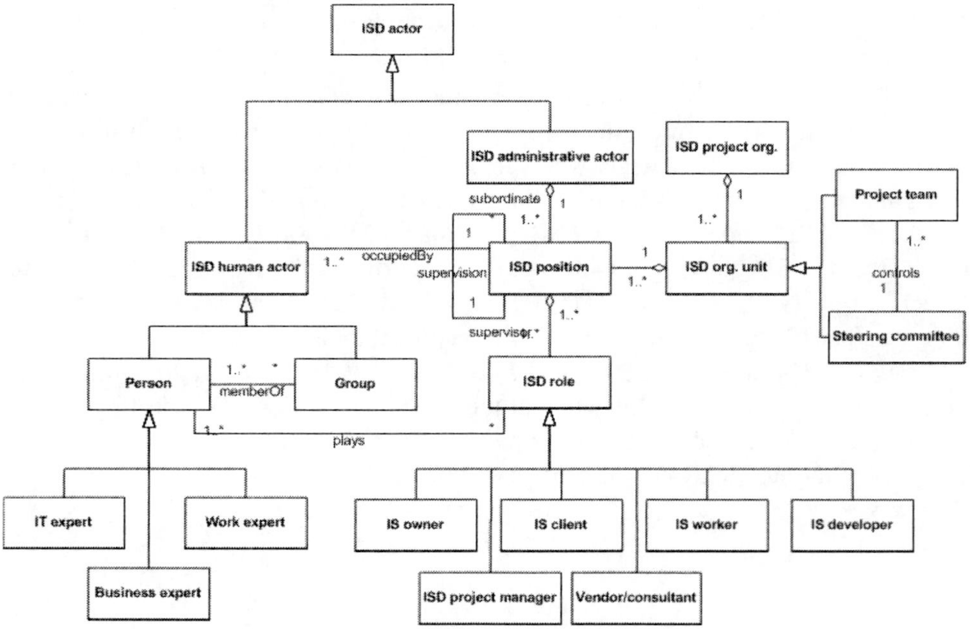

In ISD literature, ISD roles are categorized in various ways, for instance, into social roles and technical roles (Constantine, 1991). Divisions among social ISD roles, in turn, have been derived from the views of seeing ISD as a problem solving process (a problem owner and a problem solver (Vessey & Conger, 1994)), as a change process (a facilitator or a change agent, and a change implementator (Rettig & Simons, 1993)), as a political process (self-interest agents employed to perform some services on behalf of the principals (Markus & Björn-Andersen, 1987; Robey, 1984)), or as a learning process (a mentor and a student or an apprentice). The divisions among technical ISD roles have resulted from applying, for instance, a stakeholder view (e.g., Macauley, 1993), a software business view (e.g., Franckson, 1994), or an organizational view.

In this work, we base our categorization of the ISD roles on the works of Checkland (1988), Baskerville (1989), Sabherwal and Robey (1995) and Mathiassen (1998). We distinguish between six major ISD roles that unify social and technical features of ISD work. The roles are: an IS owner, an IS client, an IS worker, an IS developer, an ISD project manager, and a vendor/consultant.

An *IS owner* has a financial interest in the IS and, thereby, the responsibility for and the authority of making decisions on the IS as though it were his/her property. An IS owner does not directly intervene in ISD project work, unless the project is so large and important that it has a major impact on the organization. An *IS client* is the ISD role player for whom the IS is to be developed. They are a beneficiary or a "victim" of the IS (Graham, Henderson-Sellers, & Younessi 1997). Therefore, they are expected to be active in specifying information requirements for the IS in terms of contents, form, time, and media. An IS client also acts as an informant for inquiries on business processes, and as an acceptor of the designs of ISD deliverables (cf. the so-called client tests) and plans of re-engineering business processes and work contents (cf. Brinkkemper, 1990). An *IS worker* works with the current IS and/or is going to work with the new IS. They collect, record, store, transmit, and processe data with or without the help of the computerized information system, in order to produce information needed by IS clients. An *IS developer* attempts to satisfy the needs and requirements put forward by ISD actors in the other roles. For that purpose, their analyses IS requirements and IS goals expressed and refines them into more elaborated specifications, searches for social and technical solutions, and implements those selected. An *ISD project manager* makes plans on how to organize the ISD effort. This includes making plans on ISD phases, schedules, milestones, base lines, resource allocations, and so forth. A *vendor/consultant* role is played by a person from outside the organization. With this role, more expertise on some specific organizational or technical issues is imported to the ISD project. Expertise may be related to technologies (e.g., J2EE platforms, Web services), methods (e.g., agile methods), techniques (e.g., TQM) or the like, that is something new to the organization.

The ISD work is mostly organized in the form of a project. An *ISD project* is a temporary effort with well-defined objectives and constraints, the established organization, a budget and a schedule, launched for the accomplishment of the ISD effort. An *ISD project organization* is a composition of ISD positions, ISD roles, and ISD teams, wherein the responsibility, authority, and communication relationships are defined (cf. Fife, 1987). A large project organization is composed of several *organizational units*. The most common units in the ISD project are a steering committee and a project team. A *steering committee* carries the responsibility for the overall management of the ISD project. A *project team* is collected for the execution of the ISD effort. If a project is large, there may be a need for several teams acknowledging their share in the common responsibility for developing the IS. The day-to-day management is delegated to the project manager, who directs and controls the actions of specialists in various disciplines.

Some of the positions and roles in the ISD project are full-time vacancies due to the amount of responsibilities and time they require. Some other positions and roles do not require full-time commitment. The most suitable person is sought for each ISD position. In order to be suitable, the person's skill and experience profile has to match with the expertise profile stated for the ISD position (cf. Acuna & Juristo, 2004). Sometimes, no person with the required qualifications can be found from inside the organization, and thus an expert (e.g., a consultant) from another organization is hired.

The persons involved in ISD can be categorized into IT experts, business experts, and work experts according to their expertise. *IT experts* are persons whose education, skills, experience, as well as their former positions, are related to information technology and/or ISD methods. *Business experts* are knowledgeable in business strategies, policies, markets, competition, trends, legislation, and so on, in other words, in matters relating to ways of doing business, in general or in the organization. *Work experts* master daily routines, for instance, in marketing, invoicing, production planning, and inventory control.

ISD Action Domain

The *ISD action domain* comprises all those concepts and constructs that refer to deeds in the ISD context (Figure 4). We use the general term *ISD action* to signify those deeds. ISD actions are carried out to manage and execute an ISD effort. By them, procedures, rules, and policies are selected, customized, incorporated, implemented, and applied to produce desirable ISD deliverables. To manage this extensive variety of ISD actions, several categorizations of ISD actions and ISD processes have been presented in the literature of the field (e.g., Curtis et al., 1992; Dowson, 1987). We recognize eight fundamental ISD action structures that are orthogonal to, and highly intertwined with, one another. They are categorized into two groups:

generic action structures and ISD-specific action structures. The *generic action structures* include the decomposition structure, the control structure (i.e., sequence, selection, iteration), and the temporal structure (e.g., overlapping, parallel, disjoint). The *ISD-specific action structures* are the ISD management-execution structure, the ISD workflow structure, the ISD phase structure, and the IS modeling structure. The aforementioned ISD action structures provide a natural basis for specializing and decomposing ISD work into more specific ISD actions, if needed. Each ISD action is governed by one or more *ISD rules* with the ECAA structure (Herbst, 1995). In the following, we consider the ISD-specific action structures in more detail.

Figure 4. Meta model of the ISD action domain

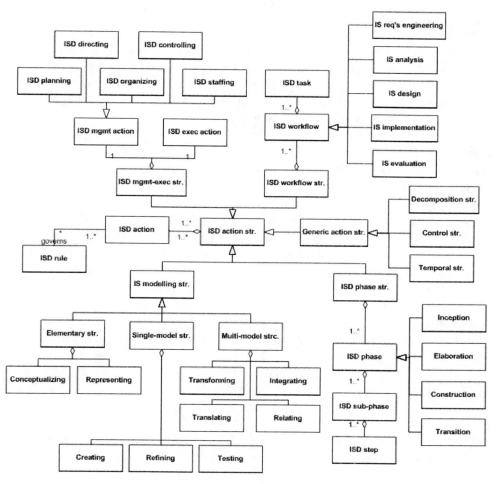

ISD Management-Execution Structure

An ISD can be seen as a functional and behavioral unity that is composed of two kinds of actions—ISD execution actions and ISD management actions. *ISD execution actions* aim to produce the required ISD deliverables under the guidance and control of ISD management. These actions include, for instance, knowledge acquisition about the current IS and problems encountered there, requirements specification for a new IS, and design and implementation of specifications into a working system. Besides the actions directly contributing to the deliverables, ISD execution actions comprise supporting actions, for instance, training and guidance of users, installation of computer-aided engineering environments, and so forth.

ISD management actions plan, organize, staff, direct, and control ISD work (Thayer, 1987). *ISD planning* refers to all those actions that specify the goals of an ISD project and the strategies, policies, programs, and procedures for achieving them. These actions involve partitioning managerial and technical requirements into measurable actions and tasks, determining milestones, priorities, and schedules, estimating necessary resources and figuring them as a budget. *ISD organizing* signifies all those actions that are needed to design an instance-level structure of ISD execution actions and authority relationships between them. These comprise aggregating actions into ISD roles and ISD positions, establishing organizational units, and specifying titles, duties, qualifications, and relationships of ISD positions. *ISD staffing* designates all those actions that are needed to fill the ISD positions and to keep them filled. These comprise, for instance, recruiting qualified people, orientating them into technical and social environment, and educating them in required methods, skills and equipment. *ISD directing* is needed for, among others, clarifying the assignments of ISD personnel, assigning actions to organizational units, teams and individuals, motivating and inspiring personnel, and resolving disagreements between personnel and between the ISD project and external stakeholders. *ISD controlling* aims to ensure that execution actions are carried out according to the plans. This includes developing standards of performance and methods for the assessments, establishing reporting and monitoring systems, measuring and auditing progress and status of a project and so on.

ISD Workflow Structure

ISD work is composed of various ISD workflows. An *ISD workflow* is a coherent composition of ISD actions, which are organized to accomplish some ISD process, share the same target of action, and produce valuable results for stakeholders. A part of an ISD workflow is called an *ISD task*. ISD workflows can be identified among the ISD management actions as well as among the ISD execution actions. In the following, we consider them in the context of the ISD execution actions.

We distinguish between five core ISD workflows: IS requirements engineering, IS analysis, IS design, IS implementation, and IS evaluation (cf. Jacobson, Booch, & Rumbaugh, 1999). Besides the core workflows, there are supporting workflows, such as configuration and change management (cf. Kruchten, 2000), but these are not discussed here.

IS requirements engineering aims to identify and elicit IS clients' and IS workers' requirements for the IS, as well as to establish and maintain, at least to some extent, agreement on what the IS should do and why. IS requirements engineering is commonly decomposed into feasibility study, requirements analysis, requirements definition, and requirements specification (Sommerville, 1998). *IS analysis* means the ISD workflow which models the problem domain. The purpose is to represent the business system in a manner that is natural and concise enough, and to make an overall description of the information system that is easy to maintain. The workflow starts with looking at the system from outside. *IS design* means the ISD workflow that models the solution domain. It involves the elicitation, innovation, and evaluation of design options in the form of IS models on various levels of abstraction. IS design looks at the system from inside. A decision is also made on which part of the system will be automated and which part is to be implemented as a manual system. *IS implementation* fleshes out the architecture and the system as a whole by carrying IS models into effect. There are two kinds of implementation actions. Technical implementation, known as construction in Iivari (1991), involves all those actions that are necessary to construct/acquire and carry into effect technical components of the IS. Organizational implementation, referred to as institutionalisation in Iivari (1991), means actions that are necessary to create and change social norms, conventions, procedures and structures for information processing. *IS evaluation* aims at assessing the current system, as well as specifications, designs and implementations made for the new system. Evaluation is based on quality criteria derived from functional and non-functional requirements.

ISD Phase Structure

ISD work is commonly organized to be carried out in sequential phases. An *ISD phase* stands for a composition of ISD actions which are executed between two milestones, and by which a well-defined set of goals is met, ISD deliverables are completed, and decisions are made on whether or not to move into the next phase (cf. Kruchten, 2000). *Milestones* are synchronization points where ISD management makes important business decisions and ISD deliverables have to be at a certain level of completion (Heym & Österle, 1992). Major milestones are used to establish baselines (see the next section for the definition of a baseline).

A large variety of phases with different names are suggested in ISD methods. Without wanting to commit to any of them, we have selected, as an example of the ISD phase structure, the set of phases defined in Jacobson et al. (1999) and Kruchten (2000). It comprises four phases: IS inception, IS elaboration, IS construction, and IS transition. *IS inception* focuses on understanding overall requirements and determining the scope of the development endeavor. The scope is specified to understand what the architecture has to cover, what the critical risks are, and to determine the boundaries for costs and schedule. IS inception resolves the feasibility of the proposed system development. In *IS elaboration* the focus is on detailed requirements engineering, but some actions of systems design and implementation aimed at prototyping can also be carried out. Prototyping is deployed to better understand IS requirements, to test the established architecture and/or to learn how to use certain tools or techniques. The phase ends with the baseline for the next phase. *IS construction* focuses on design and implementation of the system. During this phase, a software product, which is ready for the initial operational release, is produced. Also, plans for organizational changes are "operationalized" for realization. *IS transition* is entered when at least some part of the ISD baseline is mature enough to be deployed. The phase comprises, for instance, beta testing, fixing bugs, adjusting features, conversion of operational databases, and training of users and maintainers. At the end of the phase, the final product has been delivered and the new organizational arrangements are fully in operation.

IS Modeling Structures

Modeling has a focal role in the full range of ISD actions. It is a necessary and frequently used means, equally utilized in the ISD management actions and in the ISD execution actions. Here, we focus on modeling in the latter, and refer to it as *IS modeling*. The target of IS modeling can be the existing IS, or the new IS. We refer to the structures of actions targeted at the IS models as the *IS modeling structures*. There are three kinds of IS modeling structures: the elementary modeling structure, the single-model action structure, and the multi-model action structure. The *elementary modeling structure* comprises actions that are always present in IS modeling. These are conceptualizing and representing. By *conceptualizing*, relevant perceptions of the existing reality and conceptions of the imagined reality are interpreted, abstracted, and structured according to some conceptual model (cf. Falkenberg et al., 1998). *Representing* is an ISD action through which conceptions are made "visible" and suitable for communication.

The *single-model action structure* comprises IS modeling actions that involve a single model at a time. These actions are creating, refining, and testing. *Creating* is an ISD action by which an IS model is conceptualized and represented for some specific use. After creation, some corrections, modifications, and extensions are often required. These IS modeling actions are called *refining* actions. *Testing* is an ISD action by which a model is verified and/or validated against the given quality criteria (cf. Krogstie, 1995). The *multi-model action structure* comprises IS modeling actions that involve, in some way or another, two or more IS models at the same time. These actions include transforming, translating, relating, and integrating. *Transforming* is an ISD action by which conceptions structured according to one IS model are transformed into conceptions structured according to another IS model. *Translating* is an ISD action through which conceptions represented in some language are translated into another language. Two or more IS models are *related,* or mapped, to one another by finding common concepts within the models, or by defining "bridging" relationships between the concepts of the models. *Integrating* means an ISD action by which a new model is crafted by assembling together concepts and constructs of two or more other IS models.

ISD Object Domain

The *ISD object domain* comprises all those concepts and constructs that refer to something to which ISD actions are directed (Figure 5). In the current ISD frameworks, these are commonly called deliverables (Cimitile & Visaggio, 1994; Glasson, 1989; Heym & Österle, 1992), artifacts (Hruby, 2000; Jacobson et al., 1999), decisions (Rose & Jarke, 1990; Wild, Maly, & Liu, 1991), products (Aoyama, 1993; Hazeyama & Komiya, 1993; Saeki et al., 1993), work products (Firesmith & Henderson-Sellers, 1999; Henderson-Sellers & Mellor, 1999; Hidding, 1997), and design products (Olle et al., 1988). To emphasize the linguistic nature of the ISD objects and our orientation to the ISD objects in the execution part of the ISD, we use the generic term *ISD deliverable*. An ISD deliverable can be, on the elementary level, an assertion, a prediction, a plan, a rule, or a command, concerning the ISD itself, the existing IS, the new IS, the object system (OS), or the utilizing system. We use the term 'OS_{ISD} construct' to denote some part of the object systems of ISD. The *signifies relationship* expresses a semantic relationship between an ISD deliverable and an OS_{ISD} construct.

Figure 5. Meta model of the ISD object domain

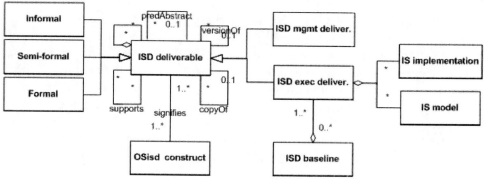

The *ISD management deliverables* mean plans for, decisions on, directives for, and assessments of goals, positions, actions, deliverables, locations, and so forth, in the ISD context. The *ISD execution deliverables* refer to descriptions about and prescriptions for why, what, and how information processing is carried out or is to be carried out in the current IS context or in a new IS context, respectively. The ISD execution deliverables comprise informal drafts and scenarios as well as more formal presentations. The former include instructions and guidelines, produced for IS actors, in the form of training materials, handbooks, and manuals. The latter are presented in *IS models* (e.g., ER schemes, DFDs, and program structure charts) or they are *IS implementations* of those models (e.g., software modules, prototypes, files, and databases).

Some of the ISD execution deliverables are specified to be parts of the ISD baselines with milestones in the project plan. An *ISD baseline* is a set of reviewed and approved ISD deliverables that represents an agreed basis for further evolution and development, and can be changed only through a formal procedure such as configuration and change management (Jacobson et al., 1999). The ISD deliverables are presented in some language(s). Presentations may be informal, semi-formal, or formal, including texts, lists, matrices, program codes, diagrams, charts, maps, pictures, voices, and videos.

The ISD deliverables are related to one another through five kinds of relationships. An ISD deliverable can be a *part of* another ISD deliverable. An ISD deliverable can be used as input to, or as a prescription for, another ISD deliverable (e.g., the *supports relationship*). That is, an ER schema is a major input to a relational schema. An ISD deliverable can be the next *version of* or a *copy of* another ISD deliverable. Finally, an ISD deliverable may be more abstract than another ISD deliverable in terms of predicate abstraction (e.g., the *predAbstract relationship*).

ISD Inter-Domain Relationships

In the previous sections, the ISD concepts and constructs have been considered from the perspective of one ISD domain at a time. The ISD domains are, however, inter-related in many ways. Figure 6 presents, on a general level, the meta model, which illustrates essential *inter-domain relationships*. In the meta model, one or more main concepts from each of the ISD domains are depicted and related to concepts of the other domains. The multiplicities associated with the relationships are omitted to keep the model simple. It is not possible here to discuss all the inter-domain relationships. There are, however, two relationships, which are worth considering in more detail. These are the viewedBy relationship and the strivesFor relationship. Through these relationships, we can highlight the nature of ISD as an organizational

Figure 6. Meta model of ISD inter-domain relationships

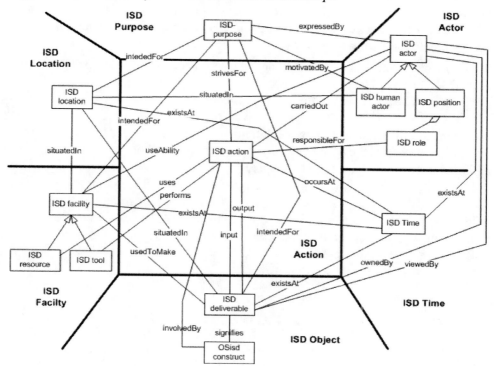

context in which ISD actors have different views and opinions and ISD actions are guided by design rationale.

The *viewedBy relationship* between an ISD deliverable and an ISD actor means that an ISD deliverable represents views, insights, or opinions of a certain ISD actor. If associated with a person or a group of persons, an ISD deliverable represents a subjective or inter-subjective view whereas, if associated with an ISD position, an ISD deliverable reflects an organizational view or a so-called "official" view. According to Stamper (1992), there is no knowledge without an agent. With this relationship, an ISD deliverable can be tied to the person or organization concerned. Through this relationship, it is also possible to bring forth differences between, and conflicts among, the views. The significance of this relationship is acknowledged especially in requirements engineering literature. Lang and Duggan (2001) identify the "proposes" relationship between "Stakeholder" and "User requirement" in the meta model for RM-tool (requirements management tool). Lee et al. (2001) argue that the requirements should be incorporated into the stakeholders who have presented them. This is important because of traceability, conflict resolving, and prioritization. Nuseibeh, Finkelstein, and Kramer (1996) outline the ViewPoints framework, which acknowledges the existence of ISD actors "who hold multiple views on a system and its domain," (p. 267). The multiple views can be specified and managed by the use of the ViewPoint pattern (Finkelstein, Kramer, Nuseibeh, Finkelstein, & Goedicke, 1992) which is related to the ViewPoint owner. The owner acts as the domain knowledge provider.

The *strivesFor relationship* between an ISD action and an ISD purpose means that an ISD action is to be conducted, is conducted, or was conducted for satisfying a certain goal. The goal may be inferred from encountered problems, specified requirements, observed opportunities, or perceived threats. The strivesFor relationship, together with the input and output relationships between the ISD actions and the ISD deliverables, can be used to express design rationale (Goldkuhl, 1991; Ramesh & Jarke, 2001). Design rationale means a "record of reasons behind the decision taken, thus providing a kind of design/project memory and a common medium of communication among different people," (Louridas & Loucopoulos, 1996, p. 1). With this knowledge, it is possible to trace reasons for the decisions made and actions taken, which is especially beneficial in requirements engineering (e.g., Nguyen & Swatman, 2003; Pohl, Dömges, & Jarke, 1997).

Comparative Analysis

The ISD literature suggests a large number of frameworks, meta models, and reference models, here called ISD artifacts, for ISD and ISD methods. In this section, we report on a comparative analysis of prominent ISD artifacts. By the analysis, we want first to find out what kinds of ISD artifacts exist, how comprehensive they are in terms of contextual features, and how they are focused on ISD domains. Second, we aim to test the usability of our ISD ontology as an analytical means for these kinds of exercises. In the following, we first categorize ISD artifacts and make the selection of artifacts for the analysis. Then, we give an overview of the selected ISD artifacts and describe the results from the overall analysis. Finally, we deepen the analysis through the four ISD domains of the ISD ontology.

Categorization and Selection of ISD Artifacts

ISD artifacts can be categorized into two main groups: those that describe and structure ISD, and those that have been developed to analyze, compare, and/or engineer ISD methods, or parts thereof. Artifacts in the first group characterize and structure ISD in terms of ISD paradigms (e.g., Hirschheim & Klein, 1989; Iivari, Hirschheim, & Klein, 1998), ISD approaches (e.g., Hirschheim, Klein, & Lyytinen, 1995; Iivari, Hirschheim & Klein, 2001; Wood-Harper & Fitzgerald, 1982), or ISD processes (e.g., Boehm, 1988; Iivari, 1990; NATURE Team, 1996). Most of the artifacts in this group have too narrow a scope or too general a view of ISD to be of interest to us. There are, however, some exceptions. For instance, Iivari (1990) presents the hierarchical spiral model, which provides an abstract explanatory model for IS/SW design process, containing strictly defined concepts and constructs in a large variety.

Another set of ISD artifacts, included in the first group, consists of meta models and ontologies for structuring specific aspects of ISD. For instance, NATURE Team (1996) proposes the process meta model, which views requirements engineering process as being composed of inter-linked contexts. OMG (2005) presents the Software Process Engineering Meta model (SPEM), which describes a concrete software development process or a family of related software development processes. Ontologies such as the Frisco framework (Falkenberg et al., 1998) and the Bunge-Wand-Weber model (e.g., Wand & Weber, 1990) cover elementary phenomena of the IS quite well, but they do not extend sufficiently to the ISD layer. There are also some ontologies that do concern systems engineering (Kishore, Zhang, & Ramesh, 2004; Kitchenham et al., 1999; Ruiz, Vizcaino, & Piattini, 2004), but their focus is on software maintenance and thus, they are too specific to serve as a generic and comprehensive basis for the conceptualization of ISD.

The ISD artifacts in the second group have been constructed for the analysis, comparison, and engineering of ISD methods. Some of them provide feature lists (e.g., Bodart et al., 1983; Karam & Casselman, 1993; Kelly, & Sherif, 1992; Maddison et al., 1984; Rzevski, 1983), taxonomies (e.g., Blum, 1994; Brandt, 1983), or frameworks (e.g., Iivari & Kerola, 1983; Jayaratna, 1994). Although these artifacts have been built with concepts referring to specific aspects of ISD, the concepts are not explicitly defined, nor are they properly structured. The same holds for contingency frameworks (e.g., Davis, 1982; Kettinger, Teng, & Guha, 1997; Lin & Ho, 1999; Punter & Lemmen, 1996; van Slooten & Brinkkemper, 1993; van Swede & van Vliet, 1993).

The second group also contains meta models that model notations and conceptual contents of ISD methods. Here, we are especially interested in those ISD artifacts that specify the conceptual contents of the ISD methods. These kinds of ISD artifacts are the "framework for understanding" of Olle et al. (1988), the framework and the reference model of Heym and Österle (1992), the meta model of Saeki et al. (1993), the framework of Song and Osterweil (1992), the framework of a situational method of Harmsen (1997), the views of ISD methods of Gupta and Prakash (2001), the conceptual model of the MMC (method for method configuration) Framework of Karlsson and Ågerfalk (2004), and the OPEN Process Framework (OPF) Meta model of Firesmith and Henderson-Sellers (2002).

We apply the following criteria in the selection of ISD artifacts for our analysis: (a) ISD artifacts describe, in a comprehensive and detailed manner, contextual phenomena of ISD, and (b) ISD artifacts are presented in an unambiguous and precise manner, preferably in a graphical notation. Based on these criteria, we decided to select the following seven ISD artifacts from the two groups (in alphabetical order): Firesmith and Henderson-Sellers (2002), Harmsen (1997), Heym and Österle (1992), Iivari (1990), NATURE Team (1996), Saeki et al. (1993), and Song and Osterweil (1992).

Overall Analysis

Here, we first present a brief overview of the selected ISD artifacts and then analyze them in terms of five aspects: purpose of use, theoretical basis, ISD approach(es) applied, representation form, and acts for validation of the artifacts.

The OPEN Process Framework (OPF) meta model of Firesmith and Henderson-Sellers (2002) defines the core process concepts (e.g., Endeavor, Language, Producer, Stage, Work Product, and Work Unit) and their most important sub-concepts and associations, needed to specify a process component. Process components can be selected, combined, customized, and instantiated to form an actual process with the method. Harmsen (1997) proposes a framework, a language, and a procedure to assemble a situational method from building blocks, called method fragments. For defining the method fragments, Harmsen (1997) specifies an ontology and a process classification system. Heym and Österle (1992) present a framework and a reference model for describing, understanding, and comparing ISD methods. The framework categorizes the aspects of ISD methods into three perspectives: application type, life cycle, and model focus. In the reference model, the methodology knowledge is decomposed and structured by five meta models. Iivari (1990) presents the hierarchical spiral model for ISD and SE, based on the conceptual framework for IS/SW product (Iivari, 1989). The NATURE Project (NATURE Team, 1996; Grosz et al., 1997) suggests the process meta model based on the novel approaches to theories underlying requirements engineering (NATURE) approach, according to which requirements engineering is modeled as a set of related contexts in which a decision is made on how to process product parts and in which order. Saeki et al. (1993) present a meta model for representing software specification and design methods, with the purpose of covering "atomic concepts" that are common to all the methods. Song and Osterweil (1992) suggest the base framework for the identification of method components that are comparable in different methods. It is composed of two parts: the type framework and the function framework.

The summary of the overall analysis of the seven ISD artifacts is presented in Table 1. The table also includes the ISD ontology. As can be seen in the table, only two of the artifacts (e.g., Iivari, 1990; NATURE Team, 1996) have been established on some theoretical grounds. Most of the artifacts have been abstracted from exist-

Table 1. Overview of the ISD artifacts

Reference	Artifact	Purpose	Theoretical basis	ISD approach	Representation	Validation
This study	ISD ontology	For understanding the ISD domain and for analyzing and constructing other ISD artifacts	Theories underlying the contextual approach, ISD theories, ISD methods	Contextual approach	Definitions in English, meta models in a graphical notation	Used as a framework in a number of comparative analyses and in the construction of methodical support for method engineering
Firesmith et al. (2002)	Process framework Meta model	For specifying process/ method components	Not mentioned	Not recognizable	Definitions in English, the Meta model in a graphical notation	Used as a basis for the repository of more than 1000 open-source reusable process/ method components, and in a number of projects
Harmsen (1997)	Ontology (MDM), Process classification system	For assembling a situational method from method fragments	Literature on existing ISD methods	Not recognizable	Definitions in English, supported with the use of first order predicate calculus	Implemented as a prototype of the Method Base System that has been used in empirical studies
Heym and Österle (1992)	Framework, Reference model	For describing, understanding, and comparing ISD methods	Not mentioned	Not recognizable	Definitions in English, the reference model in a graphical notation	Used as the data model of the MERET tool, which has been deployed in several organizations
Iivari (1990)	Hierarchical spiral model	For providing an abstract explanatory model for the IS/SW design process	Socio-cybernetics, Information economics	Transformation, learning process, and decision-oriented approaches	Definitions in English	Not mentioned
NATURE Team (1996), Grosz et al. (1997)	Process meta model	For defining way-of-working in requirements engineering	Theory of plans	Decision-oriented approach	Definitions in English, partly in a graphical notation	Widely used in succeeding projects; Prototype
Saeki et al. (1993)	Meta model	For representing software specification and design methods	Not mentioned	Transformation approach	Definitions in English, partly in a graphical notation	Used to develop representations of ISD methods; Prototype
Song and Osterweil (1992)	Framework	For identifying method components	Abstracted from existing methods	Transformation approach	Definitions in English	Not mentioned

ing ISD methods. For some artifacts, no grounds are mentioned. This situation is unsatisfactory for two reasons. First, only with a sound theoretical background can we be sure that phenomena of ISD become properly conceived, understood, and structured. Second, abstracting from existing methods in a way replicates properties of the methods and does not help recognize phenomena of ISD not addressed by the methods. We have built our ISD ontology by following the contextual approach, which has been established on several underlying theories, including semantics, pragmatics, and activity theory. In addition, we have utilized a large array of ISD literature on ISD theories and ISD methods.

In the ISD artifacts, divergent approaches are applied: a transformation approach (Iivari, 1990; Saeki et al., 1993; Song and Osterweil, 1992), a decision-oriented approach (Iivari, 1990; NATURE Team, 1996), and a learning approach (Iivari, 1990). Some of the artifacts give no preference for approaches. The ISD ontology is based on the contextual approach, thus enabling a comprehensive conceptualization of ISD. Most of the ISD artifacts have been validated by using them for intended purposes, for instance, for describing and/or integrating methods, and/or as a basis for prototypes of computer-aided method engineering (CAME) environments. The OPF meta model of Firesmith and Henderson-Sellers (2002) has been the most largely used. The ISD ontology has been used as a basis of a number of comparative analyses and in the construction of methodical support for method engineering (Leppänen, 2005a). It still needs more acts for validation.

Contextual Analysis

For the second part of the analysis, called the contextual analysis, we categorized the concepts and constructs of the selected ISD artifacts to match them with the four ISD domains of the ISD ontology (see Appendix 1 for the categorization based on the ISD action domain). The following findings and conclusions can be made from the contextual analysis. Only two artifacts (Harmsen, 1997; NATURE Team, 1996) provide, even to some extent, concepts and constructs for the ISD purpose domain. This is unfortunate when taking into account that most of the artifacts have been constructed for describing, analyzing, and comparing the ISD methods. Concepts of the ISD purpose domain are important for presenting, for instance, motivations and design rationale (Ramesh and Jarke, 2001). Three of the artifacts (Firesmith and Henderson-Sellers, 2002; Harmsen, 1997; Heym and Österle, 1992) explicitly offer concepts and constructs for the ISD actor domain. Concepts of the ISD actor domain should be included in the ISD artifacts in order to bring out, for instance, who are responsible for ISD actions, and differences between viewpoints of ISD actors (Nuseibeh et al., 1996).

Emphasis in all the artifacts is on the ISD action domain, as expected when considering the ISD approaches they apply. From the ISD action structures, the ISD management-execution structure is included in Heym and Österle (1992) and, to some extent, in NATURE Team (1996). The ISD workflow structure can be recognized in Harmsen (1997) and Heym and Österle (1992). The ISD phase structure is included in Iivari (1990) and on a general level in Heym and Österle (1992). Parts of the IS modeling structures can be found in Heym and Österle (1992), Iivari (1990), NATURE Team (1996) and Song and Osterweil (1992). The control structures are embedded in every artifact, except in Song and Osterweil (1992). Firesmith and Henderson-Sellers (2002) define a number of sub-concepts, including phase and workflow, but do not suggest any specific action structures based on them. Only four artifacts (Harmsen, 1997; Heym and Österle, 1992; Iivari, 1990; Song and Osterweil, 1992) present categorizations of ISD deliverables grounded on some specific criteria (e.g., IS perspectives, IS domains). Firesmith and Henderson-Sellers (2002) present a large array of work product types, mostly technical ones, but without any explicit categorization.

From the seven artifacts, the ontology of Harmsen (1997) appeared to be the most comprehensive in terms of contextual aspects of ISD, although it has some shortcomings in the coverage of the ISD actor domain and the ISD action domain. The artifact can also be criticized for its incoherence and ill-structuredness. The second most comprehensive is the reference model of Heym and Österle (1992). Although it lacks the concepts of the ISD purpose domain, it provides basic concepts and constructs for the three other ISD domains. The OPF meta model by Firesmith and Henderson-Sellers (2002) also ignores the ISD purpose domain, but it defines some concepts and sub-concepts for the ISD actor domain, the ISD action domain and the ISD object domain. The hierarchical spiral model by Iivari (1990) mainly focuses on the ISD action domain. In addition, it defines some concepts for the ISD object domain. The process meta model by NATURE Team (1996) introduces the notion of intention for the ISD purpose domain, ignores the ISD actor domain, and provides a number of decision-based concepts for the ISD action domain as well as a few concepts for the ISD object domain. The meta model of Saeki et al. (1993) and the framework of Song and Osterweil (1992) were found to be insufficient in all the ISD domains, although they are aimed to provide a comprehensive basis for the description, analysis, and comparison of ISD methods. They address neither the ISD purpose domain, nor the ISD actor domain. Also, the other ISD domains are inadequately covered.

Discussions and Implications

In this chapter, we have presented a coherent and comprehensive conceptualization of ISD in the form of ISD ontology. The ISD ontology is based on the contextual approach grounded on fundamental theories with special interest in contextual phenomena (Engeström, 1987; Fillmore, 1968; Levinson, 1983). Implied from the contextual approach, ISD is seen as a context composed of concepts and constructs of seven contextual domains referring to purposes, actors, actions, objects, facilities, locations, and time. For four of these domains, we have defined a wide range of concepts and constructs and presented them in meta models.

The ISD ontology differs favorably from existing ISD artifacts as the comparative analysis in the previous section showed. The current artifacts mostly lack a theoretical background, and they have mainly been abstracted from existing ISD methods. They are also narrow-scoped as regards the contextual aspects of ISD. The ISD ontology provides a large array of concepts and constructs within four contextual domains, organized into a flexible and easy-to-adapt structure.

In the literature of ontology engineering (e.g. Burton-Jones et al., 2005; Gruber, 1993; Uschold, 1996), a large variety of quality criteria for ontologies are suggested. Most commonly, these criteria comprise clarity, consistency, coherence, comprehensiveness, extendibility, and applicability. It is not possible here to consider the quality of the ISD ontology in detail in terms of all of these criteria. We can, however, say that, through the application of the contextual approach, we have pursued achievement of a conceptualization of ISD that is natural and understandable (cf. face validity), thus advancing clarity. Semi-formal meta models have helped us evaluate consistency and coherency of our ontology. We have carefully checked that there are no contradictions between the definitions of concepts and constructs (consistency), and each concept is related, directly or indirectly, to every other concept (coherence). Comprehensiveness is relative to the needs for which the ontology is used. Extendibility has been furthered by the use of a modular structure of the ontology. Our aim has been that the ISD ontology can be extended with new and more specialized concepts without the revision of existing definitions.

The ultimate measure of the quality of an ontology is, naturally, its applicability. The ISD ontology has been intended for descriptive, analytical, and constructive use. In the previous sections, we deployed the ISD ontology to analyze and compare existing ISD artifacts. As far as we know, this kind of comparative analysis has not been made before. In this analytical task, the ISD ontology appeared to be a useful means to uncover the orientation, emphases, and limitations of the ISD artifacts as regards how they reflect contextual features of ISD. We have also deployed the ISD ontology as groundwork for engineering an ISD method ontology and a methodical skeleton for method engineering (MEMES) (Leppänen, 2005a). In this construction task, the ISD ontology offered a rich set of concepts and constructs for specifying and elaborating the semantic contents of an ISD method, and helped distinguish structure and relate approaches, actions, and deliverables for MEMES.

The ISD ontology is not without limitations. It should be enhanced with concepts and constructs of the ISD facility domain, the ISD location domain, and the ISD time domain. Second, many of the concepts included in the ontology should be further specialized to cover more specific phenomena of ISD. Third, the set of constraints expressed through multiplicities in the meta models should be supplemented with more ISD specific constraints. Fourth, to help the application of the ISD ontology in different kinds of situations, it is necessary to specify perspective-based sub-sets of the ISD ontology. For instance, to analyze and construct those parts of ISD methods that concern IS analysis, it is often sufficient to use only concepts and constructs in the ISD purpose domain, the ISD action domain, and the ISD object domain. These kinds of perspective-based sub-sets have already been outlined in Leppänen (2005a). Fifth, the ISD ontology should be employed in more kinds of situations to gain stronger evidence of its applicability. This is also necessary for validating the ontology.

In future research, our aim is, besides making the ISD ontology more complete, to apply it in the analysis of empirical ISD research and ISD approaches. For the former purpose, we have collected conceptual models underlying empirical studies on "how things are in ISD practice." These models are, typically, quite specific, which hinders building an integrated understanding of the results of the studies. The ISD ontology may serve as a coherent and comprehensive foundation to define, analyze, and integrate conceptual models, in the way an ontology for software maintenance (Kitchenham et al., 1999) is suggested to be used. For the latter purpose, we will examine ISD artifacts, applying specific ISD approaches more closely to find out how their commitments are visible in aggregates of concepts within each ISD domain and in inter-domain relationships.

References

Acuna, S., & Juristo, N. (2004). Assigning people to roles in software projects. *Software—Practice and Experience, 34*(7), 675-696.

Aoyama, M. (1993). Concurrent development process model. *IEEE Software, 10*(4), 46-55.

Baskerville, R. (1989). Logical controls specification: An approach to information systems security. In H. Klein & K. Kumar (Eds.), *Proceedings of the IFIP Working Conference on Systems Development for Human Progress* (pp. 241-255). Amsterdam: Elsevier Science Publishers.

Blum, B. (1994). A taxonomy of software development methods. *Communications of the ACM, 37*(11), 82-94.

Bodart, F., Flory, A., Leonard, M., Rochefeld, A., Rolland, C., & Tardieu, H. (1983). Evaluation of CRIS 1 I.S. development methods using a three cycles framework. In T. Olle, H. Sol, & C. Tully (Eds.), *Information systems design methodologies: A feature analysis* (pp. 191-206). Amsterdam: Elsevier Science Publishers.

Boehm, B. (1988). A spiral model of software development and enhancement. *IEEE Computer, 21*(5), 61-72.

Brandt, I. (1983). A comparative study of information systems design methodologies. In T. Olle, H. Sol, & C. Tully (Eds.), *Information systems design methodologies—A feature analysis* (pp. 9-36). Amsterdam: Elsevier Science.

Brezillon, P., Pomerol, J.-Ch., & Saker I. (1998). Contextual and contextualized knowledge: An application in subway control. *International Journal of Human-Computer Studies, 48*(3), 357-373.

Brinkkemper, S. (1990). *Formalization of information systems modeling.* Unpublished dissertation thesis, University of Nijmegen, Amsterdam.

Burton-Jones, A., Storey, V., Sugumaran, V., & Ahluwalia, P. (2005). A semiotic metric suite for assessing the quality of ontologies. *Data & Knowledge Engineering, 55*(1), 84-102.

Chandrasekaran, B., Josephson, J., & Benjamins, R. (1999). What are ontologies, and why do we need them? *IEEE Intelligent Systems, 14*(1), 20-26.

Checkland, P. (1988). Information systems and system thinking: Time to unite? *International Journal of Information Management, 8*(4), 239-248.

Chung, L., Nixon, B., Yu, E., & Mylopoulos, J. (2000). *Non-functional requirements in software engineering.* Dordrecht: Kluwert.

Cimitile, A., & Visaggio, G. (1994). A formalism for structured planning of a software project. *International Journal of Software Engineering and Knowledge Engineering, 4*(2), 277-300.

Clark, H., & Carlson, T. (1981). Context for comprehension. In J. Long, & A. Baddeley (Eds.), *Attention and performance,* IX (pp. 313-330). Hillsdale, NJ: Erlbaum.

Constantine, L. (1991). Building structured open teams to work. In *Proceedings of Software Development '91.* San Francisco: Miller-Freeman.

Couger, D., Higgins, L., & McIntyre, S. (1993). (Un)structured creativity in information systems organizations. *MIS Quarterly, 17*(4), 375-397.

Curtis, B., & Kellner, M., & Over, J. (1992). Process modeling. *Comm. of the ACM, 35*(9), 75-90.

Cysneiros, L., Leite, J., & Neto, J. (2001). A framework for integrating non-functional requirements into conceptual models. *Requirements Eng.*, 6(2), 97-115.

Davis, G. (1982). Strategies for information requirements determination. *IBM Systems Journal, 21*(1), 4-30.

Dowson, M. (1987). Iteration in the software process. In *Proceedings of the 9th International Conference on Software Engineering* (pp. 36-39). New York: ACM Press.

Engeström, Y. (1987). *Learning by expanding: An activity theoretical approach to developmental research.* Helsinki: Orienta-Konsultit.

Engeström, Y. (1999). Activity theory and individual and social transformation. In Y. Engeström, R. Miettinen, & R. Punamäki (Eds.), *Perspectives on activity theory. Cambridge* (pp. 19-38). UK: Cambridge University Press.

Falkenberg, E., Hesse, W., Lindgreen, P., Nilsson, B., Oei, J., Rolland, C., Stamper, R., van Asche, F., Verrijn-Stuart, A., & Voss, K. (1998) Framework of information system concepts. *The Frisco Report (Web edition)*, IFIP.

Falkenberg, E., Nijjsen, G., Adams, A., Bradley, L., Bugeia, P., Campbell, A., Carkeet, M., Lehman, G., & Shoesmith, A. (1983). Feature analysis of ACM/PCM, CIAM, ISAC and NIAM. In T. Olle, H. Sol, & C. Tully (Eds.), *Information systems design methodologies—A feature analysis* (pp. 169-190). Amsterdam: Elsevier Science Publishers.

Fernandez-Lopez, M., Gomez-Perez, A., Pazos-Sierra, A., & Pazos-Sierra, J. (1999). Building a chemical ontology using METONTOLOGY and the ontology design environment. *IEEE Intelligent Systems & Theory Applications,* 4(1), 37-46.

Fife, D. (1987). How to know a well-organized software project when you find one. In R. Thayer (Ed.), *Tutorial: Software engineering project management* (pp. 268-276). Washington: IEEE Computer Society Press.

Fillmore, C. (1968). The case for case. In E. Bach, & R. T. Harms (Eds.), *Universals in linguistic theory* (pp. 1-88). New York: Holt, Rinehart, and Winston.

Finkelstein, A., Kramer, J., Nuseibeh, B., Finkelstein, L., & Goedicke, M. (1992). Viewpoints: A framework for integrating multiple perspectives in system development. *International Journal of Software Engineering and Knowledge Engineering, 1*(2), 31-58.

Firesmith, D., & Henderson-Sellers, B. (1999). Improvements to the OPEN process Meta model. *Journal of Object-Oriented Programming, 12*(7), 30-35.

Firesmith, D., & Henderson-Sellers, B. (2002). *The OPEN process framework. An introduction,* Harlow: Addison-Wesley.

Franckson, M. (1994). The Euromethod deliverable model and its contributions to the objectives of Euromethod. In A. Verrijn-Stuart & T. Olle (Eds.), *Methods and associated tools for the information systems life cycle* (pp. 131-150). Amsterdam: Elsevier Science Publishers.

Glasson, B. (1989). Model of system evolution. *Information and Software Technology, 31*(7), 351-356.

Goldkuhl, G. (1991). Information systems design as argumentation—An investigation into design rationale as a conceptualization of design. In K. Ivanov (Ed.), *Proceedings of the 14ᵗʰ Information Systems Research Seminar in Scandinavia (IRIS 1991)*, Umeå, Sweden.

Goldkuhl, G., & Röstling, A. (1988). *Förändringsanalysi—arbetsmetodik och förhållningssätt för goda förändringsbelust.* Lund: Studentlitterature.

Graham, I., Henderson-Sellers, B. & Younessi, H. (1997). *The OPEN process specification.* Reading: Addison-Wesley.

Grosz, G., Rolland, C., Schwer, S., Souveyet, C., Plihon, V., Si-Said, S., Achour, C., & Gnaho, C. (1997). Modelling and engineering the requirements engineering process: An overview of the NATURE approach. *Requirements Engineering, 2*(2), 115-131.

Gruber, T. (1993). A translation approach to portable ontology specification. *Knowledge Acquisition, 5*(2), 119-220.

Gruber, T. (1995). Towards principles for the design of ontologies used for knowledge sharing. *International Journal of Human-Computer Studies, 43*(5/6), 907-928.

Gupta, D., & Prakash, N. (2001). Engineering methods from method requirements specifications. *Requirements Engineering, 6*(3), 135-160.

Halliday, M. (1978). *Language as social semiotic: The social interpretation of meaning.* London: Edwards Arnold.

Harmsen, F. (1997). *Situational method engineering.* Unpublished doctoral dissertation, University of Twente, Moret, Ernst, & Young Management Consultants, The Netherlands.

Hazeyama, A., & Komiya S. (1993). Software process management system supporting the cooperation between manager and developers. In S. Brinkkemper, & F. Harmsen (Eds.), *Proc. of the Fourth Workshop on the Next Generation of CASE Tools* (pp. 183-188). Memoranda Informatica 93-32, University of Twente, The Netherlands

Henderson-Sellers, B., & Mellor, S. (1999). Tailoring process-focused OO methods. *Journal of Object-Oriented Programming, 12*(4), 40-45.

Herbst, H. (1995). A meta model for business rules in systems analysis. In J. Iivari, K. Lyytinen, & M. Rossi (Eds.), *Advanced information systems engineering* (LNCS 932, pp. 186-199). Berlin: Springer.

Heym, M., & Österle, H. (1992). A reference model for information systems development. In K. Kendall, K. Lyytinen, & J. DeGross (Eds.), *Proceedings of the IFIP WG 8.2 Working Conference on the Impacts on Computer Supported Technologies on Information Systems Development* (pp. 215-240). Amsterdam: Elsevier Science Publishers.

Hidding, G. (1997). Reinventing methodology: Who reads it and why? *Comm. of the ACM, 40*(11), 102-109.

Hirschheim, R., & Klein, H. (1989). Four paradigms of information systems development. *Comm. of the ACM, 32*(10), 1199-1216.

Hirschheim, R., Klein, H., & Lyytinen, K. (1995). *Information systems development—Conceptual and philosophical foundations*. Cambridge: Cambridge University Press.

Hruby, P. (2000). Designing customizable methodologies. *Journal of Object-Oriented Programming, 13*(8), 22-31.

IEEE (1990). *Standard glossary of software engineering terminology*. IEEE Standard 610.12-1990.

Iivari, J. (1989). Levels of abstraction as a conceptual framework for an information system. In E. Falkenberg & P. Lindgren (Eds.), *Information system concepts: An in-depth analysis* (pp. 323-352). Amsterdam: Elsevier Science Publishers.

Iivari, J. (1990). Hierarchical spiral model for information system and software development. Part 2: Design process. *Information and Software Technology, 32*(7), 450-458.

Iivari, J. (1991). A paradigmatic analysis of contemporary schools of IS development. *European Journal of Information Systems, 1*(4), 249-272.

Iivari, J., Hirschheim, R., & Klein, H. (1998). A paradigmatic analysis of contrasting IS development approaches and methodologies. *Information Systems Research*, 9(2), 164-193.

Iivari, J., Hirschheim, R., & Klein, H. (2001). A dynamic framework for classifying information systems development methodologies and approaches. *Journal of Management Information Systems*, 17(3), 179-218.

Iivari, J., & Kerola, P. (1983). A sociocybernetic framework for the feature analysis of information systems design methodologies. In T. Olle, H. Sol, & C. Tully (Eds.), *Proceedings of the IFIP WG 8.1 Working Conference on Feature Analysis of Information Systems Development Methodologies* (pp. 87-139). Amsterdam: Elsevier Science Publishers.

Jacobson, I., Booch, G., & Rumbaugh, J. (1999). *The unified software development process*. Reading: Addison-Wesley.

Jarke, M., Jeusfeld, M., & Rose, T. (1990). A software process data model for knowledge engineering in information systems. *Information Systems, 15*(1), 85-116.

Jayaratna, N. (1994). *Understanding and evaluating methodologies: NIMSAD—A systemic framework*. London: McGraw-Hill.

Karam, G. & Casselman, R. (1993). A cataloging framework for software development methods. *IEEE Computer, 26*(2), 34-46.

Karlsson, F., & Ågerfalk, P. (2004). Method configuration: Adapting to situational characteristics while creating reusable assets. *Information and Software Technology, 46*(9), 619-633.

Kavakli, V., & Loucopoulos, P. (1999). Goal-driven business process analysis application in electricity deregulation. *Information Systems, 24*(3), 187-207.

Kelly, J., & Sherif, Y. (1992). Comparison of four design methods for real-time software development. *Information and Software Technology, 34*(2), 76-82.

Kettinger, W., Teng, J., & Guha S. (1997). Business process change: A study of methodologies, techniques, and tools. *MIS Quarterly, 21*(1), 55-80.

Kishore, R., Zhang, H., & Ramesh, R. (2004). A Helix-Spindel model for ontological engineering. *Comm. of the ACM, 47*(2), 69-75.

Kitchenham, B., Travassos, H., von Mayrhauser, A., Nielssink, F., Schneiderwind, N., Singer, J., Takada, S., Vehvilainen, R., & Yang, H. (1999). Towards an ontology of software maintenance. *Journal of Software Maintenance: Research and Practice, 11*(6), 365-389.

Krogstie, J. (1995). *Conceptual modeling for computerized information systems support in organizations*. Unpublished doctoral dissertation, University of Trondheim, Norway.

Krogstie, J., & Sölvberg, A. (1996). A classification of methodological frameworks for computerized information systems support in organizations. In B. Brinkkemper, K. Lyytinen, & R. Welke (Eds.), *Proceedings of the IFIP TC8 WG 8.1/8.2 Working Conference on Method Engineering: Principles of Method Construction and Tool Support* (pp. 278-295). London: Chapman & Hall.

Kruchten, P. (2000). *The rational unified process: An introduction*. Reading: Addison-Wesley.

Kyng, M., & Mathiassen, L. (Eds.). (1997). *Computers and design in context*. Cambridge, MA: MIT Press.

Lang, M., & Duggan, J. (2001). A tool to support collaborative software requirements management. *Requirements Engineering, 6*(3), 161-172.

Lee, J., Xue, N.-L., & Kuo, J.-Y. (2001). Structuring requirement specifications with goals. *Information and Software Technology, 43*(2), 121-135.

Leont'ev, A. (1978). *Activity, consciousness, and personality*. Englewood Cliffs, NJ: Prentice-Hall.

Leppänen, M. (2005a). *An ontological framework and a methodical skeleton for method engineering.* Unpublished doctoral dissertation, University of Jyväskylä, Finland.

Leppänen, M. (2005b). A context-based enterprise ontology. In G. Guizzardi & G. Wagner (Eds.), *Proceedings of the International Workshop on Vocabularies, Ontologies, and Rules for the Enterprise (VORTE '05),* Enchede, The Netherlands (pp. 17-24).

Leppänen, M. (2005c). Conceptual analysis of current ME artifacts in terms of coverage: A contextual approach. In J. Ralyté, Per Ågerfalk, & N. Kraiem (Eds.), *Proceedings of the 1st International Workshop on Situational Requirements Engineering Processes (SREP '05),* Paris (pp. 75-90).

Leppänen, M. (2006). Contextual method integration. In *Proceedings of the Conference on Information Systems Development (ISD 2006),* Budapest, Hungary.

Levinson, S. (1983). *Pragmatics.* London: Cambridge University Press.

Lin, C.-Y., & Ho, C.-S. (1999). Generating domain-specific methodical knowledge for requirements analysis based on methodology ontology. *Information Sciences, 114*(1-4), 127-164.

Loucopoulos, P., Kavakli, V., Prekas, N., Rolland, C., Grosz, G., & Nurcan, S. (1998). *Using the EKD approach: The modelling component.* ELEKTRA—Project No. 22927, ESPRIT Programme 7.1.

Louridas, P., & Loucopoulos, P. (1996). A framework for evaluating design rationale methods. In K. Siau & Y. Wand (Eds.), *Proceedings of the Workshop on Evaluation of Modeling Methods in Systems Analysis and Design (EMMSAD '96).*

Macauley, L. (1993). Requirements capture as a cooperative activity. In *Proceedings of the IEEE International Symposium on Requirements Engineering* (pp. 174-181). IEEE Computer Science Press.

Maddison, R., Baker, G., Bhabuta, L., Fitzgerald, G., Hindle, K., Song, J., Stokes, N., & Wood, J. (1984). Feature analysis of five information system methodologies. In T. Bemelmans (Ed.), *Beyond productivity: Information systems for organizational effectiveness* (pp.277-306). Amsterdam: Elsevier Science Publishers.

Markus, M., & Björn-Andersen, L. (1987). Power over users: Its exercise by system professionals. *Comm. of the ACM, 30*(6), 498-504.

Mathiassen, L. (1998). Reflective systems development. *Scandinavian Journal of Information Systems, 10*(1/2), 67-117.

Moynihan, T. (1993). Modelling the software process in terms of the system representations and transformation steps used. *Information and Software Technology, 35*(3), 181-188.

Mylopoulos, J., Chung, L., Liao, S., & Wang, H. (2001). Exploring alternatives during requirements analysis. *IEEE Software, 18*(1), 92-96.

NATURE Team (1996). Defining visions in context: Models, processes, and tools for requirements engineering. *Information Systems, 21*(6), 515-547.

Nguyen, L., & Swatman, P. (2003). Managing the requirements engineering process. *Requirements Engineering, 8*(1), 55-68.

Nuseibeh, B., Finkelstein, A., & Kramer, J. (1996). Method engineering for multi-perspective software development. *Information and Software Technology, 38*(4), 267-274.

Olle, T., Hagelstein, J., MacDonald, I., Rolland, C., Sol, H., van Assche, F., & Verrijn-Stuart, A. (1988). *Information systems methodologies—A framework for understanding* (2nd ed.). Reading: Addison-Wesley.

OMG. (2005). *Software process engineering Meta model specification* (Version 1.1). Object Management Group.

Pohl, K. (1993). The three dimensions of requirements engineering. In C. Rolland, F. Bodart, & C. Cauvet (Eds.), *Proc. of the 5th Int. Conf. on Advanced Info. Systems Engineering (CAiSE'93)* (LNCS 685, pp. 275-292). Berlin: Springer.

Pohl, K. (1994). The three dimensions of requirements engineering: A framework and its application. *Information Systems, 19*(3), 243-258.

Pohl, K., Dömges, R., & Jarke, M. (1997). Towards method-driven trace capture. In A. Olive & J. Pastor (Eds.), *Proceedings of the 9th International Conference on Advanced Information Systems Engineering (CAiSE'97)* (pp. 103-116). Berlin: Springer.

Punter, T., & Lemmen, K. (1996). The MEMA-model: Towards a new approach for methods engineering. *Journal of Information and Software Technology, 38*(4), 295-305.

Ramesh, B., & Jarke, M. (2001). Towards reference models for requirements traceability. *IEEE Trans. on Software Engineering, 27*(1), 58-93.

Rettig, M., & Simons, G. (1993). A project planning and development process for small teams. *Comm. of the ACM, 36*(10), 45-55.

Robey, D. (1984). Conflict models for implementation research. In R. Schultz (Ed.), *Management science implementation*. New York: American Elsevier.

Rolland, R., Souveyet, C., & Ben Achour, C. (1998). Guiding goal modeling using scenarios. *IEEE Trans. on Software Engineering, 24*(12), 1055-1071.

Rolland, C., Souveyet, C., & Moreno, M. (1995). An approach for defining ways-of-working. *Information Systems, 20*(4), 337-359.

Rose, T., & Jarke, M. (1990). A decision-based configuration process model. In *Proceedings of the 12th International Conference on Software Engineering* (pp. 316-325). Los Alamitos: IEEE Computer Society Press.

Ruiz, F., Vizcaino, A., Piattini, M., & Garcia, F. (2004). An ontology for the management of software maintenance projects. *International Journal of Software Engineering and Knowledge Engineering, 14*(3), 323-349.

Rzevski, G. (1983). On the comparison of design methodologies. In T. Olle, H. Sol, & C. Tully (Eds.), *Information systems design methodologies—A feature analysis* (pp. 259-266). Amsterdam: Elsevier Science Publishers.

Sabherwal, R., & Robey, D. (1993). An empirical taxonomy of implementation processes based on sequences of events in information system development. *Organization Science, 4*(4), 548-576.

Sabherwal, R., & Robey, D. (1995). Reconciling variance and process strategies for studying information system development. *Information Systems Research, 6*(4), 303-327

Saeki, M., Iguchi, K., Wen-yin, K., & Shinokara M. (1993). A meta model for representing software specification & design methods. In N. Prakash, C. Rolland, & B. Pernici (Eds.), *Proceedings of the IFIP WG8.1 Working Conference on Information Systems Development Process* (pp. 149-166). Amsterdam: Elsevier Science Publishers.

Short, K. (1991). Methodology integration: Evolution of information engineering. *Information and Software Technology, 33*(9), 720-732.

Slooten van, K., & Brinkkemper, S. (1993). A method engineering approach to information systems development. In N. Prakash, C. Rolland, & B. Pernici (Eds.), *Proceedings of the IFIP WG8.1 Working Conference on Information Systems Development Process* (pp. 167-188). Amsterdam: Elsevier Science Publishers.

Sol, H. (1992). Information systems development: A problem solving approach. In W. Cotterman & J. Senn (Eds.), *Challenges and strategies for research in systems development* (pp. 151-161). New York: John Wiley & Sons.

Sommerville, I. (1998). *Software engineering* (5th ed.). Reading: Addison-Wesley Longman.

Söderström, E., Andersson, B., Johannesson, P., Perjons, E., & Wangler, B. (2002). Towards a framework for comparing process modeling languages. In A. Banks Pidduck, J. Mylopoulos, C. Woo, & T. Ozsu (Eds.), *Proceedings of the 14th International Conference on Advanced Information Systems Engineering (CAiSE 2002)* (pp. 600-611). Berlin: Springer-Verlag.

Song, X., & Osterweil, L. (1992). Towards objective, systematic design-method comparison. *IEEE Software, 9*(3), 43-53.

Sowa, J. (2000). *Knowledge representation—Logical, philosophical, and computational foundations*. Pacific Grove, CA: Brooks/Cole.

Sowa, J., & Zachman J. (1992). Extending and formalizing the framework for information system architecture. *IBM Systems Journal, 31*(3), 590-616.

Staab, S., Schnurr, H.P., Studer, R., & Sure, Y. (2001). Knowledge processes and ontologies. *IEEE Intelligent Systems, 16*(1), 26-34.

Stamper, R. (1975). Information science for systems analysis. In E. Mumford & H. Sackman (Eds.), *Human choice and computers* (pp. 107-120). Amsterdam: Elsevier Science Publishers.

Stamper, R. (1992). Signs, organizations, norms and information systems. In *Proceedings of the 3rd Australian Conference on Information Systems* (pp. 21-65). Department of Business Systems, Univ. of Wollongong, Australia.

Swede van, V., & van Vliet, J. (1993). A flexible framework for contingent information systems modeling. *Information and Software Technology, 35*(9), 530-548.

Thayer, R. (1987). Software engineering project management—A top-down view. In R. Thayer (Ed.), *Tutorial: Software engineering project management* (pp. 15-56). IEEE Computer Society Press.

Uschold, M. (1996). Building ontologies: Towards a unified methodology. In *Proceedings of the 16th Annual Conference of the British Computer Society Specialist Group on Expert Systems*, Cambridge, UK.

Uschold, M., & King, M. (1995). Towards a methodology for building ontologies. In *Workshop on Basic Ontological Issues in Knowledge Sharing*, Montreal, Canada.

Vessey, I., & Conger, S. (1994). Requirements specification: Learning object, process, and data methodologies. *Comm. of the ACM, 37*(5), 102-113.

Wand, Y., & Weber, R. (1990). An ontological model of an information system. *IEEE Trans. on Software Engineering, 16*(11), 1282-1292.

Webster (1989). *Webster's encyclopedic unabridged dictionary of the English language*. New York: Gramercy Books.

Weick, K. E. (1995). *Sensemaking in organizations*. CA: Sage Publications.

Weinberger, H., Te'eni, D., & Frank, A. (2003). Ontologies of organizational memory as a basis for evaluation. In *Proceedings of the 11th European Conference of Information Systems*, Naples, Italy.

Wild, C., Maly, K., & Liu, L. (1991). Decision-based software development. *Software maintenance: Research and practice, 3*(1), 17-43.

Wood-Harper, A., & Fitzgerald, G. (1982). A taxonomy of current approaches to systems analysis. *The Computer Journal, 25*(1), 12-16.

Zachman, J. (1987). A framework for information systems architecture. *IBM Systems Journal, 26*(3), 276-292.

Zultner, R. (1993). TQM for technical teams. *Comm. of the ACM, 36*(10), 79-91.

Appendix

Table 2. Summary of the concepts and relationships of the ISD action domain in the ISD artifacts

References/ Concepts	ISD Ontology	Firesmith & Henderson-Sellers (2002)	Harmsen (1997)	Heym & Österle (1992)
Generic concept	ISD action	Work unit	Process fragment	Process
Sub-concepts	ISD workflow, ISD phase, ISD process	Activity, Task, Stage, Work-flow, Phase	Process role, Basic action	Phase, Activity
ISD management-execution structure	Mgmt action: ISD planning, ISD organizing, ISD staffing, ISD directing, ISD controlling; Execution action			Decision, Planning, Control
ISD workflow structure	ISD worflow: IS req's engineering, IS analysis, IS design, IS implementation, IS evaluation	Workflow	Action type: Planning, Analysis, Synthesis, Evaluation, Implementation, Evolution	ISD stage: Analysis, Design, Construction design, Construction, Test and installation, Maintenance
ISD phase structure	ISD phase: Inception, Elaboration, Construction, Transition	Phase		Phase
IS modeling structure	Conceptualizing, Representing, Creating, Refining, Testing, Transforming, Translating, Integrating, Relating			Abstraction, Checking, Review, Form conversion
Control structures	sequence, selection, iteration	sequence iteration	precedence, choice	sequence, refinement jump, branching path, unifying path, iteration
Abstraction structures	partOf, isA, memberOf, instanceOf		contents	aggregation

continued on following page

Table 2. continued

References/Concepts	Iivari (1990)	NATURE Team (1996)	Saeki et al. (1993)	Song & Oster-weil (1992)
Generic concept	Design act	Action	Procedure	Action
Sub-concepts	Main phase, Subphase, Design act			Step
ISD management-execution structure		Plan Execution		
ISD workflow structure				
ISD phase structure	Phase structure: Org. design, Conceptual/ infological design, Datalogical/technical design, Implementation			
IS modeling structure	Diagnosis/ Design, Verification/Validation, Observation/ Analysis, Manipulation/Refinement	Transformation		Create, Modify
Control structures	iteration	precedence, alternative	precede	
Abstraction structures	component of		has	part of, is a

Chapter II

Ontological Analysis of KAOS Using Separation of References

Raimundas Matulevičius, University of Namur, Belgium

Patrick Heymans, University of Namur, Belgium

Andreas L. Opdahl, University of Bergen, Norway

Abstract

Goal modeling is emerging as a central requirements engineering (RE) technique. Unfortunately, current goal-oriented languages are not interoperable with one another or with modeling languages that address other modeling perspectives. This problematic because the emerging generation of model-driven information systems is likely to depend on coordinated use of several modeling languages to represent different perspectives of the enterprise and its proposed information system. The chapter applies a structured approach to describe a well-known goal-oriented language, KAOS, by mapping it onto a philosophically grounded ontology. The structured approach facilitates language interoperability because when other languages are described using the same approach, they become mapped onto the same ontology. The approach thereby provides an intermediate language for comparison, consistency checking, update reflection, view synchronization and, eventually, model-to-model translation, both between goal-oriented languages and between different languages.

Introduction

Goal-oriented modeling languages emerge as a promising path towards model driven technologies that can account for trust in the early development stages. For instance, goal-oriented languages are emphasized during requirements engineering (RE) to identify system vulnerabilities and design countermeasures (Liu, Yu, & Mylopoulos, 2003; van Lamsweerde, 2004; Giorgini et al., 2005), hence aiming at a trusted information system (IS) from very early development phases. Current trends towards *model-driven IS development* and *agent-oriented* IS makes it likely that the importance of goal modeling will continue to increase. One central, goal-oriented language is knowledge acquisition in automated specification (KAOS), described by Letier (2001) and van Lamsweerde (2003). In addition to the conventional *what*, it offers a multi-perspective approach to specifying the *why, who,* and *when* of enterprises and their IS. Like other modeling languages, KAOS does not support all aspects and phases of IS development equally well. For example, it offers strong support for *representing, reasoning* about, and *specifying* trust during analysis and specification, but it offers less support for *tracing* and *realizing* trust concerns during design and system generation. In addition, an intermediate language is needed to *support integrated management* of enterprise, IS, and problem domain models expressed in different languages.

This chapter presents a preliminary ontological analysis of KAOS using *separation of reference* introduced by Opdahl and Henderson-Sellers (2004, 2005a). The technique analyzes modeling languages by first breaking each construct down into its ontologically primitive parts and then mapping the parts onto a *common ontology* that elaborates the *Bunge-Wand-Weber* (BWW) *representation model* (Wand & Weber, 1993, 1995) and philosophical ontology presented by Bunge (1977, 1979). The aim is to facilitate comparison, consistency checking, update reflection, view synchronization, and eventually, model-to-model translation, both between goal-oriented languages and across language families. The current work is a part of a larger effort to establish an intermediate language that supports integrated use of enterprise models expressed in different languages. The approach used in this chapter is currently being applied to develop version two of the unified enterprise modeling language (UEML).

The chapter is structured as follows: The "Theory" section provides the theoretical research background. This third section is "Research Method." "Results" are presented in the fourth section and discussed in the fifth section, "Discussion." Finally, we conclude and give directions for future work in "Conclusion."

Theory

This section discusses KAOS' main features and introduces the UEML approach.

KAOS

In this work, we are using the KAOS definition presented by Letier (2001) and van Lamsweerde (2003) as the latest self-contained description we know. However, these sources do not take into account the most recent language extensions (van Lamsweerde, 2004). Furthermore, some aspects of KAOS addressed in these sources were willingly omitted in our analysis.

The main purpose of KAOS is to ensure that high-level goals are identified and progressively refined into precise operational statements, which are then assigned to agents of the software-to-be and its environment. Together, the two form the so-called (*composite*) *system-to-be*. In this process, various alternative goal assignments and refinements are considered until the most satisfactory solution can be chosen.

The KAOS approach consists of a *modeling language*, a *method*, and a *software environment*. In this chapter, we will consider only the KAOS *modeling language*—called KAOS, from now on. A KAOS model includes a goal model, an object model, an agent model, and an operation model. Each of them has a graphical and a textual syntax. Some constructs can be further defined using the KAOS real-time temporal logic[1] in order to facilitate rigorous reasoning. For sake of brevity, we will introduce KAOS through examples from the London Ambulance Service system, adapted from (Letier, 2001) and shown in Figure 1. Our focus is the *goal model*, but agent, object, and operation models cannot be excluded completely, as all KAOS models are interrelated.

A *goal* is a prescriptive assertion that captures an objective, which the system-to-be should meet. Goals can be classified according to one of four patterns: *maintain*, *avoid*, *achieve*, and *cease* goals. For example, goal AccurateLocationInfoOnNon-StationaryAmbulance in Figure 1 follows the *maintain* pattern in which a property always holds. AmbulanceAllocationBasedOnIncidentForm follows the *achieve* pattern, where a property eventually holds. A goal can be refined through *G-refinement*, which relates it to a set of sub-goals whose conjunction, possibly together with *domain properties*, contributes to the satisfaction of the goal. A goal can have alternative G-refinements (e.g., AccurateStationaryInfo). A set of goals is *conflicting* if these goals cannot be achieved together (e.g., LocationContactedByPhone and InformationSentByEMail). This means that, under some *boundary condition*, these goals become logically inconsistent in a considered domain.

An *object* (e.g., Ambulance in the object model in Figure 1) is a thing of interest in the system. Its instances can be distinctly identified and may evolve from state

Figure 1. KAOS model fragment for the London Ambulance Service system (Adapted from Letier, 2001)

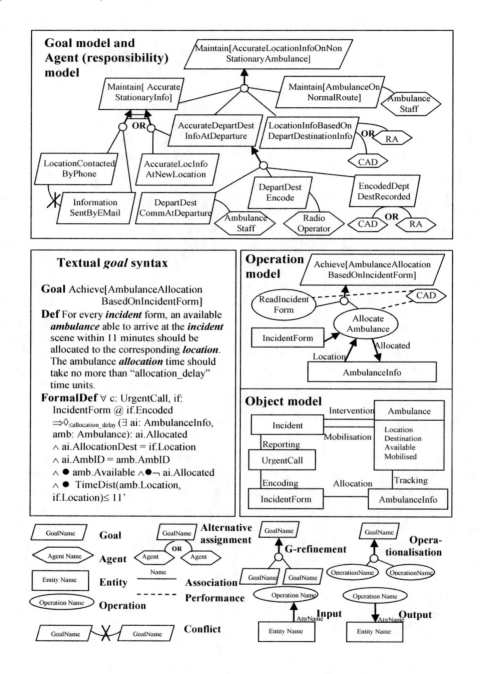

to state. Objects have *attributes*. Goals *concern* objects and attributes (see **Def** in textual goal syntax in Figure 1).

An *agent* plays a role towards a goal's satisfaction by *monitoring* or *controlling* object behaviour. Goals are refined until they are *assigned* to individual agents. A goal effectively assigned to a *software agent* (e.g., **CAD**—computer aided despatch) is called a *requirement*. A goal effectively assigned to an *environment agent* (e.g., **Ambulance Staff**) is called an *expectation* (*assumption* in (Letier, 2001)).

An *operation* is an *input-output* relation over objects. Operations are characterized textually by *domain* and *required* conditions. Whenever the required conditions are met, performing the operations satisfies the goal. If a goal is *operationalised* and has a responsible agent, the latter *performs* the operations (see operation model in Figure 1).

The UEML Approach

The UEML approach suggested by Opdahl and Henderson-Sellers (2004, 2005a), builds on the BWW model (Wand & Weber, 1993, 1995) and Bunge's (1977, 1979) ontology to describe modeling constructs in a way that facilitates precise language definition, understanding, and integration (Green & Rosemann, 2000; Evermann & Wand, 2005; Irwin & Turk, 2005; Opdahl & Henderson-Sellers, 2005b). The approach adapts BWW model analysis in two ways. Firstly, whereas the BWW model only maps a construct onto an ontological concept in general, such as class, property, state, or event, the UEML approach maps it onto a specific ontological class, property, state, or event. Secondly, whereas the BWW model usually maps a construct onto a single ontological concept, the UEML approach recognizes that a construct may represent a scene where multiple classes, properties, states, and events play parts. The UEML approach offers a structured approach to construct description, where the description of each construct is separated into descriptions of:

- **Instantiation level:** Is the construct intended to represent individual things and their particular properties, states, and events? Is it intended to represent classes and their characteristic properties, states, and events? Can it be used to represent both levels?

- **Classes:** Which thing or class of things in the problem domain is the construct intended to represent? Even when a construct primarily represents a property, state, or event, this field remains relevant because every property, state, or event must be a property in, state of, or event in, a specific thing or class. A construct definition can have several class entries because some constructs are even intended to represent more than one thing or class at the same time.

- **Properties:** Which property or properties in the problem domain is the construct intended to represent? Again, even when a construct primarily represents not a property but, for example, a state or event, this field is relevant, because every state or event pertains to one or more properties. This entry can also be repeated.

- **Behaviour:** Even when two modeling constructs are intended to represent the same properties of the same things or classes, they may be intended to represent different behaviors. For example, one modeling construct may be intended to represent just their existence, that is, a static representation. Other modeling constructs may be intended to represent a state of the classes, things or properties, an event, or a process, that is, alternative dynamic representations.

- **Modality:** Although we are used to thinking about enterprise and IS models as stating, or asserting, what is the case, not all modeling constructs are intended for stating assertions. Other types of constructs are intended to represent recommendations, obligations, permission, and so forth. The modality entry is used to identify such constructs.

The various ontological concepts—that is, the classes, properties, states and events—that are used to describe modeling constructs, are maintained in a common ontology. The common ontology was initially derived from the BWW model and Bunge's ontology and is designed to grow incrementally as additional classes, properties, states, and events are introduced in order to describe new modeling constructs. Its classes, properties, states, and events are organized in abstraction hierarchies in order to simplify ontology management and facilitate language integration. In consequence, when two modeling constructs—either from the same or from different languages—have both been described using the UEML approach, the exact relationship between them can be identified through their mappings onto the common ontology, paving the way for comparison, consistency checking, update reflection, view synchronization, and eventually, model-to-model translation.

Initial attempts to use the UEML approach were made by partners (Berio et al., 2005) of the InterOP project,[2] who applied it to describe BPMN, coloured Petri-nets, GRL, ISO/DIS 19440, UEML 1.0, selected diagram types of UML 2.0. Language descriptions are currently being negotiated and entered into the Protege-OWL based prototype tool, called *UEMLBase*.

Research Method

The research method has two main steps: (1) defining KAOS' abstract syntax and (2) applying the UEML approach to selected KAOS constructs from the abstract syntax. Getting a precise view of KAOS constructs and their interrelations was not an easy task. A part of the metamodel is exposed by Letier (2001) through structures and meta-constraints, described in conventional mathematics, but intertwined with other topics. In van Lamsweerde (2003), all focus is on the metamodel, but the author uses non-standard constructions to visualize it, omitting some multiplicities, specialization-related constraints, and abstract classes. Furthermore, integrity constraints are only given partially and informally. In order to facilitate analysis, we represented our understanding of KAOS in a UML 2.0 class diagram shown in Figure 2. [3] Our metamodel focuses on the goal model, the main object of our analysis, but also includes a few closely related constructs from the KAOS models.

Figure 2. A metamodel of the KAOS goal model (Adapted from Letier, 2001; van Lamsweerde, 2003)

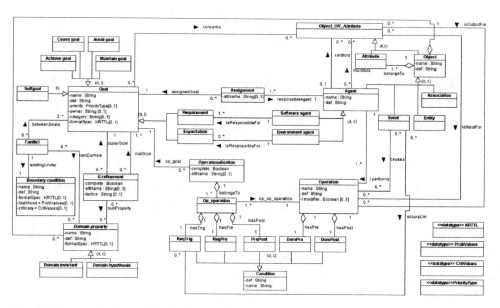

Note: Disjoint, overlapping, complete and incomplete are written d, o, c and i respectively.

Results

Table 1 outlines how the KAOS constructs have been represented in terms of the common ontology. For each construct, the table indicates: (1) the instantiation level (type or instance), (2) the primary class of things or property of this class, (2) the type of behaviour that the construct is intended to represent, and (4) modality. Although a construct may be intended to represent more than one class and/or more than one property, we have only indicated the most important ("primary") ones in the table.[4]

In order to illustrate the approach, we will present the **Goal** construct, which is central in KAOS, in greater detail. We will discuss the five parts of the UEML approach—instantiation level, classes, properties, behavior and modality—separately.

- **Instantiation level:** A Goal can be used to restrict either individual objects or objects that represent classes of individuals. The instantiation level of goal is therefore both, that is, either instance level or type level.

- **Classes:** A KAOS **Goal** says something about two things (if at the instance level) or two classes of things (if at the type level): There is the *goalOwner*, that is, the thing or class that holds the intent of reaching the **Goal**, and there is the *concernedObject*, that is, the thing or class for which a certain state must be maintained or avoided or a certain event must be achieved or ceased for the goal to be reached. In the common ontology, the *goalOwner* is mapped onto the class of *ActiveThings*, because attempting to reach a goal entails activity. Possibly, *goalOwner* can be mapped onto a more specific class of *ActorThings*, that is, *ActiveThings* that also hold **Goals**. The *concernedObject* is mapped onto the class of *ActedOnComponentThings* in the common ontology, a common subclass of *ActedOnThings* and *ComponentThings*. They are *ActedOnThings* because attempting to reach a goal entails acting on the object. They are *ComponentThings* because a *concernedObject* in KAOS is always a component of the system.

  Both the *goalOwner* and the *concernedObject* can be composite, that is, to account for complex **Goals** held by a group of people, or for goals about a collection of things/classes. However, we do not map them, even more specifically, onto the classes of *CompositeActiveThings* and *CompositeActedOnThings*, respectively, because they do not have to represent composite things.

- **Properties:** A KAOS **Goal** represents a particular group of properties of *goalOwners* and *concernedObjects*. The "primary" property represented by a KAOS **Goal** is a *complex law* property of the *goalOwner*. We call this property simply *theGoal*. It is a *law* because it restricts the states or transformations that the *concernedObject* can undergo. It is *complex* because it enforces this

Table 1. Mapping of KAOS constructs to elements of the common ontology

Construct	Inst	Primary Class/Property	Behaviour	Modality
Achieve goal	Both	Transformation law	Existence	Intent
Agent	Both	Active component thing	Existence	Fact
Assignment	Both	Complex mutual property	Existence	Fact
Avoid goal	Both	State law	Existence	Intent
Boundary condition	Both	State law	State	Fact
Cease goal	Both	Transformation law	Existence	Intent
Conflict	Both	Mutual property	Existence	Fact
Control	Both	Binding mutual property	Existence	Fact
Domain property	Both	Any property	Existence	Fact
Environment agent	Both	Active component thing	Existence	Fact
Event	Type	Changing thing	Event	Fact
Expectation	Both	Complex law property	Existence	Intent
Goal	Both	Complex law property	Existence	Intent
G-refinement	Both	Complex mutual property	Existence	Fact
Input	Type	Binding mutual property	Existence	Fact
Maintain goal	Both	State law	Existence	Intent
Monitor	Both	Binding mutual property	Existence	Fact
Object	Both	Component thing	Existence	Fact
Operation	Type	Transformation law	Process	Fact
Operationa-lisation	Both	Complex mutual property	Existence	Fact
Output	Type	Binding mutual property	Existence	Fact
Performance	Type	Complex mutual property	Existence	Fact
Requirement	Both	Complex law property	Existence	Intent
Softgoal	Both	Law property	Existence	Intent
Software agent	Both	Component software thing	Existence	Fact

restriction by restricting the various properties (or attributes) that a *concernedObject* may possess.

Figure 3 illustrates this situation informally.[5] The *goalOwner* class/thing possesses a single complex *theGoal* law property. The *concernedObject* class/thing possesses one or more *objAttribute* non-law properties. These properties are also sub-properties of *theGoal*: they are the properties that *theGoal* restricts, thereby also restricting the states and transformations that *concernedObject* can undergo. In the common ontology, *theGoal* is mapped onto *ComplexLawProperty*.

Figure 3 thus captures the gist of our interpretation of Goal, making it possible to discuss its semantics on a very detailed level, which might go into further depth:

o   A KAOS Goal has further characteristics, namely name, def, formalSpec, priority, and category, which are subproperties of the *theGoal* property too.

o   In KAOS, there is a difference between *objAttributes* that are explicitly mentioned in the Goal's def and those that are left implicit—that are not known by the analyst.

o   A KAOS Goal has even further properties, such as the ability to be assigned, refined, operationalized, and conflicting, which are left out here because they are considered in descriptions of other constructs (like Assignement, G-refinement, Operationalisation and Conflict)

- **Behavior:** The *behavior* entry for Goal is simple. A Goal just states the *existence* of property *theGoal*, as opposed to constructs that represent particular states of, or events in, one or more properties.

- **Modality:** The *modality* entry makes it clear that a Goal does not just assert a fact, but denotes the desire or *wish* of the *goalOwner* to reach *theGoal* with respect to the *concernedObject*.

The Goal subtypes MaintainGoal, AchieveGoal, AvoidGoal, and CeaseGoal, just refine the ontological grounding of their supertype by indicating which kind of law *theGoal* is. In Table 1, MaintainGoal and AvoidGoal are *state laws*, indicating the allowable (resp. forbidden) states *concernedObjects* can be in. AchieveGoal and CeaseGoal indicate that a *change* is required between a state where the *concernedObjects'* properties are false (resp. true) and one where they are true (resp. false). In BWW, this amounts to a *transformation law*.

Figure 3. The classes and properties represented by KAOS goal

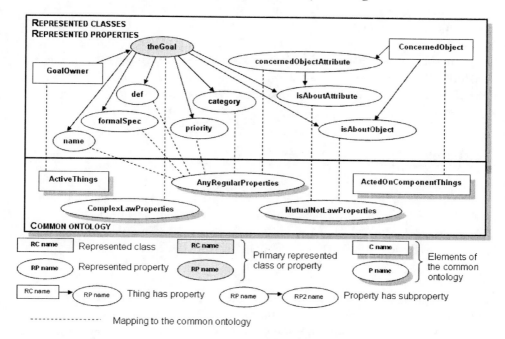

Discussion

The section discusses KAOS and the UEML approach with respect to our analysis. It also compares our approach with related work of language evaluation and integration.

KAOS

The first problem we encountered was the lack of a standard, consistent description of the KAOS syntax. Hence, our proposal for abstract syntax—a standard notation like UML class diagrams complemented with OCL constraints—could serve as a basis for a complete metamodel of KAOS. Regarding concrete syntax, we could observe variations between the sources, too. Once a metamodel is in place, concrete visualizations and variations can be established more clearly. Our major concern is semantics. KAOS goal model is now equipped with an ontological semantics defined through the UEML approach. The approach could be used to identify discrepancies in language definitions. However, this chapter concentrates on making the semantics explicit for later evaluation, comparison, and integration. Still, some observations can be made. We note the intensive use of BWW-model law, mutual and complex property to ground KAOS constructs ontologically (see Table 1). Indeed, we could observe intensive use of complex properties in previous analyses (Heymans et al., 2006; Opdahl & Henderson-Sellers, 2004), too. The use of laws might be influenced by the goal-oriented context, because all four types of KAOS goal map to law properties, elegantly matching the BWW model's distinction between state and transformation law. This demonstrates a convergence of KAOS' ontological semantics with its existing formal (modal logic-based) semantics. A detailed evaluation of KAOS will be envisaged when the other KAOS models will be analyzed.

Goal-Oriented Approaches

Besides KAOS, in more than a decade, various goal-oriented languages and methods have been proposed, most notably $i*$ (Yu, 1997), GRL (ITU, 2003), Tropos (Bresciani et al., 2004), GBRAM (Anton, 1996), NFR (Chung et al., 2000) and Lightswitch (Regev, 2003). They differ in many respects. Kavakli and Loucopoulos (2005) examine 15 of them and classify them along four dimensions: "usage" (What RE activity does goal modeling contribute to?), "subject" (What is the nature of goals?), "representation" (How are goals expressed?) and "development" (How are goal models developed and used?). The survey shows that, taken separately, each approach tends to focus only on one "usage." For example, $i*$ focuses on understanding the current organizational situation, while KAOS and NFR concentrate on relating business goals to system components. At the "subject" level, approaches use different definitions and categories of goals. At the "representation" level, approaches come with their own language syntax, semantics, and degree of formality. Two main conclusions of Kavakli and Loucopoulos (2005) survey are that, on the one hand, the research area is fragmented but, on the other hand, "contributions from different frameworks seem to complement each other." Consequently, the authors argue for more integration efforts: "By putting the various goal-based approaches together, one could obtain a stronger framework that takes advantage of the many streams of goal-oriented research," (Kavakli & Loucopoulos, 2005). In further work (Kavakli, 2002), "usage"-level integration is proposed through a unifying goal-oriented method meta-model. Processes of existing approaches were modelled as a move towards integrated goal-oriented processes. However, a main obstacle to such integration is fragmentation at the "subject" and "representation" levels. In our work, we address "*representation*" and "*subject*" levels, by providing the base for KAOS semantic integration with other languages.

Recently, a comparison of various notions of goal in RE was performed by Regev and Wegmann (2005). The authors examine the definitions of goal and related concepts found in KAOS, GBRAM, and GRL. They propose to redefine the notions based on the "regulation" concept borrowed from system theory. The work results in the definitions of, and the interrelations between, the key concepts made more precise and theoretically grounded. Further, the authors suggest formalization of definitions using the BWW model. By mapping KAOS and other goal-oriented languages to a common ontology based on BWW, we open the way for an accurate, systematic, and tool-supported comparison of notations at the syntactic and semantic levels.

IS and enterprise modeling require considering goals, but also many other perspectives like data, process, and architecture. Thus, integration is not only necessary between goal techniques, but also across different modeling perspectives. Groundbreaking work reported by (Anton et al., 1994) combined goals with scenarios to improve business process re-engineering. Others have investigated the interplay between goals and other modeling techniques (Dubois, Yu, & Petit, 1998; Mylopoulos, Kolp, & Castro, 2001; Liu & Yu, 2004; Salinesi, 2004). Three results directly concern KAOS. Van Lamsweerde and Willemet (1998) devise a procedure to infer KAOS goals from scenarios. In (Landtsheer, Letier, & van Lamsweerde, 2003), formal behavioural software specifications are built by stepwise refinement of KAOS models. Finally, Heaven and Finkelstein (2004) suggest embedding KAOS within the UML by proposing a KAOS UML profile. However, cross-language relationships are either informal (Anton et al., 1994; Liu & Yu, 2004) or ad-hoc (Dubois, Yu, & Petit, 1998; van Lamsweerde & Willemet, 1998; Mylopoulos, Kolp, & Castro, 2001; Liu & Yu, 2004). They are not based on an explicit mapping to an intermediate semantic representation. Defining KAOS as a UML profile (Heaven & Finkelstein, 2004) can make the transformation definition more standard by relying on general-purpose mechanisms developed around the UML. However, the UML definition is the source of many problematic referential issues (Krogstie, 2003; Opdahl & Henderson-Sellers, 2005b), so semantic consistency of transformations is not guaranteed.

Evaluation of the UEML Approach

The KAOS analysis indicates that the UEML approach is difficult to use because it is based on a particular way of thinking. It is hard to (1) determine exactly which language part constitutes a modeling construct; (2) find the appropriate classes, properties, states and events in the common ontology to use when describing a construct; (3) judge when to choose an existing class, property, state, or event in the ontology, and when to define a new one. In consequence, the UEML approach, with its ambition to facilitate inter-subjective construct descriptions, can produce subjective results. Problems of this kind are not surprising given that the UEML approach is ambitious and still new. We are currently looking for ways to counter them, including extended tool support, better documentation, and improving/simplifying the approach.

The KAOS analysis also highlights several advantages of the UEML approach. It offers (1) a detailed advice on how to proceed when analyzing individual language constructs; (2) construct description at a high level of detail, which tends to integrate languages at a fine-grained level, which leads to complete and easily comparable construct descriptions; (3) ontological analysis in terms of particular classes, properties, states and events, and not just in terms of the concepts in general; (4) a path towards tool supported, integrated use of models expressed in different languages, through the structured format in combination with the common ontology. Finally, it has positive externality, in the sense that each construct becomes easier to incorporate as more constructs are already added to UEML and each language becomes easier to incorporate as more languages are already added. The UEML approach offers a systematic way of revealing and managing the ontological assumptions inherent in a language.

With respect to the semiotic quality framework (Krogstie, 2003), the UEML approach suggests an analytically sound way of reaching the goals of syntactic and semantic quality. However, it leaves aside other quality types, such as pragmatic, empirical, physical, perceived, semantic and social quality.

Conclusion

We have presented our use of the UEML approach to provide a preliminary ontological grounding of the core concepts of the KAOS language. Mapping KAOS and other goal-oriented languages to a common well accepted ontological model, such as the BWW model, is a way to reduce the observed fragmentation in this research area. Once discussed, compared and validated by the community, these mappings can serve as a basis either (1) to create a unique, integrated, expressively complete[6] goal-modeling language, or (2) to devise semantic-preserving model transformations, consistency rules, or view synchronization mechanisms to cross language families and hence exchange goal models between process fragments. Model interoperability across modeling perspectives can be achieved in the same way and will be explored in the InterOP project on the basis of our results.

Currently a prototype tool, UEMLBase, is under development. It helps automate the UEML approach for defining and for finding common integration points based on the mappings. The tool will also help future negotiation of construct definitions made by different (groups of) researchers in order to reach consensus and include these constructs to the next UEML version.

Acknowledgment

This work is partially supported by the Commision of the European Communities under the sixth framework programme (InterOP Network of Excellence, Contract 508011).

References

Anton, I. (1996). Goal-based requirements analysis. In *Proceedings of the 2nd International Conference on Requirements Engineering (ICRE '96)*. IEEE Computer Society.

Anton, A. I., McCracken, W. M., & Potts, C. (1994). Goal decomposition and scenario analysis in business process reengineering. In *Proceedings of the 6th International Conference on Advanced Information Systems Engineering (CAiSE '94)* (pp. 94-104). Springer-Verlag.

Berio, G., Opdahl, A., Anaya, V., & Dassisti, M. (2005). *Deliverable DEM1*. Retrieved from www.interop-noe.org

Bresciani, P., Perini, A., Giorgini, P., Giunchiglia, F., & Mylopoulos, J. (2004). Tropos: An agent-oriented software development methodology. *Autonomous Agents and Multi-Agent Systems, 8*(3), 203-236.

Bunge, M. (1977). Ontology I: The furniture of the world. In *Treatise on basic philosophy* (Vol. 3). Boston: Reidel.

Bunge, M. (1979). Ontology II: A world of systems. In *Treatise on basic philosophy* (Vol. 4). Boston: Reidel.

Chung, K. L., Nixon, B., Mylopoulos, J., & Yu, E. (2000). *Non-functional requirements in software engineering*. Boston: Kluwer Academic Publishers.

Dubois, E., Yu, E., & Petit, M. (1998). From early to late requirements: A process-control case study. In *Proceedings of the 9th International Workshop on Software Specification and Design (IWSSD '98)*, Isobe, Japan.

Evermann J., & Wand, Y., (2005). Toward formalizing domain modeling semantics in language syntax. *IEEE Transactions on Software Engineering, 31*(1), 21-37.

Green, P., & Rosemann, M., (2000, April). Integrated process modeling: An ontological evaluation. *Information Systems, 25*(2), 73-87.

Giorgini, P., Massacci, F., Mylopoulos, J., & Zannone, N. (2005). Modeling security requirements through ownership, permission and delegation. In *Proceedings of the 13th IEEE International Conference on Requirements Engineering (RE '05)* (pp. 167-176). IEEE Computer Society.

Heaven, W., & Finkelstein, A. (2004). UML profile to support requirements engineering with KAOS. *IEE Proceedings - Software, 151*(1), 2004, 10-27.

Heymans, P., Saval G., Dallons, G., & Pollet, I. (2006). A template-based analysis of GRL. In K. Siau (Ed.), *Advanced topics in database research* (pp. 124-148). Hershey, PA: Idea Group Publishing.

Irwin, G., & Turk, D., (2005). An ontological analysis of use case modeling grammar. *Journal of AIS, 6*(1).

ITU. (2003, September). *Recommendation Z.151 (GRL)* (Version 3.0).

Kavakli, E. (2002). Goal-oriented requirements engineering: a unifying framework. *Requirements Engineering Journal, 6*(4), 237-251.

Kavakli, E., & Loucopoulos, P. (2005). Goal modeling in requirements engineering: Analysis and critique of current methods. In J. Krogstie, T. Halpin, & K. Siau (Eds.), *Information modeling methods and methodologies* (pp. 102-124). Hershey, PA: Idea Group Publishing.

Krogstie, J. (2003). Evaluating UML using a generic quality framework. In *UML and the unified process* (pp. 1-22). Hershey, PA: Idea Group Publishing.

van Lamsweerde, A., & Willemet, L. (1998). Inferring declarative requirements specifications from operational scenarios. *IEEE Transactions on Software Engineering, 24*(12), 1089-1114.

van Lamsweerde, A. (2003). *The KAOS meta-model: Ten years after.* Technical report, Universite Catholique de Louvain.

van Lamsweerde, A. (2004). Elaborating security requirements by construction of intentional anti-models. In *Proceedings of the 26th International Conference on Software Engineering (ICSE'04)* (pp. 148-157). IEEE Computer Society.

Landtsheer, R. D., Letier, E., & van Lamsweerde, A. (2003). Deriving tabular event-based specifications from goal-oriented requirements models. In *Proceedings of the 11th IEEE International Conference on Requirements Engineering (RE'03)* (pp. 200-210). IEEE Computer Society.

Letier, E. (2001). *Reasoning about agents in goal-oriented requirements engineering.* PhD thesis, Universit´e Catholique de Louvain.

Liu, L., & Yu, E. (2004). Designing information systems in social context: A goal and scenario modeling approach. *Journal of Information Systems, 29*(2), 187-203.

Liu, L., Yu, E., & Mylopoulos, J. (2003). Security and privacy requirements analysis within a social setting. In *Proceedings of the 11th IEEE International Requirements Engineering Conference (RE'03)* (pp. 151-161). IEEE Computer Society.

Mylopoulos, J., Kolp, M., & Castro, J. (2001). UML for agent-oriented development: The Tropos proposal. In *Proceedings of the 4ᵗʰ International Conference on the Unified Modeling Language, Modeling Languages, Concepts, and Tools* (pp. 422-441).

Opdahl A. L., & Henderson-Sellers B. (2004). A template for defining enterprise modelling constructs. *Journal of Database Management (JDM)*, *15*(2), 39-73.

Opdahl, A. L., & Henderson-Sellers, B. (2005a). Template-based definition of information systems and enterprise modeling constructs. In P. Green & M. Rosemann (Eds.), *Business systems analysis with ontologies*. Hershey, PA: Idea Group Publishing.

Opdahl, A. L., & Henderson-Sellers, B. (2005b). A unified modeling language without referential redundancy. *Data and Knowledge Engineering (DKE), Special issue on quality in conceptual modeling*.

Regev, G. (2003). *A systemic paradigm for early IT system requirements based on regulation principles: The Lightswitch approach*. PhD thesis, Swiss Federal Institute of Technology (EPFL).

Regev, G., & Wegmann, A. (2005, August). Where do goals come from: The underlying principles of goal-oriented requirements engineering. In *Proceedings of the 13ᵗʰ IEEE International Conference on Requirements Engineering (RE'05)*, Paris.

Salinesi, C., (2004). Authoring use cases. In I. Alexander & N. Maiden (Eds.), *Scenarios, use cases and stories through the system life-cycle*. John Wiley & Sons.

Wand, Y., & Weber, R. (1993). On the ontological expressiveness of information systems analysis and design grammars. *Journal of Information Systems, 3*, 217-237.

Wand, Y., & Weber, R. (1995). On the deep structure of information systems. *Journal of Information Systems, 5*, 203-223.

Yu, E. (1997). Towards modeling and reasoning support for early-phase requirements engineering. In *Proceedings of the 3ʳᵈ IEEE Int. Symposium on Requirements Engineering (RE'97)*, IEEE Computer Society.

Endnotes

[1]   See FormalDef in the textual goal syntax in Figure 1.

[2]   URL: http://www.interop-noe.org/

[3]   Our metamodel together with formalized integrity constraints is elaborated in a report available at http://www.info.fundp.ac.be/~rma/KAOSanalysis/KAOS-metaModel.pdf.

[4]   The complete, construct descriptions are available at http://www.info.fundp.ac.be/~rma/KAOSanalysis/KAOSconstructs.pdf.

[5]   Figure 3 simplifies an UML object diagram that instantiates the metameta model, presented by Opdahl and Henderson-Sellers (2004). Similar object diagrams are shown in (Opdahl & Henderson-Sellers, 2005a), but they are too detailed for this brief outline.

[6]   Such an integrated goal-oriented modeling language would also exhibit many other qualities (Krogstie, 2003).

Chapter III

Applying UML for Modeling the Physical Design of Data Warehouses

Sergio Luján-Mora, Universidad de Alicante, Spain

Juan Trujillo, Universidad de Alicante, Spain

Abstract

In previous work, we have shown how to use unified modeling language (UML) as the primary representation mechanism to model conceptual design, logical design, modeling of extraction, transformation, loading (ETL) processes, and defining online analytical processing (OLAP) requirements of data warehouses (DW). Continuing our work on using UML throughout the DW development lifecycle, in this chapter, we present our modeling techniques of physical design of DW using component diagrams and deployment diagrams of UML. Our approach allows the DW designer to anticipate important physical design decisions that may reduce the overall development time of a DW such as replicating dimension tables, vertical and horizontal partitioning of a fact table, and the use of particular servers for certain ETL processes. We illustrate our techniques with a case study.

Introduction

In the early 90s, Bill Inmon (Inmon, 2002) coined the term *data warehouse* (DW): "A data warehouse is a subject-oriented, integrated, time-variant, non-volatile collection of data in support of management's decisions" (p. 33). This definition contains four key elements that deserve a detailed explanation:

- **Subject orientation** means that the development of the DW will be done in order to satisfy the analytical requirements of managers that will query the DW. The topics of analysis differ and depend on the kind of business activities; for example, it can be product sales focusing on client interests in some sales company, the client behavior in utilization of different banking services, the insurance history of the clients, the railroad system utilization or changes in structure, and so forth.
- **Integration** relates to the problem that data from different operational and external systems have to be joined. In this process, some problems have to be resolved: differences in data format, data codification, synonyms (fields with different names but the same data), homonyms (fields with the same name but different meaning), multiplicity of data occurrences, nulls presence, default values selection, and so forth.
- **Non-volatility** implies data durability: Data can neither be modified nor removed.
- **Time-variation** indicates the possibility to count on different values of the same object according to its changes in time. For example, in a banking DW, the average balances of client's account during different months for the period of several years.

DWs provide organizations with historical information to support a decision. It is widely accepted that these systems are based on multidimensional (MD) modeling. Thus, research on the design of a DW has been mainly addressed from the conceptual and logical point of view through multidimensional (MD) data models (Blaschka, Sapia, Höfling, & Dinter, 1998, Abelló, Samos, & Saltor, 2001). During the few last years, few efforts have been dedicated to the modeling of the physical design (e.g., the physical structures that will host data together with their corresponding implementations) of a DW from the early stages of a DW project.

Nevertheless, the physical design of a DW is vitally important and highly influences the overall performance of the DW (Nicola & Rizvi, 2003) and the following maintenance; even more, a well-structured physical design policy can provide the perfect roadmap for implementing the whole warehouse architecture (Triantafillakis, Kanellis, & Martakos, 2004).

In some companies, the same employee may take on both the role of DW designer and DW administrator; other organizations may have separate people working on each task. Regardless of the situation, modeling the storage of the data and how it will be deployed across different components (servers, drives, and so forth) helps in the implementation and maintenance of a DW. In traditional software products or transactional databases, physical design or implementation issues are not considered until the latest stages of a software project. Then, if the final product does not satisfy user requirements, designers do a feedback taking into consideration (or at least bearing in mind) some final implementation issues.

Nevertheless, due to the specific characteristics of DWs, we can address several decisions regarding the physical design of a DW from the early stages of a DW project, with no need to leave them until the final implementation stage. DWs, mainly built for analytical reasons, are queried by final users trying to analyze historical data on which they can base their strategy decisions. Thus, the performance measure for DWs is the amount of queries that can be executed instead of the amount of processes or transactions that it supports. Moreover, the kinds of queries on DWs are demonstrated to be much more complex than the queries normally posed in transactional databases (Kimball, 2002, Poe, Klauer, & Brobst, 1998). Therefore, poor performance of queries has a worse impact in DWs than in transactional databases. Furthermore, the set of online analytical processing (OLAP) operations that users can execute with OLAP tools on DWs depends so much on the design of the DW, that is, on the multidimensional model underneath (Sapia, 1999, Trujillo, Palomar, Gómez, & Song, 2001).

Based on our experience in real world DW projects, physical storage and query performance issues can be discussed in the early stages of the project. The reason is that in DW projects, final users, analysts and business managers, DW designers, and database administrators participate, at least, in first meetings. Therefore, we believe that some decisions on the physical design of DWs can be made in the beginning. Some examples of these decision are as follows: (1) the size and the speed of the hard disk needed to deal with the fact table and the corresponding views, (2) a coherent partitioning of both fact and dimension tables based on data and user requirements (Furtado, 2006), and (3) the estimation of the workload needed and the time boundaries to accomplish it. Based on our experience, we believe that making these decisions in the early stages of a DW project will reduce the total development time of the DW.

In previous works (Luján-Mora & Trujillo, 2003, 2004), a DW development method was proposed, based on the unified modeling language (UML) (Object Management Group [OMG], 2003) and the unified process (UP) (Jacobson, Booch, & Rumbaugh, 1999), to properly design all aspects of a DW. So far, we have dealt with the modeling of different aspects of a DW by using the UML (Object Management Group [OMG], 2005b): MD modeling (Trujillo et al., 2001, Luján-Mora, Trujillo, & Song, 2002a, 2002b), modeling of the extraction, transformation, loading (ETL) processes (Trujillo & Luján-Mora, 2003), and modeling data mappings between data sources and targets (Luján-Mora, Vassiliadis, & Trujillo, 2004). In this chapter, we complement all of these previous works with a proposal to accomplish the physical design of DWs from the early stages of a DW project. To accomplish these goals, we propose the use of the *component diagrams* and *deployment diagrams* of UML. Both *component* and *deployment* diagrams must be defined at the same time by DW designers and DW administrators who will be in charge of the subsequent implementation and maintenance. This is mainly due to the fact that while the former know how to design and build a DW, the latter have a better knowledge in the corresponding implementation and the real hardware and software needs for the correct functioning of the DW.

The modeling of the physical design of a DW from the early stages of a DW project with our approach provides us with many advantages:

*   We deal with important aspects of the implementation before we start with the implementation process, and therefore, we can reduce the total development time of the DW. This is mainly due to the fact that, after the conceptual modeling has been accomplished, we can have enough information to make some decisions regarding the implementation of the DW structures, such as replicating dimension tables or designing the vertical and horizontal partitioning of a fact table (Furtado, 2006).
*   We have rapid feedback if there is a problem with the DW implementation as we can easily track a problem to find out its main reasons.
*   It facilitates communication between all people involved in the design of a DW since all of them use the same notation (based on UML) for modeling different aspects of a DW. Moreover, making sure that the crucial concepts mean the same to all groups and are not used in different ways is critical. In this way, our approach helps achieve a coherent and consistent documentation during the DW development life cycle.
*   It helps us choose both hardware and software on which we intend to implement the DW. This also allows us to compare and evaluate different configurations based on user requirements.
*   It allows us to verify that all different parts of the DW (fact and dimension tables, ETL processes, OLAP tools, and so forth) perfectly fit together.

The rest of this chapter is organized as follows. In section two, we briefly comment other works that have dealt with the conceptual, logical, and physical design and/or deployment of a DW. Section three introduces the three levels of data modeling. In section four, we briefly introduce our overall method to design all aspects of a DW. In section five, we summarize UML diagrams and we present main issues that can be specified by using both component and deployment diagrams of UML. In section six, we describe our approach for using both component and deployment diagrams for the physical design of DWs. In section seven, we provide information, in great detail, on how to use our component and deployment diagrams to implement a DW on a commercial database management server. Finally, in section eight, we present our conclusions and main future work.

Related Work

As this chapter focuses on the design of DWs, and more specifically, the physical design of DWs, the related work is organized into three subsections, about multidimensional modeling, physical design and implementation of DWs, and UML extensibility mechanisms.

Multidimensional Modeling

Several multidimensional (MD) data models have been proposed for DWs. Some of them fall into the logical level (such as the well-known star schema by (Kimball, 2002)). Others may be considered as formal models as they provide a formalism to consider main MD properties. A review of the most relevant logical and formal models can be found in Blaschka et al. (1998).

In this subsection, we will only make brief reference to the most relevant models that we consider "pure" conceptual MD models as this chapter focuses on the physical design of DWs from the early stages of a DW project. These models provide a high level of abstraction for the main MD modeling properties (e.g., facts, dimensions, classification hierarchies defined along dimensions, the additivity of measures, and so forth) and are independent from implementation issues. One interesting feature provided by these models is that they provide a set of graphical notations (such as the classical and well-known EER model) that facilitates their use and reading. These are as follows: *The Dimensional-Fact (DF) Model* by Golfarelli, Maio, and Rizzi (1998), *The Multidimensional/ER (M/ER) Model* by Sapia, Blaschka, Höfling, and Dinter (1998), *The starER Model* by Tryfona, Busborg, and Christiansen (1999), the Model proposed by Hüsemann, Lechtenbörger, and Vossen (2000), and *The Yet Another Multidimensional Model (YAM)* by Abelló, Samos, and Saltor (2002).

In the following, we further summarize YAM^2 (Abelló et al., 2002) as this is the related work most similar to ours. YAM^2 is an object-oriented model that uses UML as a notation to represent the MD data structures. However, authors only focus on the design of the DW repository and no other DW component is considered.

Furthermore, how to obtain a logical representation of the conceptual model is not described in this chapter.

One of the latest approaches in the design of data warehouses is *The Multidimensional Normal Form* by Lechtenbörger and Vossen (2003), in which the authors propose a well-structured approach to formalize the development of the DW repository. They propose a set of multidimensional normal forms in order to obtain the correct conceptual model of the DW repository from the operational data sources. Unfortunately, authors informally derive a relational representation from the conceptual model, but no formal transformations are defined to obtain this logical model.

However, none of these approaches for MD modeling considers the design of physical aspects of DWs as an important issue of their modeling, and therefore, they do not solve the problem of physical modeling from the early stages of a DW project.

Modeling of ETL Processes

Concerning the development of ETL processes, a conceptual model is proposed in Vassiliadis, Simitsis, and Skiadopoulos (2002). This model is customized for the tracing of inter-attribute relationships and the respective ETL activities in the early stages of a data warehouse project. Furthermore, the logical design of ETL scenarios is presented (Vassiliadis, Simitsis, Georgantas, Terrovitis, & Skiadopoulos, 2005). This logical design is based on a metamodel particularly customized for the definition of ETL activities by following a workflow-like approach, where the output of a certain activity can either be stored persistently or passed to a subsequent activity. A recent work (Simitsis, 2005) has proposed a formal transformation between these conceptual and logical models. However, this approach is not based on a standard like QVT (Object Management Group [OMG], 2005a).

Within our overall framework to design data warehouses, we have also developed some approaches to design ETL processes based on UML and UP. In concrete, we proposed how to accomplish the logical design of ETL processes by means of UML class diagrams (Trujillo & Luján-Mora, 2003); soon after, we proposed the conceptual modeling of ETL processes by means of data mappings between data sources and targets (Luján-Mora et al., 2004). In this latter work, we proposed the data mapping diagram, as a new UML diagram that allowed us to consider attributes as first class citizens, thereby allowing us to consider associations (e.g., mappings) between attributes.

Applying New Standard Methods in Data Warehouses

On the other hand, the model-driven architecture (MDA) is a standard frame-work for software development by using models (Object Management Group [OMG], 2006). This framework separates the specification of system functionality in a platform-independent model (PIM) from the specification of the implementation of that functionality on a specific technology in a platform-specific model (PSM). Furthermore, the system requirements are specified in a computation independent model (CIM). MDA not only allows the development of these models in a formal and integrated way by using a standard notation, but also the specification of model transformations in order to obtain the final software product. The MOF 2.0 query/ view/transformation (QVT) language (Object Management Group [OMG], 2005a) allows the formal definition of these transformations provided that the models are MOF-compliant. The main benefit of MDA is that less time and effort are needed to develop the whole software system, thus improving productivity. Furthermore, MDA provides support for system evolution, integration, interoperability, portability, adaptability, and reusability (Frankel, 2003; Kleppe, Warmer, & Bast, 2003; Mellor, Scott, Uhl, & Weise, 2004).

Considering all of these aspects, we described a MDA framework for the development of DWs (Mazon, Trujillo, Serrano, & Piattini, 2005). Every DW layer is modeled by a corresponding PIM using several UML profiles. The resulting PIMs represent conceptual models of each DW component, without any reference to a concrete target platform or a specific technology. Then, each PIM can be automatically mapped to several PSMs, depending on the required target platform, by using formal QVT transformations. Finally, each derived PSM provides the code according to a platform-specific DW implementation.

The main advantages of our framework are the following: (1) since MDA is applied, the complex task of designing the whole DW is tackled in a systematic, well-structured and standard way; (2) the design follows an integrated modeling framework, thus avoiding layer interoperability and integration problems; and (3) the DW implementation can be derived from the previously developed PIMs by using a set of clear and formal QVT transformations, thus saving time and effort.

Physical Design and Implementation Issues of Data Warehouses

Both the research community and companies have devoted little effort to the physical design of DWs from the early stages of a DW project, and incorporated it within a global method that allows the design of all main aspects of DWs. In this subsection, we are not presenting research on physical issues of DWs, such as new algorithms for defining and managing indices, view materialization, query processing or per-formance, as these and other physical aspects of DWs are out of the scope of this chapter. Instead, we will concentrate on the modeling of the physical design of DWs from the first stages of a DW project.

Kimball, Reeves, Ross, and Thornthwaite (1998) study the lifecycle of a DW and propose a method for the design, development, and deployment of a DW. They discuss the planning of the deployment of a DW and they recommend document-ing all different deployment strategies. However, they do not provide a standard technique for the formal modeling of the deployment of a DW.

Poe, Klauer, and Brobst (1998) address the design of a DW from conceptual model-ing to implementation. They propose the use of non-standard diagrams to represent the physical architecture of a DW: to represent data integration processes and to represent the relationship between the *enterprise data warehouse* and the different *data marts* that are populated from it. Nevertheless, these diagrams represent the architecture of the DW from a high level without providing different levels of detail of the subsequent implementation of the DW.

Giovinazzo (2000) discusses several aspects of a DW implementation. Although in this book, other aspects of a DW implementation such as the parallelism, the partitioning of data in a *redundant array of inexpensive disk* (RAID) system, or the use of a distributed database are addressed, authors do not provide a formal or standard technique to model all these aspects.

Finally, Rizzi (2003) states that one of the current open problems regarding DWs is the lack of a formal documentation that covers all design phases and provides multiple levels of abstraction (low level for designers and people devoted to the corresponding implementation and high level for final users). The author argues that this documentation is basic for the maintenance and the ulterior extension of the DW. In this work, three different detailed levels for DWs are proposed: *data warehouse level*, *data mart level*, and *fact level*. At the first level, the use of the deployment diagrams of UML are proposed to document a DW architecture from a high level of detail. However, these diagrams are not integrated at all with the rest of techniques, models, and/or methods used in the design of other aspects of the DW.

On the other hand, Naiburg and Maksimchuk (2001) have studied the use of UML for the design of databases. Their work is structured around the database design process; therefore, it contains a chapter devoted to database deployment. In this book, it is stated that, from the database designers' point of view, in a real database development project, "The biggest benefit in using the UML is the ability to model the tablespaces and quickly understand what tablespaces exist and how tables are partitioned across those tablespaces." On the other hand, using UML for designing databases has the advantage that a different UML diagram can be used (e.g., package diagram, class diagram, component diagram, and deployment diagram) depending on the particular aspect modelled. Many transformations between these diagrams have been widely and recently proposed (Whittle, 2000; Selonen, Koskimies, & Sakkinen, 2003).

Therefore, we argue that there is still a need for providing a standard technique that allows modeling the physical design of a DW from the early stages of a DW project. Another important issue is that this technique is integrated in an overall approach that allows coverage of other aspects of the DW design such as the conceptual or logical design of the DW or the modeling of ETL processes.

UML Extensibility Mechanism

The UML Extensibility Mechanism package is the subpackage from the UML metamodel that specifies how specific UML model elements are customized and extended with new semantics, by using stereotypes, tagged values, and constraints. A coherent set of such extensions, defined for specific purposes, constitutes a UML *profile*. For example, the UML 1.5 (Object Management Group [OMG], 2003) includes a standard profile for modeling software development processes and another one for business modeling.

A *stereotype* is a model element that defines additional values (based on tagged values), additional constraints, and optionally, a new graphical representation (an icon); a stereotype allows us to attach a new semantic meaning to a model element. A stereotype is either represented as a string between a pair of guillemots (<<>>) or rendered as a new icon.

A *tagged value* specifies a new kind of property that may be attached to a model element. A tagged value is rendered as a string enclosed by brackets ([ ]) and placed below the name of another element.

A *constraint* can be attached to any model element to refine its semantics. Warmer and Kleppe (1998) state, "A constraint is a restriction on one or more values of (part of) an object-oriented model or system" (XIX). In the UML, a constraint is rendered as a string between a pair of braces ({ }) and placed near the associated model element. A constraint on a stereotype is interpreted as a constraint on all types on which the stereotype is applied. A constraint can be defined by means of an informal explanation or by means of OCL (Warmer & Kleppe, 1998; Object Management Group [OMG], 2003) expressions. The OCL is a declarative language that allows software developers to write constraints over object models.

Figure 1. Conceptual, logical, and physical levels

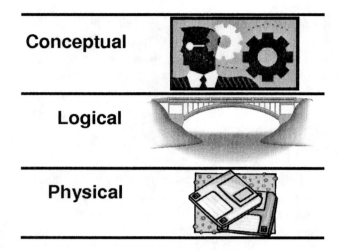

Levels of Data Modeling

"Data modeling is a technique that records the inventory, shape, size, contents, and rules of data elements used in the scope of a business process," (Allen, 2002). The result of data modeling is a kind of map (the model) that describes the data used in a process.

Traditionally, there are three levels of data modeling in databases and DW: conceptual, logical, and physical. These three levels provide a framework for developing a database structure or schema from the top down. This section will briefly explain the difference among the three and the order in which each one is created.

In Figure 1, we graphically represent the relationship among the three levels of data modeling. Whereas the conceptual level is closer to the user domain and the physical level is closer to the computer, the logical level serves as a bridge between the conceptual and the logical levels.

Conceptual Data Model

In the conceptual data model, we normally represent the important entities and the relationships among them. The goal of conceptual data modeling is to describe data in a way that is not governed by implementation-level issues and details.

The conceptual data model is closer to the problem space (the real world) than to the solution space (the implementation).

Logical Data Model

The logical data model usually includes:

*   All entities and relationships among them
*   All attributes and the corresponding datatypes for each entity
*   The primary key for each entity specified
*   Foreign keys

The goal of the logical data model is to describe the data in as much detail as possible, without regarding how they will physically be implemented in the database.

Physical Data Model

In the physical data model, we normally include the whole specification of all tables and columns, following the rules of the implementation platform.

The physical data model determines the actual design of a database. This model is the basis of the code written to create tables, views, and integrity constraints.

Data Modeling and UML

Nowadays, the dominant trend in data modeling is the object-oriented (OO) paradigm, because OO modeling supports complex and advanced data structures. The OO paradigm is semantically richer than others and it offers numerous advantages, but "the most important advantage of conceptualizing by means of an OO model is that the result is closer to the user conception," (Abelló, Samos, & Saltor, 2000, p. 3).

Figure 2. Stages of modeling and related UML constructs

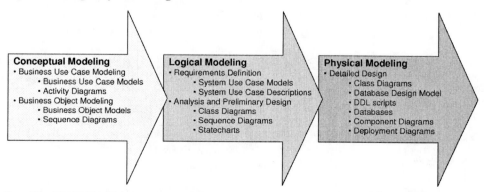

In Figure 2, we show a flow diagram adapted from Naiburg and Maksimchuk (2001). In this diagram, each level of modeling (conceptual, logical, and physical) is shown within the major activities performed and the key UML elements that support that activity.

Data Warehouse Design Framework

The architecture of a DW is usually depicted as various layers of data in which data from one layer is derived from data of the previous layer (Jarke, Lenzerini, Vassiliou, & Vassiliadis, 2003). In a previous work (Luján-Mora & Trujillo, 2004), we presented a DW development method, based on UML (Object Management Group [OMG], 2005b) and the UP (Jacobson et al., 1999), that addressed the design and development of both the DW back-end and front-end. In our approach, we considered that the development of a DW can be structured into an integrated framework with five stages and three levels that define different diagrams for the DW model, as shown in Figure 3 and summarized next:

- **Stages:** We distinguish five stages in the definition of a DW:
  - **Source:** That defines the data sources of the DW, such as OLTP systems, external data sources (syndicated data, census data), and so forth.
  - **Integration:** That defines the mapping between the data sources and the DW.
  - **Data warehouse:** That defines the structure of the DW.
  - **Customization:** That defines the mapping between the DW and the clients' structures.
  - **Client:** That defines special structures that are used by the clients to access the DW, such as data marts (DM) or OLAP applications.

Figure 3. Data warehouse design framework

	Source (S) (OLTP, external data, ...)	Integration	Data Warehouse (DW)	Customization	Client (C) (OLAP, data mining, ...)
Conceptual	SCS Class diagram Standard UML	DM Class diagram Data Mapping Profile	DWCS Class diagram Standard UML Multidimensional Profile	DM Class diagram Data Mapping Profile	CCS Class diagram Standard UML Multidimensional Profile
Logical	SLS Class diagram Different data modeling profiles	ETL Process Class diagram ETL Profile	DWLS Class diagram Different data modeling profiles	Exporting Process Class diagram ETL Profile	CLS Class diagram Different data modeling profiles
Physical	SPS Comp. & deploy. diagrams Database Deployment Profile	Transportation Diagram Deployment diagram Database Deployment Profile	DWPS Comp. & deploy. diagrams Database Deployment Profile	Transportation Diagram Deployment diagram Database Deployment Profile	CPS Comp. & deploy. diagrams Database Deployment Profile

LEGEND: CS: Conceptual Schema, LS: Logical Schema, PS: Physical Schema, Comp. & deploy: Component and deployment

- **Levels:** Each stage can be analyzed at three different levels or perspectives:
  - ○ **Conceptual:** It defines the DW from a conceptual point of view.
  - ○ **Logical:** It addresses logical aspects of the DW design, such as the definition of the ETL processes.
  - ○ **Physical:** It defines physical aspects of the DW, such as the storage of the logical structures in different disks, or the configuration of the database servers that support the DW.
- **Diagrams:** Each stage or level requires different modeling formalisms. Therefore, our approach is composed of 15 diagrams, but the DW designer does not need to define all the diagrams in each DW project. For example, if there is a straightforward mapping between the source conceptual schema (SCS) and the data warehouse conceptual schema (DWCS), the designer may not need to define the corresponding data mapping (DM). In our approach, we use UML (Object Management Group (OMG), 2005b) as the modeling language, because it provides enough expressiveness power to address all the diagrams. As UML is a general modeling language, we can use UML extension mechanisms (stereotypes, tag definitions, and constraints) to adapt UML to specific domains. A stereotype is a UML modeling element that extends the UML metamodel in a controlled way. That is, a stereotype is a specialized version of a standard UML element; a tag definition allows additional information about a standard UML element to be specified and a constraint is a rule that limits the behavior of a UML element. Figure 3 contains the following information for each diagram:
  - ○ **Name (in bold face):** This is the name we have coined for this diagram.
  - ○ **UML diagram:** This is the UML diagram we use to model this DW diagram. Currently, we use class, deployment, and component diagrams.
  - ○ **Profile (*in italic font*):** The dashed boxes show the diagrams where we propose a new profile[1] ; in the other boxes, we use a standard UML diagram or a profile from other authors.

The different diagrams of the same DW are not independent, but overlapping; they depend on each other in many ways, therefore, they can not be created in any order.[2] For example, changes in one diagram may imply changes in another, and a large portion of one diagram may be created on the basis of another diagram. For example, the data mapping (DM) is created by importing elements from the source conceptual schema (SCS) and the data warehouse conceptual schema (DWCS). Moreover, our approach is flexible in the sense that the DW designer does not need to define all the diagrams, but he or she can use what is needed when it is needed and can continue moving forward as necessary.

In previous works, we have presented some of the diagrams and the corresponding profiles shown in white dashed boxes in Figure 3: *multidimensional profile* (Luján-Mora et al., 2002a, 2002b) for the DWCS and the client conceptual schema (CCS), the *ETL profile* (Trujillo & Luján-Mora, 2003) for the ETL process and the exporting process, and the *data mapping profile* (Luján-Mora & Trujillo, 2004) for the DM between the SCS and the DWCS, and between the DWCS and the CCS. Finally, in light gray dashed boxes, we show the profile we present in this chapter, the *database deployment profile*, for modeling a DW at a physical level.

Figure 4 shows a symbolic diagram to summarize our approach and the relationships between the different diagrams (DWCS, DWLS, and DWPS):

- On the left hand side of this figure, we have represented the DWCS, which is structured into three levels: Level 1 or *Model definition*, Level 2 or *Star schema definition*, and Level 3 or *Dimension/fact definition*. The different elements drawn in this diagram are stereotyped packages and classes[3] that represent MD concepts.

- From the DWCS, we develop[4] the logical model (DWLS, represented in the middle of Figure 4) according to different options, such as ROLAP[5] (*relational OLAP*) or MOLAP[6] (*multidimensional OLAP*). In this example, we have chosen a ROLAP representation and each element corresponds to a table in the relational model.

- Finally, from the DWLS, we derive the DWPS, which is represented on the right hand side of Figure 4. The DWPS shows the physical aspects of the implementation of the DW. This diagram is divided up into two parts: the component diagram, which shows the configuration of the logical structures used to store the DW, and the deployment diagram, which specifies different aspects relative to the hardware and software configuration.

Figure 4 shows how our approach allows the designer to trace the design of an element from the conceptual to the physical level. For example, in this figure, we have drawn a cloud around different elements that represent the same entity in different diagrams.

In the following section, we summarize the basic concepts about the UML component and deployment diagrams that we apply for the physical design of DWs.

Figure 4. From the conceptual to the physical level

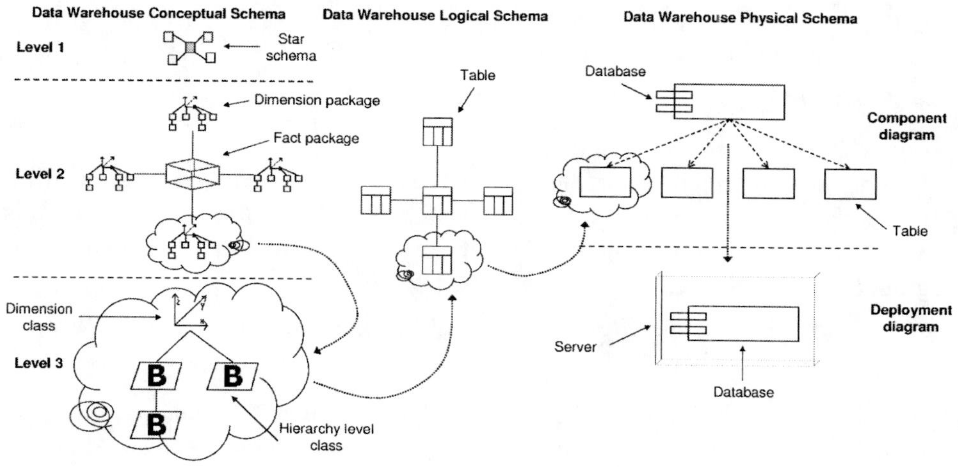

UML Diagrams

UML 2.0 (Object Management Group [OMG], 2005b) includes 13 types of different modeling diagrams. These diagrams can be hierarchically categorized into three main groups, as shown in Figure 5:

- **Structure diagrams** emphasize what things must be in the system being modeled:
  - ○ Class diagram
  - ○ Component diagram
  - ○ Object diagram
  - ○ Composite structure diagram
  - ○ Deployment diagram
  - ○ Package diagram
- **Behavior diagrams** emphasize what must happen in the system being modeled:
  - ○ Activity diagram
  - ○ Use case diagram
  - ○ State machine diagram
- **Interaction diagrams**, a subset of behavior diagrams, emphasize the flow of control and data among the things in the system being modeled:

- o   Sequence diagram
- o   Communication diagram
- o   Interaction overview diagram
- o   Timing diagram

In previous work (Luján-Mora, 2005), we have applied the class and package diagrams to model the conceptual and logical design of DWs and the use case diagrams to model users' requirements. In this chapter, we use the component and deployment diagram to model physical aspects of DWs.

According to the UML specification (Object Management Group [OMG], 2003):

Implementation diagrams show aspects of physical implementation, including the structure of components and the run-time deployment system. They come in two forms: (1) component diagrams show the structure of components, including the classifiers that specify them and the artifacts that implement them; and (2) deployment diagrams show the structure of the nodes on which the components are deployed.(p. 9)

Figure 5. Hierarchy of UML 2.0 diagrams shown as a class diagram

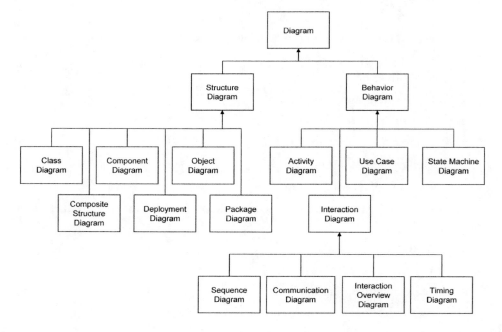

In the following subsections, we summarize the main concepts about the UML component diagram and the deployment diagram.

Component Diagram

The UML specification says that "A component represents a modular, deployable, and replaceable part of a system that encapsulates implementation and exposes a set of interfaces". Components represent physical issues such as Enterprise JavaBeans, ActiveX components, or configuration files. A component is typically specified by one or more classifiers (e.g., classes and interfaces) that reside on the component. A subset of these classifiers explicitly defines the component's external interfaces. Moreover, a component can also contain other components. However, a component does not have its own features (attributes and operations).

On the other hand, a component diagram is a graph of components connected by dependency relationships that shows how classifiers are assigned to components and how the components depend on each other. In a component diagram (Figure 6), a component is represented using a rectangular box, with two rectangles protruding from the left side.

Figure 6 shows the two different representations of a component and the classifiers it contains:

- On the left hand side of the figure, the class (Sales) that resides on the component (Facts) is shown as nested inside the component (this indicates residence and not ownership).
- On the right hand side of the figure, the class is connected to the component by a <<reside>> dependency.

Figure 6. Different component representations in a component diagram

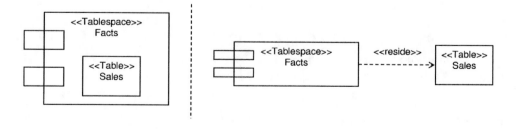

In these examples, both the component and the class are stereotyped: the component is adorned with the <<Tablespace>> stereotype and the class with the <<Table>> stereotype; these stereotypes are defined by Naiburg and Maksimchuk (2001).

Deployment Diagram

According to the UML specification, "Deployment diagrams show the configuration of run-time processing elements and the software components, processes, and objects that execute on them" (p. 617). A deployment diagram is a graph of nodes connected by communication associations. A deployment model is a collection of one or more deployment diagrams with their associated documentation.

In a deployment diagram, a node represents a piece of hardware (e.g., a computer, a device, an interface) or a software artifact (e.g., Web server, database) in the system, and it is represented by a three-dimensional cube. A node may contain components that indicate that the components run or execute on the node.

An association of nodes, which is drawn as a solid line between two nodes, indicates a line of communication between the nodes; the association may have a stereotype to indicate the nature of the communication path (e.g., the kind of channel, communication protocol or network).

There are two forms of deployment diagram:

1. **The descriptor form:** It contains types of nodes and components. This form is used as a first-cut deployment diagram during the design of a system, when there is not a complete decision about the final hardware architecture.

2. **The instance form:** It contains specific and identifiable nodes and components. This form is used to show the actual deployment of a system at a particular site. Therefore, it is normally used in the last steps of the implementation activity, when the details of the deployment site are known.

According to Ambler (2002), a deployment diagram is normally used to:

*   Explore the issues involved with installing your system into production
*   Explore the dependencies that your system has with other systems that are currently in, or planned for, your production environment
*   Depict a major deployment configuration of a business application
*   Design the hardware and software configuration of an embedded system
*   Depict the hardware/network infrastructure of an organization

UML deployment diagrams normally make extensive use of visual stereotypes because they are easy to read the diagrams at a glance. Unfortunately, there are no standard palettes of visual stereotypes for UML deployment diagrams.

As suggested by Ambler (2002), each node in a deployment diagram may have tens if not hundreds of software components deployed to it; the goal is not to depict all of them, but to depict those components that are vital to the understanding of the system.

Figure 7 shows two different representations of a node and the components it contains:

1.   On the left hand side of the figure, the component (DailySales) that is deployed on the node (DWServer) is shown as nested inside the node.

2.   On the right hand side of the figure, the component is connected to the node by a <<deploy>> dependency.

In this example, both the node and the component are stereotyped: the node with the <<Computer>> stereotype and the component with the <<Database>> stereotype. Moreover, the node DWServer contains a set of tagged values (OS, SW, CPU, and Mem) that allow the designer to describe the particular characteristics of the node.

A deployment diagram can be specified at different levels of detail. For example, Figure 8 shows two versions of the same deployment diagram. At the top of Figure 8, the software deployed in the nodes is specified by means of tagged values. Moreover, the association between the nodes is only adorned with the <<HTTP>> stereotype (*hypertext transfer protocol*), although different protocols can be used in the communication. At the bottom of Figure 8, the software deployed in the nodes

Figure 7. Different node representations in a deployment diagram

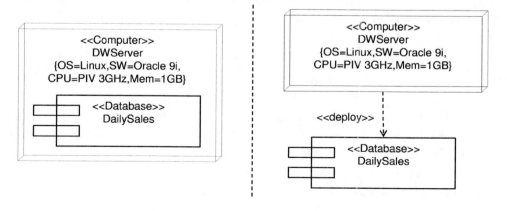

Figure 8. Different levels of detail in a deployment diagram

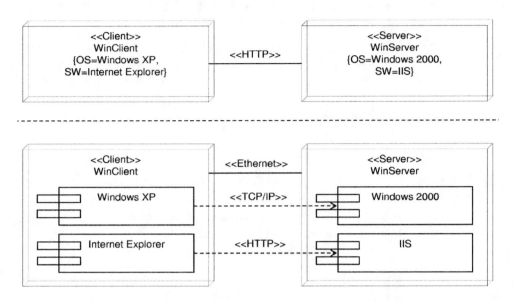

is depicted as components and different stereotyped dependencies (<<TCP/IP>> and <<HTTP>>) indicate how one component uses the services of another component. However, there are more display possibilities. For example, the designer can omit the tagged values in the diagram and capture them only in the supported documentation.

Data Warehouse Physical Design

In Section Data Warehouse Design Framework, we have briefly described our design method for DWs. Within this method, we use the component and deployment diagrams to model the physical level of DWs. To achieve this goal, we propose the following five diagrams, which correspond to the five stages presented previously:

- **Source physical schema (SPS):** It defines the physical configuration of the data sources that populate the DW.

- **Integration transportation diagram (ITD):** It defines the physical structure of the ETL processes that extract, transform, and load data into the DW. This diagram relates the SPS and the next diagram.

- **Data warehouse physical schema (DWPS):** It defines the physical structure of the DW itself.

- **Customization transportation diagram (CTD):** It defines the physical structure of the exportation processes from the DW to the specific structures employed by clients. This diagram relates the DWPS and the next diagram.
- **Client physical schema (CPS):** It defines the physical configuration of the structures employed by clients in accessing the DW.

The SPS, DWPS, and CPS are based on the UML component and deployment diagrams, whereas ITD and CTD are only based on the deployment diagrams. These diagrams reflect the modeling aspects of the storage of data (Naiburg & Maksimchuk, 2001), such as the database size, information about where the database will reside (hardware and software), partitioning of the data, properties specific to the *database management system* (DBMS) chosen, and so forth.

The five proposed diagrams use an extension of UML that we have called *database deployment profile*, which is formed by a series of stereotypes, tagged values, and constraints.

Throughout the rest of this chapter, we use an example to introduce the different diagrams we propose. This example is partly based on the enterprise DW sample database schema from Silverston, Inmon, and Graziano (1997). In this example, final users need a DW in order to analyze the main operations of the company. Because of this, the DW contains information about customers, customer invoices, budget details, products, and suppliers. Moreover, data about the employees, such as salaries, positions, and categories are also stored in the DW.

The operational data sources are stored in three servers:

1. The sales server, which contains the data about transactions and sales;
2. The CRM (*customer relationship management*) server, which contains the data about the customers who buy products;
3. The HRM (*human resource management*) server, which contains the data about employees, positions, salaries, and so forth.

Following our approach (Luján-Mora et al., 2002b), we structure the conceptual model into three levels:

- **Level 1. Model definition:** A package represents a star schema of a conceptual MD model. A dependency between two packages at this level indicates that the star schemas share at least one dimension, allowing us to consider conformed dimensions.

Figure 9. Data warehouse conceptual schema: Level 1

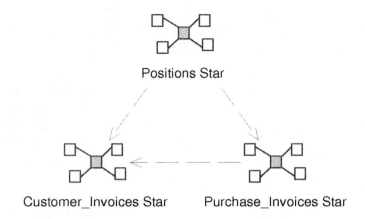

- **Level 2. Star schema definition:** A package represents a fact or a dimension of a star schema. A dependency between two dimension packages at this level indicates that the packages share at least one level of a dimension hierarchy.
- **Level 3. Dimension/fact definition:** A package is exploded into a set of classes that represents the hierarchy levels defined in a dimension package, or the whole star schema in the case of the fact package.

Figure 9 shows the first level of the DWCS, which represents the conceptual model of the DW. In our example, the first level is formed by three packages called Customer_Invoices Star, Positions Star, and Purchase_Invoices Star. A dashed arrow from one package to another denotes a dependency between packages. That is, the packages have some dimensions in common. The direction of the dependency indicates that the common dimensions shared by the two packages were first defined in the package pointed to by the arrow (to start with, we have to choose a star schema to define the dimensions, and then, the other schemas can use them with no need to define them again). If the common dimensions had been first defined in another package, the direction of the arrow would have been different. In any case, it is better to group together the definition of the common dimensions in order to reduce the number of dependencies. From now on, we will focus our discussion on the Customer_Invoices Star. This star schema represents the invoices belonging to customers.

Figure 10 shows the second level of the DWCS. The fact package, Customer_Invoices, is represented in the middle of the figure, while the dimension packages are placed around the fact package. As seen in Figure 10, a dependency is drawn from the fact package, Customer_Invoices, to each one of the dimension packages

Figure 10. Data warehouse conceptual schema: Level 2 of Customer_Invoices Star)

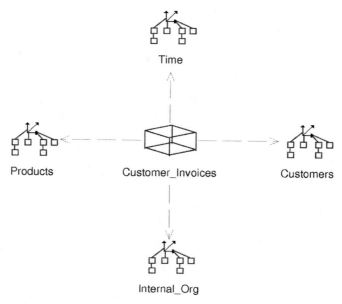

(Customers, Internal_Org, Products, and Time), because the fact package comprises the whole definition of the star schema, and therefore, uses the definitions of dimensions related to the fact. At level two, it is possible to create a dependency from a fact package to a dimension package or between dimension packages, but we do not allow a dependency from a dimension package to a fact package, since it is not semantically correct in our technique.

The content of the dimension and fact packages is represented at level three. The diagrams at this level are only comprised of classes and associations among them. Figure 11 shows the level three of the Customers dimension package (Figure 10), which contains the definition of the dimension (Customers) and the different hierarchy levels (Customer_Addresses, Customer_SED, GB_City, Postal_Code, GB_City,[7] etc.). The hierarchy of a dimension defines how the different OLAP operations (roll up, drill down, and so forth) can be applied. In a UML note, we highlight that Customer_SED (SED means *socioeconomic data*) is a *slowly changing dimension* (SCD) and some kind of solution has to be selected during the implementation (Kimball, 2002).

Figure 12 shows the level three of the Products dimension. This dimension contains two alternative hierarchies: the category of the product (Category) and the supplier of the product (Products_Supplier, City, State, and Country). In Products_Supplier hierarchy level, msrp means *manufacturer's suggested retail price* and uom is the standard *unit of measure* used for the product.

Figure 11. Data warehouse conceptual schema: Customers dimension

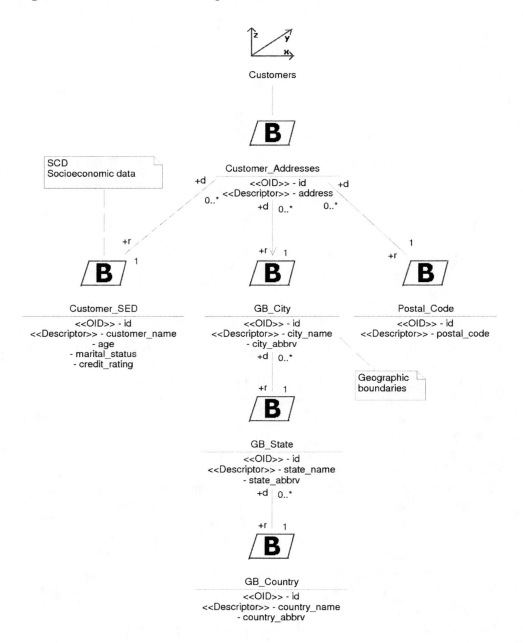

Figure 12. Data warehouse conceptual schema: Products dimension

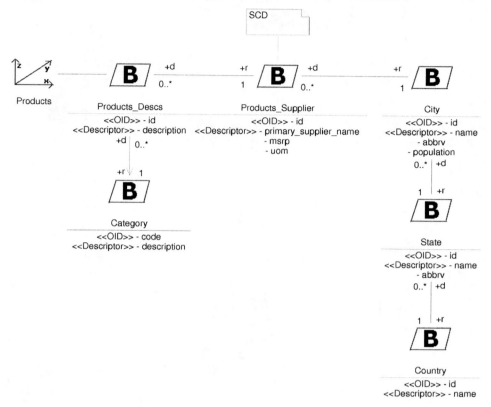

Figure 13. Data warehouse conceptual schema: Customer_Invoices fact

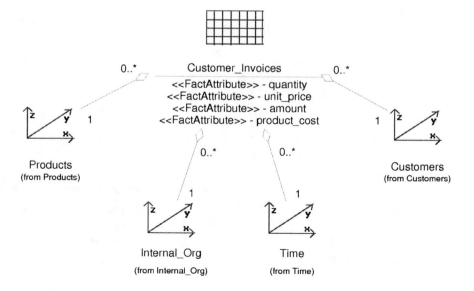

Figure 14. Logical model (ROLAP) of the data warehouse

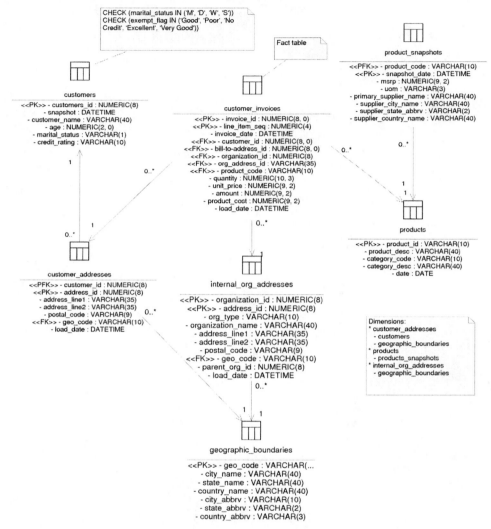

Figure 13 shows the level three of the Customer_Invoices fact package. In this package, the whole star schema is displayed: the fact class is defined in this package and the dimensions with their corresponding hierarchy levels are imported from the dimension packages. Because of this, the name of the package where they have been previously defined appears below the package name (from Products, from Internal_Org). In order to avoid a cluttered diagram, we only show the attributes of the fact class (Customer_Invoices) and we hide the attributes and the hierarchy levels of the dimensions.

Figure 14 shows the *data warehouse logical schema* (DWLS), which represents the logical model of the DW. In this example, a ROLAP system has been selected for the implementation of the DW, which means the use of the relational model in the logical design of the DW. In Figure 14, seven classes adorned with the stereotype <<Table>> are shown: customers, customer_addresses, customer_invoices, internal_org_addresses, geographic_boundaries, product_snapshots, and products.

In the customer_invoices table, the attributes customer_id, bill-to-address, organization_id, org_address_id, and product_code are the foreign keys that connect the fact table with the dimension tables, whereas the attributes quantity, unit_price, amount, and product_cost represent the measures of the fact table. The attribute invoice_date represents a degenerate dimension,[8] whereas the attribute load_date is the date the record was loaded into the DW and it is used in the refresh process.

The products and product_snapshots tables contain all the attributes of the different dimension levels (Figure 12) following the star schema approach (Kimball, 2002); some attributes have changed their names in order to avoid repeated names and some design decisions have been made. Moreover, we observe that we use UML notes to provide additional information to the diagram.

The following subsections present the five diagrams we propose for the physical design of DWs.

Source Physical Schema

The source physical schema (SPS) describes the origins of data of the DW from a physical point of view. Figure 15 shows the SPS of our example, which is formed

Figure 15. Source physical schema: Deployment diagram

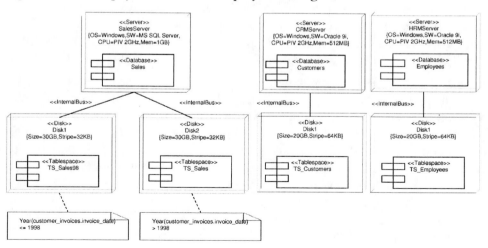

by three servers called SalesServer, CRMServer, and HRMServer..For each one of them, the hardware and software configuration is displayed by means of tagged values. The first server hosts a database called Sales, whereas the second server hosts a database called Customers.

In our *database deployment profile*, when the storage system is a *relational database management system* (RDBMS), we make use of the *UML for profile database* that defines a series of stereotypes including <<Database>>, <<Schema>>, or <<Tablespace>> (Naiburg & Maksimchuk, 2001). Moreover, we have defined our own set of stereotypes. In Figure 15, we can see the stereotypes <<Server>> that defines a computer that performs server functions, <<Disk>> to represent a physical disk drive, and <<InternalBus>> to define the type of communication between two elements. In our approach, we represent the configuration parameters of the tablespaces (e.g., size of the tablespace) by means of tagged values; however, these parameters vary greatly depending on the DBMS, so we only provide a set of common parameters. As UML is extensible, the designer can add additional tagged values as needed to accomplish all the modeling needs of a particular DBMS.

Moreover, whenever we need to specify additional information in a diagram, we make use of the UML notes to incorporate it. For example, in Figure 15 we have used two notes to indicate how the data is distributed into the two existing tablespaces; the tablespace TS_Sales98 holds the data about the sales before or in 1998, whereas the tablespace TS_Sales holds the sales after 1998.

Data Warehouse Physical Schema

The DWPS shows the physical aspects of the implementation of the DW. This diagram is divided into two parts: the component diagram and the deployment diagram. In the first diagram, the configuration of the logical structures used to store the DW is shown. For example, in Figure 16, the DW is implemented by means of a database called DWEnt, which is formed by three tablespaces called FACTS, DIMENSIONS, and INDX. The data files that the tablespaces use are given as well: FACTS.ORA, FACTS2.ORA, DIMENSIONS.ORA, DIM-PART2.ORA, and INDX01.DBF.

Figure 17 shows a part of the definition of the tablespaces: the tablespace FACTS hosts the table customer_invoices and the tablespace DIMENSIONS hosts the dimension tables customers, products, product_snapshots, and the rest of the tables (not shown in the diagram for the sake of simplicity). The notes attached to tables customer_invoices and products show the definition of the corresponding partitions. Below the name of each table, the text (from ROLAP1) is included, which indicates that the tables have been previously defined in a package called ROLAP1 (Figure 14). It is important to highlight that the logical structure defined in the DWLS are reused in this diagram and, therefore, we avoid any possibility of ambiguity or incoherence.

In the second diagram, the deployment diagram, different aspects relative to the hardware and software configuration are specified. Moreover, the physical distribution of the logical structures previously defined in the component diagrams is also represented. For example, in Figure 18, we can observe the configuration of the

Figure 16. Data warehouse physical schema: Component diagram (part 1)

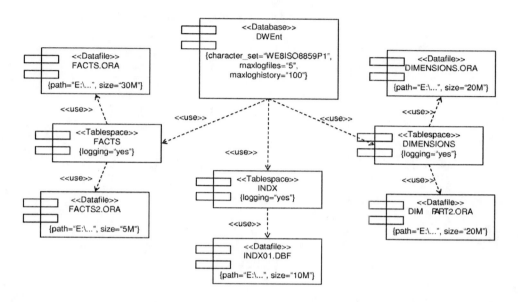

Figure 17. Data warehouse physical schema: Component diagram (part 2)

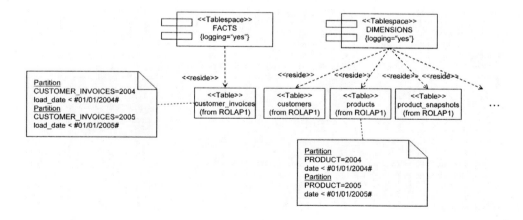

Figure 18. Data warehouse physical schema: Deployment diagram (version 1)

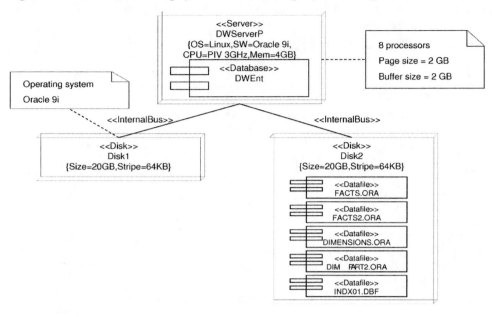

Figure 19. Data warehouse physical schema: Deployment diagram (version 2)

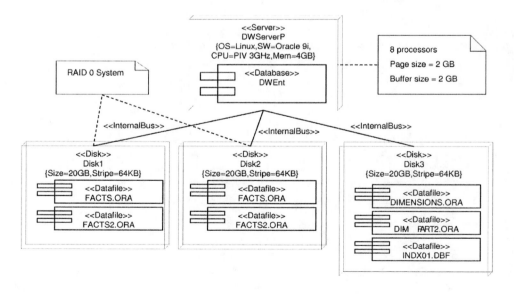

server that hosts the DW: the server is composed of two disks, one for the operating system (Linux) and the applications (Oracle) and another one for the different datafiles (FACTS.ORA, FACTS2.ORA, and so forth) that are used by the database (Figure 16).

One of the advantages of our approach is that it allows evaluation and discussion of different implementations, during the first stages in the design of a DW. In this way, the designer can anticipate some implementation or performance problems. For example, an alternative configuration of the physical structure of the DW can be established, as shown in Figure 19. In this second alternative, a RAID 0 system has been chosen to host the datafiles that are used by the tablespace FACTS, in order to improve the response time of the disk drive and the performance of the system in general. From these two alternative configurations, the DW designer and the DW administrator can discuss the pros and cons of each option.

Integration Transportation Diagram

The ITD defines the physical structure of the ETL processes used in the loading of data in the DW from the data sources. On the one hand, the data sources are represented by means of the SPS and, on the other hand, the DW is represented by means of the DWPS. Since the SPS and the DWPS have been defined previously, in this diagram they are imported.

Figure 20. Integration transportation diagram: Deployment diagram

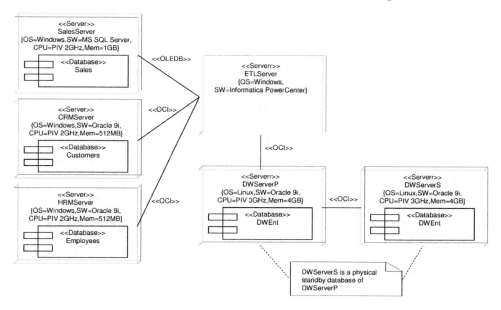

For example, the ITD for our running example is shown in Figure 20. On the left hand side of this diagram, different data source servers are represented: SalesServer, CRMServer, and HRMServer, which have been previously defined in Figure 15; on the right hand side, the DWServerP, previously defined in Figure 18, is shown. Moreover, the DWServerS, a physical standby database[9] is also included in the design.

In Figure 20, the ETLServer is introduced, an additional server that is used to execute the ETL processes. This server communicates with the rest of the servers by means of a series of specific protocols: OLEDB to communicate with SalesServer because it uses Microsoft SQLServer[10] and OCI (*Oracle Call Interface*) to communicate with CRMServer, HRMServer, and DWServer because they use Oracle.

Client Physical Schema

The CPS defines the physical structure of the specific structures that are used by the clients to access the DW. Diverse configurations exist that can be used: exportation of data to *data marts*, use of an OLAP server, and so forth. In our example, we have chosen a client/server architecture and the same DW server provides access to data for the clients. Therefore, we do not need to define a specific structure for the clients.

Figure 21. Customization transportation diagram: Deployment diagram

Customization Transportation Diagram

The CTD defines the exportation processes from the DW towards the specific structures used by the clients. In this diagram, the DW is represented by means of the DWPS and clients are represented by means of the CPS. Since the DWPS and the CPS have been previously defined, in this diagram, we do not have to define them again, but they are directly imported.

For example, in Figure 21, the CTD of our running example is shown. On the left hand side of this diagram, part of the DWPS, which has been previously defined in Figure 18, is shown. On the right hand side, three types of clients who will use the DW are shown: a Web client with operating system Apple Macintosh, a Web client with operating system Microsoft Windows and, finally, a client with a specific desktop application (MicroStrategy) with operating system Microsoft Windows. Whereas both Web clients communicate with the server by means of HTTP, the desktop client uses the *open database connectivity* (ODBC).

In the following section, we explain how to use our component and deployment diagrams to implement a DW on an Oracle database server (Oracle, 2005a, 2005b).

Implementation in Oracle

Creating a database consists basically of the following steps:

- Creating the database's datafiles (files where the database server will host the data in the database structures, such as tables, materialized views, and so forth), its control files (files where the status of the physical structure of the database is stored), and its redo log files (files that record all changes made in datafiles)
- Creating the system tablespaces
- Creating the data dictionary (tables, views, etc.)

Creating the Database

Before proceeding, we should point out that the information about the database repository to be created (Figure 16 and Figure 17) was passed to our database administrator, who created the database. Following Oracle recommendations, the database creation is an operation that should only be executed by the administrator, who is also responsible for granting database permissions to users. Then, if users need to create several databases or wish to organize a big database consisting of a considerable amount of tables, the DW administrator should organize them by specifying *tablespaces* and decide which tables to locate in each created *tablespace*. Therefore, the concept of database for Oracle is at a high administrative level, avoiding programmers and even database designers to create databases. For this reason, we do not do a deep study on the *create database* statement in this section. Instead, we will concentrate on the statements and stages that the DW designer has accomplished from our UML *component* and *deployment diagrams* described in previous sections. In the following subsections, we will show some SQL sentences automatically generated by the *Oracle Enterprise Manager Console* tool to implement the DW and some snapshots from the same tool to see the created *tablespaces*, *tables*, *indexes*, and so forth.

Creating the Tablespaces

The created database is called DWEnt. Then, the first task to accomplish is to specify the *tablespaces* where allocating the tables. As seen in Figure 16, we need to create three tablespaces: one for the facts (FACTS), another one for the dimensions (DIMENSIONS), and the last one for the indexes (INDX). Furthermore, according to the same component diagram, the tablespaces for the facts and the dimensions need to be defined in two *datafiles*. Datafiles are the logical structure in which Oracle

Figure 22. Tablespaces definition in Oracle

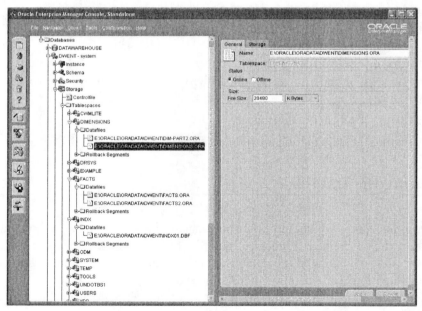

structures a database, that is, the place where allocating the structures (e.g., tables, indices, and so forth) defined within a tablespace. Due to the amount of data to be stored in the tablespaces for facts and dimensions, the designer decided to specify two datafiles for each tablespace (Figure 16).

Figure 22 shows the definition of the tablespaces as seen in the *Oracle Enterprise Console Manager*. In the following SQL statements, we can see the SQL patterns generated by this management tool for defining tablespaces. We can also notice the datafiles that will be used for the DW to store fact tables, dimension tables, views, and so on.

```
CREATE TABLESPACE "FACTS"
    LOGGING
    DATAFILE 'E:\ORACLE\ORADATA\DWENT\FACTS.ora' SIZE 30M,
    'E:\ORACLE\ORADATA\DWENT\FACTS2.ORA' SIZE 5M
    EXTENT MANAGEMENT LOCAL SEGMENT SPACE MANAGEMENT  AUTO

CREATE TABLESPACE "DIMENSIONS"
    LOGGING
    DATAFILE 'E:\ORACLE\ORADATA\DWENT\DIMENSIONS.ora' SIZE 20M,
    'E:\ORACLE\ORADATA\DWENT\DIM-PART2.ORA' SIZE 20M
    EXTENT MANAGEMENT LOCAL SEGMENT SPACE MANAGEMENT AUTO
```

Creating the Data Dictionary

Once both tablespaces and datafiles have been created within a database, the next step is to define fact and dimension tables. First of all, in the following SQL sentences, we can see how we have specified the products table. Following the DWPS from Figure 17, the table has been created partitioning it into two different partitions, once for products in year 2004 and another for new products in 2005. Furthermore, due to the fact that a partitioning has been defined, an index for the column in which we define the partitioning (e.g., date), has automatically been created. In Figure 23, we show the definition of the partition on products as it is displayed in *Oracle Enterprise Manager Console*. We can notice the definition of the two partitions (PRODUCT=2004 and PRODUCT=2005) and the definition of the index (IDX_PRODUCTS).

Figure 23. Definition of a partition on products table in Oracle

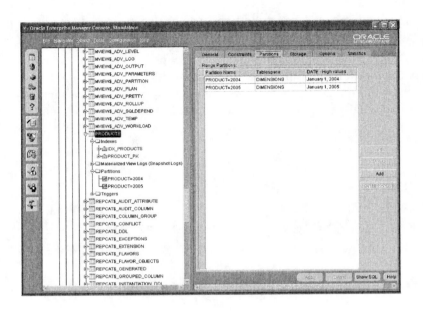

```
CREATE TABLE "SYSTEM"."PRODUCTS" (
  "PRODUCT_ID" NUMBER(10) NOT NULL,
  "PRODUCT_DESC" VARCHAR2(40) NOT NULL,
  'CATEGORY_CODE" VARCHAR2(10) NOT NULL,
  "CATEGORY_DESC" VARCHAR2(40) NOT NULL,
  "DATE" DATE NOT NULL,
  CONSTRAINT "PRODUCT_PK" PRIMARY KEY("PRODUCT_ID"))
  TABLESPACE "DIMENSIONS"
  PARTITION BY RANGE ("DATE") (PARTITION "PRODUCT=2004"
  VALUES LESS THAN  (TO_DATE('2004-1-1,' 'YYYY-MM-DD'))
  TABLESPACE "DIMENSIONS,"
  PARTITION "PRODUCT=2005"
  VALUES LESS THAN (TO_DATE('2005-1-1,' 'YYYY-MM-DD'))
  TABLESPACE 'DIMENSIONS' );
 CREATE INDEX SYSTEM.IDX_PRODUCTS ON SYSTEM.PRODUCTS ("DATE")
LOCAL
```

The SQL statements for the customers and customer_addresses tables are more simple as no partitioning was defined for these tables in Figure 17. Besides, all dimension tables are defined in the *dimension tablespace*.

```
CREATE TABLE "SYSTEM." "CUSTOMERS" (
    "CUSTOMERS_ID" NUMBER(8) NOT NULL,
    "SNAPSHOT" DATE NOT NULL,
    "CUSTOMER_NAME" VARCHAR2(40) NOT NULL,
    "AGE" NUMBER(2) NOT NULL,
    "MARITAL_STATUS" VARCHAR2(1) NOT NULL,
    "CREDIT_RATING" VARCHAR2(10) NOT NULL,
    CONSTRAINT "CUSTOMER_PK" PRIMARY KEY("CUSTOMERS_ID"))
    TABLESPACE "DIMENSIONS"


CREATE TABLE "SYSTEM." "CUSTOMER_ADDRESSES" (
    "CUSTOMER_ID" NUMBER(8) NOT NULL,
    "ADDRESS_ID" NUMBER(8) NOT NULL,
    "ADDRESS_LINE1" VARCHAR2(35) NOT NULL,
    "ADDRESS_LINE2" VARCHAR2(35) NOT NULL,
    "POSTAL_CODE" VARCHAR2(9) NOT NULL,
    CONSTRAINT "CUST_ADDRESS_PK" PRIMARY KEY("CUSTOMER_ID",
"ADDRESS_ID"),
    CONSTRAINT "CUST_ADDRESS_FK" FOREIGN KEY("CUSTOMER_ID")
    REFERENCES "SYSTEM"."CUSTOMERS"("CUSTOMERS_ID")
    TABLESPACE "DIMENSIONS"
```

Figure 24 shows the definition of the columns of the fact table customer_invoices in Oracle. Another partitioning has been created in this table. Again, our DW is intended to locate data for every year in each different partition (Figure 17), and therefore, the column in which we base our partition is load_date. Instead of the previous dimension tables, this fact table is defined in the *fact tablespace*. Moreover, the index creation SQL statement has been slightly changed because the following SQL statement has been automatically generated by the *Oracle Enterprise Manager Console*, and thus, the index name was automatically specified based on the database and table names. Then, this index name exceeded the longest index name allowed by Oracle. Therefore, the index name was manually shortened. In Figure 25, we include the definition of the partition on customer_invoices as it is shown in Oracle.

Figure 24. Defintion of customer_invoices table in Oracle

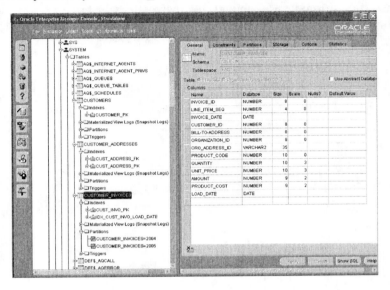

Figure 25. Definition of a partition on customer_invoices table in Oracle

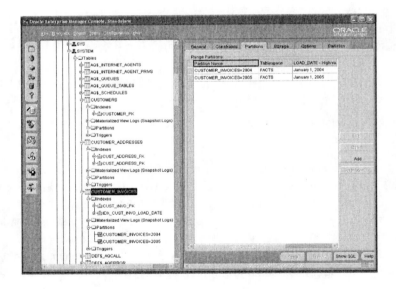

```
CREATE TABLE "SYSTEM." "CUSTOMER_INVOICES" (
  "INVOICE_ID" NUMBER(8) NOT NULL,
  "LINE_ITEM_SEQ" NUMBER(4) NOT NULL,
  "INVOICE_DATE" DATE NOT NULL,
  "CUSTOMER_ID" NUMBER(8) NOT NULL,
  "BILL-TO-ADDRESS" NUMBER(8) NOT NULL,
  "ORGANIZATION_ID" NUMBER(8) NOT NULL,
  "ORG_ADDRESS_ID" VARCHAR2(35) NOT NULL,
  "PRODUCT_CODE" NUMBER(10) NOT NULL,
  "QUANTITY" NUMBER(10, 3) NOT NULL,
  "UNIT_PRICE" NUMBER(10, 3) NOT NULL,
  "AMOUNT" NUMBER(9, 2) NOT NULL,
  "PRODUCT_COST" NUMBER(9, 2) NOT NULL,
  "LOAD_DATE" DATE NOT NULL,
  CONSTRAINT "CUST_INVO_PK" PRIMARY KEY("INVOICE_ID",
  "LINE_ITEM_SEQ"),
  CONSTRAINT "CUST_INVO_FK" FOREIGN KEY("CUSTOMER_ID",
  "BILL-TO-ADDRESS")
  REFERENCES "SYSTEM." "CUSTOMER_ADDRESSES"("CUSTOMER_ID",
  "ADDRESS_ID"),
  CONSTRAINT "CUST_INVO_FK2" FOREIGN KEY("PRODUCT_CODE")
  REFERENCES "SYSTEM." "PRODUCTS"("PRODUCT_ID"),
  CONSTRAINT "CUST_INVO_FK3" FOREIGN KEY("ORGANIZATION_ID",
  "ORG_ADDRESS_ID")
  REFERENCES"SYSTEM.""INTERNAL_ORG_ADDRESSES"("ORGANIZATION_ID",
  "ADDRESS_ID"))
  TABLESPACE "FACTS"
  PARTITION BY RANGE ("LOAD_DATE") (PARTITION
  "CUSTOMER_INVOICES=2004"
  VALUES LESS THAN  (TO_DATE('2004-1-1,' 'YYYY-MM-DD'))
  TABLESPACE "FACTS",
  PARTITION "CUSTOMER_INVOICES=2005"
  VALUES LESS THAN  (TO_DATE('2005-1-1,' 'YYYY-MM-DD'))
  TABLESPACE "FACTS" );
  CREATE INDEX SYSTEM.IDX_CUST_INVO_LOAD_DATE ON
  SYSTEM.CUSTOMER_INVOICES ("LOAD_DATE") LOCAL
```

In this section, we have shown how to accomplish the implementation of a DW from our *component* and *deployment diagrams*. We believe that the implementation issues considered in our techniques are useful for the final implementation. Even more, the DW administrator has implemented the DW according to our physical modeling schema.

Conclusion

In this chapter, we have presented an adaptation of the component and deployment diagrams of UML for the modeling of the physical design of a DW. One of the advantages of this proposal is that these diagrams are not used in an isolated way, instead they are used together with other diagrams that we use for the modeling of other aspects of a DW (conceptual and logical design, modeling of ETL processes, and so forth) in the context of our overall method for designing DW (Luján-Mora, 2005). Thanks to the use of the component and deployment diagrams, a DW designer can specify both hardware, software, and middleware needs for a DW project. The main advantages provided by our approach are as follows:

- It traces the design of a DW, from the conceptual model up to the physical model.

- It reduces the overall development cost as we accomplish implementation issues from the early stages of a DW project. We should take into account that modifying these aspects in ulterior design phases may result in increasing the total cost of the project.

- It supports different levels of abstraction, by providing different levels of details for the same diagram.

We believe that we are the first to define a DW engineering process (Luján-Mora, 2005) that addresses the design and development of both the DW back-end and front-end, from the conceptual to the physical levels. Our method provides a unifying framework that facilitates the integration of different DW models.

Future work will be focused on improving our proposal. Furthermore, we will redefine our approach by following the model-driven architecture (MDA) (Object Management Group [OMG], 2006). MDA separates the specification of system functionality from the specification of the implementation of that functionality on a specific technology platform, that is, a platform-independent model (PIM) can be transformed into multiple platform-specific models (PSMs) in order to execute on a concrete platform.

References

Abelló, A., Samos, J., & Saltor, F. (2000). Benefits of an object-oriented multi-dimensional data model. In *Proceedings of the Symposium on Objects and Databases in 14th European Conference on Object-Oriented Programming (ECOOP'00)* (Vol. 1944, p. 141-152). Sophia Antipolis and Cannes, France: Springer-Verlag.

Abelló, A., Samos, J., & Saltor, F. (2001). A framework for the classification and description of multidimensional data models. In *Proceedings of the 12ᵗʰ Internatinal Conference on Database and Expert Systems Applications (DEXA'01)* (Vol. 2113, p. 668-677). Munich, Germany: Springer-Verlag.

Abelló, A., Samos, J., & Saltor, F. (2002). YAM2 (Yet Another Multidimensional Model): An extension of UML. In *International Database Engineering & Applications Symposium (IDEAS'02)* (p. 172-181). Edmonton, Canada: IEEE Computer Society.

Allen, S. (2002). *Data modeling for everyone.* Curlingstone Publishing.

Ambler, S. (2002). *A UML profile for data modeling.* Retrieved from http://www.agiledata.org/essays/umlDataModelingProfile.html

Blaschka, M., Sapia, C., Höfling, G., & Dinter, B. (1998). Finding your way through multidimensional data models. In *Proceedings of the 9ᵗʰ International Conference on Database and Expert Systems Applications (DEXA'98)* (Vol. 1460, p. 198-203). Vienna, Austria: Springer-Verlag.

Frankel, D. (2003). *Model driven architecture. Applying MDA to enterprise computing.* Indianapolis, IN: John Wiley & Sons.

Furtado, P. (2006). Node partitioned data warehouses: Experimental evidence and improvements. *Journal of Database Management, 17*(2), 43-61.

Giovinazzo, W. (2000). *Object-oriented data warehouse design. Building a star schema.* New Jersey, USA: Prentice-Hall.

Golfarelli, M., Maio, D., & Rizzi, S. (1998). The dimensional fact model: A conceptual model for data warehouses. *International Journal of Cooperative Information Systems (IJCIS), 7*(2-3), 215-247.

Hüsemann, B., Lechtenbörger, J., & Vossen, G. (2000). Conceptual data warehouse modeling. In *Proceedings of the 2ⁿᵈ International Workshop on Design and Management of Data Warehouses (DMDW'00)* (p. 6.1-6.11). Stockholm, Sweden.

Inmon, W. (2002). *Building the Data Warehouse* (3ʳᵈ ed.). John Wiley & Sons.

Jacobson, I., Booch, G., & Rumbaugh, J. (1999). *The unified software development process.* Addison-Wesley.

Jarke, M., Lenzerini, M., Vassiliou, Y., & Vassiliadis, P. (2003). *Fundamentals of data warehouses* (2nd ed.). Springer-Verlag.

Kimball, R. (2002). *The data warehouse toolkit* (2nd ed.). John Wiley & Sons.

Kimball, R., Reeves, L., Ross, M., & Thornthwaite, W. (1998). *The data warehouse lifecycle toolkit.* John Wiley & Sons.

Kleppe, A., Warmer, J., & Bast, W. (2003). *MDA explained. The practice and promise of the model driven architecture.* Addison Wesley.

Lechtenbörger, J., & Vossen, G. (2003). Multidimensional normal forms for data warehouse design. *Information Systems, 28*(5), 415-434.

Luján-Mora, S. (2005). *Data warehouse design with UML.* Unpublished doctoral dissertation, Department of Software and Computing Systems, University of Alicante. Retrieved from http://www.dlsi.ua.es/□slujan/files/thesis.pdf

Luján-Mora, S., & Trujillo, J. (2003). A comprehensive method for data warehouse design. In *Proceedings of the 5th International Workshop on Design and Management of Data Warehouses (DMDW '03)* (p. 1.1-1.14). Berlin, Germany.

Luján-Mora, S., & Trujillo, J. (2004). A data warehouse engineering process. In *Proceedings of the 3rd Biennial International Conference on Advances in Information Systems (ADVIS '04)* (Vol. 3261, p. 14-23). Izmir, Turkey: Springer-Verlag.

Luján-Mora, S., Trujillo, J., & Song, I. (2002a). Extending UML for multidimensional modeling. In *Proceedings of the 5th International Conference on the Unified Modeling Language (UML '02)* (Vol. 2460, p. 290-304). Dresden, Germany: Springer-Verlag.

Luján-Mora, S., Trujillo, J., & Song, I. (2002b). Multidimensional modeling with UML package diagrams. In *Proceedings of the 21st International Conference on Conceptual Modeling (ER '02)* (Vol. 2503, p. 199-213). Tampere, Finland: Springer-Verlag.

Luján-Mora, S., Vassiliadis, P., & Trujillo, J. (2004). Data Mapping Diagrams for Data Warehouse Design with UML. In *Proceedings of the 23rd International Conference on Conceptual Modeling (ER '04)* (Vol. 3288, p. 191-204). Shanghai, China: Springer-Verlag.

Mazon, J., Trujillo, J., Serrano, M., & Piattini, M. (2005). Applying MDA to the development of data warehouses. In *Proceedings of the ACM Seventh International Workshop on Data Warehousing and OLAP (DOLAP 2005)* (p. 57-66). Bremen, Germany: ACM.

Mellor, S., Scott, K., Uhl, A., & Weise, D. (2004). *MDA distilled: Principles of model-driven architecture.* Addison Wesley.

Naiburg, E., & Maksimchuk, R. (2001). *UML for database design.* Addison-Wesley.

Nicola, M., & Rizvi, H. (2003). Storage layout and I/O performance in data ware-houses. In *Proceedings of the 5ᵗʰ International Workshop on Design and Management of Data Warehouses (DMDW'03)* (p. 7.1-7.9). Berlin, Germany.

Object Management Group (OMG). (2003). *Unified modeling language specification 1.5.* Retrieved from http://www.omg.org/cgi-bin/doc? formal/03-03-01

Object Management Group (OMG). (2005a). *MOF 2.0 query/view/transformation.* Retrieved from http://www.omg.org/cgi-bin/doc? ptc/2005-11-01

Object Management Group (OMG). (2005b). *UML superstructure specification, v2.0.* Retrieved from http://www.omg.org/cgi-bin/doc? formal/05-07-04

Object Management Group (OMG). (2006). *Model driven architecture (MDA) guide 1.0.1.* Retrieved from http://www.omg.org/cgi-bin/doc? omg/03-06-01

Oracle. (2005a). *Oracle database concepts 10g release 2 (10.2).* Oracle Corporation.

Oracle. (2005b). *Oracle database data warehousing guide 10g release 2 (10.2).* Oracle Corporation.

Poe, V., Klauer, P., & Brobst, S. (1998). *Building a data warehouse for decision support* (2ⁿᵈ ed.). Prentice-Hall.

Rizzi, S. (2003). Open problems in data warehousing: Eight years later. In *Proceedings of the 5ᵗʰ International Workshop on Design and Management of Data Warehouses (DMDW'03).* Berlin, Germany.

Sapia, C. (1999). On modeling and predicting query behavior in OLAP systems. In *Proceedings of the 1ˢᵗ International Workshop on Design and Management of Data Warehouses (DMDW'99)* (pp. 1-10). Heidelberg, Germany.

Sapia, C., Blaschka, M., Höfling, G., & Dinter, B. (1998). Extending the E/R model for the multidimensional paradigm. In *Proceedings of the 1ˢᵗ International Workshop on Data Warehouse and Data Mining (DWDM'98)* (Vol. 1552, pp. 105-116). Singapore: Springer-Verlag.

Selonen, P., Koskimies, K., & Sakkinen, M. (2003). Transformation between UML diagrams. *Journal of Database Management, 14*(3), 37-55.

Silverston, L., Inmon, W., & Graziano, K. (1997). *The data model resource book: A library of logical data models and data warehouse designs.* John Wiley & Sons.

Simitsis, A. (2005). Mapping conceptual to logical models for ETL processes. In *Proceedings of the ACM Seventh International Workshop on Data Warehousing and OLAP (DOLAP 2005)* (pp. 67-76). Bremen, Germany: ACM.

Triantafillakis, A., Kanellis, P., & Martakos, D. (2004). Data warehouse interoper-ability for the extended enterprise. *Journal of Database Management, 15*(3), 73-84.

Trujillo, J., & Luján-Mora, S. (2003). A UML based approach for modeling ETL processes in data warehouses. In *Proceedings of the 22ⁿᵈ International Conference on Conceptual Modeling (ER '03)* (Vol. 2813, pp. 307-320). Chicago, USA: Springer-Verlag.

Trujillo, J., Palomar, M., Gómez, J., & Song, I. (2001). Designing data warehouses with OO conceptual models. *IEEE Computer, Special Issue on Data Warehouses, 34*(12), 66-75.

Tryfona, N., Busborg, F., & Christiansen, J. (1999). StarER: A conceptual model for data warehouse design. In *Proceedings of the ACM 2ⁿᵈ International Workshop on Data Warehousing and OLAP (DOLAP '99)* (pp. 3-8). Kansas City, MO: ACM.

Vassiliadis, P., Simitsis, A., Georgantas, P., Terrovitis, M., & Skiadopoulos, S. (2005). A generic and customizable framework for the design of ETL scenarios. *Information Systems, 30*(7), 492-525.

Vassiliadis, P., Simitsis, A., & Skiadopoulos, S. (2002). Conceptual modeling for ETL processes. In *Proceedings of the ACM Fifth International Workshop on Data Warehousing and OLAP (DOLAP 2002)* (pp. 14-21). McLean, USA: ACM.

Warmer, J., & Kleppe, A. (1998). *The object constraint language. Precise modeling with UML.* Addison-Wesley.

Whittle, J. (2000). Formal approaches to systems analysis using UML: An overview. *Journal of Database Management, 11*(4), 4-13.

Endnotes

[1] A profile is an extension to the UML that uses stereotypes, tagged values, and constraints to extend the UML for specialized purposes.

[2] Due to the lack of space, we do not show the order we propose in our DW design method.

[3] An icon, a new graphical representation, can be associated to a stereotype in UML.

[4] The transformation process from the DWCS to the DWLS is outside the scope of this chapter.

[5] ROLAP is a storage model that uses tables in a relational database to store multidimensional data.

[6] MOLAP is a storage mode that uses a proprietary multidimensional structure to store multidimensional data.

[7] GB means *geographic boundaries*.

[8] Kimball (2002) coined the term *degenerate dimensions* for data items that perform much the same function as dimensions, but they are stored in the fact table and are not foreign key links through to dimension tables.

[9] A physical standby database is a byte by byte exact copy of the primary database. The primary database records all changes and sends them to the standby database. A standby database environment is meant for disastrous failures.

[10] The configuration of a server is defined by means of tagged values: OS, SW, CPU, and so forth.

Chapter IV

Supporting the Full BPM Life-Cycle Using Process Mining and Intelligent Redesign

Wil M. P. van der Aalst, Eindhoven University of Technology, The Netherlands

Mariska Netjes, Eindhoven University of Technology, The Netherlands

Hajo A. Reijers, Eindhoven University of Technology, The Netherlands

Abstract

Business process management (BPM) systems provide a broad range of facilities to enact and manage operational business processes. Ideally, these systems should provide support for the complete BPM life-cycle: (re)design, configuration, execution, control, and diagnosis of processes. However, based on an extensive evaluation of the FileNet P8 BPM Suite, we show that existing BPM tools are unable to support the full life-cycle. There are clearly gaps between the various phases (e.g., users need to transfer or interpret information without any support) and some of the phases (e.g., the redesign and diagnosis phases) are not supported sufficiently. This chapter shows that techniques for process mining and intelligent redesign can be used to offer better support for the (re)design and diagnosis phases and, thus, close the BPM life-cycle. We also briefly report on the work done in the context of the ProM tool, which is used as framework to experiment with such techniques.

Introduction

Business process management (BPM) systems can be seen as successors of workflow management (WFM) systems, which became popular in the mid-nineties. However, already in the seventies, people were working on office automation systems, which are comparable with today's WFM systems. Consider, for example, the OfficeTalk system developed by Ellis et al. at Xerox that was already able to support administrative processes based on Petri-net-based specifications of procedures (Ellis, 1979). Today, many WFM systems are available (Aalst & Hee, 2004; Jablonski & Bussler, 1996; Lawrence, 1997; Mühlen, 2004). The core functionality of these systems can be described as *the ability to support an operational business process based on an explicit process model*, that is, automating the "flow of work" without necessarily automating individual activities.

Recently, WFM vendors started to position their systems as BPM systems. We define BPM as follows: Supporting business processes using methods, techniques, and software to design, enact, control, and analyze operational processes involving humans, organizations, applications, documents, and other sources of information (Aalst, Hofstede, & Weske, 2003). This definition restricts BPM to operational processes, that is, processes at the strategic level and processes that cannot be made explicit are excluded. It also follows that systems supporting BPM need to be "process aware." After all, without information about the operational processes at hand, little support is possible. When comparing classical definitions of WFM (Lawrence, 1997) with the above definition of BPM, one could conclude that the main goal of BPM systems is to offer a broader set of functionalities and support of the whole process life-cycle. This is also the "sales pitch" that many vendors use to market their products. However, analysis of existing BPM systems shows that the functionality of these systems leaves much to be desired. In the first part of this chapter, we analyze the limitations of today's BPM systems. Based on this analysis, problems are identified and in the second part of this chapter, we show how to address these problems.

Step 1: Evaluation of the FileNet P8 BPM Suite

The first goal of this chapter is to analyze whether today's BPM systems actually support the BPM life-cycle. To do this, we use the BPM life-cycle as depicted in

Figure 1. The BPM life-cycle

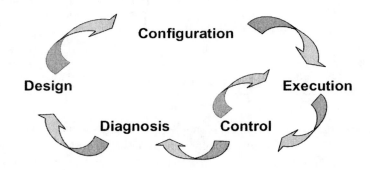

Table 1. The workflows used in our analysis

Workflow Name	Reference
Intake_Admin	(Reijers, 2003)
Credit application	(Reijers, 2003)
Intake_Meetings	(Jansen-Vullers & Reijers, 2005; Reijers, 2003)
Bank account	(Netjes, Aalst, & Reijers, 2005)
Mortgage request	(Aalst, 2001; Netjes, Vanderfeesten, & Reijers, 2006)

Figure 1. This life-cycle identifies five phases (*design, configuration, execution, control*, and *diagnosis*), which will be described later. The depicted life-cycle is an extension of the life-cycle presented in (Aalst, Hofstede, & Weske, 2003). We will discuss the desired functionality in each of the phases. To make things more concrete, we have evaluated one particular system in detail: FileNet P8 BPM Suite (Version 3.5). We have selected this system because it is considered one of the leading commercial BPM systems (Gartner, 2003, 2004, 2005). Moreover, the system is explicitly positioned by the vendor as a tool to support the whole BPM life-cycle.

We analyze the support of the FileNet P8 BPM Suite in each of the five phases shown in Figure 1. For our evaluation, we performed a full pass through these phases using five realistic workflow scenarios, each including a concrete workflow process and life-cycle context. We have used five workflows to be able to obtain additional insights, when necessary. As a starting point for our evaluation, we will assume that each workflow has already made one pass through the BPM cycle. The name and the related literature for each of the workflows is provided in Table 1.

These particular workflows have been selected because the papers describing them provide a diagnosis of the improvement points and one or more alternative designs. Also, the original workflows and the alternatives have already been tested and the underlying data were available to us.

Step 2: An Approach Based on Process Mining and Intelligent Redesign

Based on the evaluation of the FileNet P8 BPM Suite using the five workflows mentioned in Table 1, we noted that there was little support for the diagnosis and design phases in the BPM life-cycle. Moreover, the transfer of information from the run-time environment to the design-time environment is hardly supported. When looking at other BPM products, we see the same limitations. Therefore, the second part of this chapter is concerned with a more detailed analysis of these problems and a proposal for a solution addressing them. Figure 2 sketches the link between Step 1 (Evaluation of systems like the FileNet P8 BPM Suite) and Step 2 (Our proposal to address some of the problems identified). On the left-hand side of Figure 2, we highlight the part of the BPM life-cycle we consider to be most problematic and typically poorly supported by BPM systems. The right-hand side of Figure 2 shows a diagram analyzing the problem and proposing an approach based on process mining and intelligent redesign. We will elaborate on this diagram later in the chapter.

Figure 2. Problems in the BPM life-cycle related to the approach presented in this chapter

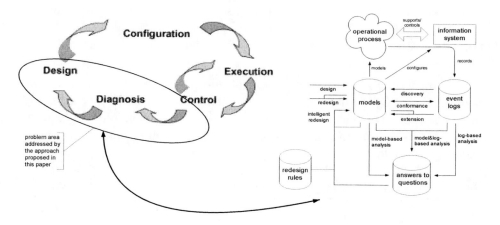

Our approach is based on the observation that there are two core problems in current BPM systems:

- **Problem 1:** The actual execution of the process supported by the BPM system is completely disconnected from the (re)design of the process. To close the BPM life-cycle, it is necessary to automatically interpret information stored in event logs and use this to discover, check, and enhance models describing what is really going on in the business process. To address this problem, we propose to use *process mining techniques* (Aalst, Weijters, & Maruster, 2004; Aalst, Reijers, & Song, 2005; Agrawal, Gunopulos, & Leymann, 1998; Cook & Wolf, 1998; Datta, 1998; Weijters & Aalst, 2003).

- **Problem 2:** BPM systems offer graphical editors and, at times, also simple analysis facilities to analyze the design (In this context, we are not referring to the verification of models, that is, the goal is not to assess the internal consistency, for instance, absence of deadlocks, but to improve the process from a business perspective.) Several BPM systems (including the FileNet P8 BPM Suite) offer basic simulation facilities. However, these facilities are typically considering a very abstract situation (with many assumptions about reality that do not hold) and provide only "what-if" analysis. This means that it is difficult to use these systems and the designer has to come up with ideas for redesigns. The goal of *intelligent redesign* is twofold. First of all, we want to use the information about the real process obtained through process mining. Second, we want to move beyond "what-if" analysis, that is, the system should automatically suggest and evaluate different redesign possibilities.

In the context of the *ProM framework* (Dongen, Medeiros, Verbeek, Weijters, & Aalst, 2005), we are developing automated support for process mining and intelligent redesign in an effort to address the two problems mentioned above. The goal of this chapter is not to provide detailed solutions, but to show the potential of truly closing the BPM life-cycle.

The remainder of this chapter is organized as follows. First we discuss related work. Then, we evaluate the FileNet P8 BPM Suite based on a generic approach, which can also be applied to other BPM systems. Based on this evaluation, we identify the main problems and propose an approach involving techniques for process mining and intelligent redesign. We end the chapter with conclusions.

Related Work

Since the early nineties, workflow technology has matured (Georgakopoulos, Hornick, & Sheth, 1995) and several textbooks have been published (e.g., Aalst & Hee, 2004; Dumas, Aalst, & Hofstede, 2005; Jablonski & Bussler, 1996; Leymann & Roller, 1999; Marinescu, 2002; Mühlen, 2004). Most of the available systems use some proprietary process modeling language and, even if systems claim to support some "standard," there are often all kinds of system-specific extensions and limitations. Petri nets have often been used as an abstraction of these languages, both for the purpose of modeling the control-flow aspects of workflows for the analysis of workflows and different workflow languages and systems (Aalst & Hee, 2004; Aalst, Hofstede, Kiepuszewski, & Barros, 2003; Dumas et al., 2005). The evaluation of workflow and BPM systems has been the domain of consultancy firms such as Gartner (Gartner, 2003, 2004, 2005) and many others. These evaluations are typically not very rigorous and lack objective criteria with respect to the functionality of systems. The *Workflow Patterns* initiative, cf. www.workflowpatterns.com, has been one of the few attempts to evaluate systems and languages in a systematic manner (Aalst et al., 2003). This chapter does not use the workflow patterns to evaluate the FileNet P8 BPM Suite because we want to look at the support of the whole BPM life-cycle. Note that the workflow patterns focus on specific aspects of the system such as the control-flow perspective, the data perspective, or the resource perspective. Therefore, we used an approach where we selected five processes (Table 1), and for each of these processes, we went through the whole BPM life-cycle.

It is impossible to give a complete overview of process mining here. Therefore, we refer to a special issue of *Computers in Industry* on process mining (Aalst & Weijters, 2004) and a survey paper (Aalst, Dongen, Herbst, Maruster, Schimm, & Weijters, 2003) for more references. We will show that process mining techniques can be split into three categories: (1) discovery, (2) conformance, and (3) extension. Techniques for *discovery* try to generate a model based on the event logs. This may be a process model (Aalst et al., 2004; Agrawal et al., 1998; Cook & Wolf, 1998; Datta, 1998; Weijters & Aalst, 2003), but also other models focusing on different perspectives (e.g., a social network (Aalst, Reijers, & Song, 2005)) can be discovered using process mining. Techniques for *conformance* checking (Rozinat & Aalst, 2006a) aim at exposing the difference between some a-priori model (e.g., a Petri net describing the control-flow) and the real process observed via the event log. Process mining techniques for model *extension* take some a-priori model (e.g., a control-flow model) and project other information on it derived from the log (e.g., A Petri net can be extended by providing a decision tree for each choice in the system) (Rozinat & Aalst, 2006b). This way, data and performance aspects can be projected on some a-priori process model obtained directly from the system or discovered through process mining.

Process mining can be seen in the broader context of business (process) intelligence (BPI) and business activity monitoring (BAM). In Grigori, Casati, Castellanos, Dayal, Sayal, and Shan (2004) Grigori, Casati, Dayal, and Shan (2001), and Sayal, Casati, Dayal, and Shan (2002), a BPI toolset on top of HP's Process Manager is described. The BPI toolset includes a so-called "BPI Process Mining Engine." In Mühlen's and Rosemann's work (2000), the authors describe the PISA tool which can be used to extract performance metrics from workflow logs. Similar diagnostics are provided by the ARIS Process Performance Manager (PPM) (IDS Scheer, 2002). The latter tool is commercially available and a customized version of PPM is the Staffware Process Monitor (SPM) (TIBCO, 2005), which is tailored towards mining Staffware logs.

Literature on "intelligent" redesign is limited (Netjes et al., 2006). Clearly, there are many techniques originating from operations management (e.g., simulation, queuing networks, and so forth) that can be applied to workflow processes (Buzacott, 1996). However, these typically only support "what-if" analysis and do not provide suggestions for improvement.

Several researchers have focused on the problem of not meeting certain deadlines in a process. For example, in Panagos and Rabinovich (1997), an approach to dynamically adjust deadlines based on costs, expected execution times, and available slack time is described. In Panagos and Rabinovich (1998), this approach is refined and supported by simulation experiments. In Eder, Panagos, and Rabinovich (1999) and Eder, Panagos, Pezewaunig, and Rabinovich (1999) the topic of capturing time constraints in workflow definitions is considered, and a PERT-like technique for the analysis of the temporal behavior of a workflow is proposed. This technique is similar to the one employed by the "prediction engine" of Staffware (Staffware, 2003). There are also several papers that address timing (e.g., determining performance indicators based on simulation or some analytical method) without considering what to do in case deadlines are not met (See (Reijers, 2003) for an overview). For example, in Zhao and Stohr (1999), different task prioritization policies are compared with respect to turnaround times.

Few of the simulation techniques and systems described in literature use historic data. Even fewer use the current state of a workflow in their analysis. A notable exception is Reijers' and Aalst's work (1999), which proposes the concept of a so-called short-term simulation, that is, a "fast forward" into the near future based on historic and current data.

Most related to the type of intelligent redesign discussed in this chapter are the redesign rules defined in Reijers' work (2003). One example of such a rule is the "knock-out rule," which describes how to reorder activities in a sequential or parallel "checking process" consisting of multiple tests (Aalst, 2001). Also related are the "Process Recombinator" tool, developed in the context of the MIT Process Handbook (Bernstein, Klein, & Malone, 1999), and the KOPeR tool (Nissen, 1998).

The Process Recombinator tool (Bernstein et al., 1999) uses the notions of process specialization and coordination mechanisms to generate new designs on the basis of a list of core activities. From these process designs, the user can select the most promising ones. The KOPeR tool (Nissen, 1998) attempts to automate three activities required for process redesign: process measurement, pathology diagnosis, and transformation matching. The idea is that a limited set of process measures (e.g., process length, process handoffs, and so forth) can be used to identify process pathologies in a given process (e.g., a problematic process structure, fragmented process flows, etc.). Then, these process pathologies can be matched to redesign transformations known to effectively deal with these pathologies. Note that the KOPeR tool only provides ideas for redesign and does not generate new designs.

Evaluation of the FileNet P8 BPM Suite

As described in the introduction, we start by analyzing the FileNet P8 BPM Suite. The main goal of this evaluation is not to discuss the specifics of this particular system, but to provide some insights into the functionality of today's BPM systems. The evaluation approach that we will present is based on the BPM life-cycle and can also be applied to other systems. We selected the FileNet P8 BPM Suite for two reasons. First of all, it is consistently ranked as one of the leading commercial BPM systems (Gartner, 2003, 2004, 2005). Second, it is representative for the current generation of BPM products. In fact, when it comes to supporting the full BPM life-cycle, we expect most systems to offer less functionality (Gartner, 2003, 2004, 2005).

Note that this section is based on an earlier evaluation of the FileNet P8 BPM Suite (Netjes, Reijers, & Aalst, 2006b).

Evaluation Approach Based on the BPM Life-Cycle

First, we present our system-independent approach to evaluate BPM systems. Pivotal to our evaluation approach is the BPM life-cycle depicted in Figure 1. Clearly, we want to evaluate the degree to which each phase is facilitated by a BPM system. Moreover, we want to asses the interoperability among phases. For instance, can information obtained or created in one phase be used in another phase? A BPM system may incorporate a simulation tool, but it may be the case that the simulation model and the model used for execution are incompatible, forcing the user to re-create models or to set parameters twice.

First, we focus on the *design phase*. In case of an already existing process, the goal of this phase is to create an alternative for the current process. This alternative should remedy the diagnosed weaknesses of the process according to the identified improvement possibilities. As indicated in Figure 1, this phase is in-between the diagnosis phase and the configuration phase, that is, input from the diagnosis phase is used to identify improvement opportunities (e.g., bottlenecks or other weaknesses) and the output is transferred towards the configuration part of the BPM system. The resulting process definition consists of the following elements (Aalst & Hee, 2004):

- **Process structure**
- **Resource structure**
- **Allocation logic**
- **Interfaces**

We would like to emphasize that a graphical editor by itself does not offer full support for the design phase. In the design phase the designer wants to experiment with designs, evaluate designs, and use input from the diagnosis phase. Some systems offer a simulation tool to support the design phase. Unfortunately, such a tool is often disconnected from the diagnosis phase, that is, it is impossible to directly use historic data (e.g., to estimate service time distributions or routing probabilities). Moreover, simulation tools typically offer only what-if analysis, that is, the designer has to come up with ideas for alternative designs and needs to analyze each alternative separately without sufficient tool support (Netjes, Vanderfeesten, & Reijers, 2006).

The *configuration phase* focuses on the detailed specification of the selected design. Note that, in the design phase, the emphasis is on the performance of the process while in the configuration phase, the emphasis shifts to the realization of the corresponding system. In principle, the design and configuration phase could use a common graphical editor, that is,, the configuration phase details the process definition created in the design phase. However, it is important that the user is not forced to bypass the editor to code parts of the process and also, that technical details do not need to be addressed in the design phase. If both phases use different tools or concepts, interoperability issues may frustrate a smooth transition from design to configuration.

In the *execution phase*, the configured workflow becomes operational by transferring the process definition to the workflow engine. For the workflow execution, not only the process definition data is required, but also context data about the environment with which the BPM system interacts. Relevant environmental aspects are:

- Information on arriving cases
- Availability and behavior of internal/external resources and services

The execution part of the BPM system captures the context data and relates it to specific instances of the workflow.

The execution of the operational business process is monitored in the *control phase*. The control part of the BPM system monitors, on the one hand, individual cases to be able to give feedback about their status and, on the other hand, aggregates execution data to be able to obtain the current performance of the workflow. The monitoring of specific cases is done with the data from individual process executions without any form of aggregation, while obtaining the performance indicators requires aggregation of these data. Information about running cases can be used as input for the diagnosis phase. However, it can also be used to make changes in the process. For example, temporary bottlenecks do not require a redesign of the process, but require the addition of resources or other direct measures (e.g., not accepting new cases). Hence, the control phase also provides input for the execution phase.

In the *diagnosis phase*, information collected in the control phase is used to reveal weaknesses in the process. In this phase, the focus is usually on aggregated performance data and not on individual cases. This is the domain of process mining (Aalst et al., 2003), business process intelligence (Grigori et al., 2004), data warehousing, and classical data mining techniques. This diagnosis information is providing ideas for redesign (e.g., bottleneck identification) and input for the analysis of redesigns (e.g., historic data) in the design phase.

As indicated, it is not sufficient to support each of the five phases in isolation: interoperability among phases is vital for the usability of a BPM system. Consider, for example, the role of simulation. In a worst case scenario, a BPM system could offer a simulation tool that, on the one hand, cannot directly read the current workflow design used for execution (or relevant information is lost in some translation) and, on the other hand, cannot use any historic data to extract information about service times, routing probabilities, workloads, or resource availability. Such a simulation tool probably offers little support for the BPM life-cycle (Reijers & Aalst, 1999).

Applying the Evaluation Approach to FileNet

We will evaluate the available BPM support by conducting a full pass through the BPM cycle with the aid of several tools from the FileNet P8 BPM Suite. We have evaluated the FileNet P8 BPM Suite, Version 3.5. The system has been used with Microsoft Windows 2000 as operating system, a Microsoft SQL Server as database, BEA Weblogic as J2EE application server, and Microsoft Internet Explorer as browser. The P8 BPM Suite consists of six parts: Workflow Management, process design, process simulation, process tracking, process analysis, and document review and approval (www.FileNet.com). The evaluation of FileNet's BPM abilities focuses on the tools supporting the first five parts. Document review and approval is not relevant for the evaluation; it only facilitates process management. In the remainder of this section, we consider FileNet's capabilities for each of the five BPM phases (design, configuration, execution, control, and diagnosis). A detailed illustration of the BPM support offered by FileNet can be found in Netjes, Reijers, and Aalst (2006a), where we present the full pass through the BPM life-cycle for one of the five workflow scenarios.

Design

We start our evaluation with the design phase. For each of the five workflow scenarios mentioned in Table 1, we would like to create an alternative workflow with help from the FileNet P8 BPM Suite. We assume these workflows have already made one pass through the BPM cycle, meaning that the original workflow model and data from execution are present in the FileNet system. A workflow model for which an alternative should be made can be loaded in the FileNet *process designer*, which, however, does not support the creation of one or more alternatives. The redesign of the original model to obtain a better performing alternative should be done manually. For each of the workflows, we take the alternatives described in the corresponding and use the *process designer* to change the original model to the alternative model. One of the alternative designs made with the *process designer*

Figure 3. Workflow model in the process designer

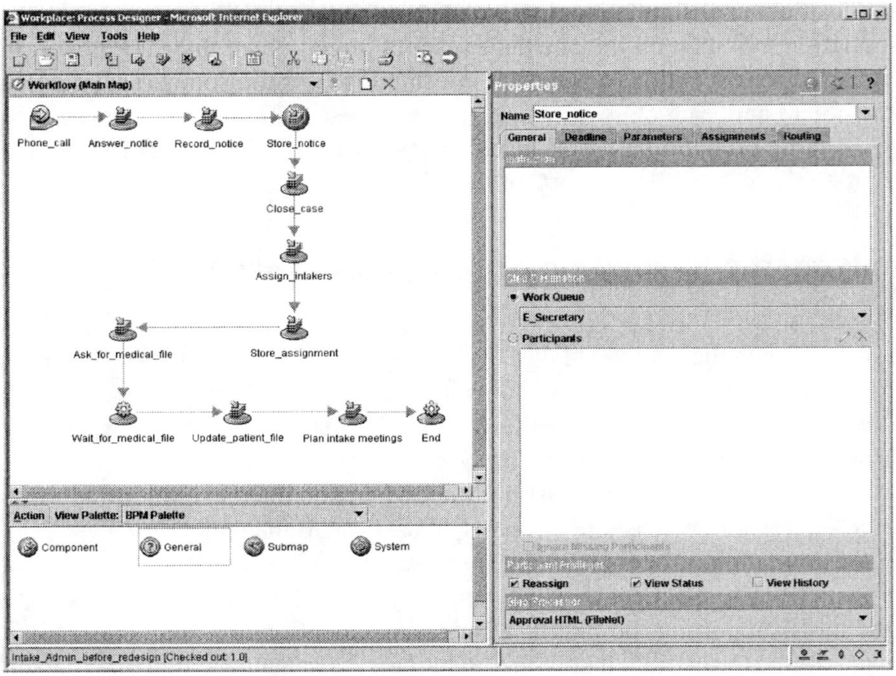

is shown in Figure 3. The depicted design presents a medical process in which a mental patient is registered and assigned to medical employees (intakers), and for which intake meetings are planned. A detailed description of the process is available in (Reijers, 2003). More information on the modeling of workflows with the FileNet *process designer* can be found in Netjes, Reijers, and Aalst (2006a).

The performance of each of the created alternatives should be evaluated to find the best alternative. For this, we use the FileNet *process simulator*. For each alternative, we create a simulation scenario for which we import the process steps, their order, and the allocation logic defined with the *process designer*. The imported data can not be changed in the *process simulator*, but a replacement can be imported from the *process designer* without the loss of settings. Other process definition data should be added to the simulation scenario manually. *Jobs* are connected to the process steps and assigned to *resources*, which are allocated according to *shifts*. The notion of *shifts* allows for the scheduling of resources over the available working hours. Relating these *jobs*, *resources*, and *shifts* to each other is rather complicated, because only one definition window can be open at the time and relations should also be indicated when defining a *job*, *resource*, or *shift*.

In addition to the definition data, there is context data required to perform a simulation. Historic data is present in the system, but it can only be used in a limited way. Historic information on arriving cases can be transferred to the *process simulator*, but all other data, like processing times and routing probabilities, should be derived from the execution data and included manually. It is only possible to provide constant values for the simulation parameters, so the simulation results will only provide a rough indication for the performance of a scenario. Simulation results are generated fast and with no additional effort. The use of the FileNet *process simulator* is explained in detail in Netjes, Reijers, and Aalst (2006a). A simulation scenario with simulation results is depicted in Figure 4. For each of the five workflows, we choose the best alternative, which we specify in detail in the configuration phase.

Configuration

The FileNet *process designer* is also used for the configuration of the chosen alternative workflows and offers interoperability between the design and the configuration phase. In the design phase, we already specified the process structure and the mapping of resources to tasks for each workflow with the *process designer*. The more complicated parts of the process structure are detailed out in the configuration phase. Each workflow model contains one or more complex constructs, but besides one construct, we have been able to configure them all with the *process designer*. The resource structure, the allocation rules, and the interfaces are defined outside the *process designer*. Defining outside the process designer allows for sharing with other processes, making the resource structure and the allocation rules reusable for other process definitions. All five workflows use the same allocation rules and some workflows have the same resource structure. The complete configuration of the five workflows, both inside and outside the *process designer*, has been done in two working days. The configuration phase is strongly supported by the FileNet P8 BPM Suite.

As closure of the configuration phase, the workflow model is checked for completeness by the system and a workflow instance could be launched to pretest the execution of the workflow. Another possible check would have been a check on the correctness of the model—conform the verification of workflow processes provided by the Woflan tool (Verbeek, Basten, & Aalst, 2001), but such a verification is not supported by the FileNet system. The configuration of the workflows is necessary for their execution.

Execution

The execution phase is started with the transfer of the workflow configurations to the FileNet *process engine*. All process definition data are transferred to the *process engine*, providing interoperability between the configuration and the execution phase. Resources work on the processes in operation via an inbox. The FileNet P8 BPM Suite offers integration with external applications, document management, integration with content management, and interaction between inter-related processes. The FileNet system supports the execution phase in an excellent way. We expected mature support for execution because this support has traditionally been the heart of a WFM system and many systems provide extended support for the execution phase. In the execution phase, context data is related to each specific instance of a workflow and this combination of definition and context data is used for the control of a workflow.

Control

In the control phase, the operational business process is monitored to follow individual cases and to obtain the performance of a workflow. The first way of monitoring is supported by the FileNet *process administrator* and the second by the *analysis engine*, providing a strong support for the control phase.

The execution data for individual cases and other workflow events are logged by the *process engine*. The history of a certain workflow, step, or work item can be tracked in the log through the FileNet *process administrator*. For the workflows with conditional routing, this gives the opportunity to determine which steps were executed for a specific case. With the *process administrator*, it can also be determined how

Figure 4. Simulation results from the process simulator

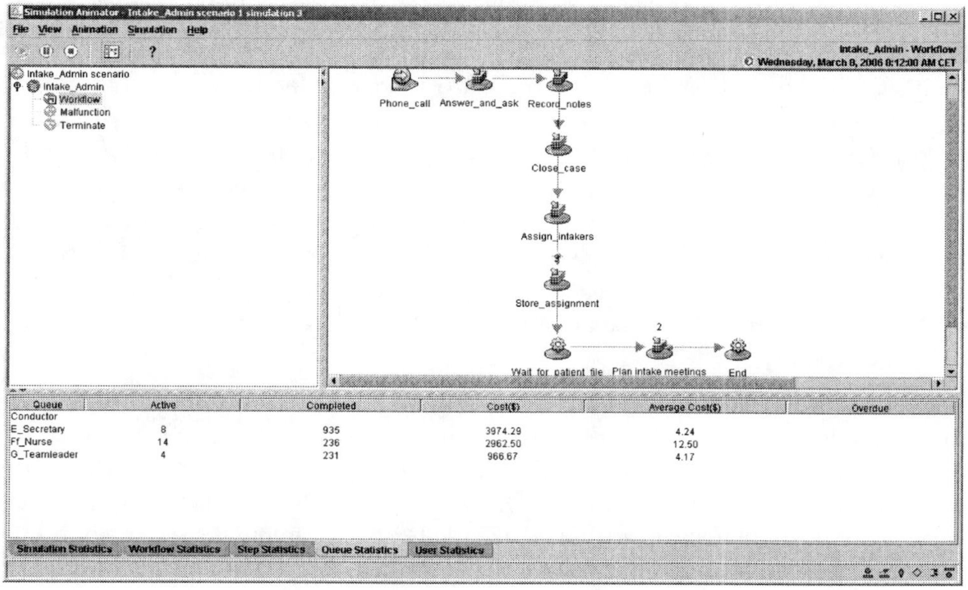

certain decisions were made during execution, allowing us to see at which point and why a certain case was rejected.

The performance of a workflow is read from aggregated execution data. The execution data present in the *process engine* is aggregated and parsed to the FileNet *analysis engine*. Interoperability exists between the execution and the control phase because all execution data necessary for control are available either through the *process engine* or the *analysis engine*. The aggregated performance data resides on a separate engine in order to not affect the performance of the *process engine*. Reporting and analysis of the aggregated data is facilitated by twenty out-of-the-box reports; each graphically presents the data related to one performance indicator. It is possible to specify custom reports, but this requires advanced Excel skills. The representation of the data can be manipulated by adjusting the detail level or by filtering the data.

An analysis of the work present in the queues gives insight in the existence of temporary bottlenecks in the process. This information is used as feedback for the execution phase. The feedback, however, is obtained from human interpretation of the analysis results and does not contain suggestions for the removal of the bottleneck. More permanent weaknesses in the process could also be revealed, based on the analysis of performance data; this is done in the diagnosis phase.

Diagnosis

In the diagnosis phase, problems and improvement possibilities are identified through analysis of the operational process. The *analysis engine* facilitates the control and the diagnosis phase, creating interoperability between the two phases. Analysis reports present an aggregated view on the performance data and weaknesses in the process are derived from this. The derivation, however, is not supported by the FileNet P8 BPM Suite and is based on human insights. A system not capable of identifying process weaknesses is certainly unable to provide improvement suggestions for these weaknesses. The FileNet P8 BPM Suite provides limited support for the diagnosis phase and the creation of ideas for process improvement should be done manually.

The ideas for redesign, generated in the diagnosis phase, could result in another pass through the BPM cycle, starting with a new design phase. When we started our pass in the design phase, it became clear that historic performance data is necessary to obtain the performance of the created redesigns with simulation. We already mentioned that only historic arrival data could be used, making the interoperability between the diagnosis and the design phase limited. We did not yet mention that data generated with simulation can also be transferred to the *analysis engine* and presented in the performance reports. This provides a comprehensive view on the simulation results. Nevertheless, presenting the correct data becomes problematic when multiple scenarios of the same simulation model have been simulated over the same simulation time. It is not possible to select the data of only one of the scenarios, while the aggregation of all simulation data leads to unusable results. The only solution for this is clearing the *analysis engine* before each new simulation run, which does not only lead to unworkable situations, but will also remove the historic execution data from the *analysis engine*.

Analysis of the Evaluation Results

The conclusions from the evaluation just described are summarized in Table 2. In Table 2, we present the support required for each phase in the BPM life-cycle and the support provided by the FileNet P8 BPM Suite. From our evaluation, we conclude that FileNet provides strong support for the configuration, the execution, and the control phase. In particular:

- The configuration phase is well supported by the *process designer*.
- The execution of the workflow is strongly supported by the *process engine*.
- The control phase is supported by the *process administrator* and the *analysis engine*.

Table 2. Summary of the evaluation

Phase	Required support	FileNet support
Design	Make redesign	"- - -"
	Model designs	Process designer
	Evaluate designs	Process simulator
	Compare designs	"- - -"
	Input from diagnosis phase available	"- - -" (only arrival data)
	Output for configuration phase available	Through process designer
Configuration	Model detailed designs	Process designer
	Input from design phase available	Through process designer
	Output for execution phase available	Transfer of process definition
Execution	Workflow engine	Process engine
	Capture context data	Process engine
	Input from configuration phase available	Transfer to process engine
	Output for control phase available	Transfer from process engine
Control	Monitor specific cases	Process administrator
	Aggregation of execution data	Analysis engine
	Monitor performance	Process analyzer
	Input from execution phase available	Transfer to analysis engine
	Output for diagnosis phase available	Through analysis engine
	Output for execution phase available	"- - -"
Diagnosis	Reveal weaknesses	Process analyzer
	Identify improvement points	"- - -"
	Input from control phase available	Through analysis engine
	Output for design phase available	"- - -"(only arrival data)

Note: - - - not supported by FileNet, should be done manually.

Less explicit support is available for the diagnosis and (re)design phase. Some support in the diagnosis phase is provided by the *process analyzer*, which gives an aggregate view on the data. However, the search for weaknesses in the process is not supported and certainly no improvement suggestions are generated. Moreover, the information provided by the *process analyzer* is limited to simple performance indicators such as flow time and utilization. There is no analysis aiming at identifying structures or patterns in the processes and the organization (e.g., social networks or deviations from the normal execution paths). Furthermore, in the design phase, the creation of the redesign alternatives is not supported. Limited support is available through the representation of the alternatives as facilitated by the *process designer* and the selection of the best alternative by the *process simulator*.

The conclusion for our interoperability evaluation is that the interoperability of the FileNet process tools is notably supported in the transitions between the design, the configuration, the execution, the control, and the diagnosis phase. At the same time, the interoperability between the diagnosis and the design phase is limited to the use of historic arrival data (present in the *analysis engine*) for the simulation. All other performance data present in the *analysis engine* can not be passed to the *process simulator* and should be copied manually. Although interoperability exists between the execution and control phase, the loop back from control to execution is not supported. In the control phase, temporary bottlenecks can be identified, but human intervention is required to interpret the findings and tune the operational process.

These insights are in line with the support that could be expected from a WFM system, as these systems are well-known for their emphasis on the configuration, execution, and control phase. Nonetheless, it is also clear that opportunities exist to improve the support that so-called BPM systems offer to execute the entire BPM life-cycle. We consider the FileNet P8 BPM Suite as a relevant benchmark for many of the other available systems, because of its broad range of features and market dominance. Yet the system is far from supporting the whole BPM life-cycle. Therefore, in the remainder, *we focus on the main problems identified, which are, limited support for the diagnosis and (re)design phase and the problematic integration of components in this part of the BPM life-cycle*. In the next section, we will argue that an approach based on state-of-the-art techniques for *process mining* and *intelligent redesign* is needed to address these problems.

An Approach Based on Process Mining and Intelligent Redesign

Based on the evaluation and analysis presented in the previous section, we now focus on the two problems mentioned in the introduction. First, we describe the two problems in more detail. Based on this, we present our ideas with respect to using process mining and intelligent redesign. Finally, we briefly discuss the ProM framework as a platform for addressing the two problems.

Figure 5. Two problems not addressed by contemporary BPM systems: (1) event logs are not used to feed the (re)design of processes and (2) the redesign is at best supported by "what-if" analysis (e.g., simulation)

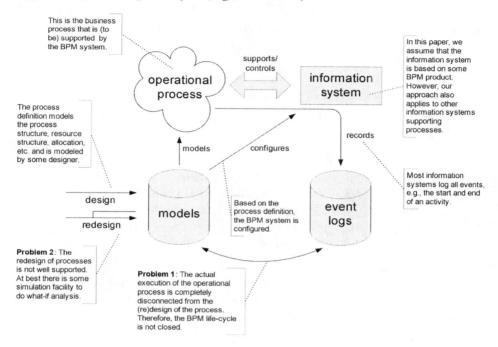

Linking Design and Reality

To clarify the two problems mentioned in the introduction and to link our proposal to the evaluation presented in the previous section, we use Figure 5.

Figure 5 shows the operational process (e.g., the flow of patients in a hospital, the handling of insurance claims, the procurement process of a multinational, and so forth) that is interacting with some information system (e.g., an ERP, CRM, PDM, BPM, or WFM system). Clearly, the information system and the operational process exchange information, for example, the system may support and/or control the processes at hand. Related to the information system and processes it supports are models and event logs. Many systems log events related to the processes they support (cf. the arrow labeled *records* in Figure 5). The role of models is more involved. Clearly, process models can be used to model the operational process for a variety of reasons. Process models can be used to analyze and optimize processes, but can also be used for guidelines, training, discussions, and so forth (cf. the arrow labeled *models* in Figure 5). However, increasingly, information systems are configured on the basis of models (cf. the arrow labeled *configures* in Figure 5). For example, consider process-aware systems (Dumas et al., 2005), ranging from workflow and BPM systems such as FileNet, Staffware, and COSA to ERP systems like SAP R/3 and PeopleSoft. Models can be prescriptive or descriptive. If they are used for configuration, they tend to be prescriptive. If they are used for other purposes (e.g., analysis, training, auditing, and so forth), they are often descriptive. In the first part of this chapter, we were focusing on prescriptive models (e.g., the process definition used by FileNet). However, it is also important to note that descriptive models play an important role when it comes to process support and improvement.

Using Figure 5, we can further detail the two problems mentioned in the introduction:

- **Problem 1:** As Figure 5 shows, the actual execution of the process supported by the BPM system is completely disconnected from the (re)design of the process. In BPM systems such as FileNet, the event logs are not related to the initial process design. Moreover, there is no support to extract knowledge from these logs to aid the redesign.

- **Problem 2:** Redesign activities are typically only supported by a graphical editor, which allows the designer to modify the existing process. This implies that the designer has to come up with ideas for process improvement. These are not suggested by the system. Moreover, at best, there is a simple simulation facility that is completely disconnected from the real operational process, that is, no information extracted from the real process is automatically used in the analysis of different redesign alternatives.

We would like to argue that the only way to address these problems is by linking *design* and *reality*, that is, as long as information about the real process (event logs) is not used by the design tool, it is not possible to close the BPM life-cycle. Therefore, we propose to use recent results achieved in the domain of *process mining* (Aalst & Weijters, 2004; Aalst et al., 2003).

Process Mining

Figure 6 shows that there are three classes of process mining techniques. This classification is based on whether there is an a-priori model and, if so, how it is used.

- **Discovery:** There is no a-priori model, that is, based on an event log, some model is constructed. For example, using the alpha algorithm (Aalst et al., 2004), a process model can be discovered, based on low-level events. There exist many techniques to automatically construct process models (e.g., in terms of a Petri net), based on some event log (Aalst et al., 2004; Agrawal et al., 1998; Cook & Wolf, 1998; Datta, 1998; Weijters & Aalst, 2003). Recently, process mining research also started to target the other perspectives (e.g., data, resources, time, and so forth). For example, the technique described in (Aalst, Reijers, & Song, 2005) can be used to construct a social network.

- **Conformance:** There is an a-priori model. This model is compared with the event log and discrepancies between the log and the model are analyzed. For example, there may be a process model indicating that purchase orders of more than one million euros require two checks. Another example is the checking of the so-called "four-eyes" principle. Conformance checking may be used to detect deviations, to locate and explain these deviations, and to measure the severity of these deviations. An example is the conformance checker described in Rozinat and Aalst (2006a), which compares the event log with some a-priori process model expressed in terms of a Petri net.

- **Extension:** There is an a-priori model. This model is extended with a new aspect or perspective, that is, the goal is not to check conformance, but to enrich the model. An example is the extension of a process model with performance data, that is, some a-priori process model is used to project the bottlenecks on. Another example is the decision miner described in Rozinat and Aalst (2006b),

Figure 6. Process mining as a means to link models and event logs

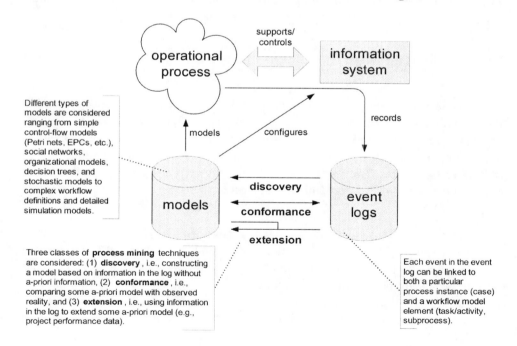

which takes an a-priori process model and analyzes every choice in the process model. For each choice, the event log is consulted to see which information is typically available the moment the choice is made. Then, classical data mining techniques are used to see which data elements influence the choice. As a result, a decision tree is generated for each choice in the process.

Note that the FileNet P8 BPM Suite does not support any form of process mining. This illustrates the missing link between the various models used in the context of a BPM system (e.g., process definitions, organizational models, simulation models, and so forth) and the real processes, as observed by the information system through its event logs. Clearly, all three classes of process mining techniques are valuable in a setting where BPM systems are used. Discovery techniques look at the process under a specific angle and reveal what is really going on. For example, by creating a social network, one can see how people work together. The construction of a process model (e.g., a Petri net) may be helpful if the process is not enforced by the information system or if one is collecting information about a process that is not yet supported by the BPM system (e.g., to generate an initial design). Conformance checking is useful to detect deviations. This information can be used to redesign the process where it does not fit or to improve the control of the system to make sure that reality follows the desired process. Finally, model extension, based on event logs, can be very valuable because it combines a-priori knowledge with real observations. This can be used to "upgrade" process models with information relevant for simulation purposes (e.g., routing probabilities, service times, inter-arrival times, and so forth) or decision support (e.g., decision analysis).

Intelligent Redesign

Although process mining is useful by itself, we believe that it is particularly powerful if it is combined with *intelligent redesign*. To illustrate this, consider Figure 7 where intelligent redesign is linked to process mining. The goal of intelligent redesign is to come up with suggestions for redesigns, based on the evaluation of all kinds of redesign possibilities. The starting point for intelligent redesign is a set of *redesign rules* (in the sense of Reijers (2003)). Each rule specifies:

*   A **precondition** describing under which circumstances the rule is applicable. For example, a redesign rule intended to make a sequential process more parallel has as a precondition that there should be a sequence of tasks where the tasks are potentially executed by different people (otherwise it makes no sense to put things in parallel). One can think of this precondition as a kind of pattern matching: potentially suboptimal structures in the process definition

(in the broadest sense. Also, interaction with other parties and organizational structures (are considered) are identified using a repository of redesign rules. Note that the patterns do not have to be of a strictly structural nature, that is, they may also refer to performance indicators as work-in-progress, flow time, utilization, service levels, and so forth.

- A **transformation** describing how the design should be changed. For example, the redesign rule intended to make a sequential process more parallel should specify how to transform a sequential process fragment into a parallel one. The transformation is typically a replacement of the pattern described in the precondition.

- A set of **intended effects**, that is, the redesign rule aims at improving some aspect of the process. The different aspects are captured in so-called performance indicators. The goal of the rule may be to improve the flow time, to reduce resource utilization, to improve quality, and so forth. Note that redesign rules often provide a tradeoff, for example, parallel processing may lead to a reduction in flow time, but at the same time increase overhead.

As an example, consider the *knock-out rule* defined in (Aalst, 2001). The knock-out rule applies to so-called "knock-out processes." The goal of a knock-out process is to decide whether the case should be accepted or rejected. To make this decision, a sequence of tasks needs to be executed. Each task has two possible results: OK or NOK (e.g., not OK). If, for a specific case (e.g., process instance), a task results in

Figure 7. Intelligent redesign linked to process mining

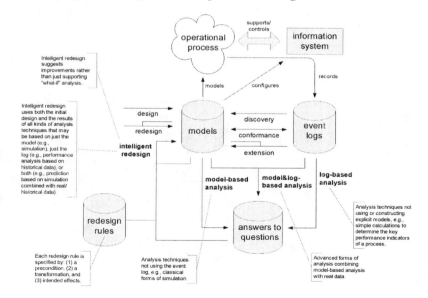

NOK, the case is rejected immediately. Only if all tasks have a positive result, the case is accepted. Many business processes have parts that can be viewed as knock-out processes. Handling an insurance claim, a request for a loan, a job application, and the reviewing of a paper for publication in a journal are typical examples of processes with a knock-out structure. Many knock-out processes are characterized by the fact that the degree of freedom with respect to the order in which tasks can be executed is quite high. Most tasks correspond to checks, which can be executed in any order. A task is *selective* if the reject probability is high. A task is *expensive* if the average processing time is high. Clearly, it is wise to start with selective tasks that are not expensive and postpone the expensive tasks, which are not selective as long as possible. This rule of thumb is captured in the following redesign rule: *Tasks sharing the same resource class should be ordered in descending order using the ratio $rp(t)/pt(t)$ to obtain an optimal process with respect to resource utilization and maximal throughput.* (Note that in this ratio, t refers to a task, $rp(t)$ is the rejection probability, that is, the percentage of cases for which t results in a NOK, and $pt(t)$ is the average processing time of task t.) It is fairly straightforward to define the knock-out rule in terms of a precondition, a transformation, and its intended effects. The precondition is the presence of a sequential process fragment consisting of different tests executed by potentially different sets of people (preferably different roles, departments, and so forth). The transformation is a reordering of activities based on the ratio $rp(t)/pt(t)$. The intended effects are a reduction of flow time and lower resource utilization.

Driven by a set of redesign rules, the following procedure is followed to support intelligent redesign:

- **Step 1. Determine applicable redesign rules:** In this first step, the preconditions of all redesign rules are checked in the context of the concrete process at hand. Note that the preconditions may also refer to the process as it is being executed, that is, the pattern matching is not limited to the process design and extends, for example, to the detection of bottle-necks and so forth.

- **Step 2. Select applicable redesign rules based on intended effects:** Based on the opportunities identified in the first step, a first selection is made. This selection is based on the expected effects of the application of the rule and what the perceived problem is. Note that the same redesign rule may be applicable at multiple places in the process. For each possible application of the rule, a selection decision needs to be made. The selection of applicable redesign rules is an interactive process, that is, the designer can guide the selection process.

- **Step 3. Create redesigns:** After selecting the applicable redesign rules, different redesigns are created. Typically, each selected redesign rule results in a redesign, that is, the rules are applied incrementally (cf. Step 5). To do this, the transformation part of the redesign rule is used.

- **Step 4. Evaluate redesigns:** After applying the redesign rules, each of the resulting redesigns is evaluated using simulation. Using simulation, the effects of applying the redesign rule in this particular context are predicted. Note that the performance indicators used to describe the intended effects of a redesign are of particular interest for this step because now the predicted effect can be measured.

- **Step 5. Select the redesigned processes:** For each redesign evaluated through simulation, two decisions need to be made: (1) Will the redesign be used for further investigation? and/or (2) Will the redesign be presented to the designer? In this step, the most promising redesigns are selected. For each redesign selected for further investigation, steps 1-5 are repeated. Moreover, all redesigns selected for presentation are collected as input for Step 6.

- **Step 6. Present the selected redesigns and their expected effects:** In the final step, the results are presented to the designer. It is the designer that selects the redesign to be used (if any). Moreover, the designer may refine a selected redesign or restart the procedure with different input.

It is important to note that both in Step 1 and in Step 4, the event logs play an important role, that is, the pattern matching in Step 1 may be partially based on performance indicators derived from the real process (e.g., a redesign rule only applies if there is some sort of problem) and the simulation in Step 4 should be based on data derived from the actual process (e.g., the arrival patterns of new cases). This is illustrated by the lower half of Figure 7. As shown, intelligent redesign is driven by the existing process design, the redesign rules, and answers to various questions. These questions relate to just the models (e.g., the process definition or the organizational model), just the event logs (e.g., flow times, frequencies, and so forth), or both (e.g., the process definition embedded in a real-life context). Figure 7 refers to answering these questions as *model-based analysis*, *log-based analysis*, and *model&log-based analysis*. An example of *model-based analysis* is the classical form of simulation, that is, based on some model completely disconnected from the run-time environment performance indicators estimation. *Log-based analysis* typically uses simple queries or calculations on some database with run-time/historic information. This is the area commonly referred to as data-warehousing, business activity monitoring, or business intelligence. *Model&log-based analysis* tries to combine some a-priori model with relevant run-time/historic information, for example, a simulation model using run-time/historic information as described in Reijers and Aalst (1999). It should be noted that *model&log-based analysis* is closely related to model extension (the third form of process mining). Note that the same information, for example, inter-arrival times of cases, may be used to extend the model (fit some stochastic distribution and add this to the simulation model) or to directly answer a question without extending the model (directly feed a log with historic inter-arrival times to the simulation engine as supported by the FileNet simulator).

Existing BPM systems provide limited support for the lower half of Figure 7. At best, they offer basic *model-based analysis* (e.g., simple simulation engine) and *log-based analysis* (e.g., basic information on the key performance indicators). There is typically no support for process mining and *model&log-based analysis*. As shown earlier, leading BPM systems such as the FileNet P8 BPM Suite only provide a basic *process designer* and a *process simulator*. Historic information on arriving cases can be transferred to the *process simulator*, but all other data, like processing times and routing probabilities, should be derived from the execution data and included manually. It is only possible to provide constant values for the simulation parameters, so the simulation results will only provide a very rough indication for the performance of a scenario. Moreover, there is no form of intelligent redesign, that is it is impossible to use redesign rules in a systematic way. The user needs to come up with redesigns and is not supported in any way.

The ProM Framework

The primary goal of this chapter is not to provide detailed solutions, but to sketch how process mining and intelligent redesign could be used to close the BPM life-cycle and to enhance systems like the FileNet P8 BPM Suite. We have been developing process mining techniques in the context of the ProM framework for several years now (Dongen et al., 2005) and recently started adding functionality to support intelligent redesign to ProM. Therefore, we briefly describe the ProM framework and some of its plug-ins.

The starting point for ProM is event logs in MXML format. The MXML format is system-independent and using ProMimport, it is possible to extract logs from a wide variety of systems, that is, systems based on products such as SAP, Peoplesoft, Staffware, FLOWer, WebSphere, YAWL, ADEPT, ARIS PPM, Caramba, InConcert, Oracle BPEL, Outlook, and tailor-made systems. It is also possible to load and/or save a variety of models, for example, EPCs (that is, event-driven process chains in different formats, for example, ARIS, ARIS PPM, EPML, and Visio), BPEL (e.g., Oracle BPEL, Websphere), YAWL, Petri nets (using different formats, e.g., PNML, TPN, etc.), CPNs (that is, colored Petri nets as supported by CPN Tools), and Protos. Currently, there are no interfaces with the FileNet P8 BPM Suite, but it would be fairly easy to make this connection (both at the model level and the event log level), since it is similar to many of the other systems already supported.

The ProM framework is open-source and plug-able, that is, people can plug-in new pieces of functionality. Some of the plug-ins are related to model transformations and various forms of model analysis (e.g., verification of soundness, analysis of

Figure 8. Based on an analysis of an event log with data on 1000 patients, various mining plug-ins are able to discover the underlying process

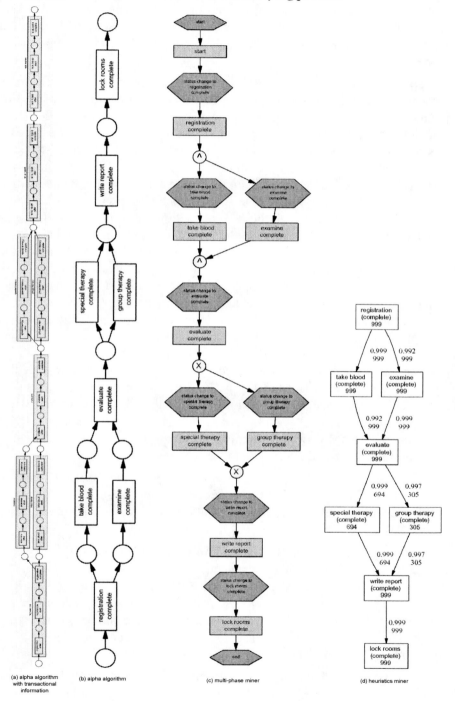

(a) alpha algorithm with transactional information

(b) alpha algorithm

(c) multi-phase miner

(d) heuristics miner

deadlocks, invariants, reductions, etc.). Most of the plug-ins, however, focus on a particular process mining technique. Currently, there are more than 100 plug-ins, of which about half are mining and analysis plug-ins. In this chapter, we distinguished three types of process mining techniques: discovery, conformance, and extension. Below, we briefly mention some of the plug-ins present in ProM to support these three types of process mining.

ProM supports many discovery algorithms. ProM currently offers eight plug-ins for discovering processes. These plug-ins use different "target formats," that is, different languages to represent the result of the discovery algorithm (e.g., Petri nets, EPCs, heuristics nets). Figure 8 shows four process models obtained using various plug-ins for control-flow discovery present in ProM. The models are based on an event log with about 20,000 events relating to about 1,000 patients. It is important to note that the process models have been generated automatically, without any a-priori information. Figure 8a shows the result obtained by applying the α algorithm (Aalst et al., 2004) to the log with the full transactional information, that is, each activity characterized by three events in the log: *offer*, *start*, and *complete*. Hence, in the resulting Petri-net, each activity is represented by three transitions. Figure 8b is also generated by the α algorithm, but now by only considering the *complete* events. Figure 8c shows the result of applying the multi-phase miner. This approach first builds a model for every instance and then starts aggregating these instance models. The native format of the multi-phase miner is the EPC language. However, the multi-phase miner can also display its results as Petri nets. In fact, in ProM, any Petri net can be converted into an EPC, YAWL model, or heuristics net and vice versa. Figure 8d shows a heuristics net discovered by the heuristics miner (Weijters & Aalst, 2003). The format is also used by the genetic miner and both are able to cope with noise. Discovery in ProM is not limited to the control-flow perspective. It is also possible to discover social networks (Aalst, Reijers, & Song, 2005) or staff assignment rules. However, a complete overview of all discovery techniques supported by ProM is outside the scope of this chapter.

ProM also has two plug-ins for conformance: the conformance checker (Rozinat & Aalst, 2006a) and the LTL checker (Aalst, Beer, & Dongen, 2005). Both are able to discover deviations between some model and the real behavior captured in the event log.

The decision miner described in Rozinat and Aalst (2006b) is an example of a plug-in that takes a process model without data and extends it with data and information about decisions. More precisely, it takes an a-priori process model and analyzes every choice in the process model. For each choice, the event log is consulted to see which information is typically available the moment the choice is made. Then, classical data mining techniques are used to see which data elements influence the choice. As a result, a decision tree is generated for each choice in the process.

In the context of intelligent redesign, it is relevant to note that it is possible to export process models in ProM to CPN Tools (CPN Group, University of Aarhus, Denmark, n.d.). The control-flow, data-flow, performance and organizational perspectives can be incorporated in a single colored Petri net (CPN) model (Jensen, 1996) that can be exported to CPN tools. CPN tools allows for various types of analysis, including state-space analysis and simulation. Using the monitoring facilities of CPN tools, it is easy to detect bottlenecks and collect all kinds of performance indicators. We believe that the combination of automatic discovery of process models, using ProM and the simulation capabilities of CPN tools, offers an innovative way to improve business processes. The initially discovered process model describes reality better than most hand-crafted simulation models. Moreover, if there is an a-priori model, it can be verified whether reality fits the model (conformance checker) or not and the model can also be extended to incorporate historic information (e.g., arrival processes and service times). The simulation models are constructed in such a way that it is easy to explore various redesigns.

ProM is available as open source software (under the common public license, CPL) and can be downloaded from www.processmining.org. It has been applied to various real-life processes, ranging from administrative processes and health-care processes to the logs of complex machines and service processes. While the process mining capabilities of ProM are very mature, the support of intelligent redesign is still in its infancy. Currently, we are adding redesign rules to ProM to support intelligent redesign.

Conclusion

In this chapter, we focused on supporting the whole BPM life-cycle consisting of the following phases: *(re)design, configuration, execution, control*, and *diagnosis*. The contribution of this chapter is twofold.

First of all, we analyzed the limitations of today's BPM systems, using the FileNet P8 BPM Suite as a representative example. We presented a generic approach to analyze the capabilities of a BPM product with respect to its support of the BPM life-cycle. We discovered several problems. It was observed that systems such as the FileNet P8 BPM Suite provide limited support for the diagnosis and (re)design phase and that the integration of the different components in this part of the BPM life-cycle is problematic (that is, results obtained in one component are not used in other components and users need to rekey and reinterpret results).

Second, based on these observations, we focused on the problematic part of the BPM life-cycle and discussed techniques that can alleviate the problems. We identified two key problems: (1) the complete disconnect between the (re)designs and reality as observed by the system through its event logs and (2) the lack of support when it comes to automatically generating redesigns based on an analysis of the current situation (that is, current design and event logs) and evaluating these results. To address these problems, we argued that techniques for process mining and intelligent redesign are needed to support the (re)design and diagnosis phases and thus, close the BPM life-cycle.

We briefly presented the ProM framework and some of its plug-ins. Currently, ProM already provides mature support for a wide variety of process mining techniques (aiming at discovery, conformance, and extension). Future work aims at strengthening the support of intelligent redesign by adding redesign plug-ins and a repository of redesign rules.

Acknowledgment

We would like to thank the consultancy and IT support staff from FileNet for their kind assistance in carrying out this study. We would also like to thank the people involved in the development of the ProM framework: Ton Weijters, Boudewijn van Dongen, Ana Karla Alves de Medeiros, Anne Rozinat, Christian Günter, Minseok Song, Laura Maruster, Eric Verbeek, Monique Jansen-Vullers, Huub de Beer, Ronny Mans, Peter van den Brand, Andriy Nikolov, Irene Vanderfeesten, et al. This research is supported by EIT and the Technology Foundation STW, applied science division of NWO and the technology program of the Dutch Ministry of Economic Affairs.

References

Aalst, W. van der (2001). Reengineering knock-out processes. *Decision Support Systems, 30*(4), 451-468.

Aalst, W. van der, Beer, H., & Dongen, B. van (2005). Process mining and verification of properties: An approach based on temporal logic. In R. Meersman & Z. Tari. et al. (Eds.), *On the Move to Meaningful Internet Systems 2005: CoopIS, DOA, and ODBASE: OTM Confederated International Conferences, CoopIS, DOA, and ODBASE 2005* (LNCS 3760, pp. 130-147). Berlin: Springer-Verlag.

Aalst, W. van der, Dongen, B. van, Herbst, J., Maruster, L., Schimm, G., & Weijters, A. (2003). Workflow mining: A survey of issues and approaches. *Data and Knowledge Engineering, 47*(2), 237-267.

Aalst, W. van der, & Hee, K. van (2004). *Workflow management: Models, methods, and systems*. Cambridge, MA: MIT Press.

Aalst, W. van der, Hofstede, A. ter, Kiepuszewski, B., & Barros, A. (2003). Workflow patterns. *Distributed and Parallel Databases, 14*(1), 5-51.

Aalst, W. van der, Hofstede, A. ter, & Weske, M. (2003). Business process management: A survey. In W. Aalst, A. Hofstede, & M. Weske (Eds.), *International Conference on Business Process Management (BPM 2003)* (LNCS 2678, pp. 1-12). Berlin: Springer-Verlag.

Aalst, W. van der, Reijers, H., & Song, M. (2005). Discovering social networks from event logs. *Computer Supported Cooperative Work*, 14(6), 549-593.

Aalst, W. van der, & Weijters, A. (Eds.). (2004). *Process mining*. Amsterdam: Elsevier Science Publishers.

Aalst, W. van der, Weijters, A., & Maruster, L. (2004). Workflow mining: Discovering process models from event logs. *IEEE Transactions on Knowledge and Data Engineering, 16*(9), 1128-1142.

Agrawal, R., Gunopulos, D., & Leymann, F. (1998). Mining process models from workflow logs. In *Sixth International Conference on Extending Database Technology* (pp. 469-483).

Bernstein, A., Klein, M., & Malone, T. (1999). The process recombinator: A tool for generating new business process ideas. In *Proceedings of ICIS 1999* (pp. 178-192).

Buzacott, J. (1996). Commonalities in reengineered business processes: Models and issues. *Management Science, 42*(5), 768-782.

Cook, J., & Wolf, A. (1998). Discovering models of software processes from event-based data. *ACM Transactions on Software Engineering and Methodology, 7*(3), 215-249.

CPN Group, University of Aarhus, Denmark. (n.d.). *CPN tools home page*. Retrieved from http://wiki.daimi.au.dk/cpntools/

Datta, A. (1998). Automating the discovery of as-is business process models: Probabilistic and algorithmic approaches. *Information Systems Research, 9*(3), 275-301.

Dongen, B. van, Medeiros, A., Verbeek, H., Weijters, A., & Aalst, W. van der (2005). The ProM framework: A new era in process mining tool support. In G. Ciardo & P. Darondeau (Eds.), *Application and Theory of Petri Nets 2005* (LNCS 3536, pp. 444-454). Berlin: Springer-Verlag.

Dumas, M., Aalst, W. van der, & Hofstede, A. ter (2005). *Process-aware information systems: Bridging people and software through process technology*. New York: Wiley & Sons.

Eder, J., Panagos, E., Pezewaunig, H., & Rabinovich, M. (1999). Time management in workflow systems. In W. Abramowicz & M. Orlowska (Eds.), *Third International Conference on Business Information Systems (BIS'99)* (pp. 265-280). Berlin: Springer-Verlag.

Eder, J., Panagos, E., & Rabinovich, M. (1999). Time constraints in workflow systems. In M. Jarke & A. Oberweis (Eds.), *Proceedings of the 11th International Conference on Advanced Information Systems Engineering (CAiSE '99)* (LNCS 1626, pp. 286-300). Berlin, Springer-Verlag.

Ellis, C. (1979). Information control nets: A mathematical model of office information flow. In *Proceedings of the Conference on Simulation, Measurement and Modeling of Computer Systems* (pp. 225-240). Boulder, CO: ACM Press.

Gartner. (2003). *Gartner's magic quadrant for pure-play BPM.* Retrieved from http://www.gartner.com

Gartner. (2004). *Gartner's magic quadrant for pure-play BPM.* Retrieved from http://www.gartner.com

Gartner. (2005). *Gartner's magic quadrant for pure-play BPM.* Retrieved from http://www.gartner.com

Georgakopoulos, D., Hornick, M., & Sheth, A. (1995). An overview of workflow management: From process modeling to workflow automation infrastructure. *Distributed and Parallel Databases, 3*, 119-153.

Grigori, D., Casati, F., Castellanos, M., Dayal, U., Sayal, M., & Shan, M. (2004). Business process intelligence. *Computers in Industry, 53*(3), 321-343.

Grigori, D., Casati, F., Dayal, U., & Shan, M. (2001). Improving business process quality through exception understanding, prediction, and prevention. In P. Apers, P. Atzeni, S. Ceri, S. Paraboschi, K. Ramamohanarao, & R. Snodgrass (Eds.), *Proceedings of 27th International Conference on Very Large Data Bases (VLDB'01)* (pp. 159-168). San Fransisco: Morgan Kaufmann.

IDS Scheer. (2002). *ARIS Process Performance Manager (ARIS PPM): Measure, analyze and optimize your business process performance* (whitepaper). Saarbruecken, Germany: DS Scheer Retrieved from http://www.ids-scheer.com

Jablonski, S., & Bussler, C. (1996). *Workflow management: Modeling concepts, architecture, and implementation.* London: International Thomson Computer Press.

Jansen-Vullers, M., & Reijers, H. (2005). Business process redesign at a mental healthcare institute: A coloured Petri net approach. In K. Jensen (Ed.), *Proceedings of the Sixth Workshop on the Practical Use of Coloured Petri Nets and CPN Tools (CPN 2005)* (Vol. 576, pp. 21-38). Aarhus, Denmark: University of Aarhus.

Jensen, K. (1996). Coloured Petri nets. In *Basic concepts, analysis methods, and practical use*. Berlin: Springer-Verlag.

Lawrence, P. (Ed.). (1997). *Workflow handbook 1997, workflow management coalition*. New York: John Wiley & Sons.

Leymann, F., & Roller, D. (1999). *Production workflow: Concepts and techniques*. NJ: Prentice-Hall.

Marinescu, D. (2002). *Internet-based workflow management: Towards a Semantic Web* (Vol. 40). New York: Wiley-Interscience.

Mühlen, M. (2004). *Workflow-based process controlling: Foundation, design and application of workflow-driven process information systems.* Berlin: Logos.

Mühlen, M., & Rosemann, M. (2000). Workflow-based process monitoring and controlling—Technical and organizational issues. In R. Sprague (Ed.), *Proceedings of the 33rd Hawaii international conference on system science (HICSS-33)* (pp. 1-10). Los Alamitos: IEEE Computer Society Press.

Netjes, M., Aalst, W. van der, & Reijers, H. (2005). Analysis of resource-constrained processes with colored Petri nets. In K. Jensen (Ed.), *Proceedings of the Sixth Workshop on the Practical Use of Coloured Petri Nets and CPN Tools (CPN 2005)* (Vol. 576, pp. 251-266). Aarhus, Denmark: University of Aarhus.

Netjes, M., Reijers, H., & Aalst, W. van der (2006a). *FileNet's BPM life-cycle support.* BPM Center Report BPM-06-07. Retrieved from BPMcenter.org.

Netjes, M., Reijers, H., & Aalst, W. van der (2006b). Supporting the BPM lifecycle with FileNet. In T. Latour & M. Petit (Eds.), *Proceedings of the EMMSAD Workshop at the 18th International Conference on Advanced Information Systems Engineering (CAiSE'06)* (pp. 497-508). Namur University Press.

Netjes, M., Vanderfeesten, I., & Reijers, H. (2006). "Intelligent" tools for workflow process redesign: A research agenda. In C. Bussler & A. Haller (Eds.), *Business process management workshops (BPM 2005)* (LNCS 3812, pp. 444-453). Berlin: Springer-Verlag.

Nissen, M. (1998). Redesigning reengineering through measurement-driven inference. *MIS Quarterly, 22*(4), 509-534.

Panagos, E., & Rabinovich, M. (1997). Escalations in workflow management systems. In *Proceedings of the Workshop on Databases: Active and Real Time (DART-96)* (pp. 25-28). New York: ACM.

Panagos, E., & Rabinovich, M. (1998). Reducing escalation-related costs in WFMSs. In *Workflow management systems and interoperability* (pp. 107-127). Berlin: Springer-Verlag.

Reijers, H. (2003). *Design and control of workflow processes: Business process management for the service industry* (LNCS Vol. 2617). Berlin: Springer-Verlag.

Reijers, H., & Aalst, W. van der (1999). Short-term simulation: Bridging the gap between operational control and strategic decision making. In M. Hamza (Ed.), *Proceedings of the IASTED International Conference on Modelling and Simulation* (pp. 417-421). Anaheim, CA: IASTED/Acta Press.

Rozinat, A., & Aalst, W. van der (2006a). Conformance testing: Measuring the fit and appropriateness of event logs and process models. In C. Bussler & A. Haller (Eds.), *Business Process Management Workshops (BPM 2005)* (LNCS 3812, pp. 163-176). Berlin: Springer-Verlag.

Rozinat, A., & Aalst, W. van der (2006b). Decision mining in ProM. In S. Dustdar, J. Faideiro, & A. Sheth (Eds.), *International Conference on Business Process Management (BPM 2006)* (LNCS 4102, pp. 420-425). Berlin: Springer-Verlag.

Sayal, M., Casati, F., Dayal, U., & Shan, M. (2002). Business process cockpit. In *Proceedings of 28th International Conference on Very Large Data Bases (VLDB'02)* (pp. 880-883). San Francisco: Morgan Kaufmann.

Staffware. (2003). *Staffware process suite version 2* (white paper). Maidenhead, UK.

TIBCO. (2005). *TIBCO Staffware Process Monitor (SPM)*. Retrieved from http://www.tibco.com

Verbeek, H., Basten, T., & Aalst, W. van der (2001). Diagnosing workflow processes using Woflan. *The Computer Journal, 44*(4), 246-279.

Weijters, A., & Aalst, W. van der (2003). Rediscovering workflow models from event-based data using little thumb. *Integrated Computer-Aided Engineering, 10*(2), 151-162.

Zhao, J., & Stohr, E. (1999). Temporal workflow management in a claim handling system. In *Proceedings of the Iwnternational Joint Conference on Work Activities Coordination and Collaboration (WACC'99)* (pp. 187-195). New York: ACM.

Chapter V

Efficient Placement and Processing in Shared-Nothing Data Warehouses

Pedro Nuno San-Bento Furtado, Universidade de Coimbra, Portugal

Abstract

Some businesses generate giga or even terabytes of historical data that can be orga-nized and analyzed for better decision making. This poses issues concerning systems and software for efficient processing over such data. While the traditional solution to this problem involves costly hardware and software, we focus on strategies for running large data warehouses over low-cost, non-dedicated nodes in a local-area network (LAN) and non-proprietary software. Once such a technology is in place, every data warehouse will be able to run in a small cost environment, but the sys-tem must be able to choose its placement and processing for maximum efficiency. We discuss the basic system architecture and the design of the data placement and processing strategy. We compare the shortcomings of a basic horizontal partitioning for the environment, with a simple design that produces efficient placements. Our discussion and results provide important insight into how low-cost efficient data warehouse systems can be obtained.

Introduction

Software and hardware suppliers typically differentiate their offer in order to increase their market share and profits, with the most demanding "high-end" applications and systems topping prices and profit margins. On the other hand, lean organizations are increasingly wary of investments into software and systems with large total cost of ownership (TOC) and unpredictable returns. This is why low-cost reliable solutions are an important and useful challenge generically and, in particular, in the highly-demanding data warehousing environment. Data warehouses are specialized databases that pose relevant challenges in what concerns performance. A system may store many hundreds of gigabytes of data, and still the user requires a fast answer to any analysis that he may be interested in from that data. Several performance optimizing structures exist, such as specialized indexing and materialized views, and they are increasingly implemented in database systems to speed up computations. Some computations may be very fast, using a specific index or materialized view, but may take minutes or even hours otherwise. Parallel architectures and parallel processing are another very relevant choice that can be used in conjunction with those structures to deliver very good performance for any operation. The choice of parallel architecture has implications on data partitioning, placement, and parallel query processing algorithms (DeWitt & Gray, 1992). The system is only as fast as the slowest components dictate, so they must be designed to avoid bottlenecks and there are specific data and control overheads that must be taken into account. A shared-disk system is a good example of architecture in which storage devices, interconnections, network cards, and I/O buses should all be dimensioned to avoid bottlenecks, which is typically expensive.

Today, virtually all organizations already possess a shared-nothing parallel system composed of their desktop computers in a local area network (LAN) or, if necessary, can buy low-cost computers, link them together in a LAN and, this way, build a low-cost parallel system. Therefore, the challenge is to run a large data warehouse in such an environment, while still guaranteeing efficiency. This is an environment where the performance of data interchange between nodes may vary widely, which means that data placement is a very relevant issue in such a context. In this chapter, we are concerned with the basic system architecture to allow data processing in such an environment, and the specific issues of how data can be efficiently divided into the nodes (data placement) and processed in a system that can run heterogeneous database servers. The fact that the system runs heterogeneous servers means that there is no database server-embedded query processor and optimizer, but rather a simpler global query processor. We consider as basic data placement primitives, horizontal partitioning and replication of data sets and analyze a simple replication-oriented approach, its advantages and shortcomings and, then also, analyze our proposal of an improved simple, but efficient placement strategy. The results we discuss in this chapter provide valuable insight into the major issues in node-partitioned data warehouses and were useful for part of the design of the query processor of the data warehouse parallel architecture (DWPA, 2005). The objective of this system is to be able to adapt automatically to run anywhere, with any software and environment. Research issues associated with this context, including autonomic and adaptable functionality and availability, are the subject of our current and future research within the DWPA project.

Background

Data warehouses are based on a large central repository of historical data that may have several hundreds of gigabytes and specific analysis-oriented data marts stored and analyzed using some non-relational multidimensional engine (Kimball, Reeves, Ross, & Thornthwaite, 1998). Our emphasis is on the central repository, organized as a relational schema. Such schemas are typically read-only, with multidimensional characteristics: large central fact relations containing several measurements (e.g., the amount of sales) and a size of up to hundreds or thousands of gigabytes are related to dimensions (e.g., shop, client, product, supplier). The measurements of the central facts are related to specific combinations of dimension values (e.g., sales of a product from a supplier, in one shop and for an individual client). Online analytical processing (OLAP) refers to analysis queries that are posed to the data warehouse by business analyzers to extract the information they need. These queries may be quite complex, with joins involving multiple relations and aggregations, while the user typically sits waiting for the results and posing additional queries to analyze various details in an interactive experience that must be efficient. To speedup query response times, some research in recent years has focused on ad-hoc star join processing in data warehouses. Specialized structures, such as materialized views (Rousopoulos, 1998) and specialized indexes (O'Neil & Graefe, 1995; Chan & Ioannidis, 1998), have been proposed to improve response time. Although these structures are useful in a context in which queries are known in advance, this is not the case when ad-hoc queries are posed. Therefore, parallel approaches are important, as they can be used alone or in conjunction with specialized structures to provide efficient processing for any query pattern at any time.

The choice of a shared-nothing architecture to hold and process such data, while justified by the low-cost, ubiquitous characteristics of such architecture, poses a relevant issue, as nodes may need to exchange massive quantities of data during the processing of the queries.

In the past, there has been significant research activity around the main data placement and processing issues that arise over a shared-nothing architecture. One such problem concerns the cost of processing joins over partitioned data. The most promising solutions to this issue involve hash-partitioning large relations into nodes in order to minimize data exchange requirements (Kitsuregawa, Tanaka, & Motooka, 1983; DeWitt & Gerber, 1985) and applying parallel hash-join algorithms, also reviewed in Yu and Meng (1998). These strategies typically allocate a hash range to each processor, which builds a hash table and hashes relation fragments accordingly. In a shared-nothing environment, it often becomes necessary to exchange data between nodes in order to send tuples into the node that has been allocated the corresponding hash-value range for the join attribute. This process is called partitioning, if the relation is not partitioned yet, or repartitioning, if the relation is already partitioned, but must be reorganized. Both operations can be costly because they may require heavy data exchange over the network connecting the nodes.

Data placement (we also use the term "data partitioning" in this context) refers to organizing the data into the nodes in a manner that favors efficient processing. The data placement strategy is applied initially and also periodically to reorganize the data according to query patterns so that the most efficient system results. Williams and Zhou (1998) review five major data placement strategies (size-based, access frequency-based, and network traffic based) and conclude experimentally that the way data is placed in a shared-nothing environment can have considerable effect on performance. Hua and Lee (1990) use variable partitioning (size and access frequency-based) and conclude that partitioning increases throughput for short transactions, but complex transactions involving several large joins result in reduced throughput with increased partitioning.

Some of the most promising partitioning and placement approaches focus on query Workload-based Partitioning choice (Zilio, Jhingram, & Padmanabhan, 1994; Rao, Zhang, Megiddo, & Lohman, 2002). These strategies use the query workload to determine the most appropriate partitioning attributes, which should be related to typical query access patterns. While they are targeted at generic parallel databases and may require tight integration with a specific cost predictor and optimizer (Rao et al., 2002), our proposals envision data placement and query processing in node-partitioned data warehouses with independent, possibly heterogeneous database servers, nodes, and systems (Furtado, 2004a; Furtado, 2004b; Furtado, 2004c).

Considering that the major bottleneck in many non-dedicated systems may be the interconnection between computer nodes and that data warehouses are mostly read-only, it is important to consider different degrees of replication that might decrease significantly the amount of data that needs to be exchanged between nodes (Furtado, 2006), as well as early-selection bitmap-based strategies that may minimize the amount of data that needs to be exchanged (Furtado, 2007; O'Neil & Graefe, 1995; Saborit, Mulero, & Pey, 2003).

Architecture, Partitioning, and Processing

In this section, we introduce the rudiments of the architecture, partitioning and processing in the data warehouse parallel architecture (DWPA, 2005). Figure 1 illustrates the basic DWPA architecture for the shared-nothing, node partitioned data warehouse, which can run in any number of computers interconnected by a LAN. It includes three major entities implemented as services: Submitter, Executor, and the DWPA Manager. Submitters are simple services that may reside in any computer, do not require an underlying database server, and submit queries to the system. The query may be submitted from a submitter console application or from other applications through an API. Once submitted, the query is parsed and transformed into high-level actions by a query planner. These actions are then transformed into command lists for each executor service. Executors are services that maintain local database sessions and control the execution of commands locally and the data exchange with other nodes. Finally, the DWPA manager is a node which controls the whole system (it can be replicated for fault tolerance reasons), maintaining registries with necessary information for the whole system. When nodes enter the system, they contact the DWPA manager to register themselves and to obtain all the necessary information. In DWPA, any computer can assume any role as long as it runs the corresponding service.

Figure 1. The DWPA architecture

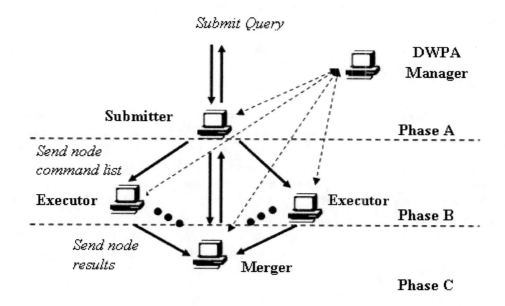

We will now describe basic query processing functionality. For simplicity, we start with the simplest possible example. Consider a single very large relation R partitioned into n nodes and a sum query over some attribute x of the relation. Formula (1) states that the sum of attribute x over all nodes is simply the sum of the sums of x in each node:

$$\sum x = \sum_{\text{all nodes}} \sum_{\text{over node } i} (x)$$

(1)

The implementation of this very basic operation in DWPA involves the submitter parsing the initial query *sum(x) from R* and producing command lists for every node with the following operations:

1. A local query: *sum(x) as sumx from R_{local}*
2. Data transfer commands for every executor node: send *sumx* to merger node
3. A merge query for the merger node: *sum(sumx) from partial_results*
4. Signal the submitter to pull the results

The Merger node is an Executor that is chosen for merging the partial results, if necessary. The query processing steps depend heavily on the placement layout of the data on the nodes. For instance, if relation R is replicated into all nodes or placed in a single node, the commands will be (executed in a single node):

1. A local query: *sum(x) as sumx from R_{local}*
2. Signal the submitter to pull the results

More generically, Figure 2 shows a set of query processing steps that may be necessary in the processing of each query using DWPA (some queries may not require all these steps). Steps S1 to S4 represent the parsing and planning of queries, the generation of lists of commands for the executor nodes, and the sending of those commands to executors. Steps E1 to E4 represent the processing of the local queries within executor nodes, data exchanges between them, and either sending the results to a merger node or signalling to the submitter that he can get the results. The merger node steps include a redistribution step, EM3, which may be necessary for processing nested queries (for some queries containing sub-queries, in which case more than one processing cycle may be required).

Figure 2. Query processing architecture (QPA) within DWPA

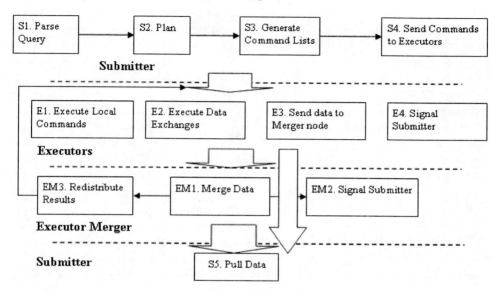

In this section, we introduced the DWPA architecture and query processor. The objective of the next section is to show the design of a basic partitioning and processing strategy for the data warehouse that minimizes data transfer costs and uses the query processing blocks illustrated in Figure 2.

Basic Star Partitioning

We use the terms partitioning and placement interchangeably and simplify the discussion by considering only one group of nodes (all nodes) and homogeneity between nodes, in order to concentrate on the core partitioning and processing issues (assuming heterogeneous nodes, the system would have to balance the amount of data into nodes according to performance metrics). In a partitioning scheme, each relation can be partitioned (divided into partitions or fragments), replicated (copied in its entirety into all nodes), or placed into a single node of a group of nodes. When partitioned, relations are horizontally-divided into fragments using round-robin, random, range, or hash-based schemes.

Next, we analyze the partitioning issue, considering the data warehouse organization. The star schema (Kimball, 1996) is part of the typical data organization in a data warehouse, representing a multidimensional logic with a large central fact table and

Figure 3. Star partitioning

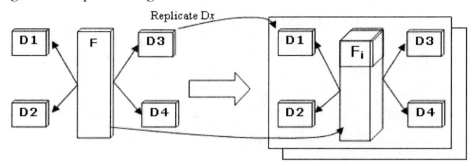

smaller dimension tables. Facts are typically very large relations with hundreds of gigabytes of historical details. Dimensions are smaller relations identifying entities by means of several descriptive properties.

In that context, a basic placement strategy for the simple star schema replicates dimensions and fully-partitions the large central fact horizontally and randomly. Figure 3 illustrates this simple strategy, which we name *"star partitioning,"* in which the large fact F is partitioned into node fragments F_i and dimensions D are replicated into all nodes. Very small dimensions can even be cached into memory for faster access and join processing.

Heavy replication of dimensions is feasible because the data is not constantly changed and the only refresh is based on periodically loading new data. Under this scheme, facts can be partitioned using a random or round-robin partitioning strategy.

The main reason for this placement is to be able to simultaneously parallelize the processing of the largest relation and, at the same time, process time consuming operations (e.g., joins and aggregations) locally at each node, therefore minimizing inter-node communication. In this way, query processing does not become a large burden to the network and it is less dependent on network bandwidth and data exchange handling issues. Next, we show why this strategy minimizes inter-node communication, using a simple query example. Each node processes its part of the query independently, so that the system may achieve a speedup that is expected to be near to linear with the number of nodes. Consider a simple OLAP query formulated as:

OP(…)

JOIN (F, D1, …, Dn)

GROUP (G1,..Gm);

where OP is an aggregation operator such as SUM, COUNT. Each node needs to apply exactly the same initial query on its partial data and the results are merged by applying the same query again at the merging node with the partial results coming from the processing nodes. The independent execution of partial joins by nodes is supported by the fact that all but one of the relations in the star (that is, all dimensions) are replicated into all nodes, which is similar to the rationale of the Partition and Replicate Strategy (PRS) (Yu, Guh, Brill, & Chen, 1989), although, in that case, the initial placement of relations was different. Considering a single fully-partitioned relation R_i (with partitions R_{ij}) and all the remaining ones (R_l, $l=1$ to n: $l \neq i$) replicated into all nodes, the relevant join property that allows joins to be processed by nodes independently from each other is:

$$R_1 \bowtie \ldots \bowtie R_i \bowtie \ldots \bowtie R_n = U_{j \text{ over all nodes}} R_1 \bowtie \ldots \bowtie R_{ij} \bowtie \ldots \bowtie R_n \qquad (2)$$

Additionally, even though expression (2) includes a union operator, many other operators denoted here as OP() can be applied before the partial results are collected by some node to process the union of the partial results, due to the property in (3):

$$OP(R_1 \bowtie \ldots \bowtie R_i \bowtie \ldots \bowtie R_n) = OP(U_{j \text{ over all nodes}} R_1 \bowtie \ldots \bowtie R_{ij} \bowtie \ldots \bowtie R_n) =$$
$$= OP_y[U_{j \text{ over all nodes}} OP_x(R_1 \bowtie \ldots \bowtie R_{ij} \bowtie \ldots \bowtie R_n)] \qquad (3)$$

In this expression, OP_x is an operator applied locally at each node and OP_y is a global merge operator. The set OP_x and OP_y replace OP. Expressions (2) and (3) allow each node to compute part of joins and aggregations over the data it holds, independently from the other nodes. Then the partial results from all nodes are merged in a final step. Figure 4 shows an SQL example of the processing strategy.

As shown in the example of Figure 4, aggregations over a fact A(F,Dx,...,Dy) can be processed independently in each node, followed by merging (union_all) of the partial result sets and re-applying of the aggregation query over the merged result set. Aggregation primitives are computed at each node. The most common primitives are: LINEAR SUM (LS=SUM(X)); SUM_OF_SQUARES (SS=SUM(X2)); number of elements (N), and extremes MAX and MIN. For the most common aggregation operators, the final aggregation function is shown in Figure 5.

This basic placement and query processing strategy is very simple and returns good results for the basic star schema with small dimensions. In the next section, we analyze its performance and show why a more flexible alternative is required.

Figure 4. Typical query processing with basic partitioning

```
SELECT avg(a), group_attributes
JOIN fact, dimensions
CONDITIONS (e.g. where x=3)
GROUPBY group_attributes;
```

```
SELECT sum(a), count(*), g_attrs
JOIN fact, dimensions
CONDITIONS (e.g. where x=3)
GROUPBY g_attrs;
```

```
SELECT sum(sums) / sum(counts), g_attrs
JOIN UNION results, dimensions
CONDITIONS (e.g. where x=3)
GROUPBY g_attrs;
```

Figure 5. Computation of aggregation from primitives

$$COUNT = N = \Sigma_{all\_nodes}\, n_{node_i} \tag{4}$$

$$SUM = LS = \Sigma_{all\_nodes}\, LS_{node_i} \tag{5}$$

$$AVERAGE = \Sigma_{all\_nodes}\, LS_{node_i} \,/\, \Sigma_{all\_nodes}\, N_{node_i} \tag{6}$$

$$STDDEV = \sqrt{\frac{(\sum SS_{node_i} - \sum LS_{node_i}^{\ 2}\,/\,N)}{N}} \tag{7}$$

$$MAX = MAX(MAX_{node_i}),\ MIN = MIN\,(MIN_{node_i}) \tag{8}$$

Experimental Evidence on Star Partitioning

Consider the schema and query set of the decision support performance benchmark TPC-H (TPC) in Figure 6 as an example. TPC-H is a multidimensional schema and a plausible historical record of a company business activity, therefore a plausible data warehouse. However, its "dimensions" are not very small and it contains several large relations, which are frequently involved in joins. The schema represents ordering and selling activity (LI-lineitem, O-orders, PS-partsupp, P-part, S-supplier, C-customer), where relations such as LI, O, PS, and even P are quite large. There are also two very small relations, NATION and REGION, not depicted in the figure, as they are very small and can be readily replicated into all nodes.

Figure 7 shows the result of applying the basic star partitioning over TPC-H. In this and following figures, filled objects represent replicated relations and (partially) unfilled ones represent partitioned relations. Fact relations LI and PS would be partitioned (randomly or round-robin) and the remaining relations would be replicated into all nodes, together with relation sizes considering TPC-H with 50GB.

Experiments were run on the TPC-H schema (50GB) and query set over 25 nodes. For these experiments, we measured processing and data exchange time on a node with a 32-bit 866 MHz CPU, three IDE hard disks (2x40 GB, 1x80GB), 512 MB of RAM, and a modern DBMS in a 100Mbps switched network. We have analyzed

Figure 6. TPC-H schema and relation sizes (Qualitative judgement)

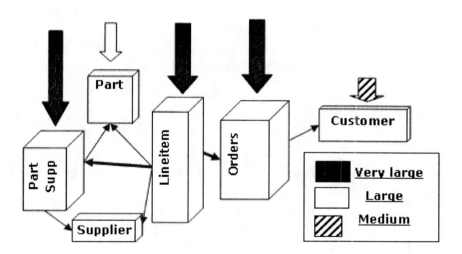

Figure 7. Star partitioning over TPC-H

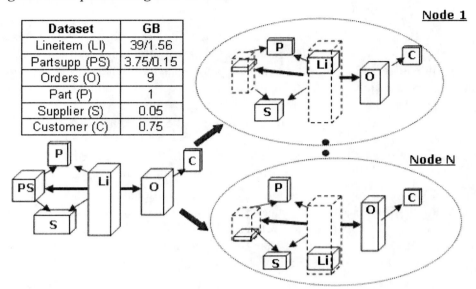

Dataset	GB
Lineitem (LI)	39/1.56
Partsupp (PS)	3.75/0.15
Orders (O)	9
Part (P)	1
Supplier (S)	0.05
Customer (C)	0.75

the results obtained by the runs. For the sake of our discussion, we organized the results into groups that provide evidence of a relationship between the placement and sizes of the relations that are accessed and the speedup that can be obtained. For details on the structure of individual queries of TPC-H, please refer to the specification of TPC-H in (TPC).

The following results compare the speedup of a single node, 50GB system, with a 25 node 50GB system, using the Star Partitioning of Figure 7. The speedup is measured as:

Speedup = Execution Time(single node)/Execution Time (25 nodes)   (9)

Figure 8a shows the speedup obtained for a set of queries accessing only relation LI or LI and S, as depicted in bold in Figure 8b.

This kind of results obtained for queries Q1, Q6, and Q15 are the most desirable ones because, considering that there are 25 nodes, a speedup in the vicinity of 25 is more or less linear. In practice, the speedup can be much more than linear in some cases because, when a single node is used to hold the 50GB data set, operations such as joins and sorts are very slow, as they require a lot of temporary disk storage, with the corresponding writes and reads.

Figure 9 shows queries whose speedup was between 6 and 15, and the corresponding typical access pattern. These queries have in common the fact that, besides the partitioned LI relation, they also access a full P relation, whose size is comparable to the LI fragment size. Instead of taking full advantage of the partitioning of relations, the fact that P is replicated means that the speedup decreases to levels that are significantly lower than 25 times (the linear speedup for a system with 25 nodes).

The remaining queries all obtained a very low speedup. Figure 10 shows queries that achieved speedups in the interval from 2 to 6. Their common and most relevant access pattern is that, besides LI, they also access the O relation, which is quite large and totally replicated into all nodes under this scheme. Some of these queries also access relations P and C, which are also replicated, further downgrading the performance of the system.

Figure 8. Large speedup queries and corresponding access pattern: (a) speedup results, (b) query pattern

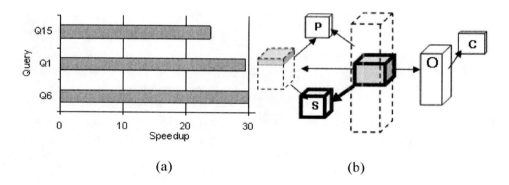

(a)   (b)

Figure 9. Medium speedup queries and corresponding access pattern: (a) speedup results, (b) query pattern

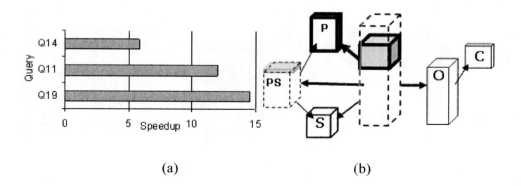

(a)   (b)

Figure 10. Low speedup queries and corresponding access pattern: (a) speedup results, (b) query pattern

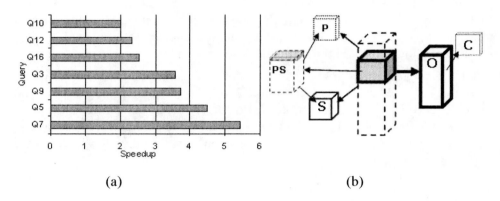

(a)   (b)

These results suggest that a more flexible partitioning strategy should be sought after. In the next section, we analyze the theoretical issues underlying a possible solution to this problem and then present a solution.

Model and Costs

From these experimental results, we conclude that the basic placement strategy is not adequate to store these complex schemas and query workloads because, although the facts are partitioned, reasonably large relations such as O and P are replicated into all nodes. We did not take sufficient advantage of the 25 nodes because we had to deal with full dimensions.

This discussion can also be represented using a mathematical model. Consider relations R_1 and R_2, N nodes, and a simplified linear cost model accounting for processing and joining costs (the only variable considered is the size of the relations). With this model, the cost of processing relation R_i is αR_i (α is a constant factor); the cost of processing a fragment is $\alpha R_i/N$; and the cost of joining R_1 to R_2 is $\alpha(R_1 + R_2)$. With N nodes, we would like to process only 1/N of the data in each node, resulting in about N times speedup:

$$\alpha \times \left(\frac{R_1}{N} + \frac{R_2}{N} \right), \alpha \ const = \frac{1}{N} \alpha \times (R_1 + R_2) \qquad (10)$$

However, we have replicated relations, which change the expression to:

$$\alpha \times \left(\frac{R_1}{N} + R_2 \right), \alpha \ const \tag{11}$$

The amount of speedup degradation depends on the size of R_2 relative to R_1/N. If replicated relations included in the expression are very large in comparison to fragments, the speedup will be very small.

Our next objective is to analyze alternative solutions to the problem, considering that our aim is to increase the degree of partitioning. Consider relations or more generically data sets R_1 and R_2 that must be joined by an equi-join key as part of the execution plan: $R_1 \bowtie_A R_2$. Also, consider that R_1 is fully horizontally partitioned into all nodes or into a node group. Each node out of N should process only 1/N of the total work in order to take full advantage of parallel execution. If both relations are partitioned by the same equi-join key and (hash) ranges (equi-partitioned), the join can be processed as a "**Local or Co-located Join**" (LocalJ) and this is the fastest alternative. The expression $R_1 \bowtie_A R_2$ is processed as $(R_{11} \bowtie_A R_{21}) \ U \ ... \ U \ (R_{1n} \bowtie_A R_{2n})$; each part of this expression is in a different node because as the two relations are partitioned by the equi-join key, the join between two fragments in different nodes is an empty set (e.g. $R_{11} \bowtie_A R_{22} = \phi$). Otherwise, at least one of the relations must be moved. If only one of the relations or neither is partitioned on the join key, we can dynamically repartition on the same join key and proceed with the parallel equi-join—this is the "**Repartitioned Join**" (RpartJ). The repartitioning is accounted as an extra overhead, which increases total work and response time and is dependent on data buffering and communication-related overheads. On the other hand, if one of the relations is replicated by placement, the join can proceed independently at all nodes, regardless of the partitioning key for the other relation. This is the "**Replicated Join**" (ReplicaJ). In a replicated join, the expression $R_1 \bowtie_A R_2$ is processed as $(R_{11} \bowtie_A R_2) \ U \ ...$ $U \ (R_{1n} \bowtie_A R_2)$. LocalJ requires the data sets involved in the join to be co-located. When trying to co-locate partitions from multiple relations, the partitioning issue that arises is that it is often necessary to choose which join will be co-located. For example, consider the join: $R_1 \bowtie_A R_2 \bowtie_B R_3$. In this case, R_2 will either be partitioned on A, in which case it will be co-located with R_1, or on B, in which case it will be co-located with R_3 (we can also partition R_2 by both attributes, but this does not result in co-location).

In multidimensional schemas of data warehouses, the partitioning issue is raised as some relations (e.g., facts) typically hold several foreign keys to other relations (e.g., dimensions). In order to choose the most appropriate partitioning alternative, we must use a strategy such as workload-based partitioning we discussed in Furtado (2004c). The idea is to choose partitioning keys that "maximize" the amount of LocalJ as opposed to RpartJ by looking at the query workload. But the discussion is not limited to determining which partitioning key should be used for each relation because, in some cases, it may be preferable not to partition at all. If the interconnections are slow or the available bandwidth is small, a replication strategy requiring no or little data exchange between nodes may be preferable, as ReplicaJ requires no data repartitioning. This is also the case for relations that are small in comparison to the data set that would need to be repartitioned to join with them, as it avoids potentially large partitioning overheads (Furtado, 2005b).

A basic knowledge of the costs that are involved in processing a query over DWPA is also useful for the formulation of an effective partitioning strategy. Next, we discuss briefly the most relevant costs incurred in this context. Given that most relations become partitioned, the main processing costs, listed next, are partitioning, repartitioning, data communication, and local processing costs.

- **Partitioning cost (PC):** Partitioning a relation consists of retrieving the relation from secondary memory, dividing it into fragments by applying a hash function to a join attribute, and assigning buffers for the data to send to other nodes. This involves scanning the relation only once. The partitioning cost is monotonically increasing on the relation size. Since there can be two or more relations to be partitioned and they can be processed in parallel in two or more nodes, the partition cost for a given query is the largest partition cost among the nodes participating simultaneously.

- **Repartitioning cost (RC):** Repartitioning is similar to partitioning, but involves a fragment in each node instead of the whole relation. It is used to re-organize the partitioned relation, hashing on a different equi-join attribute. The fragments resulting from this repartitioning need to be redistributed to other nodes to process a hash-join.

- **Data communication cost (DC):** The data communication cost is monotonically increasing with the size of the data transferred and equal between any number of nodes. We assume a switched network, as this allows different pairs of nodes to send data simultaneously (with no collisions). This, in turn, allows the repartitioning algorithm to be implemented more efficiently.

- **Local processing cost (LC):** The local processing cost for the join operation typically depends on whether the join is supported by fast access paths, such as indexes and the size of the relations participating in the join. The local processing cost should also account for other operations performed locally. For simplicity, we assume that these costs also increase monotonically on the relation sizes, although in practice this depends on several parameters, including memory buffer limitations.

- **Merging cost (MC):** The merging cost is related to applying a final query to the collected partial results at the merging node.

We define weighting parameters (Sasha & Wang, 1991): a partitioning cost weight, β, and a local processing weight, α, so that β/α denotes the ratio of partitioning costs to local processing costs (e.g., ~2 (Sasha & Wang, 1991)). Considering large relations with size R_i, N nodes and the linear cost model described above, we can obtain a simple expression for the cost of processing joins, when repartitioning is required versus the cost when the relations are already equi-partitioned. For simplicity, the following expressions consider only two large relations. The fragment size is R_i/N. The join-processing cost for queries requiring the join between equi-partitioned large relations and replicated small relations r_i is:

$$\text{Join Cost with Equi-partitioned Relations} = \alpha \times \left(\frac{R_1}{N} + \frac{R_2}{N} + r_1 + \dots + r_l \right) \quad (12)$$

The cost when large relations are not equi-partitioned on a switched network includes repartitioning and local processing cost factors with corresponding weights as shown in (13). The IR symbol in the repartitioning cost factor is an intermediate result from doing independently a locally-processable part of the joins (those involving replicated and equi-partitioned relations) at all nodes. The IR must then be repartitioned. The value IR/N is the fraction of the IR that is at each node. About 1/N of that fraction (1/N x IR/N) has the correct hash-value for the node, therefore requiring no repartitioning.

$$\textit{join cost with repartitioning} = \left(\frac{IR}{N} - \frac{IR}{N^2} \right) \times \beta + \alpha \times \left(\frac{R_1}{N} + \frac{R_2}{N} + r_1 + \dots + r_l \right) \quad (13)$$

The increase in cost of (13) over (12) is therefore:

$$\textit{cost increase of repartitioned join} = \left(\frac{IR}{N} - \frac{IR}{N^2} \right) \times \beta \quad (14)$$

This overhead depends on the size of IR and is avoided whenever the relations to be joined are equi-partitioned by the appropriate join attribute.

The discussion of this section clarified the costs involved in processing the query and in particular joins. In the next section, we propose modifications to star partitioning and processing that reduce the performance limitations by considering the workload and relation sizes and taking full advantage of partitioning options.

Workload-Based Star Partitioning

An improved partitioning scheme should take into consideration relation sizes, joins between relations, and the query workload characteristics to improve query processing performance. From the discussion of the previous sections, it is clear that large relations should be partitioned. In this sense, a small relation is one whose average contribution to join processing time costs, considering the workload, is less than a configurable threshold value (e.g., 5%). As discussed in the previous section, when more than one relation is partitioned, it is important to promote local joins over repartitioned joins for the most frequent and costly joins, in order to reduce query processing costs. This implies a determination of the most advantageous partitioning attributes and the use of hash or range partitioning, instead of round-robin or random strategy, to enable equi-partitioning of relations. The algorithm should be simple and independent of specific database servers because DWPA can run on completely heterogeneous systems. The placement strategy described next can easily be automated:

- **Dimensions:** Non-small dimensions are hash-partitioned by their primary key. This is because the primary key of dimensions is expected to be used in every equi-join with facts. The references from fact to dimensions correspond to foreign keys on the fact referencing those equi-join primary keys of the dimensions.

- **Facts:** The objective is to find the hash-partitioning attribute that minimizes repartitioning costs. A reasonable approximation to this objective is to determine the most frequent equi-join attribute used by the relation. To do this, the placement strategy looks at the frequency of access to other partitioned relations and chooses the most frequent equi-join attribute with those relations as the partitioning attribute.

By co-locating relation fragments that are frequent equi-join targets, this simple strategy minimizes repartitioning requirements.

Next, we apply this placement strategy to the TPC-H schema. We arbitrated small as less than 1GB for TPC-H 50GB, so that dimensions C and S are considered small and replicated. This assumption is enough for us to show the advantages of the strategy, but we point out that smaller thresholds allow further speedup in systems with many nodes. Figure 11 shows that in what concerns dimensions, relations S and C are replicated, and P is partitioned by P_key. The O relation, if considered a dimension, is immediately partitioned by the O_key attribute. This relation could also be considered a fact because it links to dimension C, but the resulting partitioning would be the same if it were considered a fact. Finally, facts should be partitioned

Figure 11. Workload-based star partitioning results

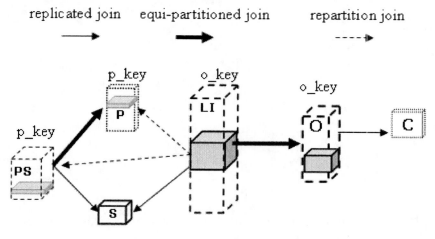

according to the most frequent join. Considering the TPC-H workload, fact LI is most frequently joined to O and, therefore, should be partitioned by O_key. Fact PS is partitioned by P_key, as shown in Figure 11. This partitioning resulted in two sets of equi-partitioned relations (LI, O), (PS, P) and a set of replicated dimensions (S, C). Joins between relations, within each of these sets, can be done without repartitioning and joins with any of the (small) replicated relations can also be done without any repartitioning. Repartitioning becomes necessary when elements from the first and second sets above are joined.

This partitioning algorithm requires modifications to the basic query processing strategy. Recall that the Submitter determines command lists for the Executors and sends them to all nodes participating in the processing of the query. Executors submit the local query and send partial results into the merger node if necessary, which applies a merge query and signals the Submitter to pull the results. These QPA steps are summarized next:

1.   Submitter generates and sends commands to executors.
2.   Executors apply a local query.
3.   Executors send results to merger.
4.   Merger applies merge query.

Under the workload-based star partitioning and processing approach, queries involving only replicated and/or equi-partitioned joins are processed as described above.

Figure 12. Query processing steps for aggregation query

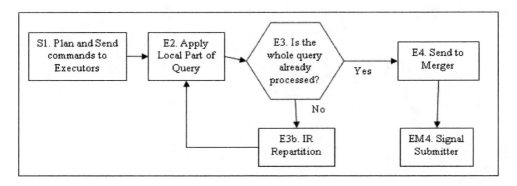

Figure 13. TPC-H speedup on star partitioning vs workload-based partitioning

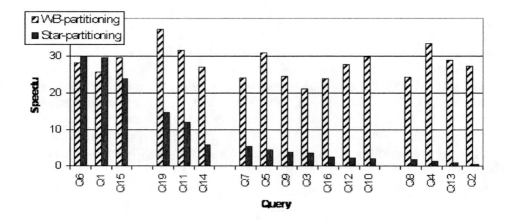

However, queries that access partitioned relations that are not all equi-partitioned require some extra steps. In this case, the query is divided into a set of partial queries that each involves only a "*locally-processable part of the query*," that is, queries that reference only datasets that are either replicated or equi-partitioned. These datasets include both relations and repartitioned intermediate results from previous partial queries. Repartitioning commands are added to re-hash those intermediate results. Steps E2, E3, and E3b of Figure 12 illustrate the processing of these partial steps. The precise execution plan is determined in step S1 by evaluating all the alternative execution plans with the simple cost model described in section 6.

Figure 13 shows our experimental speedup results, considering 25 nodes and the basic TPC-H configuration described previously. The two strategies shown are the basic—*star partitioning*—and the improved one—*workload-based partitioning*.

Most queries exhibit near to linear speedup, when the improved strategy is used.

The major improvements in Figure 13 have to do with the fact that the O relation is no longer fully replicated, being instead, partitioned by the equi-join key to LI. Other queries benefited from PS being equi-partitioned with P. At the same time, queries that were the fastest under the basic placement strategy (Figure 13a) are still as fast because they access partitioned relations in both cases.

While the most important performance issue in the initial replicated placement scheme was the need to process large full relations at each node, repartitioning requirements could be an important overhead in the improved partitioning and placement scheme. However, not only is it possible that many queries do not require repartitioning, but also, repartitioning is, in fact, much less expensive than having (possibly very) large relations completely replicated.

Figure 14 shows the repartitioning overhead of the improved, workload-based partitioning and its comparison to the overhead of using the basic star-partitioning approach instead. In Figure 14, the ratio RT/TC concerns workload-based partitioning and shows the repartitioning overhead (repartitioning cost RC) as a percentage of the total query runtime (Total Cost TC) for queries that required repartitioning. The comparison with the basic star-partitioning is made through the value RT/TC (Replicated), which is the ratio of repartitioning overhead (repartitioning cost RC) in the workload-based approach to the total query runtime for the basic star-partitioning approach, where all except one relation are replicated (total cost TC(replicated)). The conclusion is that the repartitioning cost was a reasonably small fraction of the total runtime cost for all these queries, except Q9 where it was about 30% of the total runtime cost. But even in that case, this repartitioning overhead represented only a small fraction when compared with the total cost of the basic star-partitioning approach.

In summary, after applying the simple improved partitioning strategy, the performance results improved significantly. Most queries required no repartitioning at all with the improved placement and those which did require repartitioning still

Figure 14. Repartitioning overhead (% of runtime cost)

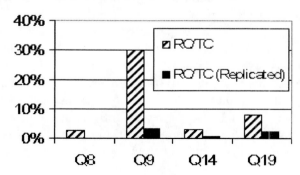

obtained a speedup that was orders of magnitude faster than the initial replicated placement scheme.

Future Work and Trends

The placement and processing issues discussed in this chapter are part of the basic design for the Data Warehouse Parallel Architecture Project (DWPA, 2005). They are also part of the query processor of DWPA. DWPA focuses on architectural characteristics, automatic reorganization, load balancing, response time prediction, and automatic adaptability for the low-cost Node Partitioned Data Warehouse. These are in line with current and future trends on database research in related issues, which include database self-tuning and auto-configuration (Chaudhuri & Weikum, 2002; Weikum, Moenkeberg, Hasse, & Zabback, 2002; Schiefer & Valentin, 1999). DWPA has also produced results concerning highly-efficient replication and the use of specialized join bitmap indexes to avoid repartitioning overheads (Furtado, 2006). Further research is necessary in adaptability issues in the DWPA context.

There is also a market trend towards more and more open-source software, including open-source database engines being deployed in organizations. Organizations also become increasingly cost-conscious—in both hardware and software platforms. In this context, the DWPA concept of an architecture that can run anywhere efficiently and adaptively also seems to be in line with current trends. Besides, many of the issues discussed in this chapter can also be applied to other parallel architectures that are increasingly deployed, in particular symmetric multiprocessors (SMP) and clusters of SMPs.

Conclusion

We have discussed placement and processing design issues for low-cost alternatives to specialized, fast and fully-dedicated, parallel hardware to handle large data warehouses. The idea is to design the system with special care, concerning partitioning for placement and reorganization. We have analyzed a basic and simple partitioning scheme—star partitioning—and related processing issues, and gained insight into the problems that such a simple strategy runs into. Our objective was to design a system that would be independent of database servers or, indeed, any other piece of software and that could run efficiently in any environment, including slow interconnections. We have proposed a workload-based partitioning approach, which proved experimentally to be very efficient and to overcome the issues raised with the basic star-partitioned approach. The whole discussion and results given are important building block elements for the construction of low-cost, highly scalable and efficient data warehouse systems.

Acknowledgment

The work in this chapter was partially supported by project Auto-DWPA: Research and Development Project POSI/EIA/57974/2004 of FCT "Fundação para a Ciência e a Tecnologia," Portugal, 2004/2007.

References

Chan, C.-Y., & Ioannidis, Y. E. (1998). Bitmap index design and evaluation. In *Proceedings of the International Conference on the Management of Data* (pp. 355-366).

Chaudhuri, S., & Weikum, G. (2002). Rethinking database system architecture: Towards a self-tuning, RISC-style database system. In *Proceedings of Very Large Databases Conference*.

Chaudhuri, S., Narasayya, V., & Ramamurthy, R. (2004). Estimating progress of execution for SQL queries. In *Proceedings of the ACM International Conference on Data Management*, Paris.

Copeland, G., & Keller, T. (1989). A comparison of high-availability media recovery techniques. In *Proceedings of the ACM International Conference on Management of Data*.

Coulon, C., Pacitti, E., & Valduriez, P. (2004). Scaling up the preventive replication of autonomous databases in cluster systems. In *Proceedings of the 6th International Vecpar Conference*, Valencia, Spain.

DeWitt, D., & Gray, J. (1992). The future of high performance database processing. *Communications of the ACM 35*(6).

DWPA. (2005). *DWPA Research and Development Project POSI/EIA/57974/2004 of FCT Fundação para a Ciência e a Tecnologia*, Portugal.

Furtado, P. (2004a). Hash-based placement and processing for efficient node partitioned query-intensive databases. In *Proceedings of the Tenth International Conference on Parallel and Distributed Systems*, NewPort Beach, CA (pp. 127-134).

Furtado, P. (2004b). Workload-based placement and join processing in node-partitioned data warehouses. In *Proceedings of the International Conference on Data Warehousing and Knowledge Discovery*, Zaragoza, Spain (pp. 38-47).

Furtado, P. (2004c). Experimental evidence on partitioning in parallel data warehouses. In *Proceedings of the ACM DOLAP 04—Workshop of the International Conference on Information and Knowledge Management*, Washington.

Furtado, P. (2005). Efficiently processing query-intensive databases over a non-dedicated local network. In *Proceedings of the 19th International Parallel and Distributed Processing Symposium*, Denver, CO.

Furtado, P. (2005b). The issue of large relations in node-partitioned data warehouses. *Proceedings of the International Conference on Database Systems for Advanced Applications*, Beijing, China.

Furtado, P. (2005c). Replication in node partitioned data warehouses. In *Proceedings of the VLDB Ws. on Design, Implementation, and Deployment of Database Replication*. Trondheim, Norway.

Furtado, P. (2006). Node partitioned data warehouses: Experimental evidence and improvements. *Journal of Database Management*, 17(2), 42-60.

Furtado, P. (2007). Efficient and robust node-partitioned data warehouses. To appear in *Data Warehouses and Olap, Wrembel, Robert (EDT)/ Koncilia, Christian (EDT)*. Idea Group.

Hsiao, H., & DeWitt, D. (1990). Chained declustering: A new availability strategy for multi-processor database machines. In *Proceedings from International Conference on Data Engineering*.

Hsiao, H., & DeWitt, D. (1990b). *Replicated data management in the gamma database machine.* Presented at the Workshop on the Management of Replicated Data.

Hsiao, H., & DeWitt, D. J. (1991). A performance study of three high availability data replication strategies. In *Proceedings of the Parallel and Distributed Systems*.

Hua, K. A., & Lee, C. (1990). An adaptive data placement scheme for parallel database computer systems. In *Proceedings of the Sixteenth Very Large Data Bases Conference* (pp. 493-506), Brisbane, Queensland, Australia.

Kimball, R., Reeves, L., Ross, M., & Thornthwaite, W. (1998). *The data warehouse life cycle toolkit*. John Wiley & Sons.

Kitsuregawa, M., Tanaka, H., & Motooka, T. (1983). Application of hash to database machine and its architecture. *New Generation Computing, 1*(1), 63-74.

Lin, Y., Kemme, B., & Jimenez-Peris, R. (2005). Consistent data replication: Is it feasible in WANs? In *Proceedings of the 11th International Europar Conference*, Lisboa, Portugal.

Luo, G., Naughton, J. F., Ellmann, C. J., & Watzke, M. W. (2004). Toward a progress indicator for database queries. In *Proceedings of the ACM International Conference on Data Management*, Paris.

O'Neil, P., & Graefe, G. (1995). Multi-table joins through bitmapped join indices. *SIGMOD Record, 24*(3), 8-11.

Pacitti, E., Özsu, M., & Coulon, C. (2003). Preventive multi-master replication in a cluster of autonomous databases. In *Proceedings of the 9th International Europar Conference*, Klagenfurt, Austria.

Patterson, D. A., Gibson, G., & Katz, R. H. (1998). A case for redundant arrays of inexpensive disks (raid). In *Proceedings of the International Conference on Management of Data*, Chicago (pp. 109-116).

Rao, J., Zhang, C., Megiddo, N., & Lohman, G. (2002). Automating physical database design in a parallel database. In *Proceedings of the ACM International Conference on Management of Data*, Madison, WI (pp. 558-569).

Rousopoulos, R. (1998). Materialized views and data warehouses. *SIGMOD Record, 27*(1), 21-26.

Saborit, J. A., Mulero, V. M., & Pey, J. L. (2003). Pushing down bit filters in the pipelined execution of large queries. In *Proceedings of the International Conference Europar* (pp. 328-337).

Sasha, D., & Wang, T. (1991). Optimizing equijoin queries in distributed databases where relations are hash partitioned. *ACM Transactions on Database System, 16*(2), 279-308.

Schiefer, B., & Valentin, G. (1999). DB2 universal database performance tuning. *IEEE Data Engineering Bulletin, 22*(2), 12-19.

Shatdal, A., & Naughton, J. (1995). Adaptive parallel aggregation algorithms. In *Proceedings of the 1995 International Conference on Management of Data*, San Jose, CA (pp. 104-114).

Tandem (1987). NonStop SQL, a distributed, high-performance, high-reliability implementation of SQL. *Workshop on High Performance Transactional Systems*, CA.

Teradata (1985). *Teradata DBC/1012 database computer system manual 2.0, C10-0001-02*. Teradata.

TPC (1989). *TPC benchmark H, transaction processing council*. Retrieved from http://www.tpc.org/

Valduriez, P., & Ozsu, M. (1999). *Principles of parallel and distributed database systems* (3rd ed.). Prentice-Hall.

Weikum, G., Moenkeberg, A., Hasse, C., & Zabback, P. (2002). Self-tuning database technology and information services: From wishful thinking to viable engineering. In *Proceedings of the Very Large Database Conference*.

Williams, M., & Zhou, S. (1998). Data placement in parallel database systems. Parallel database techniques. *IEEE Computer Society Press*, 203-219.

Yu, C. T., Guh, K. C., Brill, D., & Chen, A. L. P. (1989). Partition strategy for distributed query processing in fast local networks. *IEEE Transactions on Software Engineering, 15*(6), 780-793.

Yu, C. T., & Meng, W. (1998). *Principles of database query processing for advanced applications*. Morgan Kaufmann.

Zilio, D. C., Jhingran, A., & Padmanabhan, S. (1994). *Partitioning key selection for a shared-nothing parallel database system* (IBM Research Report RC 19820 [87739]).

Chapter VI

Factors Affecting Design Decisions for Customer Relationship Management Data

Colleen Cunningham, Drexel University, USA
Il-Yeol Song, Drexel University, USA

Abstract

Customer relationship management (CRM) is a strategy that integrates concepts of knowledge management, data mining, and data warehousing in order to support an organization's decision-making process to retain long-term and profitable relationships with its customers. Key factors for successfully implementing CRM (e.g., data quality issues, organizational readiness, customer strategies, selection of appropriate KPIs, and the design of the data warehouse model) are discussed with the main thrust of the chapter focusing on CRM analyses and the impact of those analyses on CRM data warehousing design decisions. This chapter then presents a robust multidimensional starter model that supports CRM analyses. Additional research contributions include the introduction of two new measures, percent success ratio and CRM suitability ratio by which CRM models can be evaluated, the identification/classification of CRM queries, and a preliminary heuristic for designing data warehouses to support CRM analyses.

Introduction

It is far more expensive for companies to acquire new customers than it is to retain existing customers. In fact, acquiring new customers can cost five times more than it costs to retain current customers (Massey, Montoya-Weiss, & Holcom, 2001). Furthermore, according to Winer (2001), repeat customers can generate more than twice as much gross income as new customers. Companies have realized that instead of treating all customers equally, it is more effective to invest in customers that are valuable or potentially valuable, while limiting their investments in non-valuable customers (that is, not all relationships are profitable or desirable). As a result of these types of findings as well as the fact that customers want to be served according to their individual and unique needs, companies need to develop and manage their relationships with their customers such that the relationships are long-term and profitable. Therefore, companies are turning to customer relationship management (CRM) techniques and CRM-supported technologies.

By utilizing a data warehouse, companies can make decisions about customer-specific strategies such as customer profiling, customer segmentation, and cross-selling analysis. For example, a company can use a data warehouse to determine its customers' historic and future values and to segment its customer base. Table 1 shows four quadrants of customer segmentation: (1) customers that should be eliminated (that is, they cost more than what they generate in revenues); (2) customers with whom the relationship should be re-engineered (that is, those that have the potential to be valuable, but may require the company's encouragement, cooperation, and/or management); (3) customers that the company should engage; and (4) customers in which the company should invest (Buttle, 1999; Verhoef & Donkers, 2001).

The company could then use the corresponding strategies, as depicted in Table 2, to manage the customer relationships. Table 1 and Table 2 are only examples of the types of segmentation that can be performed with a data warehouse. However, if used, a word of caution should be taken before categorizing a customer into Segment I because that segment can be further segmented into (a) those customers that serve as benchmarks for more valuable customers, (b) those customers that provide the company with ideas for product improvements or efficiency improvements, and (c) those customers that do not have any value to the company.

It is important to point out that customer segmentation can be further complicated by the concept of extended households. The term *extended household* refers to the relationship that exists between companies (e.g., parent company and subsidiary). The analysis of the relationships that exist between customers (that is, lines of potential customer influence) is known as household analysis. It is important to understand and manage extended households because a company's decision to treat a member of one segment potentially could have a negative impact on a related customer. For example, if a customer is in a non-profitable segment, then the company may

Table 1. Customer segments

		Historic Value	
		Low	High
Future Value	High	II. Re-Engineer	IV. Invest
	Low	I. Eliminate	III. Engage

Table 2. Corresponding segmentation strategies

		Historic Value	
		Low	High
Future Value	High	Up-sell & cross-sell activities and add value	Treat with priority and preferential; retention strategies; loyalty programs
	Low	Reduce costs and increase prices	Engage customer to find new opportunities in order to sustain loyalty

decide to increase the customer's price. However, if the company is aware that the same non- profitable customer has influence over another customer (e.g., a parent or small business) that is in a more profitable segment, then the company may decide to not increase the customer's price rather than to risk losing both of the customers. Clearly, these social networks of influence are important for companies to identify and manage because of the impact that they can have on the company's ability to retain customers.

Currently, however, there are no agreed upon standardized rules for how to design a data warehouse to support CRM. However, the design of the CRM data warehouse model directly impacts an organization's ability to readily perform analyses that are specific to CRM. Subsequently, the design of the CRM data warehouse model contributes to the success or failure of CRM. Thus, the ultimate long-term purpose of our study is to systematically examine CRM factors that affect design decisions for CRM data warehouses in order to build a taxonomy of CRM analyses, and to determine the impact of those analyses on CRM data warehousing design decisions.

The taxonomy and heuristics for CRM data warehousing design decisions then could be used to guide CRM initiatives and to design and implement CRM data warehouses. The taxonomy also could be used to customize a starter model for a company's specific CRM requirements within a given industry. Furthermore, that taxonomy also would serve as a guideline for companies in the selection and evaluation of CRM data warehouses and related technologies. In order to objectively quantify the completeness and suitability of the proposed CRM model (and alternative models), we propose two new metrics: *CRM success ratio* ($r_{success}$) and *CRM suitability ratio* ($r_{suitability}$). The *CRM success ratio* ($r_{success}$) is defined as the ratio of queries that successfully executed to the total number of queries issued against the model. A query is executed successfully if the results that are returned are meaningful to the analyst. The CRM success ratio can not only be used to evaluate our proposed CRM model, but it also can be used to evaluate other CRM data warehouse models, as well. The range of values for $r_{success}$ is between 0 and 1. The larger the value of *rsuccess*, the more successful the model. The following equation defines the CRM success ratio:

$$r_{success} = Qp / Qn \qquad (1)$$

where Qp is the total number of queries that successfully executed against the model and Qn is the total number of queries issued against the model.

The *CRM suitability ratio* ($r_{suitability}$) is defined as the ratio of the sum of the individual suitability scores to the sum of the number of applicable categories. The following equation defines the CRM suitability ratio:

$$r_{suitability} = \Sigma^{N}_{i=1} (XiCi) / N \qquad (2)$$

where N is the total number of applicable analysis criteria, C is the individual score for each analysis capability, and X is the weight assigned to each analysis capability. The range of values for the $r_{suitability}$ ratio is between 0 and 1, with values closer to 1 being more suitable. Unlike the $r_{success}$ ratio, which can be used to evaluate and compare the richness and completeness of CRM data warehouse models, the $r_{suitability}$ ratio, however, can be used to help companies to determine the suitability of the model based upon the contextual priorities of the decision makers (that is, based upon the company-specific CRM needs). We utilize the two metrics to evaluate the proposed CRM data warehouse model in our case study implementation.

A brief review of CRM literature is presented in the next section. The main thrust of the chapter is presented in several sections. The section on schema design introduces the analytical CRM analyses requirements that the data warehouse must support as well as provides guidelines for designing the fact tables and the dimensions (that is, issues and problems). The experiment, which is subsequently described with the results in the following section, tests the completeness of the proposed model. The flexibility of the model, the utilization of the CRM analyses, as well as the initial heuristics for designing a CRM data warehouse are presented in the discussion (that is, the solution and recommendations). Finally, the research contributions and future work are discussed in the conclusions.

Background

Customer relationship management (CRM), which is also known as relationship marketing and customer management, evolved from Sales Force Automation (Imhoff, Loftis, & Geiger, 2001; Spangler, May, & Vargas, 1999). There are many different definitions of customer relationship management (CRM). Some define it as merely a business strategy (Jackson, 2005), while others define it as a data-driven approach to assess customers current needs and profitability (Fitzgibbon & White, 2005). Paas and Kuijlen (2001) provide a summary of some of the common variations of CRM: operational CRM (O-CRM), which focuses on the business processes; analytical CRM (A-CRM), which focuses on applying analytical tools to transactional data; collaborative CRM (C-CRM), which focuses on collaboration between the customer and the company; and e-commerce CRM (E-CRM), which focuses on Web-based interactions with customers. Those definitions, however, only represent a partial view of CRM. In our earlier work (Cunningham, Song, Jung, & Chen, 2003), we defined a more complete definition of CRM as a data-driven strategy that utilizes organizational knowledge and technology in order to enable proactive and profitable long-term relationships with customers. It integrates the use of knowledge management, or organizational knowledge, and technologies to enable organizations to make decisions about, among other things, product offerings, marketing strategies, and customer interactions.

One of the major drivers of CRM is the need to understand behavioral loyalty, which deals with customers making repeat purchases (Ryals, 2003; Fitzgibbon & White, 2005). Another major driver of CRM is the shift in marketing paradigms from mass marketing to target marketing to the customer-centric, one-to-one marketing (known as relationship marketing) (Bose, 2002). Mass marketing is a product-focused approach that allows companies to reach a wide audience with little or no research, irrespective of the consumer's individual needs. Unlike mass marketing, target marketing focuses on marketing to segmented groups that share a similar set of characteristics (e.g., demographic information and purchasing habits). While both approaches are cost-effective, they do not allow for personalization. On the other hand, one-to one marketing (relationship marketing) enables companies to treat customers individually, according to their unique needs. Since not all relationships are profitable or desirable, relationship marketing allows companies to focus on customers that have the best potential lifetime value.

In the literature, researchers use the total historical value and the total potential future value to analyze the customer lifetime value (CLV). In fact, managing the CLV is essential to the success of CRM strategies because companies that understand and utilize CLV are 60% more profitable than those that do not (Bose, 2002; Kale, 2004). Moreover, failing to understand CLV is considered one of the seven deadly sins of CRM (Kale, 2004). There are many ways to define and calculate CLV (Hawkes, 2000; Hwang, Jung & Suh, 2004; Jain & Singh, 2002; Rosset, Neumann, Eick & Vatnik, 2003). For the purposes of this chapter, CLV is the sum of the total historical value and the total potential value for each customer. The following equation defines the *total historical value*:

$$\text{Historical Value} = \Sigma^N_{i=1} (\text{Revenue}_j - \text{Cost}_j) \tag{3}$$

where j is the individual products that the customer has purchased.

In equation (3), the historical value is computed by summing the difference between the revenue and total cost over every product (j) that the customer has purchased in the past. The cost would include such things as product cost, distribution cost, and overhead cost. Using the same calculation as defined by Hwang et al. (2004), the following equation defines the *potential future value* for a customer:

$$\text{Potential Future Value} = \Sigma^N_{i=1} (\text{Probability}_j \text{ X Profitability}_j) \tag{4}$$

where j is the individual products that the customer potentially could purchase.

In equation (4), the profitability represents the expected revenues minus the sum of the expected costs that would be incurred in order to gain the additional revenues. The probability represents the likelihood that the customer would purchase the product. Thus, the total potential future value would be the sum of individual potential future values of each product that the customer could potentially purchase. The sum of all of the individual customer lifetime values is known as *customer equity* (Rust, Lemon, & Zeithaml, 2004).

One of the goals of companies should be to increase their customer equity from one year to the next. By incorporating the ability to compute the CLV into the CRM data warehouse, companies can utilize the CRM data warehouse to determine their customer growth.

While companies realize that there are benefits of CRM, many have not actually achieved the full benefits of implementing CRM. In fact, recent statistics indicate that between 50% and 80% of CRM initiatives fail, due to inappropriate or incomplete CRM processes and poor selection of technologies (Myron & Ganeshram, 2002; Panker, 2002). One of the key factors in successfully implementing CRM is having the appropriate customer strategies, before rolling out a CRM solution (Rigby,

Reichheld, & Schefter, 2002). In order to identify the appropriate customer-specific approach for managing individual customers, we first must classify customers into one of the four quadrants in Table 1 and subsequently apply the appropriate strategy. Some of the strategies for managing the customers have been identified in Buttle (1999); Verhoef and Donkers (2001), Ang and Taylor (2005), and Xevelonakis (2005). Table 2 summarizes some of the common strategies.

Companies use key performance indicators (KPIs) to not only manage the strategies, but also to identify areas that could be improved. Specific KPIs should relate to the goals of the organization. For example, if a company wants to minimize the number of late deliveries, then an on-time delivery KPI should be selected. Some known KPIs that are relevant to CRM include, but are not limited to, margins, on-time deliveries, late-deliveries, and customer retention rates. Other KPIs that are relevant to CRM include, but are not limited to, marketing cost, number and value of new customers gained, complaint numbers, and customer satisfaction rates (Kellen, 2002). Furthermore, Hansotia (2004) identified some additional key customer metrics that should be monitored, which include, but are not limited to: attrition rates, revenue as a percentage of total marketing cost, operating cost per customer, total cost per customer, cash flow per customer, and average revenue per customer. Roberts et al. (2005) also identified some KPIs by functional area: revenue per sales person, average speed of reply, increase in CLV, increase in number of high value customers, and customer satisfaction.

It is important to note that the ability to properly analyze the KPIs is dependent upon data quality. Poor data quality is often sited as one of the reasons that the corporate data warehouse is not used (Payton & Zahay, 2003; Fitzgibbon & White, 2005; Reid & Catterall, 2005). Poor data quality can result in losses for companies. According to Chettayar (2002), companies can loose 10-25% of their revenues due to poor data quality, which results in as much as $600 billion per year for U.S. companies. Data quality issues can range from inaccurate data to missing data to duplicate customer records to outliers.

Given the range of decisions that the CRM data warehouse must be able to support, and given the potential impact on companies' profitability, it is imperative that the data are accurate. The data that are used in the CRM analyses originate from disparate data sources that must be integrated into the data warehouse. Under such circumstances, the issue of dirty data arises. Analyzing dirty data, particularly in the context of systems that support corporate decision-making processes (e.g., CRM analyses and subsequent decisions), would result in unreliable results and potentially inappropriate decisions. As such, ensuring data quality within the data warehouse is important to the overall success of subsequent CRM analyses and decisions. Data quality should not be considered a one-time exercise conducted only when data are loaded into the data warehouse. Rather, there should be a continuous and systematic data quality improvement process (Lee, Pipino, Strong, & Wang, 2004; Shankaranarayan, Ziad, & Wang, 2003; Reid & Catterall, 2005).

One way of minimizing data quality issues is to carefully document the business rules and data formats that then can be used to ensure that those requirements are enforced. Too often, however, thorough documentation of the business rules and data formats is not available in a corporate setting. Therefore, routine data quality audits should be performed on the data in the CRM model in order to identify data quality issues that are not addressed during the ETL process. For example, missing data can be identified during data quality audits and consequently addressed by consulting with a domain expert.

Some forms of dirty data (e.g., outliers) can be identified using data mining techniques and statistical analysis, while other forms of dirty data (e.g., missing data values) are more problematic. Although Dasu, Vesonder, and Wright (2003) assert that data quality issues are application-specific, Kim, Choi, Kim, and Lee (2003) developed a taxonomy of dirty data and identified methods for addressing dirty data based upon their taxonomy. Kim et al. (2003) identified three broad categories of dirty data: (1) missing data; (2) not missing, but wrong data; and (3) not missing and not wrong, but unusable data. Although Kim et al. (2003) identified three broad categories of dirty data and further decomposed each category of dirty data, they did not, however, include composite types of dirty data. They provided some suggestions to address the issue of dirty data that can be used to clean dirty data in the CRM model during the ETL process. For example, the use of constraints can be valuable for avoiding instances of missing data (e.g., not null constraints) or incorrect data (e.g., domain ranges and check constraints). It is important to point out that the ability to enforce integrity constraints on inconsistent spatial data (e.g., geographical data such as sales territory alignments) and outdated temporal data is not supported in current database management systems.

Koslowsky (2002) summarized some of the most common ways of handling missing data. Those methods include: (1) mean substitution, (2) group mean substitution, (3) median substitution, (4) listwise deletion, and (5) pairwise deletion. *Mean substitution* is the approach most often used, and involves substituting the average value for missing values. This method should only be used if few records have missing values. *Group mean substitution* involves computing the average based on a logical grouping (e.g., averages by gender, and so forth) and substituting the group average whenever missing values occur for the specified group. It is generally a better approach than the mean substitution approach. *Median substitution* involves substituting the median value for missing values, and is most appropriate when the averages are skewed. *Listwise deletion* involves deleting (or ignoring) records that have missing data, and is only appropriate if few records are missing data. *Pairwise deletion* involves ignoring the specific data element that has missing values for many records.

Reid and Catterall (2005) also suggested incorporating performance measurements and rewards as incentives for employees in the call center to enter accurate data. Additionally, they suggested implementing data validation rules during the data entry process. They also suggested establishing a data management strategy program, including a *data governor* that has ultimate responsibility for data quality.

It is important to note that, while it is outside the scope of this chapter, organizational readiness is another key factor in successfully implementing CRM (Jackson, 2005; Roberts et al., 2005; Hansotia, 2004). Organizational readiness means that the corporate culture, operational structure, and organizational structure need to be customer-centric and aligned with the strategies, which often involves reengineering some business processes.

In addition to having the appropriate differentiated customer strategies, selecting the appropriate KPIs, and addressing data quality issues, the design of the CRM data warehouse model also contributes to the success or failure of CRM. Fitzgibbon and White (2005) found that companies need a "single view of the customer" (p. 9). In fact, Paas and Kuijlen (2001) identified the specifications for the data warehouse and the data mining and business intelligence tools as two key steps in successfully implementing CRM. Similarly, Plakoyiannaki and Tzokas (2002) and Alvarez, Raeside, and Jones (2006) also identified analytical capabilities as an essential component of CRM. Roberts et al. (2005) and Jackson (2005) also found that the analyses are important to the success of CRM because they allow companies to monitor and adjust their CRM programs. Moreover, Alvarez et al. (2006) found that companies that effectively used customer data performed well with respect to business performance metrics.

Schema Design for CRM

While it is clear from the literature review that the design of the data warehouse and analysis capabilities are essential to the success of CRM, there are no agreed upon standardized rules for how to design a data warehouse to support CRM. Yet, the design of the CRM data warehouse model directly impacts an organization's ability to readily perform analyses that are specific to CRM. Therefore, the main thrust of this chapter focuses on not only the analyses that are relevant to CRM, but also on how to design data warehouses to support CRM analyses.

Specifically, since the first step in any design methodology is to understand the requirements, the minimum requirements for CRM analyses are presented in the "CRM Analysis Requirements" section. The specific CRM analysis requirements as well as the need to classify customers according to the four CRM quadrants presented in Table 1 are then used to identify the specific fact tables and dimensions. The heuristics (or guidelines) for modeling the fact tables and dimensions are then explored in the design rationale for the fact tables and design rationale for the dimensions subsections.

CRM Analysis Requirements

The purpose of a data warehouse is not just to store data, but rather to facilitate decision making. As such, the first step to designing the schema for the CRM data warehouse is to identify the different types of analyses that are relevant to CRM. For example, some typical CRM analyses that have been identified include customer profitability analysis, churn analysis, channel analysis, product profitability analysis, customer scoring, and campaign management.

In addition to identifying what CRM analyses the data warehouse needs to support, we also must understand how the data analyses are used by the business users. Often, understanding the business use of the data analyses provides additional insights as to how the data should be structured, including the identification of additional attributes that should be included in the model.

Once the specific types of CRM analyses as well as the intended uses of those analyses have been identified, they can be decomposed into the data points that are needed to support the analyses. Moreover, additional data points also can be identified from both experience and literature (Boon, Corbitt, & Parker, 2002; Kellen, 2002; Rust et al., 2004). It should be noted that the additional data points could include non-transactional information such as customer complaints, support calls, and other useful information that is relevant for managing the customer relationships. Furthermore, the non-transactional information could exist in a variety of formats, such as video and graphics (Bose, 2002). Such data formats are beyond the scope of this chapter. Table 3 identifies the types of analyses that are relevant to CRM as well as some of the data maintenance issues that must be considered. In other words, Table 3 identifies the minimum design requirements for a CRM data warehouse (DW). It should be noted that there is no significance to the order in which the items are listed in Table 3. The design rationale in the following section is based on the minimum design requirements in Table 3.

Design Rationale for the Fact Tables

The model needs to have fact tables that can be used to compute the historical and future values for each customer, because they are used to classify customers. As such, the model consists of a profitability fact table, a future value fact table, a customer service fact table, and various dimensions, which are defined in Table 4. We note that not all of the fact tables and dimensions are included in Figure 1.

The profitability fact table includes the attributes (e.g., revenues and all costs—distribution, marketing, overhead, and product) that are required to compute the historical profitability of each transaction in the profitability fact table with the minimum number of joins. That, in turn, improves the performance when querying the data

Table 3. Minimum design requirements for CRM DWs

No.	Analysis Type/Data Maintenance	Description
3.1	Customer Profitability	Ability to determine profitability of each customer
3.2	Product Profitability	Ability to determine profitability of each product
3.3	Market Profitability	Ability to determine profitability of each market
3.4	Campaign Analysis	Ability to evaluate different campaigns and responses over time
3.5	Channel Analysis	Ability to evaluate the profitability of each channel (e.g., stores, web, phone, and so forth)
3.6	Customer Retention	Ability to track customer retention
3.7	Customer Attrition	Ability to identify root causes for customer attrition
3.8	Customer Scoring	Ability to score customers
3.9	Household Analysis	Ability to associate customers with multiple extended household accounts.
3.10	Customer Segmentation	Ability to segment customers into multiple customer segmentations
3.11	Customer Loyalty	Ability to understand loyalty patterns among different relationship groups
3.12	Demographic Analysis	Ability to perform demographic analysis
3.13	Trend Analysis	Ability to perform trend analysis
3.14	Product Delivery Performance	Ability to evaluate on-time, late, and early product deliveries
3.15	Product Returns	Ability to analyze the reasons for and the impact of products being returned
3.16	Customer Service Analysis	Ability to track and analyze customer satisfaction, the average cost of interacting with the customer, the time it takes to resolve customer complaints, and so forth
3.17	Up-selling Analysis	Ability to analyze opportunities for customers to buy larger volumes of a product or a product with a higher profitability margin
3.18	Cross-selling Analysis	Ability to identify additional types of products that customers could purchase, which they currently are not purchasing
3.19	Web Analysis	Ability to analyze metrics for Web site
3.20	Data Maintenance	Ability to maintain the history of customer segments and scores
3.21	Data Maintenance	Ability to integrate data from multiple sources, including external sources
3.22	Data Maintenance	Ability to efficiently update/maintain data

Table 4. Starter model dimension definitions

Dimension Name	Dimension Definition
Channel Dimension	Stores the different modes for interacting with customers
Customer Dimension	Stores the static information about the customer
Customer Behavior Dimension	Stores the dynamic scoring attributes of the customer
Customer Demographics Dimension	Stores the dynamic demographic characteristics of the customer
CustomerExistence	Tracks the periods in which the customer is a valid
CustomerMarket	Tracks changes in the relationship between the customer and market dimensions
Comments Dimension	Stores the reasons for customer attrition and product returns
Company Representative	Stores the company representatives (sales representatives)
County Demographics Dimension	Stores external demographics about the counties
Extended Household	Represents the fact that the customer may belong to one or more extended households.
Market Dimension	The organizational hierarchy & regions in which the customer belongs
Product Dimension	Represents the products that the company sells
ProductExistence	Tracks the periods in which the products are valid
Promotion dimension	Represents the promotions that the company offers
Prospect	Stores information about prospects
Scenario Dimension	Used to analyze hypothetical up-selling and cross-selling scenarios
Supplier Dimension	Represents the vendors that supply the products
Time Dimension	The universal times used throughout the schema
Time Dimension	Universal dates used throughout the schema

warehouse. Additionally, storing the detailed transactions facilitates the ability to compute the CLV for each customer across each product. Moreover, the model depicted in Figure 1 can be used to calculate KPIs for delivery, such as the number of on-time items and the number of damage-free items. The complement measures are calculated by subtracting the explicitly stored KPI measures from the total quantity. These KPIs are important to track and manage because they can help organizations to identify internal areas for process improvements and ultimately influence customer satisfaction and possibly customer retention. The customer service fact table contains information about each interaction with the customer, including the cost of the interaction, the time to resolve the complaint, and a count of customer satisfaction or dissatisfaction. The total historical value of each customer is computed by summing the historical value of each transaction (that is., the net revenue from the profitability fact table) and then subtracting the sum of the cost of interacting with the customer (that is, the service cost from the customer service fact table).

In accordance with equation (4), the future value fact table stores measures that are needed to compute the potential future lifetime value for each customer. For example, among other things, the future value fact table contains the expected gross revenue, costs, expected purchasing frequency, and the probability of gaining additional revenue. It also contains other descriptive attributes that can be used to analyze and categorize the customer's future lifetime value. The customer lifetime value, which is used to classify each customer in one of the four quadrants in Table 1, is computed by summing the historical value for each customer and the future value for each customer.

Design Rationale for the Dimensions

Dimensions are very important to a data warehouse because they allow the users to easily browse the content of the data warehouse.

Special treatment of certain types of dimensions must be taken into consideration for CRM analyses. Each of those dimension types, and their special treatments, are discussed in the following subsections.

Existence Dimensions and Time

Customer relationship management is a process. As with any business process, the RM process needs to be changed periodically to reflect changes in and additions to the business process (e.g., organizational restructuring due to territory realignments or mergers and acquisitions, new or modified business rules, changes in strategic focus, and modified or new analysis requirements). Thus, time is an inherent part of business systems and must be modeled in the data warehouse. Traditionally, the time dimension primarily participates in a relationship with the fact tables only. Additionally, there are two ways of handling temporal changes: tuple versioning and attribute versioning (Allen & March, 2003). Tuple versioning (or row time stamping) is used in multiple ways to record (1) changes in the active state of a dimension, (2) changes to the values of attributes, and (3) changes in relationships (Todman, 2001). As such, traditional tuple versioning has limitations within the context of CRM. For example, periods of customer inactivity can be determined only by identifying two consecutive tuples where there is a gap in the timestamp. Additionally, queries that involve durations may be spread over many tuples, which would make the SQL statement complex with slow response times (Todman, 2001).

In order to alleviate the issues with traditional time stamping in the context of CRM, each dimension is examined carefully to determine if the dimension (1) contains attributes whose complete set of historical values have to be maintained, or (2) is subject to discontinuous existence (that is, only valid for specific periods).

If either (1) or (2) is applicable, then a separate dimension called an existence dimension is created. The existence dimensions are implemented as outriggers, and two relationships are created between the time dimension and each outrigger dimension. The two relationships are formed in order to record the date period in which the data instances are valid. In doing so, this facilitates the ability to perform state duration queries and transition detection queries (Todman, 2001). State duration queries contain a time period (start date and end date) in the where clause of the query, whereas transition detection queries identify a change by identifying consecutive periods for the same dimension (Todman, 2001).

Careful consideration is given to this step in the design process because the fact table only can capture historical values when a transaction occurs. Unfortunately, the reality is that there may be periods of inactivity, which would mean that any changes that occur during those periods of inactivity would not be recorded in the data warehouse. This would, in turn, impact the types of analyses that could be done, since one cannot analyze data that one has not recorded.

Mini-Dimensions

If a dimension contains attributes that are likely to change at a different rate than the other attributes within the dimension, then a separate dimension is created as a mini-dimension. The new dimensions are implemented as mini-dimensions as opposed to outriggers in order to allow the user to readily browse the fact table. One benefit of this approach is that the history of the changes in the customer's behavior scores and demographics are stored as part of the fact table, which facilitates robust analyses without requiring the use of Type 1, 2, or 3 techniques (Kimball & Ross, 2002) for the customer demographics or customer behavior dimensions.

Customer Dimension

The customer must be at the heart of the customer-centric data warehouse. As such, careful attention must be given to the design of the customer dimension, which will force attention on the customer. Direct relationships are formed between the customer dimension and the sales representative, market, comment, and time dimensions in order to allow the user to readily determine the most current values for the sales representative, market, activation date, attrition date, and attrition comments by simply browsing the customer dimension, without having to include a time constraint in the query statement.

Other Dimensions

There is a household dimension as well as an extended household dimension in order to analyze the potential lines of influence that exist between customers. In accordance with the types of CRM analyses that the data warehouse must support, other dimensions are identified according to the dimensions along which the fact tables are analyzed. For example, other dimensions include the product, supplier, channel, promotion, market, and sales representative dimensions in order to facilitate the CRM analyses described in the "CRM Analysis Requirements" section.

As a result of this approach to modeling the dimensions, the only slowly changing dimensions in the model are the county demographics dimension, the product dimension, the supplier dimension, and the customer dimension. The model depicted in Figure 1, which is based upon the minimum design requirements and the design rationale presented in this section, is tested to determine its completeness and flexibility for CRM analyses. The experiment that is used to test the model is described in the following section.

Figure 1. Proposed CRM data warehouse model

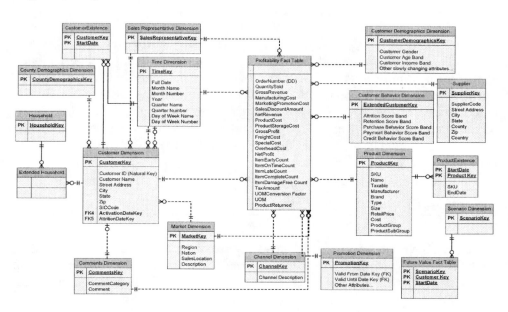

Experiment

The purpose of the experiment is to test the completeness and flexibility of the proposed CRM data warehouse model. Our hypothesis is that the proposed data warehouse starter model has a positive impact on the ability to perform CRM analyses. The implementation, methodology, and selection of the queries that are used in the experiment to test our hypothesis as well as the results are discussed in the specific subsections that follow.

Implementation

We perform a case study to test the validity of our proposed starter model. The proposed CRM data warehouse model is implemented in SQL Server 2000 running on a Windows 2000 server. The hardware computer is a DELL 1650 database server with a single processor and 2.0 MHz. The schema is populated with 1,685,809 rows of data from a manufacturing company.

Methodology

In the experiment, a series of CRM queries are executed against the proposed data warehouse schema. The success rate of the proposed schema is computed as a ratio of the number of successful queries executed, divided by the total number of queries used in the investigation. Furthermore, the proposed CRM data warehouse model is tested to determine if it could or could not perform the analyses listed in Table 3. For each analysis in Table 3 that the model could perform, it is given a score of one point; otherwise, the model is given a score of zero points. The sum of the points for the model is computed in order to determine an overall CRM-analysis capability score. The selection of the queries that are used to study the model is discussed in the following section.

Selection of Queries to Test

Since we believe that the proposed data warehouse starter model has a positive impact on the ability to perform CRM analyses, special care was taken in the selection of the queries used for testing in order to avoid any biases in the types of queries used to test the model. Stratified random sampling is used to select the specific queries for the experiment. The stratified random sampling is conducted as follows: (1) representative queries for CRM are gathered from literature and experience; (2) the queries are grouped into categories based upon the nature of the query; (3) within each category, each query is numbered; (4) a random number generator is used to select queries from each category; and (5) the queries whose assigned number corresponds to the number generated by the random number generator are selected. The specific queries that are selected are listed in Table 5. It is important to note that since the queries are randomly selected from a pool of CRM-related queries, it is possible that the $r_{success}$ ratio can be less than one for our proposed model. It is also important to note that the representative CRM queries are queries that equally apply to different industries and not queries that are specific to only one industry. This aspect of the sampling procedure is important in order to make generalizations about the characteristics of the data warehouse schema that should be present in order to perform CRM analyses across different industries.

Results

Our preliminary finding is that the proposed CRM data warehouse model can be used to successfully perform CRM analyses. Based upon the sample queries, our model has a value of 1 and 0.93 for the $r_{success}$ and $r_{suitability}$ ratios, respectively. The individual scores for successfully executing the queries against the model are listed in Table 5. The individual and cumulative scores for the suitability of the proposed CRM data warehouse model are listed in Table 6. It should be noted that there is no significance to the order in which the items are listed in the table. The scores for items 6.1 through 6.11 in Table 6 are based upon whether or not queries are successfully executed in those categories. The scores for items 14 and 15 are determined while loading data from multiple sources and updating customer scores. Each of the queries that were successfully executed in the experiment is discussed in further detail in the following section in order to highlight the completeness and flexibility of the model.

Discussion

General Discussion

In addition to discussing the completeness and flexibility of the model, this section also presents potential uses of the specific analyses, including KPIs. This section also describes the data quality issues pertaining to CRM data warehouses before presenting a summary of the heuristics for designing data warehouses to support CRM analyses.

Model Completeness and Flexibility

The starter model depicted in Figure 1 can be used for a variety of CRM analyses, including customer profitability analysis, household profitability analysis, demographics profitability analysis, product profitability analysis, channel profitability analysis, and promotion profitability analysis simply by including the appropriate dimensions in the query statement. Furthermore, each query can be modified to include additional measures and descriptions simply by including additional fields from the fact table and the dimensions. Some of those queries are discussed next.

Table 5. Sample CRM analyses

No.	Category	Analysis	Pass	Fail
5.1	Channel Analysis	Which distribution channels contribute the greatest revenue and gross margin?	1	0
5.2	Order Delivery Performance	How do early, on time, and late order shipment rates for this year compare to last year?	1	0
5.3	Order Delivery Performance & Channel Analysis	How do order shipment rates (early, on time, late) for this year compare to last year by channel?	1	0
5.4	Customer Profitability Analysis	Which customers are most profitable, based upon gross margin and revenue?	1	0
5.5	Customer Profitability Analysis	What are the customers' sales and margin trends?	1	0
5.6	Customer Retention	How many unique customers are purchasing this year compared to last year?	1	0
5.7	Market Profitability Analysis	Which markets are most profitable overall?	1	0
5.8	Market Profitability Analysis	Which products in which markets are most profitable?	1	0
5.9	Product Profitability Analysis	Which products are the most profitable?	1	0
5.10	Product Profitability Analysis	What is the lifetime value of each product?	1	0
5.11	Returns Analysis	What are the top 10 reasons that customers return products?	1	0
5.12	Returns Analysis	What is the impact of the value of the returned products on revenues?	1	0
5.13	Returns Analysis	What is the trend for product returns by customers by product by reason?	1	0
5.14	Customer Attrition	What are the top 10 reasons for customer attrition?	1	0
5.15	Customer Attrition	What is the impact of the value of the customers that have left on revenues?	1	0
5.16	Campaign Analysis	What is the ROI of marketing efforts?	1	0
5.17	Costs per Customer	What are the costs per customer?	1	0
5.18	Employee Efficiency	How much revenue does each sales agent generate?	1	0

Table 6. Sample suitability for CRM analyses scores

No.	Criteria	Score
6.1	Ability to track retention	1
6.2	Ability to identify root causes for customer attrition	1
6.3	Ability to score customers	1
6.4	Ability to associate customers with multiple extended household accounts	1
6.5	Ability to segment customers into multiple customer segmentations	1
6.6	Ability to maintain the history of customer segments and scores	1
6.7	Ability to evaluate different campaigns and responses over time	1
6.8	Ability to analyze metrics for Web site	0
6.9	Ability to understand loyalty patterns among different relationship groups	1
6.10	Ability to perform demographic analysis	1
6.11	Ability to perform trend analysis	1
6.12	Ability to perform customer profitability analysis	1
6.13	Ability to perform product profitability analysis	1
6.14	Ability to integrate data from multiple sources, including external sources	1
6.15	Ability to efficiently update/maintain data	1
	Total	14

Figure 2. Customer profitability analysis query: Which customers are most profitable based upon gross margin and revenue?

```
SELECT b.CustomerKey, b.CustomerName,
Sum(a.GrossRevenue) AS TotalRevenue,
Sum(a.GrossProfit) AS TotalGrossProfit,
TotalGrossProfit/TotalRevenue AS GrossMargin
FROM tblProfitabilityFactTable a, tblCustomer b
WHERE b.CustomerKey=a.CustomerKey
GROUP BY b.CustomerKey, b.CustomerName
ORDER BY Sum(a.GrossRevenue) DESC;
```

Figure 3. Product profitability analysis query: Which products in which markets are most profitable?

```
SELECT c.Year, b.MarketKey, b.LocationCode,
b.Location, b.Description, b.CompetitorName,
d.ProductCode, d.Name, Sum(a.GrossRevenue) AS
TotalRevenue, Sum(a.GrossProfit) AS TotalGrossProfit,
TotalGrossProfit/TotalRevenue AS GrossMargin
FROM tblProfitabilityFactTable a, tblMarket b,
tblTimeDimension c, tblProductDimension d
WHERE b.MarketKey=a.MarketKey And
a.TimeKey=c.TimeKey And
a.ProductKey=d.ProductKey
GROUP BY c.Year, b.MarketKey, b.LocationCode,
b.Location, b.Description, b.CompetitorName,
d.ProductKey, d.ProductCode, d.Name, b.MarketKey
ORDER BY Sum(a.GrossRevenue) DESC;
```

The SQL statement in Figure 2 is used to identify the most profitable customers, based upon total revenue and gross margin. By excluding the time dimension, the customer profitability SQL statement identifies the customer's historical lifetime value to the company. This is an important analysis that, in conjunction with the customer's future value and the customer service interaction costs, is used to classify customers in one of the four CRM quadrants (Table 1), which subsequently can be used to determine the appropriate strategy for managing the customer.

The SQL statement in Figure 3 is used to determine the margins for each product and subsequently identifies products that potentially may be eliminated from the company's product line. The ability to be able to determine the lifetime value of each product (irrespective of market) merely by modifying the SQL statement in Figure 3 to exclude the product code further illustrates the flexibility and robustness of the proposed CRM model.

The SQL statement in Figure 4 is used to determine and compare key performance indicators (KPIs) for overall on-time, early, and late shipment percentages for different years. By modifying the statement in Figure 4 to include the channel dimension, the performance of each channel from one year to the next is determined. The modified SQL statement can be seen in Figure 5.

The SQL statement in Figure 6 is used to determine the overall profitability of each market. By eliminating the market key from the SQL statement, the profitability for each location is obtained for each location within the organizational hierarchy that is defined in the market dimension.

The SQL statement in Figure 7 demonstrates that by including the product code from the product dimension in the previous SQL statement, the profitability of each product by market is obtained.

The SQL statement in Figure 8 is used to determine the top reasons for product returns. In this case, the basis for the top reasons is merely the count of the number of reasons that products are returned. By first grouping the products that are returned according to the reason for their return and the product code, and then including the number of returns, revenue, gross profit, and gross margin for each group, the SQL statement in Figure 8 identifies areas upon which the company should improve in order to minimize the number of returns and to improve overall customer

Figure 4. Order delivery performance query: How do early, on time, and late order shipment rates for this year compare to last year?

```
SELECT b.Year, Sum(a.ItemOnTimeCount) AS
OnTime, Sum(a.ItemEarlyCount) AS
Early, Sum(a.ItemLateCount) AS Late,
Sum(a.ItemOnTimeCount+a.ItemEarlyCount+a.ItemLate
Count) AS TotalCount,
OnTime/Late*100 AS PercentOnTime,
Early/TotalCount*100 AS PercentEarly,
Late/TotalCount*100 AS PercentLate
FROM tblProfitabilityFactTable a, tblTimeDimension b
WHERE b.TimeKey = a.TimeKey
GROUP BY b.Year;
```

Figure 5. Order delivery performance and channel analysis query: How do order shipment rates (early, on-time, late) for this year compare to last year by channel?

```
SELECT b.Year, c.ChannelCode,
Sum(a.ItemOnTimeCount) AS OnTime,
Sum(a.ItemEarlyCount) AS Early,
Sum(a.ItemLateCount) AS Late,
Sum(a.ItemOnTimeCount+a.ItemEarlyCount+a.ItemLate
Count) AS TotalCount,
OnTime/Late*100 AS PercentOnTime,
Early/TotalCount*100 AS PercentEarly,
Late/TotalCount*100 AS PercentLate
FROM tblProfitabilityFactTable a, tblTimeDimension b,
tblChannelDimension c
WHERE b.TimeKey=a.TimeKey And c.ChannelKey =
a.ChannelKey
GROUP BY b.Year, c.ChannelCode;
```

Figure 6. Market profitability analysis query: Which markets are most profitable overall?

```
SELECT c.Year, b.MarketKey, b.LocationCode,
b.Location, b.Description,
b.CompetitorName, Sum(a.GrossRevenue) AS
TotalRevenue, Sum(a.GrossProfit) AS
TotalGrossProfit, TotalGrossProfit/TotalRevenue AS
GrossMargin
FROM tblProfitabilityFactTable a, tblMarket b,
tblTimeDimension c
WHERE b.MarketKey=a.MarketKey And
a.TimeKey=c.TimeKey
GROUP BY c.Year, b.MarketKey, b.LocationCode,
b.Location, b.Description,
b.CompetitorName, b.MarketKey
ORDER BY Sum(a.GrossRevenue) DESC;
```

satisfaction. Specifically, since companies have limited resources, a company can use the result set to create Pareto charts according to the most frequently occurring problems that have the largest associated gross profits. Management teams then can use the Pareto charts to determine which problems to address first with corrective actions. It should be noted that in order to facilitate quick identification of the most frequently occurring problems that have the largest associated gross profits, the SQL statement in Figure 8 includes an ORDER BY clause. Furthermore, simply by modifying the SQL statement in Figure 8 to include the year of the transaction from the profitability fact table in the SELECT clause and the GROUP BY clause, companies can use the results of the modified query to monitor the trend of return reasons over time. Stated differently, companies can use the results of the modified query statement to monitor the impact of the corrective actions over time. Not only can the return analyses be used to monitor the impact of corrective actions, but they also can be used to identify improvement targets, which can be tied to employee (and/or departmental) performance goals.

The SQL statement listed in Figure 9 is used to determine the impact of the returned products on revenues. The SQL statement listed in Figure 10 is used to identify the trend for product returns by customer, by product, and by reason. The results can be used to identify whether or not a problem is systematic across all customers, many customers, or a few specific customers. This query also can be used to help management make an informed decision with respect to allocating resources to address problems that lead to customers returning products. Additionally, the results can be used by the sales team to gain further insights into why their customers have returned products. The sales team potentially can use that information to work with the

Figure 7. Product profitability analysis query: Which products in which markets are most profitable?

```
SELECT c.Year, b.MarketKey, b.LocationCode,
b.Location, b.Description,
b.CompetitorName, d.ProductCode, d.Name,
Sum(a.GrossRevenue) AS TotalRevenue,
Sum(a.GrossProfit) AS TotalGrossProfit,
TotalGrossProfit/TotalRevenue AS
GrossMargin
FROM tblProfitabilityFactTable a, tblMarket b,
tblTimeDimension c,
tblProductDimension d
WHERE b.MarketKey=a.MarketKey And
a.TimeKey=c.TimeKey And
a.ProductKey=d.ProductKey
GROUP BY c.Year, b.MarketKey, b.LocationCode,
b.Location, b.Description,
b.CompetitorName, d.ProductKey, d.ProductCode,
d.Name, b.MarketKey
ORDER BY Sum(a.GrossRevenue) DESC;
```

Figure 8. Returns analysis: What are the top reasons that customers return products?

```
SELECT b.CommentsKey, c.ProductCode, c.Name,
d.Comment, Sum(a.GrossRevenue)
AS TotalRevenue, Sum(a.GrossProfit) AS
TotalGrossProfit,
TotalGrossProfit/TotalRevenue AS GrossMargin,
Count(*) AS MembershipCount
FROM tblProfitabilityFactTable a, tblTimeDimension
b, tblProductDimension c,
tblCommentDimension d
WHERE a.TimeKey=b.TimeKey And
a.ProductKey=c.ProductKey And
a.CommentsKey=d.CommentsKey And
a.ProductReturned=Yes
GROUP BY d.CommentsKey, c.ProductCode, c.Name,
d.Comment, c.ProductKey
ORDER BY Count(*) DESC, Sum(a.GrossProfit)
DESC;
```

Figure 9. What is the impact of the value of the returned products on revenues?

```
SELECT b.CommentsKey, c.ProductCode, c.Name,
d.Comment, Sum(a.GrossRevenue)
AS TotalRevenue, Sum(a.GrossProfit) AS
TotalGrossProfit,
TotalGrossProfit/TotalRevenue AS GrossMargin,
Count(*) AS MembershipCount
FROM tblProfitabilityFactTable a, tblTimeDimension b,
tblProductDimension c,
tblCommentDimension d
WHERE a.TimeKey=b.TimeKey And
a.ProductKey=c.ProductKey And
a.CommentsKey=d.CommentsKey And
a.ProductReturned=Yes
GROUP BY d.CommentsKey, c.ProductCode, c.Name,
d.Comment, c.ProductKey
ORDER BY Count(*) DESC;
```

Figure 10. What is the trend for product returns by customers by product by reason?

```
SELECT e.CustomerName, b.Year, b.CommentsKey,
c.ProductCode, c.Name,
d.Comment, Sum(a.GrossRevenue) AS TotalRevenue,
Sum(a.GrossProfit) AS
TotalGrossProfit, TotalGrossProfit/TotalRevenue AS
GrossMargin, Count(*) AS
MembershipCount
FROM tblProfitabilityFactTable a, tblTimeDimension b,
tblProductDimension c,
tblCommentDimension d, tblCustomerDimension e
WHERE a.TimeKey=b.TimeKey And
a.ProductKey=c.ProductKey And
a.CommentsKey=d.CommentsKey And a.ProductReturned=Yes
GROUP BY e.CustomerName, b.Year, d.CommentsKey,
c.ProductCode, c.Name,
d.Comment, c.ProductKey
ORDER BY Count(*) DESC, Sum(a.GrossProfit) DESC;
```

Figure 11. What are the top 10 reasons for customer attrition?

```
SELECT b.Comment, Count(a.CommentsKey) AS
FROM tblCustomer AS a, tblCommentDimension
WHERE a.CommentsKey=b.CommentsKey
GROUP BY b.Comment
ORDER BY Count(a.CommentsKey) DESC;
```

Figure 12. What is the impact of the value of the customers that have left on revenues?

```
SELECT b.Comment, Count(a.CommentsKey) AS
NumberOfTransactions,
Sum(c.GrossRevenue) AS TotalGrossRevenue
FROM tblCustomer AS a, tblCommentDimension AS b,
tblProfitabilityFactTable AS c
WHERE a.CommentsKey=b.CommentsKey AND
c.CustomerKey=a.CustomerKey
GROUP BY b.Comment
ORDER BY Count(a.CommentsKey) DESC;
```

Figure 13. What is the effectiveness of the marketing campaigns?

```
SELECT e.CustomerName, b.Year,
Sum(a.GrossRevenue) AS TotalRevenue,
Sum(a.GrossProfit) AS TotalGrossProfit,
TotalGrossProfit/TotalRevenue AS GrossMargin,
Sum(a.MarketingPromotionCost) AS
TotalMarketingCost, TotalRevenue/TotalMarketingCost
AS MarketingEffectiveness
FROM tblProfitabilityFactTable a, tblTimeDimension b,
tblCustomerDimension e
WHERE a.TimeKey=b.TimeKey And
a.CustomerKey=e.CustomerKey
GROUP BY e.CustomerName, b.Year;
```

Figure 14. What are the costs per customer?

```
SELECT e.CustomerName, b.Year,
Sum(a.GrossRevenue) AS TotalRevenue,
Sum(a.GrossProfit) AS TotalGrossProfit,
TotalGrossProfit/TotalRevenue AS GrossMargin,
Sum(a.MarketingPromotionCost) AS
TotalMarketingCost, Sum(a.ManufacturingCost) AS
TotalManufacturingCost, Sum(a.ProductStorageCost)
AS TotalProductStorageCost,
Sum(a.MarketingPromotionCost +
a.ManufacturingCost + a.ProductStorageCost) AS
TotalCost, TotalRevenue/TotalMarketingCost AS
MarketingEffectiveness, TotalRevenue/TotalCost AS
RevPerCosts
FROM tblProfitabilityFactTable a, tblTimeDimension
b, tblCustomerDimension e
WHERE a.TimeKey=b.TimeKey And
a.CustomerKey=e.CustomerKey
GROUP BY e.CustomerName, b.Year;
```

Figure 15. How much revenue does each sales agent generate?

```
SELECT b.Year, e.SalesRepresentativeKey,
e.LastName, Sum(a.GrossRevenue) AS TotalRevenue,
Sum(a.GrossProfit) AS TotalGrossProfit,
TotalGrossProfit/TotalRevenue AS GrossMargin
FROM tblProfitabilityFactTable a, tblTimeDimension
b, tblSalesRepresentativeDimension e
WHERE a.TimeKey=b.TimeKey And
a.SalesRepresentativeKey=e.SalesRepresentativeKey
GROUP BY b.Year, e.LastName
ORDER BY b.Year, GrossMargin, e.LastName;
```

customer to resolve the issue(s) in cases where the customer repeatedly has returned products for reasons that cannot be considered the company's mistake. Alternatively, the sales team can use the results to identify accounts that could (should) be charged additional fees if the customer repeatedly returns products. The SQL statement in Figure 11 is used to identify the top reasons for customer attrition.

Figure 12 is used to analyze the impact of customer attrition on the total revenues. By analyzing customer attrition, companies can gain further insights into areas for improvement in order to reduce the attrition rate and thereby improve its overall company value.

Figure 13 is used to analyze the effectiveness of marketing campaigns by computing the revenues as a percentage of the total marketing cost per customer. The SQL statement in Figure 14 can be used to identify the cost of doing business with each customer. The SQL statement in Figure 15 can be used to identify the top performing Sales Representatives by revenue. However, the SQL statement in Figure 15 can also be used to identify the top performing Sales Representative by gross margin, which is a more important KPI than revenue because it is very important for companies to not only grow, but to grow profitably. This can subsequently be used to facilitate non-threatening/non-embarrassing and open discussions (e.g., lessons learned) between the top performing sales agents and the other sales agents. It would also allow companies to link and measure the performance of sales agents as it relates to the profitability objectives of the organization. Table 7 summarizes some of the possible uses for the CRM analyses that are presented in Table 5.

Table 7. Initial taxonomy of CRM analyses

#	Decision Class	Category	Analysis	Potential Use(s)	KPI
1	S	Channel Analysis	Which distribution channels contribute the greatest revenue and gross margin?	Resource allocation	
2	S & T	Order Delivery Performance	How do early, on time, and late order shipment rates for this year compare to last year?	Setting performance goals	early delivery, on-time delivery, late delivery
3	S	Order Delivery Performance & Channel Analysis	How do order shipment rates (early, on time, late) for this year compare to last year by channel?	Setting performance goals, monitoring trends	early delivery, on-time delivery, late delivery
4	S	Customer Profitability Analysis	Which customers are most profitable based upon gross margin and revenue?	Classify customers	gross margin, revenue
5	S	Customer Profitability Analysis	What are the customers'- sales and margin trends?	Classify customers	gross margin, revenue
6	S	Customer Retention	How many unique customers are purchasing this year compared to last year?	Identify the threshold to overcome with new customers	unique customers/year
7	S & T	Market Profitability Analysis	Which markets are most profitable overall?	Setting performance goals, allocate marketing resources	gross margin/market
8	S & T	Market Profitability Analysis	Which products in which markets are most profitable?	Setting performance goals, allocate marketing resources	gross margin/ products/ market
9	S & T	Product Profitability Analysis	Which products are the most profitable?	Managing product cost constraints, identify products to potentially eliminate from product line	gross margin/ product
10	S & T	Product Profitability Analysis	What is the lifetime value of each product?	Managing product cost constraints, identify products to potentially eliminate from product line	gross margin/ product
11	S & T	Returns Analysis	What are the top 10 reasons that customers return products?	Create Pareto charts to identify problems to correct, setting performance goals	count
12	S & T	Returns Analysis	What is the impact of the value of the returned products on revenues?	Create Pareto charts to identify problems to correct, setting performance goals	count, revenue, profit

Note: S = strategic and T = tactical

continued on following page

Table 7. continued

#	Decision Class	Category	Analysis	Potential Use(s)	KPI
13	S & T	Returns Analysis	What is the trend for product returns by customers by product by reason?	Create Pareto charts to identify problems to correct, setting performance goals, identify problematic accounts (identify customers that may leave), assess additional service fees	count, revenue, profit
14	S & T	Customer Attrition	What are the top 10 reasons for customer attrition?	Insights for process improvements	attrition rate
15	S & T	Customer Attrition	What is the impact of the value of the customers that have left on revenues?	Insights for process improvements	attrition rate
16	S	Campaign Analysis	What is the ROI of marketing efforts?	Insights into the effectiveness of marketing	Total revenue/ marketing costs
17	S & T	Costs per Customer	What are the costs per customer?	Insights into what it really costs to do business with each individual customer; can be used as the basis for segmenting customers in order to subsequently apply the appropriate strategy	Total revenue/total costs
18	T	Employee Efficiency	How much revenue does each sales agent generate?	Identification of the top performing sales agents	Gross margin per sales agent; revenue per sales agent

Initial Heuristics for Designing CRM Data Warehouses

Once the types of CRM analyses that the data warehouse needs to be able to support have been identified, the data points have been identified, and the granularity has been selected, the next step is designing the data warehouse model to support the analyses that were identified. Based upon our initial findings, Table 8 lists initial heuristics for designing a data warehouse in order to successfully support CRM analyses.

Table 8. Initial heuristics for designing CRM DWs

#	Heuristic	Benefit
1	Include all attributes required to compute the profitability of each individual transaction in the fact table(s)	The ability to generate a profit and loss statement for each transaction, which can then be analyzed along any dimension
2	Each dimension that will be used to analyze the Profitability fact table should be directly related to the fact table	Provides improved query performance by allowing the use of simplified queries (that is, support browsing data)
3	Pay careful attention to the Customer dimension	It forces attention to the customer to the center of CRM
4	Create a relationship between the Customer dimension and the Market and Sales Representative dimensions	Provides the ability to quickly determine the current market and Sales Representative for the customer by merely browsing the Customer dimension
5	Include the attrition date and reason for attrition attributes in the Customer dimension	Provides the ability to quickly determine if a customer is no longer a customer by browsing the Customer dimension only
6	Attributes that are likely to change at a different rate than other attributes in the same dimension should be in a separate dimension	Minimize the number of updates
7	Create a separate *existence* dimension for any entity that can have a discontinuous existence	Provides the ability to track the periods in which the instance of the entity is valid (needed to support some temporal queries)
8	Create a separate *existence* dimension for any attribute whose historical values must be kept	Provides the ability to track accurate historical values, even during periods of inactivity
9	Create a relationship between the Time dimension and each *existence* dimension	Provides the ability to perform temporal queries efficiently, using descriptive attributes of the Time dimension
10	*Existence* dimensions should be in a direct relationship with their respective original dimensions	
11	There should always be a CustomerExistence dimension	The ability to track and perform analyses on customer attrition
12	If some products are either seasonal or if it is necessary to determine when products where discontinued, then create a ProductExistence dimension	The ability to perform analyses for seasonal and discontinued products
13	There should be a Household dimension and an ExtendedHousehold dimension	Provides the ability to perform Household analyses
14	The organizational hierarchical structure can be contained in one *Market* dimension	Provides the ability to maintain a history of the organizational changes, and the ability to perform analyses according to the organizational structure

Conclusion

In this chapter, we first presented the key drivers and factors for successfully implementing CRM. Then, we presented the design implications that CRM poses to data warehousing and then proposed a robust multidimensional starter model that supports CRM analyses. Based upon sample queries, our model has a value of 1 and 0.93 for the $r_{success}$ and $r_{suitability}$ ratios, respectively. Our study shows that our starter model can be used to analyze various profitability analyses such as customer profitability analysis, market profitability analysis, product profitability analysis, and channel profitability analysis. In fact, the model has the flexibility to analyze both trends and overall lifetime value of customers, markets, channels, and products simply by including or excluding the time dimension in the SQL statements. Since the model captures rich descriptive non-numeric information that can be included in the query statement, the proposed model can return results that the user easily can understand.

It should be noted that such rich information can then be used in data mining algorithms for such things as category labels. As such, we have demonstrated that the robust proposed model can be used to perform CRM analyses. Our contributions also include the identification of and classification of CRM queries and their uses, including KPIs; the introduction of a sampling technique to select the queries with which the model is tested; the introduction of two measures (percent success ratio and CRM suitability ratio) by which CRM data warehouse models can be evaluated; and the identification of the initial heuristics for designing a data warehouse to support CRM. Finally, in terms of future work, we plan to classify and test additional CRM analyses, evaluate alternative models using the same set of queries and the $r_{success}$ and $r_{suitability}$ ratios, identify materialized views that are relevant to CRM, and explore CRM query optimization.

References

Allen, G. N., & March, S. T. (2003). Modeling temporal dynamics for business systems. *Journal of Database Management, 14*(3), 21-36.

Alvarez, J. G., Raeside, R., & Jones, W. B. (2006). The importance of analysis and planning in customer relationship marketing : Verification of the need for customer intelligence and modelling. *Journal of Database Marketing & Customer Strategy Management, 13*(3), 222-230.

Ang, L. & Taylor, B. (2005). Managing customer profitability using portfolio matrices. *Journal of Database Marketing & Customer Strategy Management, 12*(4), 298-304.

Boon, O., Corbitt, B., & Parker, C. (2002). Conceptualising the requirements of CRM from an organizational perspective: A review of the literature. In *Proceedings of 7ᵗʰ Australian Workshop on Requirements Engineering (AWRE2002)*, Melbourne, Australia.

Bose, R. (2002). Customer relationship management: Key components for IT success. *Industrial Management & Data Systems, 102*(2), 89-97.

Buttle, F. (1999). The S.C.O.P.E. of customer relationship management. *International Journal of Customer Relationship Management, 1*(4), 327-337.

Chetteyar, K. (2002). Using customer information effectively. *Financial Executive, 18*(3), 42-43.

Cunningham, C., Song, I-Y., Jung, J. T., & Chen, P. (2003). Design and research implications of customer relationship management on data warehousing and CRM decisions. In M. Khosrow-Pour (Ed.), *Information technology & organizations: Trends, issues, challenges & solutions, 2003 Information Resources Management Association International Conference (IRMA 2003)* (pp. 82-85). Hershey, PA: Idea Group Publishing.

Dasu, T., Vesonder, G. T., & Wright, J. R. (2003). Data quality through knowledge engineering. In *Proceedings of SIGKDD '03*, Washington, DC.

Fitzgibbon, C., & White, L. (2005). The role of attitudinal loyalty in the development of customer relationship management strategy within service firms. *Journal of Financial Services Marketing, 9*(3), 214-230.

Hansotia, B. (2004). Customer metrics and organizational alignment for maximizing customer equity. *Journal of Database Marketing & Customer Strategy Management, 12*(1), 9-20.

Hawkes, V. A. (2000). The heart of the matter: The challenge of customer lifetime value. *CRM Forum Resources, 13,* 1-10.

Hwang, H., Jung, T., & Suh, E. (2004). An LTV model and customer segmentation based on customer value: A case study on the wireless telecommunication industry. *Expert Systems with Applications, 26,* 181-188.

Imhoff, C., Loftis, L., & Geiger, J.G. (2001). *Building the customer-centric enterprise*. New York: Wiley Computer Publishing.

Jackson, T. W. (2005). CRM: From "art to science." *Journal of Database Marketing & Customer Strategy Management, 13*(1), 76-92.

Jain, D., & Singh, S. (2002). Customer lifetime value research in marketing: A review and future direction. *Journal of Interactive Marketing, 16*(2), 34-46.

Kale, S. H. (2004, September/October). CRM failure and the seven deadly sins. *Marketing Management*, 42-46.

Kellen, V. (2002). *CRM measurement frameworks*. Retrieved from http://www.kellen.net/crmmeas.htm

Kim, W., Choi, B., Kim, S., & Lee, D. (2003). A taxonomy of dirty data. *Data Mining and Knowledge Discovery, 7*, 81-99.

Kimball, R., & Ross, M. (2002). *The data warehouse toolkit* (2nd ed.). New York: Wiley Computer Publishing.

Koslowsky, S. (2002). The case of the missing data. *Journal of Database Marketing, 9*(4), 312-318.

Lee, Y. W., Pipino, L., Strong, D. M., & Wang, R. Y. (2004). Process-embedded data integrity. *Journal of Database Management, 15*(1), 87-103.

Massey, A. P., Montoya-Weiss, M. M., & Holcom, K. (2001). Re-engineering the customer relationship: Leveraging knowledge assets at IBM. *Decision Support Systems, 32*(2), 155-170.

Myron, D., & Ganeshram, R. (2002). The truth about CRM success & failure. *CRM Magazine*. Retrieval from http://www.destinationcrm.com/articles/default.asp?ArticleID=2370

Panker, J. (2002). Are reports of CRM failure greatly exaggerated? *SearchCRM.com*. Retrieved from http://searchcrm.techtarget.com/originalContent/0,289142,sid11_gci834332,00.html

Payton, F. C., & Zahay, D. (2003). Understanding why marketing does not use the corporate data warehouse for CRM applications. *Journal of Database Marketing, 10*(4), 315-326.

Pass, L., & Kuijlen, T. (2001). Towards a general definition of customer relationship management. *Journal of Database Marketing, 9*(1), 51-60.

Plakoyiannaki, E., & Tzokas, N. (2002). Customer relationship management: A capabilities portfolio perspective. *Journal of Database Management, 9*(3), 228-237.

Reid, A., & Catterall, M. (2005). Invisible data quality issues in a CRM implementation. *Journal of Database Marketing & Customer Strategy Management, 12*(4), 305-314.

Rigby, D. K., Reichheld, F. F., & Schefter, P. (2002). Avoid the four perils of CRM. *Harvard Business Review*, February, 101-109.

Roberts, M. L., Liu, R. R., & Hazard, K. (2005). Strategy technology and organisational alignment: Key components of CRM success. *Journal of Database Marketing & Customer Strategy Management, 12*(4), 315-326.

Ryals, L. (2003). Creating profitable customers through the magic of data mining. *Journal of Targeting, Measurement, and Analysis for Marketing, 11*(4), 343-349.

Rosset, S., Neumann, E., Eick, U., & Vatnik, N. (2003). Customer lifetime value models for decision support. *Data Mining and Knowledge Discovery, 7*, 321-339.

Rust, R. T., Lemon, K. N., & Zeithaml, V. A. (2004). Return on marketing: Using customer equity to focus marketing strategy. *Journal of Marketing, 68*(1), 109-139.

Shankaranarayan, G., Ziad, M., & Wang, R. Y. (2003). Managing data quality in dynamic decision environments: An information product approach. *Journal of Database Management, 14*(4), 14-32.

Spangler, W. E., May, J. H., & Vargas, L. G., Choosing data-mining methods for multiple classification: Representational and performance measurement implications for decision support. *Journal of Management Information Systems, 16*(1), 37-62.

Todman, C. (2001). *Designing a data warehouse*. Upper Saddle River, NJ: Prentice Hall.

Verhoef, P. C., & Donkers, B. (2001). Predicting customer potential value: An application in the insurance industry. *Decision Support Systems, 32*(2), 189-199.

Winer, R. S. (2001). A framework for customer relationship management. *California Management Review, 43*(4), 89-108.

Xevelonakis, E. (2005). Developing retention strategies based on customer profitability in telecommunications: An empirical study. *Journal of Database Marketing & Customer Strategy Management, 12*(3), 226-242.

Chapter VII

Effective Processing of XML-Extended OLAP Queries Based on a Physical Algebra

Xuepeng Yin, Aalborg University, Denmark

Torben Bach Pedersen, Aalborg University, Denmark

Abstract

In today's OLAP systems, physically integrating fast-changing data, for example., stock quotes, into a cube is complex and time-consuming. This data is likely to be available in XML format on the World Wide Web (WWW); thus, instead of physical integration, making XML data logically federated with OLAP systems is desirable. In this chapter, we extend previous work on the logical federation of OLAP and XML data sources by presenting simplified query semantics, a physical query algebra and a robust OLAP-XML query engine as well as the query evaluation techniques. Performance experiments with a prototypical implementation suggest that the performance for OLAP-XML federations is comparable to queries on physically integrated data.

Introduction

Online analytical processing (OLAP) technology enables data warehouses to be used effectively for online analysis, providing rapid responses to iterative complex analytical queries. Usually, an OLAP system contains a large amount of data, but dynamic data, for example, stock prices, is not handled well in current OLAP systems. To an OLAP system, a well-designed dimensional hierarchy and a large quantity of pre-aggregated data are the keys. However, trying to maintain these two factors, when integrating fast-changing data physically into a cube, is complex and time-consuming, or even impossible. However, the advent of XML makes it very possible that this data is available in XML format on the WWW. Thus, making XML data accessible to OLAP systems is greatly needed.

Our overall solution is to logically federate the OLAP and XML data sources. This approach decorates the OLAP cube with virtual dimensions, allowing selections and aggregations to be performed over the decorated cube. In this chapter, we describe the foundation of a robust federation query engine with the focus on query evaluation, which includes the query semantics, a physical algebra, and query evaluation techniques. First, a query semantics that simplifies earlier definitions (Pedersen, Riis, & Pedersen, 2002) is proposed. Here, redundant and repeated logical operators are removed and a concise and compact logical query plan can be generated, after a federation query is analyzed. Second, a physical query algebra, unlike the previous logical algebra, is able to model the real execution tasks of a federation query. Here, all concrete data retrieval and manipulation operations in the federation are integrated. This means that we obtain a much more precise foundation for performing query optimization and cost estimation. Third, the detailed description of the query evaluation introduces how the modeled execution tasks of a query plan are performed, including the concrete evaluation algorithms and techniques for each physical operator and the general algorithm that organizes and integrates the execution of the operators in a whole plan. In addition, algebra-based query optimization techniques, including the architecture of the optimizer, cost estimation of physical operators, and plans, also are presented. Experiments with the query engine suggest that the query performance of the federation approach is comparable to physical integration.

Related Work

There has been a great deal of previous work on data integration, for instance, on relational data (Chen, Wu, Wang, & Mao, 2006; Hellerstein, Stonebraker, & Caccia, 1999; IBM, n.d.; Oracle, 2005), semi-structured data (Chawathe, Garcia-Molina,

Hammer, Ireland, Papakonstantinou, Ullman, et al., 1994; Li & An, 2005; Nicolle, Yétongnon, & Simon, 2003; Yang, Lee, Ling, & Dobbie, 2005), a combination of relational and semi-structured data (Goldman & Widom, 2000; Lahiri, Abiteboul, & Widom, 1999), a combination of relational and unstructured data (Mansuri & Sarawagi, 2006), a combination of object-oriented and semi-structured data (Bae, Kim, & Huh, 2003), and an integration of remote data warehouses by hyper materialized views (Triantafillakis, Kanellis, & Martakos, 2004). Li and An (2005) built a multidimensional model of the diverse XML data sources in UML, which then enables OLAP operations over the integrated XML data through the information within the UML diagram (e.g., retrieval paths). Yang et al. (2005) also integrated XML data, focusing on an algorithm that rewrites queries on the integrated views to query the underlying source repositories. Reveliotis and Carey (2006) used XQuery and XML schema for data and meta data integration of various data sources, including relational, Web service, function-based, and file-based data, where meta data of different data sources conformed to a uniformed framework. However, none of these previously mentioned work handles the advanced issues related to OLAP systems, for example, automatic and correct aggregation and dimensions with hierarchies.

Pérez, Llavori, Aramburu, and Pederson (2005) integrated a corporate warehouse with text-rich XML documents, where the XML data is always first extracted into a context warehouse and then maintained by complex Information Retrieval (Baeza-Yates & Ribeiro-Neto, 1999) techniques, whereas our solution provides fast and flexible access to structured XML data, thereby enabling more efficient analysis on today's fast changing data. Some work concerns integrating OLAP and object databases (Gu, Pedersen, & Shoshani, 2000; Pedersen, Shoshani, Gu, & Jensen, 2000), which demands rigid schemas (that is, data is represented by classes and connected by complex associations). Cabibbo and Torlone (2005) proposed the methods of integrating heterogeneous multidimensional databases, where data is of good quality, structured in a rather uniform way, and most importantly, static. Zaman and Schneider (2005) also integrated static relational and multidimensional data and presented SQL to MDX translation algorithms; however, the multidimensional data is viewed in a rather relational way and the solution does not support OLAP queries. In comparison, using XML as data source, as we do, enables the federation to be applied on any data as long as the data allows XML wrapping, greatly enlarging the applicability.

Our previous work (Pedersen et al., 2002) presents a logical federation of OLAP and XML systems, where a logical algebra defines the query semantics and a partial straightforward implementation. Our most related work (Yin & Pedersen, 2004; Yin & Pedersen, 2006) introduces a physical query algebra, and the query evaluation, cost estimation, and optimization techniques are implemented in a robust OLAP-XML federation query engine. This chapter further extends (Yin & Pedersen, 2006) by introducing novel logical-to-physical plan conversion techniques, which convert logical operators in a logical plan into physical operators that are needed to make the plan executable by the query evaluator.

The chapter is organized as follows. First, we introduce an example cube and XML document used in the illustrations. Then, an overview of the overall architecture of the federation and the federation query language is given. We define the formal representation of the federation and the federation queries using the logical algebra. Then, the physical algebra is introduced, which includes the definitions of the physical operators, logical-to-physical conversion, and examples. In the following sections, we present the query evaluation and optimization techniques, including algorithms, component query construction, and examples. The experiments in performance study compare the performance between the logical and physical federations, whereas the last section offers conclusions about the current OLAP-XML federation and indicates future work that extends the query optimization and evaluation techniques.

Case Study

The TPC-H-based (Transaction Processing Performance Council, 2004) database used in the experiments and illustrations is shown in Figure 1. The OLAP database, called TC, is characterized by a supplier dimension, a parts dimension, an order dimension, and a time dimension. For each line item, Quantity and ExtendedPrice are measured. An example fact table is shown in Table 1. The XML document is composed of the nation codes and public population data about nations in millions. An example of the document is illustrated in Figure 2, where each Nation element contains two sub-elements, NationName and Population. We use the listed three lines as the example data in this chapter. To connect the dimension values of the level Nation and the populations, a link, *Nlink*, is defined, which maps dimension values for Nation in the cube to the nodes Nation in the XML document. The next section uses the example cube and XML document to illustrate the federation query language.

Figure 1. Cube schema

Dimensions:	*Suppliers*	*Parts*	*Orders*	*Time*
	AllSuppliers	AllParts		AllTime
	|	|		|
	Region	Manufacturer	All Orders	Year
	|	|	|	|
	Nation	Brand	Customer	Month
	|	|	|	|
	Supplier	Part	Order	Day
Measures:	Quantity,	ExtPrice		

Figure 2. Part of the XML data

```
<Nations>
  <Nation><NationName>DK</NationName><Population>5.3</Population></Nation>
  <Nation><NationName>CN</NationName><Population>1264.5</Population></Nation>
  <Nation><NationName>UK</NationName><Population>19.1</Population></Nation>
     •
     •
     •
</Nations>
```

Federation Overview

In this section, we give an overview of the prototypical OLAP- XML federation system, the federation query language, and the basic query evaluation process.

The overall architecture of the federation system is shown in Figure 5. Besides the OLAP and the XML components, three auxiliary components have been introduced to hold meta data, link data, and temporary data. Queries are posed to the query engine, which coordinates the execution of queries in the components. In the prototype, MS SQL Server 2000 Enterprise Edition with SP3 is used. More specifically, the temporary component is the temporary database on SQL Server, and the OLAP component uses MS Analysis Services (AS), and is queried with SQL (Microsoft, 2005b). The XML component is the local file system based on the XML data retrieved from the Web with MS OPENXML (Microsoft, 2002b) on top. Figure 3 shows a screen shot of the prototypical query engine. The prototype was programmed in MS Visual J++ 6.0 with component object model (COM) interfaces (Microsoft, 2005a) to take advantage of the existing relational, multidimensional database and XML technologies from Microsoft. Using the query engine, users can pose queries in the *query* tab and execute the query by pressing the button with a red flash. The *query plan* tab in the middle shows the execution plan of the posed query. To its right is the *query result* tab, where the result data is shown in table format. Messages indicating the processing progress of the posed query are shown in the bottom text box. The current prototype does not have a sophisticated interface and is only used for experimental purposes. The core techniques will later be integrated with the business analysis products of a Danish business intelligence (BI) tool vendor, TARGIT (Pedersen, Pedersen, & Pedersen, 2004).

The federation query language is called "XML-extended multidimensional SQL" (SQL_{xm}), which has basic clauses similar to SQL (that is, SELECT, FROM, WHERE, GROUP BY, and HAVING) and uses *level expressions* (defined later) for referencing external XML data. Figure 4 is an example SQL_{xm} query based on the cube in Figure 1, where the *roll-up expression* "Brand(Part)" rolls up to the Brand level from the Part level, and the level expression "Nation[ANY]/Nlink/Population" connects the dimension level Nation and the decoration XML data Population with a link, *Nlink*.

As shown in Figure 5, the query engine has three components: query analyzer, query optimizer, and query evaluator. The query engine parses and analyzes the given query, and generates the initial logical plan. The plan is expressed in the logical algebra. The query optimizer generates a plan space for the initial plan, where all the logical plans produce the same output as the original one. Furthermore, the optimizer converts all the logical plans into physical plans by converting the logical operators into physical operators. Then, costs of the plans can be estimated. Finally, the optimizer searches for the best execution plan that has the least evaluation time

Table 1. The fact table

Quantity	ExtPrice	Supplier	Part	Order	Day
17	17954	S1	P3	11	2/12/1996
36	73638	S2	P5	18	5/2/1992
28	29983	S2	P4	42	30/3/1994
2	2388	S3	P3	4	8/12/1996
26	26374	S4	P2	20	10/11/1993

Figure 3. The GUI of the federation query engine

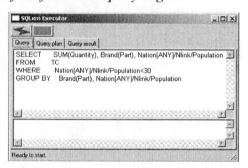

Figure 4. An example SQL$_{xm}$ query

SELECT	SUM(Quantity),Brand(Part),
FROM	TC
WHERE	Nation[ANY]/Nlink/Population < 30
GROUP BY	Brand(Part),Nation[ANY]/Nlink/Population

Figure 5. Architecture of the OLAP-XML federation system

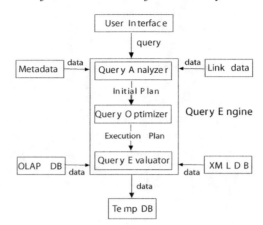

and passes the plan on to the query evaluator. The evaluator executes the operators in the given plan and generates the final result. Generally, the component queries are evaluated in the OLAP and XML components in parallel and the results of these queries are transferred to the temporary component for further processing. Sometimes the selection predicates on level expressions can be re-written to new predicates with only references to dimension values and constants and, therefore, can be evaluated in the OLAP component. We term this technique *inlining*. Therefore, in such a situation, some XML queries have to be evaluated before the construction of OLAP queries in order to re-write the predicates. Moreover, the underlying OLAP cube may be sliced and aggregated, which leads to less inter-component data transfer. There are also physical operators, in the execution plan, that model the processing of the temporary data in the temporary component, where SQL operations are used to process the gathered data. The next section formalizes the terms introduced informally in this section.

Data Models

The *cube model* is defined in terms of a multidimensional *cube* consisting of a *cube name, dimensions,* and a *fact table*. Each dimension comprises two partially ordered sets (posets), representing hierarchies of *levels* and the ordering of dimension values. Each level is associated with a set of dimension values. That is, a *dimension D_i* is a two-tuple (L_{D_i}, E_{D_i}), where L_{D_i} is a poset of levels and E_{D_i} is a poset of dimension values. L_{D_i} is the four-tuple $(LS_i, \sqsubseteq_i, \top_i, \bot_i)$, where $LS_i = \{l_{i1}, ..., l_{ik}\}$ is a set of levels, l_{ij} $(1 \leq j \leq k)$ is a level name, and $\sqsubseteq_i$ is a *partial order* on these levels. $\bot_i$ is the bottom level, while $\top_i$ is the unique ALL level. We shall use $l_{ij} \in D_i$ as a shorthand meaning that the level l_{ij} belongs to the poset of levels in dimension D_i. The partial order of levels is the containment-ship between two levels in the same dimension (that is, $l_{i1} \sqsubseteq_i l_{i2}$ holds if elements in L_{i2} can be said to contain the elements in L_{i1}). Here, L_{ik} is the set of dimension values of level l_{ik}, which is $L_{ik} = \{e_{ik_1}, ..., e_{ikl_{ik}}\}$. Similarly, we say that $e_1 \sqsubseteq_{D_i} e_2$, if e_1 is logically contained in e_2 and $l_{ij} \sqsubseteq_i l_{ik}$ for $e_1 \in L_{ij}$ and $e_2 \in L_{ik}$. For example, we say 01.21.2000 $\sqsubseteq_{D_{Time}}$ 2000 because the day 01.21.2000 is contained in the year 2000. E_{D_i} is a poset $(\cup_j L_{ij}, \sqsubseteq_{D_i})$ consisting of the set of all dimension values in the dimension and a partial ordering defined on these. For each level l, we assume a function Roll-up l : $L \times LS_i \mapsto \mathcal{P}(D_i)$, which, given a dimension value in L and a level in LS_i, returns the value's ancestor in the level; that is, Roll-up$_l(e_{ik_h}, l_{ij}) = \{e'| e_{ik_h} \sqsubseteq_{D_i} e' \wedge e' \in L_{ij}\}$. A roll-up expression $l_{ij}(l_{ik})$ uses the Roll-up function to aggregate the cube from a lower level l_{ik} to a higher level l_{ij}, i.e., $l_{ik} \sqsubseteq_i l_{ij} \wedge l_{ik} \neq l_{ij}$.

A fact table F is a relation containing one attribute for each dimension and one attribute for each measure. Thus, $F = \{(e_{\perp_1}, ..., e_{\perp_n}, v_1, ..., v_m)| (e_{\perp_1}, ..., e_{\perp_n}) \in \perp_1 \times ... \times \perp_n \wedge (v_1, ..., v_m) \in M \subseteq T_1 \times ... \times T_m\}$, where $n \geq 1$, $m \geq 1$, and T_j is the domain value for the jth measure. We will also refer to the jth measure as $M_j = \{(e_{\perp_1}, ..., e_{\perp_n}, v_j)\}$. Each measure M_j is associated with a default aggregate function $f_j : \mathcal{P}(T_j) \mapsto T_j$, where the input is a multi-set. Aggregate functions ignore NULL values as in SQL. There may be NULL values for measures in the logical definition, but in a physical implementation, only the non-empty tuples would be stored in the fact table. An n-dimensional cube, C, is given as: $C = (N, D, F)$, where N is the cube name, $D = \{D_1, ..., D_n\}$ is a set of dimensions, and F is the fact table. A federation is the data structure on which we perform logical federation operations, for example, selections, aggregations and decorations. A federation $\mathcal{F}$ is a three-tuple: $\mathcal{F} = (C, Links, X)$, where C is an OLAP cube, X are the referred XML documents, and $Links$ is a set of links (see below) between levels in C and documents in X.

A link is a relation that connects dimension values with nodes in XML documents. For example, a link $Nlink = \{(DK, n1), (CN, n2), (UK, n3)\}$ maps each dimension value to a node in the example XML document. Here, $n1$ is the Nation node with the sub-node NationName having the string value DK, $n2$ is the Nation node with the sub-node NationName having the string value CN, and similarly for $n3$.

An XPath expression (Clark & DeRose, 2005) is a path that selects a set of nodes in an XML document. To allow references to XML data in SQL$_{XM}$ queries, links are used with XPath expressions to define level expressions. A level expression $l[SEM]/link/xp$ consists of a starting level l, a decoration semantic modifier, SEM, a link $link$ from l to nodes in one or more XML documents, and a relative XPath expression xp, which is applied to these nodes to identify new nodes. For example, $Nation[ANY]/Nlink/Population$ links the dimension value "DK" with its population data "5.3" (million), which is the string value of the node Population in the context of $n1$. *SEM* represents the decoration semantics, ALL, ANY, and CONCAT, which specify how many decoration values should be used when several of them are found for a dimension value through *link* and *xp*. The ALL semantics connect each dimension value with all the linked decoration values, and the ANY semantics just use an arbitrary decoration value for each dimension value, whereas the CONCAT semantics concatenate all the possible decoration values into one.

A hierarchy is strict if no dimension value has more than one parent value from the same level (Lenz & Shoshani, 1997). Non-strict hierarchy can lead to incorrect aggregation over a dimension (e.g., some lower-level values will be double-counted). Three types of data are distinguished: c, data that may not be aggregated because fact data is duplicated and may cause incorrect aggregation, α, data that may be averaged but not added, and Σ, data that may also be added. A function AggType: $\{M_1, ..., M_m\} \times D \mapsto \{\Sigma, \alpha, c\}$ returns the aggregation type of a measure M_j when aggregated in a dimension $D_i \in D$. Considering only the standard SQL functions, we have that $\Sigma = \{SUM, AVG, MAX, MIN, COUNT\}$, $\alpha = \{AVG, MAX, MIN, COUNT\}$, and $c = \varnothing$. The next section presents the representations of federation queries in terms of logical operators using the symbols defined above.

Logical Algebra and Query Semantics

In previous work (Pedersen et al., 2002), a logical algebra over federations was proposed, which is the basis of our work here. In this section, a brief background introduction to the logical algebra and the original SQL_{XM} query semantics are given. We then propose a simplified version of the original query semantics. The following list summarizes the logical operators.

- A decoration operator, $\delta_{l_2[SEM]/link/xp}$, builds a decoration dimension using the XML data referenced by a level expression. The decoration dimension consists of the unique top level, and the mid-level, which is also called the *decoration level*, which is composed of external XML data (e.g., Population for Nation[ANY]/Nlink/Population). The bottom level to which the starting level of the level expression (e.g., Nation for Nation[ANY]/Nlink/Population) belongs is defined as the bottom level of the decoration dimension. The mid-level decorates the measures of the OLAP database through the bottom level, whose values and their ancestors in the mid-level are related using the relationship defined by the level expression. The decoration operator enables the external XML data to become a virtual part of the cube, thereby allowing the following operations involving XML data to be performed on the federation.

- A federation selection, $\sigma_{Fed[\theta]}$, allows the facts from the cube to be filtered using the external XML data as well as the regular cube data. The predicate can reference any dimension levels in the federation, including the decoration levels made of XML data in the form of level expressions. After selection, the cube schema is not changed. Only facts in the fact table are affected.

- The federation generalized projection, $\prod_{Fed[\mathcal{L}]<F(M)>}$, also let the federated cube be aggregated over the external XML data. Here, $\mathcal{L}$ is a set of levels to which the federated cube will be rolled up, or intuitively the levels in the GROUP BY clause where level expressions can be present. $F(M)$ is a set of aggregate functions over the specified measures, that is, the aggregates in the SELECT clause. Given a set of argument levels, the generalized projection first removes the dimensions for which no argument levels are present (like the SQL projection), and then each dimension is rolled up to the specified level, replacing the original dimension values in the facts by their ancestor values in the levels in $\mathcal{L}$. Finally, facts in the fact table are grouped, the specified measures are aggregated, and other measures not specified in the arguments are removed.

The semantics of an SQL_{XM} query can be expressed in terms of the algebra defined above. In the following, suppose: $\mathcal{F} = (C, Links, X)$ is a federation. $\{\bot_p, ..., \bot_q\} \subseteq \{\bot_1, ..., \bot_n\}$ and $\{l_s, ..., l_t\}$ are levels in C such that $\bot_s \sqsubseteq_s l_s \wedge \bot_s \neq l_s, ..., \bot_t \sqsubseteq l_t \wedge \bot_t \neq l_t$. le is used to represent a level expression, $l[SEM]/link/xp$, where SEM is the semantic modifier, l is a level in C, $link \in Links$ is a link from l to documents in X, and xp is an XPath expression. $pred_{where}$ represents the predicates in the WHERE clause. $pred_{having}$ represents the predicates in the HAVING clause. $LE_{\Pi} = \{le_{u_\Pi}, ..., le_{v_\Pi}\}$ are the level expressions in the SELECT and GROUP BY clause. $LE_{\sigma_{where}}$ are the level expressions in the WHERE clause. $LE_{\sigma_{having}}$ are the level expressions in the HAVING clause. $f_x, ..., f_y$ are the aggregation functions. A sequence of decoration operations is denoted by Δ; that is: $\Delta_{\{le_i, ..., le_j\}}(\mathcal{F}) = \delta_{le_i}(...(\delta_{le_j}(\mathcal{F}))...)$. Here is a prototypical SQL_{XM} query:

SELECT	$f_x(M_x), ..., f_y(M_y), \bot_p, ..., \bot_q, l_s(\bot_s), ..., l_t(\bot_t), le_{u_\Pi}, ..., le_{v_\Pi}$
FROM	$\mathcal{F}$
WHERE	$pred_{where}$
GROUP BY	$\bot_p, ..., \bot_q, l_s(\bot_s), ..., l_t(\bot_t), le_{u_\Pi}, ..., le_{v_\Pi}$
HAVING	$pred_{having}$

which can be represented in the following logical algebra (Pedersen et al., 2002):

$$\Pi_{Fed[\perp_p, \, ..., \, \perp_q, \, l_s\,(\perp_s), \, ..., \, l_t\,(\perp_t), \, le_{u_\Pi}, \, ..., \, le_{v_\Pi}]} <f_x(M_x), \, ..., f_y\,(M_y)> ($$

$$\sigma_{Fed[pred_{having}]} ($$

$$\Delta_{LE_{\sigma_{having}}} ($$

$$\Pi_{Fed[\perp_p, \, ..., \, \perp_q, \, l_s\,(\perp_s), \, ..., \, l_t\,(\perp_t), \, le_{u_\Pi}, \, ..., \, le_{v_\Pi}]} <f_x(M_x), \, ..., f_y\,(M_y)> ($$

$$\Delta_{LE_\Pi} (\sigma_{Fed[pred_{where}]}(\Delta_{LE_{\sigma_{where}}} (\mathcal{F})))))$$

The semantics implies an SQL_{XM} query, which can be evaluated in four major steps. First, the cube is sliced as specified in the WHERE clause, possibly requiring decorations with XML data. Second, the cube is decorated for the level expressions in the SELECT and GROUP BY clauses, and then all dimensions, including the new ones, are rolled up to the levels specified in the GROUP BY clause. Third, the resulting cube is sliced according to the predicate in the HAVING clause, which may require additional decorations. Fourth, the top generalized projection projects the decorations not required by the SELECT and GROUP BY clause and gives the final result cube. The following section introduces a simplified representation of the query semantics.

Simplified Query Semantics

The query semantics have a great impact on the initial plan, as the semantics take the form of a logical query tree after an SQL_{XM} query is parsed and analyzed. As the semantics indicate, duplicate decoration operators are generated when a level expression exists in several sub-clauses (e.g., the SELECT and the WHERE clauses). As the algebra shows, an operator takes an input federation and generates a new one. Thus, repeated operators can then be detected by examining the input and output federations.

The simplified query semantics can be constructed by removing the redundant operators that do not change the cube semantics. An operator that generates the same federation as the input federation is redundant. Thus, the plan without redundant operators is more compact, and sometimes considerably smaller than the unsimplified version. This simplification benefits the performance of the query processing. First, during the query optimization, the equivalent plans in the plan space can be enumerated much faster. Intuitively, this process can be thought of as the combinations of operators. The fewer operators a plan has, the fewer combinations it results in. Second, smaller plans lead to less logical-to-physical conversion and cost-estimation time. Third, during evaluation, no duplicate data is retrieved, thereby leading to high reusability, and more importantly, less resource consumption (e.g., CPU, I/O, and storage). The simplified algebraic query representation is:

Figure 6. The initial logical query plan

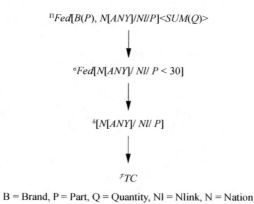

$$^{\Pi}Fed[B(P),\ N[ANY]/Nl/P]<SUM(Q)>$$

$$^{\sigma}Fed[N[ANY]/\ Nl/\ P < 30]$$

$$^{\delta}[N[ANY]/\ Nl/\ P]$$

$$^{\mathcal{F}}TC$$

B = Brand, P = Part, Q = Quantity, Nl = Nlink, N = Nation

$$\sigma_{Fed[pred_{having}]}\Big(\\ \quad \Pi_{Fed[\perp_p,\ ...,\ \perp_q,\ l_s(\perp_s),\ ...,\ l_t(\perp_t),\ le_{u_\Pi},\ ...,\ le_{v_\Pi}]\ <fx(Mx),\ ...,\ fy(My)>}\Big(\\ \qquad \Delta_{LE_{\Pi,\delta}}\Big(\\ \qquad\quad \sigma_{Fed[pred_{where}]}\big(\Delta_{LE_{\sigma_{where}}}(\mathcal{F})\big)\Big)\Big)\Big)$$

Here, $LE_{\Pi,\delta}$ is a set of the decoration operators that are referenced by the SELECT and GROUP BY clauses only, that is $LE_{\Pi,\delta} \subseteq LE_{\Pi} \wedge LE_{\Pi,\delta} \cap LE_{where} - \varnothing$. Moreover, an instance of a decoration operator for a specific level expression is unique. In other words, when a virtual dimension for a level expression already exists in the federation, no decoration operator building the same dimension is needed again. Therefore, some of the decoration operators for the WHERE clause may build the virtual dimensions required by the SELECT and GROUP BY clauses as well; that is, $LE_{\Pi} \setminus LE_{\Pi,\delta} \subseteq LE_{\sigma_{where}}$. $\Delta_{pred_{having}}$ is removed because predicates on level expressions in the HAVING clause can be put in the WHERE clause. The original top generalized projection is also removed because the HAVING clause does not change the cube schema. The simplified logical plan tree for the query in Figure 4 is shown in Figure 6, where only one decoration, $\delta_{N[ANY]/Nl/P}$, exists below the federation selection, although referenced by two federation operators. The next section presents the physical algebra modeling and the execution of federation queries.

Physical Algebra

As shown in Figure 5, an execution plan is produced by the query optimizer, which is used to guide the evaluator about when, where, and how the data retrieval and manipulation operations should be performed. An execution plan is an SQL_{XM} query tree expressed in the physical algebra. The logical semantics of a query imply the main phases of the query evaluation, whereas a physical query tree is integrated with more detailed evaluation operations. In this section, we introduce the new physical algebra operators and the new semantics of the existing federation operators, and then show an example of a logical plan and its corresponding physical plan.

The federation decorates OLAP data in the temporary component using the decoration XML data, which then enables selections and aggregations over the decorated temporary fact data. Therefore, the temporary component plays an important role at evaluation time. Before we describe the physical operators, we extend the original federation to an extended form, on which our physical algebra is based. An extended federation is $\mathcal{F}_{TC,ext} = (C, Links, X, T)$, where C is a cube, $Links$ is a set of links between levels in C and documents in X, and T is a set of temporary tables.

Querying the OLAP Component

Cube operators include cube selection and cube generalized projection. They are used to model the OLAP component query, which is used to retrieve the cube data from the OLAP database. The cube selection operator, σ_{Cube}, is much like a logical federation selection operator, but has no references to level expressions in the predicates. A cube selection only affects the tuples in the fact table, thereby returning a cube with the same fact type and the same set of dimensions.

Example 1

Suppose the extended federation $\mathcal{F}_{ext}$ has the cube schema and the fact table in the example cube, TC. The cube selection operator $\sigma_{Cube[Supplier = \text{`S1'} OR Supplier = \text{`S2'}]}(\mathcal{F}_{TC,ext})$ $= \mathcal{F}_{TC,ext}$ slices the cube so that only the data for the suppliers S1 and S2 in the fact table are retained. The resulting fact table is shown in Table 2.

Table 2. The fact table after selection

Quantity	ExtPrice	Supplier	Part	Order	Day
17	17954	S1	P3	11	02/12/1996
36	73638	S2	P5	18	05/02/1992
28	29983	S2	P4	42	30/03/1994

Definition 1 (Cube Selection)

Let $\mathcal{F}_{ext} = (C, Links, X, T)$ be an extended federation and let θ be a predicate over the set of levels $\{l_1, ..., l_k\}$ and measures $M_1, ..., M_m$. A cube selection is: $\sigma_{Cube[\theta]}(\mathcal{F}_{ext}) = (C', Links, X, T)$, where the cube is $C' = (N, D, F')$ and the new fact table is $F' = \{t'_1, ..., t'_j\}$. If $t_i = (e_{\perp_1}, ..., e_{\perp_n}, v_1, ..., v_m) \in F$ is an input fact tuple, then the corresponding fact tuple in the output fact table is $-30 = t_i$ if $\theta(t_i) = tt$; otherwise, $t'_i = (e_{\perp_1}, ..., e_{\perp_n}, NULL, ..., NULL)$.

The cube generalized projection operator Π_{Cube} rolls up the cube, aggregates measures over the specified levels, and, at the same time, removes unspecified dimensions and measures from a cube. Intuitively, it can be looked at as a SELECT statement with a GROUP BY clause in SQL. The difference between a cube and a federation generalized projection operator is that the first one does not involve external XML data or level expressions and is executed in the OLAP component. Intuitively, the levels specified as parameters to the operator become the new bottom levels of their dimensions, and all other dimensions are rolled up to the top level and removed. Each new measure value is calculated by applying the given aggregate function to the corresponding value for all tuples in the fact table containing old bottom values that roll up to the new bottom values. To ensure safe aggregation in the case of non-strict hierarchies (e.g., a dimension value has two parent values), we explicitly check for this in each dimension. If a roll-up along some dimension duplicates facts, we disallow further aggregation along that dimension by setting the aggregation type to c.

Example 2

Suppose the extended federation $\mathcal{F}_{TC,ext}$ has the cube schema and the fact table in the example cube, TC. The cube generalized projection operator $\Pi_{Cube[Supplier]<SUM(Quantity)}{}_>(\mathcal{F}_{TC,ext}) = \mathcal{F}_{TC,ext}$ rolls up the cube to the level Supplier and calculates the Quantity per Supplier. After the projection, only the measure Quantity and the dimension Suppliers are retained, of which the bottom level is Supplier. The result fact table is shown in Table 3.

Table 3. The fact table after the cube generalized projection

Quantity	Supplier
17	S1
64	S2
2	S3
26	S4

Definition 2. (Cube Generalized Projection)

Let $\mathcal{F}_{ext} = (C, \textit{Links}, X, T)$ be an extended federation. Let $l_{i_1}, ..., l_{i_k}$ be levels in C such that, at most, one level from each dimension occurs. The measures $\{M_{j_1}, ..., M_{j_l}\} \subseteq \{M_1, ..., M_m\}$ are kept in the cube and $f_{j_1}, ..., f_{j_l}$ are the given aggregate functions for the specified measures, such that $\forall D'_g \in \{D_g \mid D_g \in D \wedge \perp_g \notin \{l_{i_1}, ..., l_{i_k}\}\} \forall f_{j_h} \in \{f_{j_1}, ..., f_{j_l}\}(f_{j_h} \in \text{AggType}(M_{j_h}, D'_g))$, meaning that the specified aggregate functions are allowed to be applied. The cube generalized projection operator Π_{Cube} over a cube C is then defined as: $\Pi_{Cube[li1, ..., lik] < fj1 (Mj1), ..., fjl(Mjl)>} (\mathcal{F}_{ext}) = (C', \textit{Links}, X, T)$, where $C' = (N, D', F')$, and $D'_{i_h} = (L'_{D_{i_h}}, E'_{D_{i_h}})$ for $h \in \{1, ..., k\}$. The new poset of levels in the remaining dimensions is $L'_{D_{i_h}} = (LS'_{i_h}, \sqsubseteq'_{i_h}, \top_{i_h}, l_{i_h})$, where $LS'_{i_h} = \{l_{i_h P} \mid l_{i_h P} \in LS_{i_h} \wedge l_{i_h} \sqsubseteq_{i_h} l_{i_h P}\}$ and $\sqsubseteq'_{i_h} = \sqsubseteq_{i_h | LS'_{i_h}}$. Moreover, $E'_{D_{i_h}} = (\bigcup_{l_{i_h} \in LS'_{i_h}} L_{i_h}, \sqsubseteq_{D_{i_h} |}$

$\bigcup_{l_{i_h} \in LS_{i_h}} L_{i_h})$, where L_{i_h} is the set of dimension values of the level l_{i_h}. The new fact table is: $F' = \{(e'_{\perp_{i_1}}, ..., e'_{\perp_{i_k}}, v'_{j_1}, ..., v'_{j_l}) \mid e'_{\perp_{i_g}} \in L_{i_g} \wedge v'_{j_h} = f_{M_{j_h}} (\{v \mid (e_{\perp_1}, ..., e_{\perp_n}, v) \in M_{j_h} \wedge (e'_{\perp_{i_1}}, ..., e'_{\perp_{i_k}}) \in \text{Roll-up}_{\perp_{i_1}} (e_{\perp_{i_1}}, l_{i_1}) \times ... \times \text{Roll-up}_{\perp_{i_k}} (e_{\perp_{i_k}}, l_{i_k})\})\}$. Furthermore, the aggregation type is set to c by $\text{AggType}(M_{j_h}, D'_{i_g}) = c$, if $\exists (e_{\perp_1}, ..., e_{\perp_n}, v_j) \in M_{j_h} \exists e \in \{e_{\perp_1}, ..., e_{\perp_n}\}(\| \text{Roll-up} \perp_{i_g} (e, l_{i_g})\| > 1 \wedge v_j \neq \text{NULL})$.

Data Transfer Between Components

This section presents the definitions of fact-, dimension-, and XML-transfer operators. These operators are used to transfer data between components. The fact-transfer operator transfers fact data from the OLAP to the temporary component, whereas a dimension-transfer operator only transfers dimension data. An XML-transfer operator connects the temporary and XML components, transferring the referenced XML data into a temporary table.

In a physical execution plan, the fact-transfer operator is above the cube and below the federation operators. The resulting fact data from the cube operators is transferred to the temporary component through the fact-transfer operator. Thereafter, SQL operations (e.g., selections and joins) can be performed over the temporary fact table.

Definition 3. (Fact-Transfer)

Let $\mathcal{F}_{ext} = (C, \textit{Links}, X, T)$ be an extended federation. The fact-transfer operator is: $\phi(\mathcal{F}_{ext}) = (C, \textit{Links}, X, T')$, where $T' = T \cup \{R_F\}$ and R_F is the copy of the fact table in the temporary component.

Table 4. The temporary table for Nation and Supplier

Nation	Supplier
DK	S1
DK	S2
CN	S3
UK	S4

When a non-bottom level is referred by the federation operations in the temporary component, dimension values of the non-bottom level are required. The dimension transfer operator ω is used, at this time, to load the dimension values for the given dimension levels into a table in the temporary component, which then can be used by federation selection and generalized projection operators.

Example 3

A roll-up expression, Nation(Supplier), yields a dimension transfer. The two input parameters are Nation and Supplier. The dimension values for the two levels are loaded into a temporary table R_1 shown in Table 4.

Definition 4. (Dimension-Transfer)

Let $\mathcal{F}_{ext} = (C, Links, X, T)$ be an extended federation, where the cube is $C = (N, D, F)$. Let l_{ix}, l_{iy} be two levels in dimension D_i, where $l_{ix} \sqsubseteq_i l_{iy}$ and $l_{ix} \neq l_{iy}$. The dimension-transfer operator is defined as: $\omega_{[l_{ix}, l_{iy}]}(\mathcal{F}_{ext}) = (C, Links, X, T')$, where $T' = T \cup \{R\}$ and $R = \{(e_{ix}, e_{iy}) | e_{ix} \in L_{ix} \wedge e_{ix} \sqsubseteq_{D_i} e_{iy}\}$.

In the following, a temporary table for l_{ix} and l_{iy} by a dimension-transfer operator is denoted as $R_{\omega[l_{ix}, l_{iy}]}$. The temporary table R_1 in Example 3 can be denoted as $R_{\omega\,[Supplier, Nation]}$. According to the definition, the temporary component T' has a new element, $R_{\omega\,[Supplier, Nation]}$.

At query evaluation time, the XML data is needed in the temporary component to allow decoration, grouping, or selection on the cube according to the referenced level expressions. Intuitively, the XML-transfer operator connects the temporary component and the XML component, transferring the XML data into the temporary component. The input parameter is a level expression, which specifies the dimension values to be decorated, the corresponding decoration XML values selected by the relative XPath expression, and the link in the level expression. The operator yields a new table in the temporary component.

Definition 5. (XML-Transfer)

Let $\mathcal{F}_{ext} = (C, Links, X, T)$ be an extended federation, where $C = (N, D, F)$. Let $l_z[SEM]/link/xp$ be a level expression, where $l_z \in D_z$, $link \in Links$ is a link from l_z to X, and xp is an XPath expression over X. The XML-transfer operator is defined as: $\tau_{l_z[SEM]/link/xp}(\mathcal{F}_{ext}) = (C, Links, X, T')$, where $T' = T \cup \{R\}$. Here, R has the schema (l_z, l_{xp}) and is the temporary table containing the decorated dimension values and the decoration XML values found through the XML documents with the decoration semantics specified by the semantic modifier *SEM*. At evaluation time, the ALL semantics yield the temporary table having multiple rows with the same dimension value but different decoration values, whereas the table for the ANY semantics has only one row for a dimension value and an arbitrary decoration value linked through the level expression. Similarly, a dimension value decorated with the CONCAT semantics also takes up one row, but the decoration column is the concatenation of all the decoration values. In the following, *Strval* returns the string value of a node and *Concat* concatenates a set of strings. R is denoted as $R_{\tau_{l_z[SEM]/link/xp}}$ and defined formally as $R_{\tau_{l_z[SEM]/link/xp}} =$

- $\{(e_z, e_{xp}) | \forall (e_z, s) \in link(\forall s' \in xp(s)(e_{xp} = StrVal(s')))\}$, if $SEM = ALL$.
- $\{(e_z, e_{xp}) | \exists (e_z, s) \in link(e_{xp} = StrVal(s') for\ some\ s' \in xp(s))\}$, if $SEM = ANY$.
- $\{(e_z, e_{xp}) | (e_z, s) \in link \wedge e_{xp} = Concat(StrVal(s_1), ..., StrVal(S_k)) \wedge S_i \in S_{e_z}\}$, where $S_{e_z} = \{s | \forall (e_z, s') \in link(s \in xp(s'))\}$, for each $e_z \in L_z$, if $SEM = CONCAT$.

Example 4

The operator $\tau_{Nation[ANY]/Nlink/Population}(\mathcal{F}_{TC,ext})$ generates $\mathcal{F}'_{TC,ext} = (C, Links, X, T')$, where T' contains a new temporary table $R_{\tau_{Nation[ANY]/Nlink/Population}}$. The table has two columns: one for the dimension values of Nation and the other for the decoration values Population. A decoration value is the string value of a Population node in the context of the XML nodes in *Nlink*. Each nation has one and only one population as specified by the decoration semantics, ANY. The result temporary table $R_{\tau_{Nation[ANY]/Nlink/Population}}$, using the XML data from Figure 2, is shown in Table 5.

Querying the Temporary Component

This section presents the definitions of the operators that are performed in the temporary component. They are decoration, federation selection, and generalized

Table 5. The temporary table for Nation and Population

Nation	Population
DK	5.3
CN	1264.5
UK	19.1

projection operators, which allow the OLAP data to be decorated, selected, and grouped by the external XML data.

The cube is decorated in the temporary component using the decoration operator δ. The operator generates a decoration dimension, which is derived according to the cube definition that the fact table contains the bottom levels of all dimensions. Therefore, the new dimension has the unique top level, the middle decoration level, and the bottom level of the dimension containing the decorated level. Therefore, the new dimension has the same aggregation type as the referred dimension with each measure. Values of the levels are derived from a temporary decoration dimension table, which is composed of the decoration values and the bottom values of the referred dimension. Moreover, since the cube definition does not allow duplicate dimensions, no changes are made if an identical dimension already exists in the cube. At evaluation time of the decoration operator, the temporary table created by the XML-transfer operator having the same input level expression is used. The new dimension follows the same decoration semantics specified by the level expression. Correct aggregations on such a decoration dimension are ensured by the federation generalized projection operator in Definition 8. A physical decoration operator may have more than one child operator, which could be an XML-transfer operator with the same level expression as the input parameter, thereby providing the XML data in a temporary table.

Example 5

The decoration operator for *Nation[ANY]/Nlink/Population* generates a decoration dimension containing the top level ⊤, the middle level Population, and the bottom level Supplier, which is the bottom level of the dimension having the starting level Nation. The dimension values are derived from the result of a SQL inner join on the temporary tables of Examples 3 and 4. The dimension hierarchy is strict, since a supplier in a nation only has one corresponding population number. Figure 7 shows the dimension hierarchy and the temporary dimension table.

Figure 7. The decoration dimension and the temporary decoration dimension table Supplier/Population

Supplier	Population
S1	5.3
S2	5.3
S3	1264.5
S4	19.1

Definition 6. (Decoration)

Let Op_1, ..., Op_n be the child operators of a decoration operator $\delta_{l_z[SEM]/link/xp}$ and $(C, Links, X, T_1)$, ..., $(C, Links, X, T_n)$ be their output federations, where $C = (N, D, F)$. Let $l_z[SEM]/link/xp$ be a level expression, where $l_z \in D_z$, $link \in Links$ is a link from l_z to X and xp is an XPath expression over X. The physical decoration operator is defined as: $\delta_{l_z[SEM]/link/xp}(\mathcal{F}_{ext}) = (C', Links, X, T')$ where $\mathcal{F}_{ext} = (C', Links, X, T)$ is the input and $T = T_1 \cup ... \cup T_n$ is the union of the temporary tables from the child operators. In the output federation, $T' = T \cup \{R_{D_{n+1}}\}$, $R_{D_{n+1}}$ is a temporary decoration dimension table holding the dimension values of the bottom level $\perp_z$ and the XML level l_{xp}. In addition, n is the number of the existing dimensions prior to the decoration. More precisely, suppose $R_{\tau_{lz[SEM]/link/xp}} \in T$ is a temporary table loaded by an XML-transfer operator and $R_{\omega_{[\perp_z, lz]}}$ is a temporary table loaded by a dimension-transfer operator; then, $R_{D_{n+1}} = R_{\tau_{lz[SEM]/link/xp}}$ if $l_z = \perp_z$, meaning that the table yielded by the XML-transfer already contains the required data and can be used directly. Otherwise, $R_{D_{n+1}} = \pi_{\perp_z, l_{xp}}(R_{\tau_{lz[SEM]/link/xp}} \bowtie R_{\omega_{[\perp_z, lz]}})$ if $\perp_z \sqsubseteq_z l_z$ and $\perp_z \neq l_z$, where π is the regular SQL projection and $\bowtie$ is the natural join. The resulting cube is given by: $C' = (N, D', F)$, where $D' = \{D_1, ..., D_n\} \cup \{D_{n+1}\}$ and $D_{n+1} = \{L_{D_{n+1}}, E_{D_{n+1}}\}$. Here, $L_{D_{n+1}} = (LS_{n+1}, \sqsubseteq_{n+1}, \top_{n+1}, \perp_{n+1})$, where $LS_{n+1} = \{\top_{n+1}, l_{xp}, \perp_{n+1}\}$, $\sqsubseteq_{n+1} = \{\sqsubseteq_{n+1} = \{(\perp_{n+1}, l_{xp}), (l_{xp}, \top_{n+1}), (\perp_{n+1}, \top_{n+1})\}$, and $\perp_{n+1} = \perp_z$. The poset of dimension values is $E_{D_{n+1}} = (\bigcup_{(e_i, e_j) \in R_{D_{n+1}}} \{e_i, e_j\} \cup \{\top_{n+1}\}, \sqsubseteq_{D_{n+1}})$, where the partial order is $\sqsubseteq_{D_{n+1}} = \{(e_{\perp_{n+1}}, e_{xp}) \mid (e_1, e_2) \in R_{D_{n+1}} \wedge e_{\perp_{n+1}} = e_1 \wedge e_{xp} = e_2\} \cup \{(e_{\perp_{n+1}}, \top_{n+1}) \mid (e_1, e_2) \in R_{D_{n+1}} \wedge e_{\perp_{n+1}} = e_1\} \cup \{(e_{xp}, \top n+1) \mid (e_1, e_2) \in R_{D_{n+1}} \wedge e_{xp} = e_2\}$. For each measure M_h in M, the aggregation type of D_{n+1} is: AggType(M_h, D_z).

Intuitively, the physical federation selection operator σ_{Fed} is a SQL selection over the join of several tables, including the fact table, decoration dimension tables, and temporary dimension tables for non-bottom levels referenced by the predicate. Similarly to the cube selection, the federation selection returns a cube with the same fact types and the same set of dimensions, and only affects the tuples of the fact table, in the temporary component. A federation selection operator may have several child operators (e.g., dimension-transfer and decoration operators) to provide

Figure 8. The SQL query and the resulting fact table

			Quantity	ExtPrice	Supplier	Part	Order	Day
SELECT	Fact.*		17	17954	S1	P3	11	2/12/1996
ROM	Fact F, Supplier/ Population P		36	73638	S2	P5	18	5/2/1992
WHERE	F. Supplier = P.Supplier		28	29983	S2	P4	42	30/3/1994
	AND P.Population<30		26	26374	S4	P2	20	10/11/1993

the values required by the predicate. The temporary tables produced by the child operators are collected and will be used in the join.

Example 6

Suppose the temporary fact table in $\mathcal{F}_{TC,ext}$ is the copy of the fact table in Table 1. For the federation selection operator over $\mathcal{F}_{TC,ext}$, $\sigma_{Fed[Nation[ANY]/Nlink / Population < 30]}(\mathcal{F}_{TC,ext})$, the decoration values, Population, are needed to filter the fact data. Therefore, a SQL SELECT statement is issued against the join of the temporary decoration dimension table in Figure 7 and the temporary fact table, with the predicate on the decoration level and the join predicate in the WHERE clause, besides all the columns from the fact table. See Figure 8 for the query and the fact table.

Definition 7. (Federation Selection)

Let Op_1, ..., Op_n be the child operators of a federation selection operator and $(C, Links, X, T_1)$, ..., $(C, Links, X, T_n)$ be their output federations, where $C = (N, D, F)$. Let θ be a predicate over the levels in C. The federation selection operator is defined as: $\sigma_{Fed[\theta]}(\mathcal{F}_{ext}) = (C', Links, X, T')$, where $\mathcal{F}_{ext} = (C, Links, X, T)$ is the input and $T = T_1 \cup ... \cup T_n$ is the union of the temporary tables from the child operators. In the output federation, $T' = T \setminus \{R_F\} \cup \{R'_F\}$ means the temporary fact table R_F is replaced by R'_F. The resulting cube is $C' = (N, D, F')$, where the new fact table is $F' = \{t_i \mid t_i \in R'_F\}$. Suppose S_θ is the set of levels referenced by θ, then $R'_F = \sigma_\theta(R_F)$, if $S_\theta = \{\perp_1, ..., \perp_l\}$, meaning the predicates only contain the bottom levels. Otherwise, if S_θ has roll-up or level expressions, that is, $\{l_x(l_{\perp_x}), ..., l_y(l_{\perp_y})\} \subseteq S_\theta$, and $\{l_u[SEM_j]/ link_j / xp_j, ..., l_v [SEM_k]/ link_k / xp_k\} \subseteq S_\theta$, then $R'_F = \pi_{R_F\cdot}(\sigma_\theta(R_F \bowtie R_{\omega[\perp_x,}$
$l_x]} \bowtie ... \bowtie R_{\omega[\perp_y, l_y]} \bowtie R_{\tau_{l_u[SEM_j]/ linkj / xpj}} \bowtie ... \bowtie R_{\tau_{l_v[SEM]/link_k / xp_k}}))$.

Similar to the federation selection, the federation generalized projection operator Π_{Fed} is also implemented as a SELECT statement over temporary tables. Specifically, a roll-up operation is a join between the fact table and the temporary table containing the bottom level and the target level, where the common bottom level is the key of the join. Likewise, showing the decoration values together with OLAP values in the result also can be seen as a roll-up from the bottom level to the decoration level of a decoration dimension. Finally, an SQL aggregation calculates the given aggregate functions of the measures over the grouped facts according to the SELECT and GROUP BY arguments. Note that when performing roll-up operations, correct aggregation must be ensured by detecting hierarchy strictness explicitly (e.g., the dimension values of the two levels). If a roll-up, along some dimension, duplicates facts, we disallow further aggregation along that dimension by setting the aggregation type to not available.

Example 7

Suppose the temporary fact table in $\mathcal{F}_{TC,ext}$ is the copy of the fact table in Table 1. For $\Pi_{Fed[Nation[ANY]/Nlink/ Population]<SUM(Quantity)>}(\mathcal{F}_{TC,ext})$, the temporary dimension table containing values of Population and Supplier is needed to perform the roll-up, while the other dimensions and measures (not specified in the SELECT clause) will be removed from the cube. Therefore, a SQL query is issued against the temporary table from Figure 7 and the temporary fact table with only Population and SUM(Quantity) in the SELECT and GROUP BY clauses. Table Supplier/Population is strict, therefore further aggregation is allowed along this decoration dimension. See Figure 9 for the query and the fact table.

Definition 8. (Federation Generalized Projection)

Let Op_1, ..., Op_n be the child operators of a federation generalized projection operator. $(C, Links, X, T_1)$, ..., $(C, Links, X, T_n)$ are their output federations, where the cube is $C = (N, D, F)$. Let $\perp_p, ..., \perp_q$ be bottom levels, and let $l_s(\perp_s), ..., l_t(\perp_t)$ be roll-up expressions. Let $D_p, ..., D_k$ be the dimensions built for the level expressions $l_u[SEM_j]/link_j/xp_j, ..., l_v[SEM_k]/link_k/xp_k$. Furthermore, let $f_x, ..., f_y$ be aggregate functions over the levels $\{M_x, ..., M_y\} \subseteq \{M_1, ..., M_m\}$ such that $\forall f_z \in \{f_x, ..., f_y\} \ \forall D_g \in \{D_s, ..., D_t, D_j, ..., D_k\}(f_z \in AggType(M_z, D_g))$ holds. The federation generalized projection operator

Figure 9. The SQL query and the resulting fact table

SELECT	SUM (Quantity),		Quantity	Population
FROM	Fact F,		81	5.3
	Supplier/Population P		2	1264.5
WHERE	F.Supplier=P.Supplier		26	19.1
GROUP BY	Population			

Π_{Fed} is defined as: $\Pi_{Fed[\perp_{p}, \, ..., \, \perp_{q}, \, l_{s}(\perp_{s}), \, ..., \, l_{t}(\perp_{t}), \, l_{u}[SEM_{j}]/link_{j}/xp_{j}, \, ..., \, l_{v}[SEM_{k}]/link_{k}/xp_{k}]<f_{x}(M_{x}), \, ..., \, f_{y}(M_{y})>}(\mathcal{F}_{ext})$
$= (C', \textit{Links}, X, T')$, where $\mathcal{F}_{ext} = (C, \textit{Links}, X, T)$ is the input and $T = T_{1} \cup \, ... \cup T_{n}$ is
the union of the temporary tables from the child operators. In the output federation,
$C' = (N, D', F')$ is the updated cube. After the projection, only the temporary table
containing the values required by the federation projection are retained; that is, T'
$= \{R'_{F}, R_{\omega[\perp_{s}, \, l_{s}]}, \, ..., R_{\omega[\perp_{t}, \, l_{t}]}, R_{D_{j}}, \, ..., R_{D_{k}}\}$, where $R_{D_{j}}, \, ..., R_{D_{k}}$ are built by the decoration
operators for $l_{u}[SEM_{j}] \, Link_{j}/xp_{j}, \, ..., l_{v}[SEM_{k}]link_{k}/xp_{k}$. Unspecified dimensions are also
rolled up to the top level and removed. Therefore, the set of dimensions is given as:
$D' = \{D_{p}, \, ..., D_{q}, D'_{s}, \, ..., D'_{t}, D'_{j}, \, ..., D'_{k}\}$, where the hierarchies of levels, the ordering
of dimension values, and the aggregation types are updated in the same way as for the
cube generalized projection. Moreover, the fact table is given as: $F' = \{t_{i} \mid t_{i} \in R'_{F}\}$,
where the temporary fact table is $R'_{F} = \{t_{i} \mid t_{i} \in {}_{\perp_{p}, \, ..., \, \perp_{q}, \, l_{s}, \, ..., \, l_{t}, \, l_{xp_{j}}, \, ..., \, l_{xp_{k}}} \mathcal{G}_{f_{x}(M_{x}), ..., f_{y}(M_{y})}(R_{F,}$
${}_{intermediate})\}$, and the intermediate table is $R_{F,intermediate} = R_{F} \bowtie R_{\omega[\perp_{s}, l_{s}]} \bowtie \, ... \bowtie R_{\omega[\perp_{t}, l_{t}]} \bowtie R_{D_{j}}$
$\bowtie \, ... \bowtie R_{D_{k}}$, where $\mathcal{G}$ is the SQL aggregation.

Inlining XML Data

The inlining operator ι is used to re-write the selection predicates such that a referenced level expression can be integrated into a predicate by creating a more complex
predicate that contains only references to regular dimension levels and constants.
Without inlining, the OLAP and XML components can be accessed in parallel, followed by computation of the final result in the temporary component (e.g., selection
of the OLAP data according to XML data). Therefore, when selection predicates
refer to decoration values, a large amount of OLAP data has to be transferred into
the temporary component before it could be filtered. In this situation, it is often
advantageous to make the OLAP query dependent on the XML queries. That is,
for the predicates referring to level expressions, the XML and dimension values
linked by the level expressions are first retrieved. After this, the level expressions
are inlined into the predicates, which then only refer to dimension levels and constants, but have the identical effects as the original ones. Thus, the selection can be
performed over the cube, thereby reducing the cube size effectively before the data
is transferred to the temporary component.

Example 8

For "Nation[ANY]/Nlink/Population<30," the decoration data and the decorated
dimension values are retrieved from the XML-transfer operator in Example 4. Using
the result, the predicate is transformed to "Nation='DK' OR Nation='UK'."

Definition 9. (Inlining)

Let θ_1, ..., θ_n be predicates referencing level expressions. θ_i has the following possible forms:

1. $l_z[SEM]\,/\,link\,/\,xp\,po\,K$, where K is a constant,
2. $l_z[SEM]\,/\,link\,/\,xp\,po\,l_w$, where l_w is a level,
3. $l_z[SEM]\,/\,link\,/\,xp\,po\,M$ where M is a measure,
4. $l_z[SEM_1]\,/\,link_1\,/\,xp_1\,po\,l_w[SEM_2]\,/\,link_2\,/\,xp_2$,
5. $l_z[SEM]\,/\,link\,/\,xp\,IN\,(K_1,\,...,\,K_n)$, where K_i is aconstant value,
6. $NOT\,(\theta_{i1})$,
7. $\theta_{i1}\,bo\,\theta_{i2}$,

where the binary operator *bo* is AND or OR, the predicate operator *po* is one of the following: =, <, >, <>, >=, <=, and LIKE. Let $\mathcal{F} = (C, Links, X)$ be a federation, where $C = (N, D, F)$ is the original cube. $l_1/link_1/xp_1$, ..., $l_k\,/\,link_m\,/xp_m$ are the level expressions referenced by θ_1, ..., θ_n. The ι operator is defined as: $\iota_{[\theta_1,\,...,\,\theta_n]}(\tau$ $_{l_j/link_1/xp_1}(\mathcal{F}_{ext,\,1})$, ..., $\tau_{l_k/link_m/xp_m}(\mathcal{F}_{ext,\,m})) = (C, Links, X, T')$, where $\mathcal{F}_{ext,\,i} = \{C, Links, X, T_i\}$ is an extended federation with a temporary component T_i, which is an empty set, and $(\tau_{lj/link1/xp1}(\mathcal{F}_{ext,\,1})$, ..., $\tau_{lk\,/\,linkm\,/xpm}(\mathcal{F}_{ext,\,m}))$ are the child XML-transfers used to load decoration values referenced by the level expressions into T_i, $1 \le i \le m$. The resulting temporary component T' has new temporary tables, that is, $T' = T \cup \{R_{\tau_{l_j/\,link_1\,/\,xp_1}}, ..., R_{\tau_{l_k/link_m/xp_m}}\}$. The inlining operator is positioned at the bottom of a physical plan above the XML-transfer operators and re-writes the predicates in its parameter list to θ_1, ..., θ_n. As a consequence, the other occurrences of these predicates in the plan change accordingly. To provide the decoration values required by the inlining operator, the child XML-transfer operators are always evaluated first, the rest of the plan is evaluated after the inlining processes are finished. The transforming function $\mathcal{T}(\theta_i)$ re-writes θ_i to θ'_i, which returns the new predicate for each listed form, respectively. That is, $\theta'_i =$

1. $l_z\,IN\,(t_1,\,...,\,t_n)$, where $t_i \in \{e_z\,|\,(e_z, e_{xp}) \in R_{\tau_{l_z[SEM]/\,link\,/\,xp}} \wedge e_{xp}\,po\,K = true\}$.
2. $l_z = e_{z1}\,AND\,e_{xp1}\,po\,l_w\,OR\,...\,OR\,l_z = e_{zn}\,AND\,e_{xpn}\,po\,l_w$, where $(e_{zi}, e_{xpi}) \in R_{\tau_{l_z[SEM]/\,link\,/\,xp}}$.
3. $l_z = e_{z1}\,AND\,e_{xp1}\,po\,M\,OR\,...\,OR\,l_z = e_{zn}\,AND\,e_{xpn}\,po\,M$, where $(e_{zi}, e_{xpi}) \in R_{\tau_{l_z[SEM]/\,link\,/\,xp}}$.
4. $l_z = e_{z1}\,AND\,l_w = e_{w1}\,OR\,...\,OR\,l_z = e_{zn}\,AND\,l_w = e_{wn}$, where $(e_{zi}, e_{xp_1i}, e_{wi}, e_{xp_2i}) \in R_{\tau_{l_z[SEM]/}}$ $_{link_1\,/\,xp_1} \times R_{\tau_{l_w[SEM]/\,link_2\,/\,xp_2}}$ and $e_{xp_1i}\,po\,e_{xp_2i} = true$.

5. $T(l_z[SEM]/\ link/\ xp = K_1)\ OR\ ...\ OR\ T(l_z[SEM]/\ link/\ xp = K_n)$

6. $NOT(T(\theta_{i1}))$.

7. $T(\theta_{i1})\ bo\ T(\theta_{i2})$.

Example 9.

In this example, we show a logical plan and its corresponding physical plan. The plan is enumerated by the query optimizer for the query in Figure 4. The plan is selected so that it is possible to show more physical operators. The logical plan always yields a unique physical plan. A logical operator in a certain context only can be converted to one corresponding physical operator accompanied by other operators that provide data or construct new predicates. Therefore, a logical plan can be deterministically converted to a physical plan.

In the logical plan in Figure 10, the predicate "$(N/Nl/P < 30)$'" is marked to be re-written and no longer refers to the level expression at evaluation time. It means the federation selection then can be executed directly in the OLAP component. The bottom two federation operators perform the selection and partial aggregation on the federation before the cube is decorated. Besides the measure Quantity, only the dimensions Part and Suppliers are retained after the projection, but it still allows the decoration afterwards. The top federation generalized projection operator rolls up the dimensions to the specified levels and calculates the aggregate functions over the specified measure.

The corresponding physical plan is shown to the right. The plan is evaluated in a bottom-up fashion. The XML-transfer operator retrieves the dimension values and their decoration data, followed by the inlining operator that is required by the predicate in the logical plan, which is marked to be re-written. After the predicate is re-written by the inlining operator, the cube selection slices the cube using the new predicates, followed by the cube generalized projection operator, which rolls up the cube to levels Brand and Nation. As an optimized plan, it aggregates the cube as much as possible. Therefore, unspecified dimensions are rolled up to the top level. The dimension Part is rolled up to Brand as it is required in the SELECT clause. The dimension Suppliers is rolled up to Nation and it is still possible to perform the decoration afterwards. The two cube operators are converted from the two corresponding federation operators at the bottom of the logical plan, which do not refer to external data and can be evaluated in the OLAP component to reduce the data transferred between components. The fact-transfer operator is responsible for transferring the returned OLAP data to the temporary component after the cube operators process the cube. The decoration and the federation generalized projection operators are performed in the temporary component. Since the starting level Nation is the current bottom level of Suppliers and "Nation[ANY]/Nlink/Population" is already evaluated by the bottom XML-transfer operator, the decoration operator uses the dimension values for Nation from *Nlink* directly and the corresponding population data in the XML document to generate the decoration dimension. If the bottom level is Supplier, a dimension-transfer is required as a child operator of δ to create a table for Nation and Supplier, which is then joined with the table for the level expression to create the decoration dimension linking the facts and the decoration data. The top federation generalized projection operator utilizes SQL operations to roll up the cube, furthermore, to the decoration level Population.

Converting Logical Plans to Physical Plans

This section describes the conversion of logical query plans into query plans expressed in the physical algebra. The conversions use physical operators to replace

Figure 10. A logical plan and its corresponding physical plan

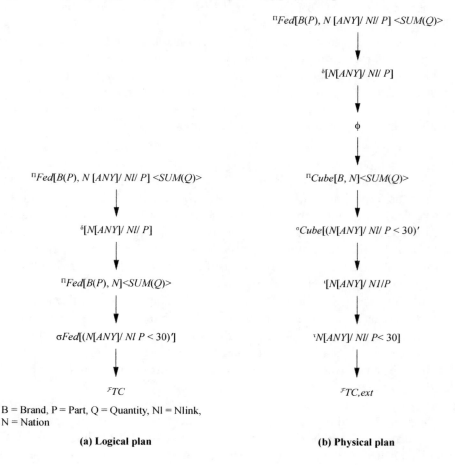

B = Brand, P = Part, Q = Quantity, Nl = Nlink,
N = Nation

(a) Logical plan   **(b) Physical plan**

the logical operators in order to integrate more operational details (e.g., predicate rewriting and intermediate table generations). In the following, we introduce the general principles of conversion/expansion for each logical operator, together with the examples referencing the plans in Figure 10.

Expanding Logical Decoration

According to Definition 6, a temporary table or a join of two temporary tables is needed to generate a decoration dimension having the decoration level and the bottom level, which will be used as the key to join the temporary fact table. Therefore, transfer operators (that is, XML-transfer and dimension-transfer) are generated as child operators below a decoration operator, when temporary tables containing the desired values are not present.

For example, the logical decoration operator $\delta_{Nation[ANY]/\ Nlink/\ Population}$ in Figure 10(a) yields the decoration operator in the corresponding physical plan in Figure 10(b). The dimension-transfer operator is not needed because the starting level Nation of the level expression is now the bottom level of the dimension Supplier and the values for Nation can be retrieved from the link data. Since the required XML-transfer operator $\tau_{Nation[ANY]/\ Nlink/\ Population}$ is already present at the bottom of the physical plan, the temporary table it generates can be directly used by the decoration operator.

Converting Logical Federation Generalized Projection and Selection to Physical Operators

The physical federation generalized projection and selection operators need to join the fact table with temporary tables to roll up the cube to, or evaluate the predicate on higher levels (that is, the levels whose values do not exist in the temporary fact table). For example, in the process of converting a logical federation generalized projection operator, new dimension-transfer operators are created as child operators to load the dimension values for the non-bottom levels in the logical federation projection's parameters, if the required temporary values do not exist in the temporary component.

The top federation generalized projection operator in Figure 10(a) is converted to the operator at the top of the corresponding physical plan in Figure 10(b). Because the lower federation generalized projection operator in the logical plan has already rolled up the dimension Parts to the level Brand, there is no dimension-transfer operators below the physical federation generalized projection.

Replacing Federation Generalized Projection and Federation with Cube Operators

A logical federation selection can be replaced by a cube selection if the federation selection operator does not reference level expressions (that is, selection can be performed directly in the OLAP component when no external XML data is required). A logical federation selection can also be replaced if the predicate is rewritten at execution time to reference only dimension values. Using cube operators can reduce the amount of data being transferred between the OLAP and the temporary components. Similarly, a logical federation generalized projection can be replaced by a cube generalized projection when no level expressions are referenced.

For example, the logical federation selection and generalized projection operators in Figure 10(a) are replaced by the cube selection and generalized projection operators in Figure 10(b), respectively. Note that, in the physical plan, the roll-up expression Brand(Part) in the parameters of the logical federation generalized projection operator is simplified to Brand, since the OLAP component, unlike the temporary component, can handle the roll-up operation directly (see the following).

Generating an Inlining Operator

An inlining operator is needed to rewrite a predicate of a federation selection to reference only dimension levels and constants at execution time. Additionally, an XML-transfer operator is also required to extract the XML data in order for the inlining operator to rewrite the predicate.

For example, the federation selection operator in Figure 10(a) is first replaced by the cube selection operator in Figure 10(b). Then, the inlining operator is generated below to instantiate the inlining process. The bottom XML-transfer operator loads the dimension values for the starting level and the decoration XML data into the table $R_{Nation[ANY]/ Nlink/ Population}$, which later is used by the decoration operator above to build the decoration dimension. At execution time, the inlining operator will first rewrite the marked predicate. Then, the cube selection can be executed in the OLAP component.

Generation of Fact-Transfer Operator

In a physical query tree, the fact-transfer operator is used to separate the operations in the OLAP component and the temporary component. Facts are copied to the temporary component after the OLAP cube is sliced or aggregated, which enables further operations (e.g., the decoration) to be performed in the temporary component. When no decoration operators exist in the plan, it means the cube data does not need to federate with external data and the plan can be executed entirely in the OLAP component. The fact-transfer operator in this case is used to generate the final query result in the temporary database. Note that the federation selection operators with predicates referencing measures cannot be executed in the OLAP component by the current query engine (due to a limitation in MS SQL server, see below); therefore, they cannot be put below the fact-transfer operator.

For example, a fact-transfer operator is generated below the decoration operator in the plan in Figure 10(b) to separate the operations in the temporary component from the lower two cube operations. At execution time, the fact-transfer operator transfers the result of the lower operators to the temporary component, thereby enabling the higher operations.

Query Evaluation

This section describes how the query result is produced, given a physical plan. We first present the general evaluation process of a physical plan and then go into details about how each physical operator executes.

The Evaluation Algorithm

The general evaluation algorithm is shown in pseudo-code in Figure 11. The physical plan in Figure 10 shows an execution plan tree, where a leaf is an extended federation. In lines 2 and 3, the algorithm just returns when it reaches the bottom of a plan tree, which is always a federation, as no operations need to be performed on these. When the algorithm returns from the bottom, the real execution starts. The algorithm follows the idea of the conventional pull-based iterator model (Graefe, 1993), where the lower part of the plan tree provides data for higher operators. However, data is not directly transferred between operators through pipes. Instead, temporary tables are used. A set, *TempTable*, is used to record the temporary tables. Sibling operators in the plan tree can be evaluated in parallel; therefore, a multi-threaded technique is adopted in implementation, as line 5 shows. After all the sub-threads are finished, the real execution of *Op* begins. Here, component queries are constructed and evaluated in the appropriate component. Data can also be transferred into temporary tables. After the execution, the output is inserted into *TempTable*. For some operators (e.g., a dimension-transfer), the result might be a real table. However, for a federation selection or generalized projection, as Examples 6 and 7 have shown, it might be a query string, which then can be nested into the query string of a higher operator and evaluated later in batch mode. Moreover, a cube selection only yields the WHERE clause of an OLAP component query. Therefore, an item in *TempTable* might represent a real table name, a complete query string, or even a part of query (see the following).

We now describe the details of operator evaluation (that is, line 8 in the evaluation algorithm) for each operator, using the existing techniques provided by MS SQL Server and XML. Later, an example will be shown to demonstrate the evaluation of the operators in the context of a complete physical plan.

XML-Transfer

The current implementation of the XML-transfer operator only supports the links where a dimension value is only paired with one XML node (e.g., *Nlink*). Specifically, the operator uses a stored procedure to execute an INSERT INTO statement, which is extended with an OPENXML function mapping an XML document into a table through a schema definition. For example, for the XML-transfer operator $\tau_{Nation[ANY]/\ Nlink/\ Population}$, the query is as follows:

INSERT INTO	tmp_population
SELECT	DISTINCT *
FROM	OPENXML(@*hdoc*,'/Nations/Nation',2)
	WITH(NationName varchar(25), Population float)
WHERE	NationName in ('DK', 'CN', 'UK')

where tmp_population is the temporary table containing the nation codes and population data, @*hdoc* is the handle of the document, '/Nations/Nation' specifies all the <Nation> nodes in the XML document, and in the WITH clause the sub-nodes of the <Nation> nodes are specified as the columns of the temporary table, where NationName and Population contain the linked nation codes and the population data for decoration, respectively. The WHERE clause filters out the <Nation> nodes that are not included in *Nlink* , ensuring that only the interesting data is copied.

Inlining

An inlining operator first uses the ADO Recordset objects to load the decoration values from the temporary tables into main memory, rewrites the predicates, and then replaces all the occurrences of the rewritten predicates with the new predicates. The pseudo-code in Figure 12 shows the transforming function for rewriting predicates. Here, the data type of the predicates is String as in Java. A new predicate can be constructed by connecting several sub-predicates with the operator "+," which

Figure 11. The evaluation algorithm

```
void OpEvaluation(Operator Op)
1.      {
2.         if Op is a ℱ_ext
3.         return;
4.         get all the child operators Op_1, ..., Op_n below Op;
5.         perform each OpEvaluation(Op_i) in separate threads;
6.         wait until all threads return;
7.         find the required tables in TempTable;
8.         execute Op;
9.         add an entry for the output in TempTable;
10.        return;
11.     }
```

is similar to the binary string operator in Java. The input θ_i is a parameter of the inlining operator $\iota_{[\theta_1, ..., \theta_n]}$. *bo* and the predicate operator *po* are as defined in Definition 9. The possible forms of θ_i are listed in Definition 9. Each form is handled with the appropriate procedure, which generally is performed in two steps: first, the required data for θ_i is retrieved, and then the new predicate, θ'_p, is constructed for the respective form.

For form 1 of θ_p, where a constant is involved, the predicate can be partially evaluated on the temporary table, meaning that the decoration XML data are compared with the constant, and only the dimension values paired with the satisfying decoration values are retrieved. Similarly, a predicate in form 4 first can be partially evaluated on a Cartesian product of the two temporary tables $R_{\tau_{l_z}[SEM]/link_1/xp_1}$ and $R_{\tau_{l_w}[SEM]/link_2/xp_2}$ before the new predicate is constructed. For forms 2 and 3, the predicates cannot be evaluated, and all the dimension values of l_z and the decoration values must be retrieved to construct the new predicate with the names of the involved level and measure, respectively. For the rest of the forms, the rewritePredicate function is called recursively to first construct the component predicates of θ_i.

Cube Selection and Cube Generalized Projection

The cube operators use the OLAP component queries to select and aggregate the cube, which, in the current implementation, is the abbreviated SQL SELECT statement supported by MS Analysis Services. Although as two different operators, the cube selection and generalized projection operators only construct one entire OLAP query. That is, the selection operator generates the WHERE clause with the parameter as the argument predicate, whereas the projection operator forms the other clauses (e.g., the SELECT and GROUP BY clauses) with the specified levels and aggregate functions as arguments. Generally, the operators in the form $\Pi_{Cube[\mathcal{L}]}$ $_{< F(M) >} (\sigma_{Cube[\theta]}(\mathcal{F}_{ext}))$ construct the following query, where N is the name of the cube C in $\mathcal{F}_{ext} = (C, Links, X, T)$.

SELECT	$F(M), \mathcal{L}$
FROM	N
WHERE	θ
GROUP BY	$\mathcal{L}$

The same query is also used for the operators in the form $\sigma_{Cube[\theta]}(\Pi_{Cube[\mathcal{L}] < F(M) >}(\mathcal{F}_{ext}))$. Note that the HAVING clause is not supported, due to a limitation in Analysis Services. Therefore, the predicate θ can only reference base measures. The selection on aggregated measures is performed in the temporary component by a federation selection (see the following), which is not a noticeably expensive alternative because the fact tuples copied into the temporary component already are aggregated and reduced by the OLAP query.

If no cube selection operator exists in the plan, the WHERE clause no longer is required, otherwise, if several selection operators exist, the predicates then are combined into one predicate. If no cube generalized projection operators exist in the plan, the SELECT clause will select everything, which is a "*" argument. However, only one cube generalized projecton operator can exist in a query plan because, during plan optimization, the equivalent plans are pruned such that the plans having multiple cube generalized projection operators are removed, and only the plan with the top cube generalized projection operator is retained. The reason is that the top projection always aggregates the cube to the same levels, no matter how many cube generalized projection yielding low-level aggregates exist below, and intermediate cubes should try to be avoided to save the execution time.

Fact-Transfer

The fact-transfer operator copies the fact data into the temporary component using a pass-through query, which is a SQL SELECT INTO statement extended by the MS TransactSQL function OPENQUERY (Microsoft, 2002a), where one of the parameters is the query constructed for the cube operators described above. Generally, the fact-transfer over the cube operators is in the form $\phi(\Pi_{Cube[\mathcal{L}] < F(M) >} (\sigma_{Cube[\theta]}(\mathcal{F}_{ext})))$, which leads to the following query, where OLAP_SVR is the OLAP component. Note that the outer SELECT statement contains a GROUP BY clause, and the SELECT clause repeats the arguments of the inner SELECT clause, $F(M)$ and $\mathcal{L}$.

Figure 12. Transforming the predicates

```
1.    String rewritePredicate(String θi) {
2.        declare the new predicate θ'i as an empty string;
3.        switch(the form of θi)
4.        {
5.        case 1:
6.            retrieve ez's in all the pairs (ez, exp) from the temporary table such
              that "exp po K" evaluates to true;
7.            construct θi according to Definition 9;
8.            break;
9.        case 2:
10.       case 3:
11.           retrieve all the (ez, exp) pairs in the temporary table;
12.           construct θ'i for the respective form;
13.           break;
14.       case 4:
15.           retrieve ezi and ewi in all the tuples (ezi, exp1i, ewi, exp2i) such that
```

$$(e_{zi}, e_{xp_1i}, e_{wi}, e_{xp_2i}) \in R_{\tau l_z[SEM]/\ link_1\ /\ xp_1} \times R_{\tau l_w[SEM]/\ link_2\ /\ xp_2}\ and\ ``e_{xp_1i}\ po\ e_{xp_2i}"$$

```
              evaluates to true;
16.           construct θ'i according to Definition 9;
17.           break;
18.       case 5:
19.           θ'i=rewritePredicate("lz[SEM]/ link/ xp = K1")+" OR "+...+" OR "+
              rewritePredicate("lz[SEM]/ link/ xp = Kn");
20.           break;
21.       case 6:
22.           θ'i="NOT"+rewritePredicate(θi1);
23.           break;
24.       case 7:
25.           θ'i=rewritePredicate(θi1)+" po "+rewritePredicate(θi2);
26.       }
27.       return θ'i;}
```

```
SELECT        F(M), L
INTO          tmp_facts
FROM          OPENQUERY(OLAP_SVR,
                        SELECT     F(M), L
                        FROM       N
                        WHERE      θ
                        GROUP BY   L
GROUP BY      L
```

As stated by the article (Microsoft, 2002a), because there is a limitation in Analysis Services that causes GROUP BY and DISTINCT queries to produce multiple rows that satisfy the grouping and/or distinct functions (instead of just one), it is necessary to reduce the tuples by coalescing the returned tuples from the OPENQUERY function in the temporary component. For example, in the query below, the result set of the inner OLAP query is a union of the results of the OLAP queries using the predicates, "Nation='DK'" and "Nation='UK'" in the WHERE clause individually; therefore, the outer query must perform an aggregation in the temporary component to coalesce the rows returned for the same grouping values (that is, Customer).

```
SELECT        SUM(Quantity), Customer
INTO          tmp_facts
FROM          OPENQUERY(OLAP_SVR,
                        SELECT     SUM(Quantity), Customer
                        FROM       TC
                        WHERE      Nation='DK' OR Nation='UK'
                        GROUP  BY  Customer)
GROUP BY      Customer
```

Therefore, the general form of the constructed OLAP query guarantees the correctness of the aggregation. However, the temporary aggregation can be avoided if the grouping values for the returned sub-sets are disjoint. For example, the predicates in the following query construct two disjoint sets of values for the grouping attributes Customer and Nation; therefore, the union of the result sets can be inserted into the temporary fact table directly.

```
SELECT        *
INTO          tmp_facts
FROM          OPENQUERY(OLAP_SVR,
                        SELECT        SUM(Quantity), Customer, Nation
                        FROM          TC
                        WHERE         Nation='DK' OR Nation='UK'
                        GROUP BY      Customer, Nation)
```

For a query plan without both cube selection and generalized projection operators, the following query ,which does not perform any aggregations in the OLAP component, is used because no OLAP data is required to be selected and aggregated.

```
SELECT        *
INTO          tmp_facts
FROM          OPENQUERY(OLAP_SVR,
                        SELECT        *
                        FROM          N)
```

The SELECT INTO statement is executed in the temporary component, whereas the OPENQUERY function sends the SQL command to the OLAP component and returns the requested data to the outer SELECT INTO query, which then inserts the fact data into a temporary fact table. Therefore, cube selection and generalized projection operators are not evaluated against the OLAP cube until the fact-transfer operator is reached.

Dimension-Transfer

The dimension-transfer operator is basically a special fact-transfer operator that copies OLAP data into the temporary component. However, unlike the regular fact-transfer, it only copies dimension values rather than the fact data. The query nested into the OPENQUERY function is a SELECT statement that retrieves the dimension values for the two levels l_{ix} and l_{iy} specified by $\omega_{[l_{ix}, l_{iy}]}$. The entire SELECT INTO query is in the general form below, where tmp_dim$_i$ is the temporary table's name. Note that the outer SELECT clause performs an additional DISTINCT operation on the data retrieved by the OPENQUERY function. This is due to the same reason as for the additional GROUP BY clause in the query constructed by the fact-transfer operator. The extra DISTINCT operation ensures the correctness of the result.

SELECT	DISTINCT *
INTO	tmp_dim$_i$
FROM	OPENQUERY(OLAP_SVR,
	SELECT DISTINCT l_{ix}, l_{iy}
	FROM N)

Decoration

A decoration operator $\delta_{l_z[SEM]/\ link/\ xp}$ uses a SQL SELECT INTO statement to create a decoration dimension table defined as $R_{D_{n+1}}$ in Definition 6, containing the data for the bottom level $\bot_z$ and the middle level l_{xp} of the decoration dimension. If the starting level l_z of the level expression $l_z[SEM]/\ link/\ xp$ is the bottom level $\bot_z$, then the values of the two levels l_{xp} and $\bot_z$ are the data yielded by the level expression through an XML-transfer operator, $\tau_{l_z[SEM]/\ link/\ xp}$, which loads the data for l_z and l_{xp} into $R_{\tau_{l_z[SEM]/\ link/\ xp}}$ as defined in Definition 5. In this case, the table $R_{\tau_{l_z[SEM]/\ link/\ xp}}$ is used as the decoration dimension table. If $l_z \neq \bot_z$, the table created by the dimension-transfer operator $\omega_{[\bot_z,\ l_z]}$ must be used to join with $R_{\tau_{l_z[SEM]/\ link/\ xp}}$ to yield the right dimension table. Therefore, the following SQL query is used, where tmp_dim$_{xp}$ is the decoration dimension table.

SELECT	$\bot_z, l_{xp}$
INTO	tmp_dim$_{xp}$
FROM	$R_{\tau_{l_z[SEM]/\ link/\ xp}}$ AS R_1, $R_{\omega_{[\bot_z,\ l_z]}}$ AS R_2
WHERE	$R_1.l_z = R_2.l_z$

Federation Selection

As shown in Example 6, a federation selection operator uses a SQL SELECT query to filter the facts in the temporary fact table. Since a federation selection operator does not change the fact types, the SELECT clause selects all the columns using the "*" expression. A new temporary table is specified by the INTO clause with the table name. When data in dimension tables (including the decoration dimension tables) are involved in the select condition as in Example 6, the tables containing the requested data must be joined with the temporary fact table, yielding the WHERE clause containing the join predicates and the selection predicate θ. The SQL query for a federation selection σ_θ is shown next, where R_1 is the temporary fact table and $l_{R_1 R_i}$ is the common attribute of the tables R_1 and R_i.

SELECT R_1

INTO   tmp_fact

FROM $R_1, ..., R_n$

WHERE $R_1.l_{R_1 R_2} = R_2.l_{R_1 R_2}$ AND ... AND $R_1.l_{R_1 R_n} = R_n.l_{R_1 R_n}$ AND θ

If the predicate θ references a regular dimension level l_{iy} higher than the level l_{ix} from the same dimension in the temporary fact table, a temporary dimension table, $R_i(l_{ix}, l_{iy})$, created by the dimension-transfer operator, $\omega_{[l_{ix}, l_{iy}]}$, is required. In this case, $l_{R_1 R_i}$ is the lower level l_{ix}, which exists in both R_1 and R_i. If $R_j(\perp_z, l_{xp})$ is a decoration dimension table created by the decoration operator $\delta_{l_z[SEM]/\ link/\ xp}$, and if the level expression $l_z[SEM]/\ link/\ xp$ is referenced by θ, then $l^z_{R_1 R_j}$ is $\perp_z$, which also exists in the fact table and represents the bottom level of the decoration dimension. If no roll-up or level expressions are involved in the selection, then $n = 1$, meaning that the selection can be performed directly on the temporary fact table.

Federation Generalized Projection

A federation generalized projection operator also is implemented using an SQL SELECT statement. Similar to the query constructed for a federation selection, the FROM clause also contains the tables having the requested data by the generalized projection operator. The only difference is that the WHERE clause is not needed, but the arguments of the SELECT clause are, instead, the levels and aggregate functions specified by the parameters. The general form of the query for the operator, $\Pi_{Fed[\mathcal{L}]<F(M)>}$, is shown next, where $F(M)$ represents the aggregate functions on the specified measures and $\mathcal{L}$ are the levels to which the cube is aggregated. The participating tables, R_1, ..., R_n, are the same as defined for the federation selection operator.

SELECT $F(M)$, $\mathcal{L}$

INTO   tmp_fact

FROM $R_1, ..., R_n$

WHERE $R_1.l_{R_1 R_2} = R_2.l_{R_1 R_2}$ AND ... AND $R_1.l_{R_1 R_n} = R_n.l_{R_1 R_n}$

GROUP BY $\mathcal{L}$

To reduce the temporary intermediate tables, we try to evaluate the SQL queries in batch-mode or to reconstruct them into one, although each SQL query constructed by a federation selection or a generalized projection operator in a plan is itself executable against the existing temporary tables. For example, when a query constructed for a federation selection is returned to the higher federation generalized projection operator, the WHERE clause is taken out and combined with the WHERE clause of the query for the generalized projection, and all the tables required by the two operators are included in the FROM clause. The general form for such two operators is $\Pi_{Fed[\mathcal{L}]<F(M)>}(\sigma_{Fed[\theta]}(\mathcal{F}_{ext}))$, yielding:

```
SELECT      F(M), L
INTO        tmp_fact
FROM        R_1, ..., R_n
WHERE       R_1.l_{R_1 R_2} = R_2.l_{R_1 R_2} AND ... AND R_1.l_{R_1 R_n} = R_n.l_{R_1 R_n} AND θ
GROUP BY    L
```

If there is a federation selection operator, $\sigma_{Fed[\theta_M]}$, referencing aggregated measures above the federation generalized projection operator, the HAVING clause, HAVING θ_M, must be added to the above query.

Example 10

In this example, we show how the physical plan in Figure 10 is evaluated step by step. Figure 13 shows (bottom-up) the operators in the order of execution and the items in the set *TempTable* during the evaluation. Before the evaluation starts, *TempTable* is empty, represented by the empty set at the bottom of the plan. The evaluation algorithm goes recursively down to the bottom of the plan tree and then evaluates the operators bottom-up. The first evaluated operator is the XML-transfer operator, $\tau_{N[ANY]/NI/P}$, which executes the INSERT INTO statement shown as follows.

```
INSERT INTO tmp_population
SELECT      DISTINCT  *
FROM        OPENXML(@hdoc, '/Nations/Nation',2)
            WITH( NationName   varchar(25), Population   float)
WHERE       NationName in ('DK', 'CN', 'UK')
```

Then, the set *TempTable* is updated with the first item $\mathcal{T}_{\tau_{N[ANY]/\,Nl/\,P}}$, which is a two-tuple $(R_\tau, \tau_{N[ANY]/\,Nl/\,P})$, where the first element R_τ (shown in Table 5) is the temporary table and the second is its creator, the operator, $\tau_{N[ANY]/\,Nl/\,P}$. In practice, a tuple, $\mathcal{T}$, is implemented as a Java class containing (1) a string variable representing a table name or a query string, (2) an Operator object pointing at the creator, and 3) an integer specifying the type of the value assigned to the string (e.g., a table name or a query string). The table, R_τ, consists of the nation codes and their corresponding population data, which are used to re-write the predicate, $N[ANY]/\,Nl/\,P < 30$. After the inlining operator $\iota_{N[ANY]/\,Nl/\,P\,<\,30}$, the selection predicate is re-written and the new predicate, Nation='DK' OR Nation='UK' , replaces the occurrence of the old predicate in the above cube selection operator. The next operator, $\sigma_{Cube\,[Nation\,=\,'DK'\,OR\,Nation\,=\,'UK']}$ (in short, σ_{Cube}), adds a new tuple $\mathcal{T}_{\sigma_{Cube}}$ =("WHERE Nation='DK' OR Nation='UK' ", σ_{Cube} to *TempTable*, where the first element is the sub-clause of the OLAP query yielded by the cube selection operator. The federation generalized projection operator above $\Pi_{Cube[B,\,N]\,<SUM\,(Q)>}$ (in short, Π_{Cube}) constructs a complete OLAP component query, based on $\mathcal{T}_{\sigma_{Cube}}$ and adds $\mathcal{T}_{\Pi_{Cube}} = (Q_1, \Pi_{Cube})$ into *TempTable*, where Q_1 is the following query:

```
SELECT      SUM(Quantity), Brand, Nation
FROM        TC
WHERE       Nation='DK' OR Nation='UK'
GROUP BY    Brand, Nation
```

which is then wrapped by the above fact-transfer operator in the OPENQUERY function to form a SELECT INTO statement executed by MS SQL Server as a whole. The query is:

```
SELECT      *
INTO        tmp_facts
FROM        OPENQUERY( OLAP_SVR,
                    SELECT      SUM(Quantity), Brand, Nation
                    FROM        TC
                    WHERE       Nation='DK' OR Nation='UK'
                    GROUP BY    Brand, Nation)
```

Figure 13. Plan evaluation example

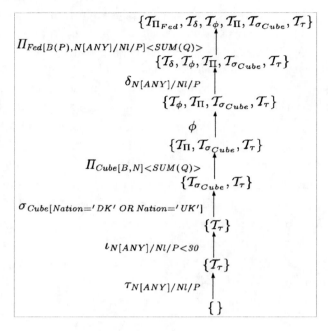

Table 6. The temporary fact table, F

Quantity	Nation	Brand
17	DK	B1
36	DK	B4
28	DK	B1
26	UK	B4

Table 7. The temporary fact table, F'

Quantity	Population	Brand
45	5.3	B1
36	5.3	B4
26	19.1	B4

which only contains one GROUP BY clause because the returned result is correct without an additional aggregation in the temporary component. The data returned by the OLAP query is inserted into the temporary fact table, F, shown in Table 6. Therefore, the new item added into *TempTable* is $T_\varphi = (F, \phi)$, where F is the name of the temporary fact table. The following operator, $\delta_{N[ANY]/NI/P}$ (in short, δ), uses R_τ created by the XML-transfer operator directly as the decoration dimension table without any additional operations in the temporary component because R_τ contains data for the dimension level Nation, which is now the bottom level after the cube operators. The new item, T_δ, yielded by δ in *TempTable* is (R_τ, δ), where the table R_τ is used as the decoration dimension table. The top federation generalized operator rolls up the decoration dimension to Population, which, in practice, is a join between F and R_τ. The sum of the quantity also is calculated for each group specified by the grouping attributes, Brand and Population. The following query is used to perform the above operations:

SELECT	SUM(Quantity), Brand, Population
INTO	F'
FROM	F, R_τ
WHERE	F.Nation = R_τ.Nation
GROUP BY	Brand, Population

The last tuple added into *TempTable* is $T_{\Pi_{Fed}} = (F', \Pi_{Fed})$, where F' is the new temporary fact table. The evaluation of the plan is now finished and F' is the result, shown in Table 7.

Query Optimization

After introducing the process of producing the query result of a plan, we now describe a more advanced topic: how the query result can be produced faster. In this section, we first present the cost-based query optimizer, including the architecture and the overall plan optimization process. Since the optimizer selects the best plan with respect to the estimated cheapest cost, we then further describe the cost estimation algorithm and strategies of the physical operators and plans.

Figure 14. Inner structure of the query optimizer

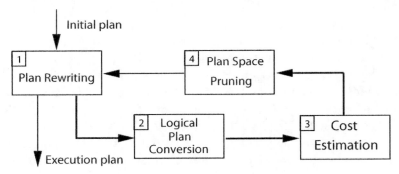

Architecture of the Optimizer

The optimizer is based on the Volcano optimizer (Graefe & McKenna, 1993), where queries are optimized in two stages. Figure 14 shows the structure of the optimizer. The first phase, plan re-writing, is similar to the first stage of Volcano, where, for the input plan, the entire plan space, consisting of the equivalent logical plans producing the same output, is generated. During the second stage of Volcano, the search for the best physical plan is performed, where various implementation rules are used to replace operators by algorithms and the costs of diverse sub-plans are estimated. However, in our optimizer, Phases 2, 3, and 4, all together, although similar to the second stage of Volcano, do not select the final physical plan, but, instead, perform pruning on the plan space of the enumerated logical plans in Phase 1, which then are used to rewrite plans again by Phase 1 in the next iteration. Conversion into physical plans in Phase 2 is straightforward, as every logical operator can be deterministically implemented by one algorithm. After Phase 2, each logical plan is integrated with real execution tasks. Therefore, the evaluation cost can be explicitly estimated. This is achieved in Phase 3 in order to perform cost-based plan space pruning in Phase 4. As the logical plans are considerably smaller than physical plans, plan enumeration is made much faster by enumerating logical rather than physical plans, boosting the overall optimization speed.

The optimization for the initial plan is performed operator by operator through a bottom-up fashion. Therefore, the process iterates through the four phases several times. An operator constructs new trees on top of the result plans from the previous iteration, generates the logical plan space, and proceeds until the pruning phase is finished. The resulting plans are then passed on to the operator mentioned before in the original plan, which starts another iteration. Therefore, the process of iterations goes on until it reaches the top. When the pruned plan space for the root operator is generated, the physical plan with the least cost is selected as the execution plan.

Figure 15. Estimating the cost of a physical plan

```
double generateCost(Operator Op)
1.      {
2.          let subTreeCost = 0 be the initial
            maximal cost of the sub-plan trees;
3.          if Op is a F_ext
4.          return 0;
5.          get all the child operators Op_1, ..., Op_n below Op;
6.          for each operator Op_i
7.          tempCost=generateCost(Op_i);
8.          if tempCost > subTreeCost
9.          subTreeCost = tempCost
10.         if an operator Op' same as Op has not
            been estimated before
11.         return generateOpCost(Op) + subTreeCost;
12.         else
13.         return the cost of Op' + subTreeCost;
14.     }
```

Cost Estimation of a Plan

Basically, a physical plan for a federation query and the evaluation algorithm suggest how the cost can be estimated. That is, the cost of a query plan is the cost of the root operator plus the maximal evaluation time of the sub-plans. However, to give an intuitive overview, we divide the total cost to the time for inlining, OLAP query evaluation and data transfer, and producing the final result in the temporary component. For a query plan on which the inlining technique is applied, references to level expressions can be inlined into the selection predicates and, therefore, can be evaluated in the OLAP component. Therefore, the first period of the evaluation time is spent on the inlining process (that is, XML query evaluation), XML data transfer, and predicate re-writing. The second period of the total time starts from query evaluation in the OLAP component until the data is transferred into the temporary component. However, for the queries not inlining all the level expressions in the selection predicates, it is the time for the slowest retrieval of data from the OLAP and XML components. Finally, the sum of the previous two periods plus the time for producing the final result in the temporary component gives the total time.

The cost estimation algorithm, generateCost, in Figure 15 estimates the cost of the plan rooted at the operator, Op, whereas the function, generateOpCost, estimates the cost of a single operator. Line 2 defines a new variable subTreeCost to be the cost of the sub-plan below Op or the maximal cost of the sub-plans if Op has multiple child operators. As in line 2 in Figure 11, when a federation is reached, no operations are performed; thus, the returned cost is zero. Lines 6 and 7 estimate the cost of the sub-plans one by one. According to lines 5 and 6 in the evaluation algorithm, the sub-plans rooted at the child operators of Op are evaluated in parallel, and Op does not execute until all the evaluation threads finish. Therefore, subTreeCost is assigned the maximal cost of the sub-plans. Lines 10 to 13 calculate and return the cost of the whole plan, CP_{Op}, which is $C_{Op} + MAX(CP_{Op_1}, ..., CP_{Op_1})$, where C_{Op} is the cost of the operator, Op, and CP_{Op_1} is the cost of the plan rooted at the operator Op_i. Note that an optimization method is used at lines 10 and 11, such that the algorithm does not estimate the cost of an operator, if the cost of an identical operator was estimated before. From the descriptions of the optimizer structure above, we know that before the plan pruning phase, the enumerated plans from the first phase may contain the same operators. For example, the XML-transfer operator, $\tau_{N[ANY]/NI/P}$, in the physical plan in Figure 10, is always required by any physical plan to load the XML decoration values. Therefore, when the physical plans for all the enumerated logical plans are cost-estimated, the cost of the operators like $\tau_{N[ANY]/NI/P}$, which exist in many plans and have exactly the same parameters, can be estimated only once for the first time of the operator's appearance. The function, generateOpCost, estimates the cost of the input operator and registers it in a hash table; therefore, later, when an identical operator is reached, an entry for the operator can be found in the hash table and its cost can be used directly.

For example, the cost estimation process for the physical plan in Figure 10 starts from the XML-transfer operator, after the algorithm first goes down to the bottom. Since all the operators are at the same branch, the costs of the operators are accumulated as the cost estimation algorithm moves up to the top. Therefore, the cost of the plan is the sum of the costs of all of the operators.

Cost Estimation of Operators

In the current implementation, the cost of a physical operator is approximately the execution time of its evaluation method introduced earlier. The costs are rough estimations, but effective enough to support the choice of relatively cheapest plan.

The cost of an XML-transfer operator is approximated as the product of the XML-to-relational data transfer rate and the size of the data to be loaded into the temporary component. Similarly, the cost of a dimension-transfer operator is the product of the size of the dimension values and the OLAP-to-relational data transfer rate. For an inlining operator, the construction of the new predicate is performed in memory, which takes a relatively trivial amount of time compared to I/O operations. Therefore, the cost of an inlining operator is approximately the time for performing lines 6, 11, or 15 of the transforming function in Figure 12 for the respective forms of the input predicate (that is, the time for loading the required data from the temporary component into memory, which is the product of the size of the required data and the relational-to-memory transfer rate). The cost parameters (e.g., the transfer rates) are estimated through *probing queries* (Zhu & Larson, 1996) and stored as constants in meta data. Later, in a more advanced implementation, a dynamic statistics manager can be used to pose the inexpensive probing queries when the system load is low to determine the cost parameters.

The cube operators, as described earlier, do not perform any operations against the real data, except for constructing OLAP component queries, which is trivial in terms of execution time. The fact-transfer operator executes the constructed query; therefore, the fact-transfer operator's cost shall include the processing time for the OLAP query. However, experiments have shown that the cost is spent mostly on data transfer between the temporary and OLAP components for the fact-transfer operators using the pass-though queries. Therefore, the cost of the fact-transfer operator is estimated as the data transfer time in a similar way to the XML-transfer operators, except that the size of the fact data to be transferred must first be estimated through the cube selection and generalized projection operators in the plan. The size of the fact data to be transferred is approximately the product of (1) the size of the original cube, which is approximately the size of the fact table; (2) the selectivity ratio of the cube selection; and (3) the roll-up fraction of the cube generalized projection, which is estimated by dividing the number of the distinct tuples after the projection with the original number of facts (Shukla, Deshpande, Naughton, & Ramasamy, 1996). For the case where no cube operators exist in a physical plan, the cost of a fact-transfer operator is the size of the original fact table divided by the OLAP-to-relational data transfer rate. The federation selection and generalized projection operators are implemented through SQL queries. Therefore, the cost of these operators is estimated as the cost of the composing SQL operations through the methods described in Elmasri and Navathe (2000) and in Silberschatz, Korth, and Sudarshan (2002). In the following, we present the experimental results to show the performance of the federation query engine with the above technologies.

Performance Study

The experiments were performed on a machine with an Intel Pentium III 800Mhz CPU, 512MB of RAM, 30 GB of disk, and 4096MB of page file. The OS is Microsoft Windows 2000 server with SP4. The example cube used in the experiments is shown in Figure 1 . The cube is based on about 100MB of data, generated using the TPC-H benchmark. The following experiments observe the federation with respect to the effectiveness of the federation system. Thus, we compare the performance

Table 8. Query types and their attribute values

type	no_of_dim	dim1	dim2	dim1level	dim2level
1	1	Suppliers		Nation	
2	1	Suppliers		Supplier	
3	1	Parts		Brand	
4	1	Parts		Part	
5	2	Suppliers	Parts	Nation	Brand
6	2	Suppliers	Parts	Supplier	Brand
7	2	Suppliers	Parts	Nation	Part
8	2	Suppliers	Parts	Supplier	Part
9	2	Suppliers	Orders	Nation	Customer
10	2	Suppliers	Orders	Supplier	Customer
11	2	Suppliers	Orders	Nation	Order
12	2	Suppliers	Orders	Supplier	Order
13	2	Parts	Orders	Brand	Customer
14	2	Parts	Orders	Part	Customer
15	2	Parts	Orders	Brand	Order
16	2	Parts	Orders	Part	Order

when the external XML data is in (1) the XML component (federated), (2) in the local, relational temporary component (cached), and (3) physically integrated in the OLAP cube itself (integrated).

The performance of 16 different query types was measured. The query types all aggregate fact data, but vary in a) whether one or two dimensions are used in the query, b) which dimensions are used, and c) which levels in these dimensions are used. Each query type is formed with the attributes: *no_of_dim* for the number of dimensions mentioned in the SELECT clause with a maximum value of two, *dim1* and *dim2* for the dimension names, and *dim1level* and *dim2level* for the argument levels in the SELECT clause. The query types are enumerated and numbered according to the sizes of the participating dimensions. In the TC cube, the dimensions participating in the queries are Suppliers, Parts, and Orders, in ascending order by size. Thus, the query types represent expected complexity. Table 8 shows the different attributes of each query type. Two different XML documents were used: a large (11.4 MB) document about orders and their priorities and a small (2KB) document about nations and their populations, both generated from the TPC-H benchmark. For the small document, the WHERE clause has a 10% selectivity. For the large one, the WHERE clause has a 0.1% selectivity. The selectivity does not affect the relative

Figure 16. Comparisons of the queries involving the federated, cached or integrated 11.4MB XML data

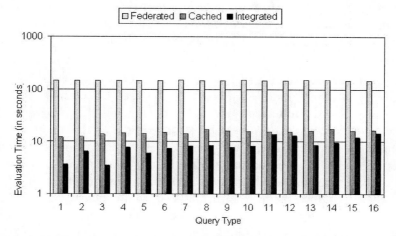

Figure 17. Comparisons of the queries involving the federated or integrated 2KB XML data

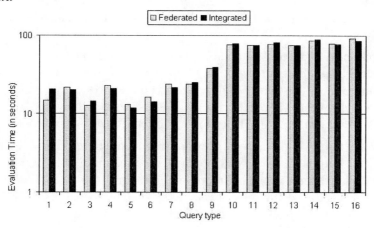

performance of the queries on the federated, cached, and integrated data originating from the same XML document, as long as the same selectivity is used.

The bar charts in Figures 16 and 17 show the performance of the queries using the federated, cached, or integrated XML data. The X axis represents the query type, and the Y axis represents the execution time in seconds. In most of the times, the execution time grows slightly when the type number is increased. The query types are organized in such a way that queries with larger type numbers tend to return more data than the smaller ones. For example, query type 1 rolls up the small-est dimension to the middle level and removes all the other dimensions, whereas query type 2 rolls up to a relatively lower level, which leads to a larger cube for the result values. The dimension Orders is much larger than the other two dimensions, therefore, queries leaving this dimension in the cube yield a lot more data than the others and take more execution time (e.g., query types 9 to 16 in Figure 17). Therefore, the charts show: the more the cube is reduced by aggregation, the better the query performs.

As Figure 16 indicates, the cost of querying the federation exceeds the cost of querying the physical integration by a factor of 10 to 20. The Cached bars stay in between, but much closer to the Integrated. The queries involving federated XML data are evaluated in three sequential tasks. First, load the XML data into the temporary component and rewrite the predicate. Second, perform the selection and aggregation in the OLAP component and then load the values into the temporary component. Third, generate the final result in the temporary component. The first task takes much more time (about 135 seconds) so that the other two are relatively trivial. Therefore, the queries on federations seem to take approximately the same evaluation time. The queries involving cached XML data skip the first part of the first task and rewrite the predicates using the cached XML data, thereby boosting the execution speed. The queries referencing the dimension values that are the integrated XML data skip the first step and, thereby, are evaluated mostly in the OLAP component.

The chart in Figure 17 demonstrates comparisons of queries on two other federated/ integrated levels. The chart suggests that querying the logical federation with a virtual dimension has almost the same performance as on the physically integrated cube, when the amount of the XML data is small (that is, a few kilobytes). Therefore, a federation involving such XML data can be queried just as if it were a local cube.

However, when the XML documents grow larger and larger, retrieving XML values is becoming the bottleneck for processing the federation queries. Experiments have shown that the performance can be improved by caching the external data; that is, the XML data can be stored in relational tables, thereby reducing the time for decorating the cube for the queries using these data. Based on the strategies proposed by Pedersen et al. (2004) in handling external XML data sources under different circumstances, the cached XML data can be used by queries and provide efficient access to external data for analysis, when, for example, the data is not out of date. In summary, the federation is good for a small amount of XML data. However, more efficient query performance can be gained by caching the external data locally, which will become the most common case in the applications of OLAP-XML federations. All in all, the logical approach can be a practical alternative for flexible online analysis involving external fast-changing data.

Conclusion and Future Work

Current OLAP systems have a common problem in physically integrating fast-changing data. As external data will most often be available in XML format, a logical integration of OLAP and XML data is desirable.

In this chapter, we present a robust OLAP-XML federation query engine with (1) a simplified logical query semantics, yielding more compact and concise logical query plans for OLAP-XML federation queries; (2) a set of physical operators to model the actual query execution tasks precisely and the logical-to-physical conversion principles; (3) the query evaluation, including the adopted relational, multi-dimension database and XML techniques, component query construction, and evaluation algorithms for physical operators and query plans; (4) query optimization, including the architecture of the optimizer and cost estimation of physical operators and plans; and (5) a performance study showing the effectiveness of our approach.

We believe we are the first to implement a robust query engine that analyzes, optimizes, and evaluates XML-extended OLAP queries. Also, we believe we are the first to introduce the query evaluation of these queries, including the detailed techniques and algorithms.

Future work will be focused on improving the query engine by developing more advanced query optimization techniques, cost estimation techniques, and query evaluation techniques (e.g., a more efficient search algorithm for query enumeration, more accurate cost formulas, and more efficient OLAP and XML data loading techniques). Furthermore, we will integrate the improved federation query engine into the business analysis products of a BI tool vendor, TARGIT.

Acknowledgment

This work was supported by the Danish Research Council for Technology and Production Sciences under grant no. 26-02-0277.

References

Bae, K. I., Kim, J. H., & Huh, S. Y. (2003). Federated process framework in a virtual enterprise using an object-oriented database and extensible markup language. *Journal of Database Management, 14*(1), 27-47.

Baeza-Yates, R. A., & Ribeiro-Neto, B. A. (1999). *Modern Information Retrieval.* ACM Press/Addison-Wesley.

Cabibbo, L., & Torlone, R. (2005). Integrating heterogeneous multidimensional databases. In *Proceedings of SSDBM*, Santa Barbara, CA (pp. 205-214).

Clark, J., & DeRose, S. (2005). *XML path language (XPath).* Retrieved July 02, 2006 from http://www.w3.org/TR/xpath

Chawathe, S., Garcia-Molina, H., Hammer, J., Ireland, K., Papakonstantinou Y., Ullman, J.D., et al. (1994). The TSIMMIS project: Integration of heterogeneous information sources. In *Proc. of IDS of Japan*, Tokyo, Japan (pp. 7-18).

Chen, H., Wu, Z., Wang, H., & Mao, Y. (2006). RDF/RDFS-based relational database integration. In *Proceedings of ICDE*, Los Alamitos, CA (pp. 94).

Elmasri, R., & Navathe, S. B. (2000). *Fundamentals of database systems.* Menlo Park, CA: Addison-Wesley.

Graefe, G. (1993). Query evaluation techniques for large databases. *ACM Computing Surveys, 25*(2), 73-170.

Graefe, G., & McKenna, W. J. (1993). The volcano optimizer generator: Extensibility and efficient search. In *Proceedings of ICDE*, Vienna, Austria (pp. 209-218).

Goldman, R., & Widom, J. (2000). WSQ/DSQ: A practical approach for combined querying of databases and the Web. In *Proceedings of SIGMOD*, Dallas, TX (pp. 285-296).

Gu, J., Pedersen, T. B., & Shoshani, A. (2000). OLAP++: Powerful and easy-to-use federations of OLAP and object databases. In *Proceedings of VLDB*, Cairo, Egypt (pp. 599-602).

Hellerstein, J. M., Stonebraker, M., & Caccia, R. (1999). Independent, open enterprise data integration. *IEEE Data Engineering Bulletin, 22*(1), 43-49.

IBM. (n.d.). *Information integrator.* Retrieved July 02, 2006 from http://www-306.ibm.com/software/data/integration.

Li, A., & An, A. (2005). Representing UML snowflake diagram from integrating XML data using XML schema. In *Proc. of DEEC*, Los Alamitos, CA (pp. 103-111).

Lahiri, T., Abiteboul, S., & Widom, J. (1999). Ozone-Integrating semistructured and structured data. In *Proceedings of DBPL*, Kinloch Rannoch, Scotland (pp. 297-323).

Lenz, H., & Shoshani, A. (1997). Summarizability in OLAP and statistical data bases. In *Proceedings of SSDBM*, Olympia, WA (pp. 39-48).

Mansuri, R. M., & Sarawagi, S. (2006). Integrating unstructured data into relational databases. In *Proceedings of ICDE*, Los Alamitos, CA (p. 29).

Microsoft. (2002a). *Passing queries from SQL server to a linked analysis server.* Retrieved July 2, 2006, from http://msdn.microsoft.com/library/default. asp?url=/library/en-us/olapdmpr/prsql_4vxv.asp

Microsoft. (2002b). *Performing bulk load of XML data.* Retrieved July 2, 2006, from http://msdn.microsoft.com/library/en-us/sqlxml3/htm/bulkload_7pv0.asp

Microsoft. (2005a). *COM: Component object model technologies.* Retrieved July 2, 2006, from http://www.microsoft.com/com

Microsoft. (2005b). *Supported SQL SELECT syntax.* Retrieved July 2, 2006, from http://msdn.microsoft.com/library/default.asp?url=/library/en-us/olapdmpr/ prsql_70e0.asp

Nicolle, C., Yétongnon, K., & Simon, J. C. (2003). XML integration and toolkit for B2B applications. *Journal of Database Management, 14*(4),33-58.

Oracle. (2005). *Gateways.* Retrieved July 2, 2006, from http://www.oracle.com/ gateways

Pedersen, D., Pedersen, J., & Pedersen, T. B. (2004). Integrating XML data in the TARGIT OLAP system. In *Proceedings of ICDE*, Boston (pp. 778-781).

Pedersen, D., Riis, K., & Pedersen, T. B. (2002). XML-extended OLAP querying. In *Proceedings of SSDBM*, Edinburgh, Scotland (pp. 195-206).

Pedersen, T. B., Shoshani, A., Gu, J., & Jensen, C. S. (2000). Extending OLAP querying to external object databases. In *Proc. of CIKM*, McLean, VA (pp. 405-413).

Pérez, J. M., Llavori, R. B., Aramburu, M. J., & Pedersen, T. B. (2005). A relevance-extended multi-dimensional model for a date warehouse contextualized with documents. In *Proceedings of DOLAP*, Bremen, Germany (pp. 19-28).

Reveliotis, P., & Carey, M. (2006). Your enterprise on Xquery and XML-based data and meta data integration. In *Proceedings of ICDEW*, Los Alamitos, CA (p. 80).

Shukla, A., Deshpande, P., Naughton, J. F., & Ramasamy, K. (1996). Storage estimation for multidimensional aggregates in the presence of hierarchies. In *Proceedings of VLDB*, Bombay, India (pp. 522-531).

Silberschatz, A., Korth, H. F., & Sudarshan, S. (2002). *Database system concepts.* New York : McGraw-Hill.

Transaction Processing Performance Council. (2004). *TPC-H.* Retrieved July 02, 2006, from http://www.tpc.org/tpch

Triantafillakis, A., Kanellis, P., & Martakos, D. (2004). Data warehouse interoperability for the extended enterprise. *Journal of Database Management, 15*(3), 73-84.

Yang, X., Lee, M., Ling, T. W, & Dobbie, G. (2005). A semantic approach to query rewriting for integrated XML data. In *Proceedings of ER*, Klagenfurt, Austria (pp. 417-432).

Yin, X., & Pedersen, T. B. (2004). Evaluating XML-extended OLAP queries based on a physical algebra. In *Proceedings of DOLAP*, Washington, DC (pp. 73-82).

Yin, X., & Pedersen, T. B. (2006). Evaluating XML-extended OLAP queries based on a physical algebra. *Journal of Database Management, 17*(2), 85-116.

Zaman, K. A., & Schneider, D. A. (2005). Modeling and query multidimensional data sources in Siebel analytics: A federated relational system. In *Proceedings of SIGMOD*, Baltimore (pp. 822-827).

Zhu, Q., & Larson, P. Å. (1996). Global query processing and optimization in the CORDS multidatabase system. In *Proceedings of PDCS*, Dijon, France (pp. 640-646).

Chapter VIII

Is There a Difference Between the Theoretical and Practical Complexity of UML?

Keng Siau, University of Nebraska – Lincoln, USA

John Erickson, University of Nebraska at Omaha, USA

Lih Yunn Lee, University of Nebraska – Lincoln, USA

Abstract

An on-going and major problem faced by information systems developers and business users alike is reaching a clear and consensual understanding of the system by both groups. This can be difficult because the businesses are (typically) process driven, while the systems are (increasingly) object-oriented. Enter modeling. Modeling is one way of presenting complex information in a way that enhances or eases understanding. But, even models can be extremely complex, and the underlying tools and modeling languages are not any less complex. This chapter investigates the possibility that modeling languages can be simplified by considering that not all of the "words" in the language are used all of the time. If theoretical (maximum) represents all the words in a modeling language, then this chapter suggests that there might exist a more use-based (we name it practical complexity) subset that represents an easier to learn and use subcomponent of the language.

Introduction

The move toward objected-oriented (OO) programming languages by application developers, in the past decade, has addressed a number of important issues, but, simultaneously, presented other problems to systems developers. One of the top issues confronting developers is that the systems resulting from the shift are quite naturally object-oriented systems. While that may not sound like a big problem at first glance, the fact that much of the systems analysis and design is still being conducted, at least partially, from a structured or more "traditional" perspective. At best, this leaves the (typically business) clients in a bit of a state of cognitive dissonance, and, to a certain extent, developers and programmers also, when it comes to understanding and explaining the systems.

The differences between the structured and OO methodologies are quite pronounced in some ways. As a response to these problems and issues, object-oriented systems analysis and design gradually emerged from object-oriented programming. Not that this made the situation entirely better, since there have been more than 50 OO methodologies proposed and used since 1990. However, over time, three of those modeling methodologies were combined and merged to form a new analysis and design technique called the unified modeling language (UML) (Booch et al., 1999). UML 1.5 consisted of nine distinct diagramming techniques designed to support object-oriented systems development, while UML 2.0 has increased the number of diagramming techniques to 13. The Object Management Group (OMG) adopted the UML language as a standard in 1997. Since that time, a growing number of researchers and practitioners have found UML to be extremely heavy and complex, both to learn and to use. In addition, and perhaps just as importantly, many of the UML constructs have been found to be ambiguous as to meaning and clarity. (Siau, Erickson, & Lee, 2002; Siau & Loo, 2002; Siau & Lee, 2005). Support for extensions to allow UML to be used in a variety of domains was also extremely lacking in versions 1.X, but this concern has begun to be addressed in version 2.0.

Siau and Cao (2001) used the complexity metrics developed by Rossi and Brinkkemper (1996) to analyze the nine diagramming techniques in UML and compared them to other modeling methods. Here, we offer the idea that the complexity metrics developed by Rossi and Brinkkemper (1996) and used to analyze UML (Siau & Cao, 2001) can be seen to do two tasks with regards to understanding and quantifying the complexity of UML. First, this approach identifies one level of complexity, what could be considered as the theoretical or maximum complexity of the UML modeling techniques. This level of complexity is composed using all of the constructs from the meta-model, as proposed by Rossi and Brinkkemper (1996). The term meta-model refers to a model of the model. For example, in the case of UML, it means a description of all possible constructs in each diagramming technique, in terms of three components: object types, relationship types, and property types.

Second, the reason this represents the theoretical upper limit of UML complexity is because the metrics are formulated and calculated based on the total number of objects, relationships, and property types in the modeling techniques. So, this defines theoretical complexity as the maximum upper limit of the complexity of the modeling technique, in this case, UML, by taking into account all its objects, relationships, and property types.

On the basis of theoretical complexity, other levels of complexity can be defined and analyzed. In particular, a second level of complexity—a more practical complexity—can be defined by realizing that not all of the meta-model constructs will be used simultaneously or in all projects, and further, that these various constructs represent varying degrees of importance to different systems and modelers. In such cases, equal weighting among the constructs cannot necessarily be assumed. For example, developers modeling an enterprise system could find at least some real time constructs in a state machine diagram less important than the flow of information as depicted in an activity diagram. Based on these premises, practical complexity must be a subset of theoretical complexity and can only be less than or equal to theoretical complexity.

The idea presented here is to use the complexity metrics to take into account the actual usage/practice of the modeling method. In other words, rather than using the metrics to simply calculate theoretical complexity, the practical complexity of a modeling methodology can be estimated based on how the real world practitioners—UML users—in this case, actually use the language. This should provide a more realistic estimation of the complexity users actually face in the field and, in addition, should complement the theoretical complexity estimate. As will be seen later, UML has been criticized for being overly complex, and the theoretical complexity metrics bear this out; however, if the UML that people learn and use does not make use of all constructs all of the time, then it is perhaps not out of line to conjecture that UML, while undoubtedly complex, is not as complex and difficult to learn and use as the metrical analyses, completed to date, indicate. If so, this research can be used to suggest better ways of learning and using UML.

Related and Relevant Research

Complexity can take many forms. For the purposes of this exposition, complexity can be examined via two separate, but closely related, perspectives. The first is cognitive complexity, which essentially means human perception and comprehension. In this context, cognitive complexity can be defined as the mental burden people face as they work with systems development constructs. A second definition useful here is generally called structural complexity, and is related to the physical properties of the

Figure 1. (Adapted from Briand, Wüst, & Lounis, 1999)

diagramming techniques found in modeling approaches (such as UML diagrams). To further enhance the ideas of cognitive and structural complexity, and to try to show a possible link between the two, the definition of structural complexity as proposed by Briand, Wüst, and Lounis (1999) is useful. Their definition illustrates that the physical (structural) complexity of diagrams can affect the cognitive complexity faced by the humans using the diagrams as aids to understanding and/or developing systems (see Figure 1).

Since cognitive complexity, as defined here, is difficult and even impossible to measure, structural complexity will be used as a surroagate explanatory vehicle for cognitive complexity. Rossi and Brinkkemper (1996) formulated seventeen distinct definitions relating to the structural complexity of each diagramming technique

Figure 2. A class diagram example

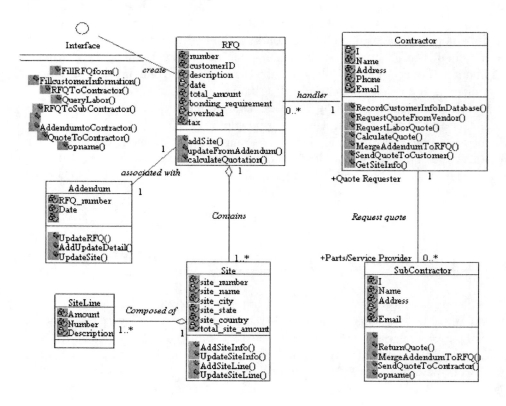

(modeling methodology). Using all available constructs laid out in the meta-model, these metrical constructs form a quantitative estimate of the total structural complexity of the diagramming technique. Recall that this has been previously identified as theoretical complexity. Structural complexity is a part of the structural characteristics of the information or modeling system, and for this research refers to the elements or constructs that comprise a given diagramming technique. These constructs would include meta-construct types such as objects (classes, and interfaces), properties (class names, attributes, methods, and roles), and relationships and associations (aggregations generalizations, specializations).

For example, the class diagram in Figure 2 above uses a number of constructs to present the information. There are six classes and one interface. The classes each have a name, attributes, and methods (that is, the RFQ class has eight attributes—number, customerID...tax; three methods—addSite(), updateFromAddendum(), and calculateQuotation()). In addition, the class has relationships with other classes (Contractor, Site, and Addendum) and with the (Customer) Interface.

A class diagram was chosen as a representative diagram, since class diagrams have a relatively long history of use in both objected-oriented programming and (database) systems development; however, the other nine UML diagrams can also be analyzed in this fashion. Note that even though this (real-world) diagram conveys a relative high volume of information to a person looking at the diagram, it does not use all of the constructs listed as possible (see Appendix A for a comprehensive list of UML constructs), which this research takes to represent theoretical complexity.

The list of UML constructs in Appendix A is taken from Siau and Cao's (2001) results, and was developed using Rossi and Brinkkemper's (1996) rubric for estimating the complexity of modeling methods. Rossi and Brinkkemper's approach to defining structural complexity was not developed for a specific methodology, but rather was created to allow complexity to be estimated regardless of the methodology. A benefit of this framework is that it permits different methodologies to be compared on an equal basis. The Rossi and Brinkkemper metrics serve as the operational definition (as well as a measure) of the structural complexity of diagrams, which can be equated with theoretical complexity.

Past MIS research has generally avoided the topic of complexity, probably because of the difficulties in defining as well as measuring it. For example, Kim, Hahn and Hahn (2000) studied diagrams, and cognitive diagrammatic reasoning enforced interpretation time limits on the subjects in their experiment (their design used time as a constraint). In this context, the time it takes for user cognition and comprehension to occur can be seen as (an admittedly imperfect) surrogate for complexity. Mcleod and Roeleveld (2002) referred to the relationship between interpretation time and complexity by contending that a person's "... ability to learn a concept quickly ... depends heavily on the complexity of the model." That implies that there is a relationship between interpretation time and complexity. Vessey and Conger

(1994) used time as a measure of interpretation, and Zendler, Pfeiffer, Eicks, and Lehner (2001) also used time necessary to structure an application as a construct. However, neither group considered complexity of interpretation directly as part of their research. While none of the above research projects were explicitly designed to study complexity, the complexity of the information conveyed in the various diagramming techniques was nevertheless a factor the researchers had considered.

In terms of why complexity is important in a modeling methodological setting, Rossi and Brinkkemper (1996) proposed that measurement of complexity is important because researchers have typically thought that complexity is closely related to how easy a specific method is to use and, also, how easy the method is to learn. These are definitely important to developers in the real world. Finally, Rossi and Brinkkemper also noted that the measured complexity of a given system does not solely translate into less complex methods being superior to more complex methodologies.

Siau and Cao (2001) compared UML's complexity with 36 distinct modeling techniques from 14 different methodologies as well as each of the 14 methodologies

Table 1. UML complexity analysis results for each diagram type (Adapted from Siau & Cao, 2001)

Technique/Diagram	$n(O_T)$	$n(R_T)$	$n(P_T)$	$\overline{P}_O(M_T)$	$\overline{P}_R(M_T)$	$\overline{R}_O(M_T)$	$\overline{C}(M_T)$	$C`(M_T)$
Class	7	18	18	1.71	1.22	2.57	0.1	**26.40**
Use Case	6	6	6	1	0.83	1	0.17	**10.39**
Activity	8	5	6	0.75	0.2	0.63	0.13	11.18
Sequence	6	1	5	0.67	6	0.17	0.13	7.87
Collaboration	4	1	7	1	8	0.25	0.14	8.12
Object	3	1	5	1.67	3	0.33	0.33	5.92
StateChart	10	4	11	1	0.5	0.40	0.09	15.39
Component	8	10	9	1	3.6	1.25	0.11	15.65
Deployment	5	7	5	1	1.14	1.40	0.2	9.95

Note:

$n(O_T)$: *count of object types per technique*

$n(R_T)$: *count of relationship types per technique*

$n(P_T)$: *count of property types per technique*

$\overline{P}_O(M_T)$: *average number of properties for a given object type*

$\overline{P}_R(M_T)$: *average number of properties per relationship type*

$\overline{R}_O(M_T)$: *number of relationship types that can be connected to a certain object type*

$\overline{C}(M_T)$: *average complexity for the entire technique*

$C`(M_T)$: *total conceptual complexity of the technique*

in aggregate. Siau and Cao's (2001) work includes the unsurprising finding that UML is much more complex (from 2 to 11 times more complex) in aggregate than any of the other 13 methods. This highlights one of the most often cited problems regarding UML—it can be extremely difficult to learn. Consider this from a cognitive perspective. The physical human short term memory is quite limited for a variety of reasons. Miller (1956) proposed that humans can hold in our short-term memories (short term working memory, STWM) a total of between five and nine items simultaneously. Miller (1956) spent a great deal of effort on establishing those cognitive limits, and his findings have become accepted norms on the subject. So, when viewed from the perspective of cognitive limitations, and since UML has been measured as 2-11 times more complex than other methodologies, it can appear even more difficult to master.

Siau and Cao's (2001) UML complexity analysis results for each diagram type are shown in Table 1.

Theoretical Foundation

Domain experts in systems development must depend on their own automaticized expert knowledge of systems analysis and development processes, in order to fully comprehend the functionalities that the users tell them they must have in a system. Users are usually neither domain experts nor technically proficient, and thus, in general, do not have a clear technical understanding of what information systems really do or how they do what they do. Therefore, the systems analysts, as domain experts, must be able to operate on two levels simultaneously as they interview users regarding system requirements. That is, the analysts must be able to listen to the (non-technical) requirements as presented by users, simultaneously develop an understanding of the underlying technical requirements of each proposed system element, and process that information into forms that the user can understand as the interview with the user progresses.

Ericsson and Kintsch (1995) have proposed an extension to STWM, which they call long term working memory (LTWM). According to Ericsson and Kintsch, LTWM is a part of long-term memory (LTM) that acts almost like (STWM). In this model, domain experts can very quickly recall information relevant to their area of expertise. The relevant information recall is a bit slower than STWM recall speeds, but appears to be significantly faster than LTM recall speeds. Of course, LTWM only works for experts in their domain areas, or possibly others, such as experienced users, who have high automaticity for certain tasks. LTWM would help to explain why it is important to interview users from different areas of organizations as part of the analysis process. Users, especially experienced users, will likely have highly valuable information regarding existing systems processes (that is, "how things are done here"), therefore, it is critical for the analysts to capture this information during the interview process.

LTWM is an important concept to consider when thinking about human cognitive limitations regarding information processing, and especially as related to task complexity. What the idea of LTWM conveys is that automaticity can greatly extend the short-term memory limitations of domain experts. LTWM addresses the problem of the information processing bottleneck, and suggests that as people learn even very complex materials, they can somewhat overcome some of their own cognitive limitations. This also implies that a person can more easily learn a very complex methodology, such as UML, by assimilating a small or relatively small part of the overall methodology by using LTWM. In the end, if one comprehension task is simpler relative to another comprehension task, it will consume fewer resources (processing time, long-term production activation and retrieval, and short-term memory), and thus take less overall time to process.

Drawing once again on the systems analysis domain, we can see how critical it is that those who develop the modeling techniques and methods do not make them too complex. The reasoning works as follows. As domain experts, developers have their expertise of the methods and techniques to draw upon, will likely have participated in many systems development efforts, and will have years of experience. So, these experts have highly developed and specialized stores of domain knowledge at their disposal, and will be able to quickly recall from LTWM far more of that domain knowledge than the typical end-user likely knows about systems development methods and techniques. That means that what may be glaringly apparent to the systems developers may by quite complex and simply beyond the processing capacity of typical end-users, since systems development methods and techniques are not their domain of expertise. This points to the importance of studying systems development methods and techniques. It also stresses the importance of studying complexity, not only from the viewpoint of developers, but more importantly, also from the perspectives of end-users.

Research Question and Hypothesis

If theoretical complexity predicts complexity encountered by subjects in practice (that is, practical complexity), we would expect to observe roughly the same degree of differences between use case and class diagrams in empirical studies as those determined by the complexity indices provided by Siau and Cao (2001). For example, Siau and Cao's (2001) results indicate that class diagrams are roughly 2.5 times more complex than use case diagrams. In other words, if theoretical and practical complexities measure the same construct, as subjects interpret the two diagrams in an experimental context, we would expect to find that class diagrams take roughly 2.5 times longer than use case diagrams to interpret. So we can form a hypothesis that practical complexity is not less than theoretical complexity. If class diagrams are indeed much more complex than use case diagrams, then it should be possible to empirically test using a time construct as a relative surrogate of complexity. Therefore, it should follow that if class diagrams are indeed more complex than use case diagrams, then it should take longer for study subjects to interpret class diagrams than use case diagrams.

Research Methodology and Design

The data is secondary, from an experiment conducted by a graduate student on volunteer subjects who had completed a one-semester UML course at a large [U.S.] midwestern university. Class and use case diagrams from two different problem domains—a bank and a music club—were the objects of interpretation. One of the problem domains, the music club, is more complex than the other (See diagrams 1 to 4 in Appendix B). Each subject was given at random, either a class diagram or a use case diagram from one of the two systems, and asked to think-aloud while they interpreted the diagram. Once finished with the diagram, subjects were given the complementary diagram (that is, a use case diagram on the same domain if s/he was given a class diagram previously and vice versa) and asked to continue the interpretation with both diagrams. Then, the process was completed for the second system (that is, a repeated design (see Table 2). The entire session was audio taped. Thirty one subjects participated in the study, but times for two of the subjects were unobtainable because of problems with the audiotapes, leaving a usable sample size of 29.

Table 2.

TREATMENT	DOMAIN	
	BANK – ATM	**MUSIC CLUB**
1	*_CD,_ then CD and UC	*_UC,_ then UC and CD
2	*_UC,_ then UC and CD	*_CD,_ then CD and UC

*Note: Original research design (CD=class diagram; UC = use case diagram), *Indicates the data used for this research*

The tapes were not timed as part of the original experiment. For this research, interpretation times were obtained by simply timing the taped interpretation of the first diagram for each problem domain. Only the first interpretation for each problem domain was used (as indicated by * in Table 1) because the second part of the experiment involved using both use case and class diagrams simultaneously. Time was measured to the nearest second.

Results and Discussion

For analysis purposes, the time data was normalized to remove the effects of the different system complexity discussed previously. This was accomplished by dividing the time by the number of possible constructs in the respective diagrams, resulting in a measure of the analysis time per construct, and making an "apples-to-apples" comparison of the different diagram types realistic and possible.

Once the data was normalized, it appeared that there were two outlier points (more than three standard deviations form the mean), which could have exerted undue influence on the final results; these points were removed from the data set for the statistical analysis. See Figure 4.

Figure 3. Scatter plot

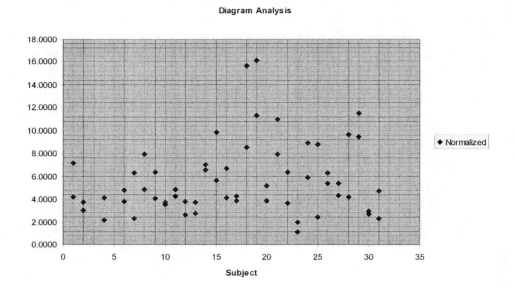

Figure 4. Descriptives

					95% Confidence Interval for			
1	27	5.4269963	3.4474058	.6634536	4.0632480	6.7907446	1.97440	16.08700
2	26	5.7584769	3.1405098	.6159046	4.4899976	7.0269563	1.08700	11.51280
Total	53	5.5896094	3.2729227	.4495705	4.6874802	6.4917387	1.08700	16.08700

Figure 5. Test of homogeneity of variances

Levene			
.542	1	51	.465

Figure 6. ANOVA

	Sum of				
Between Groups	1.455	1	1.455	.134	.716
Within Groups	555.570	51	10.894		
Total	557.025	52			

Figure 5 presents the descriptive statistics for the data set, where group 1 indicates class diagrams and group 2 indicates use case diagrams. Figure 6 shows the results of the homogeneity of variances test between the two groups. Generally, the omnibus F-test is relatively robust to differences in group variances, if the groups are the same size. In this case, the group sizes are different, and so the Levene's results are arguably more important to consider. However, the results are non-significant at the 0.05 level, which means that we may have some confidence in the F-test.

The one-way analysis of variance conducted indicates a non-significant result for the interpretation times for the two diagram types. See ANOVA results in Figure 7. Since there are just two groups, the one-way ANOVA produces the same results as a t-test.

Thus, we reject the null hypothesis and conclude that practical complexity is not equal to theoretical complexity. This also indicates that theoretical complexity might not be an accurate measure of practical complexity, since there is no significant difference between use case and class diagrams in our empirical study, but there are substantial differences between use case and class diagrams in the complexity indices. This suggests that a different set of metrics for practical complexity might be warranted.

There are several possible reasons for the inadequacy of theoretical complexity in estimating practical complexity. First, although Siau and Cao's (2001) complexity indices indicated that class diagrams are about 2.5 times more complex than use case diagrams, the analysis was based on all objects, relationships, and property types as formulated by Rossi and Brinkkemper (1996). In practice, not all constructs in each diagram are used all of the time. For example, the class diagram can contain many relationship types (e.g., association, aggregation, composition, generalization, dependency) and objects (e.g., abstract class, notes, constraints, packages, subsystems, interface), but a typical class diagram only uses a subset of these. As such, theoretical complexity may not be the best measure of the complexity that a user will encounter in practice.

Second, one of the typical reasons for complexity is the limitation of short-term memory. Miller (1956) argued that the bottleneck in human cognition is the limitation of seven plus or minus two chunks of information in short-term memory. Although short-term memory is a concern, decomposing a complex problem into sub-problems can alleviate the limitation (Siau, 1999; Siau, Wand, & Benbasat, 1997). For example, when the subjects were asked to understand the class diagram, which can have many object, relationship, and property types, the subjects would not attempt to understand every element in the class diagram simultaneously. S/he would decompose the diagram into manageable sub-diagrams and understand each sub-diagram in turn. In this case, the short-term memory limitation is partially overcome. Current complexity metrics do not take this into account. The ability for us to decompose complex problems into sub-problems needs to be factored in complexity metrics formulation.

Third, there might be a need to assign weights to different constructs. For example, a construct that is more likely to result in a short-term memory problem should be weighted more in the complexity metrics than one that is less likely to result in a short-term memory constraint. With respect to UML, for example, we would argue that objects are less likely, when compared to relationships, to result in short-term memory constraint as they are more or less "independent." Relationships, on the other hand, need to be interpreted with associated objects to make sense. Hence, one relationship will consume more short-term memory resources than an object.

Finally, and perhaps most importantly, we may also argue from an 80/20 perspective that practical complexity is more relevant to systems development than theoretical complexity. In essence, the 80/20 rule of thumb (Kobryn, 2002) says that 80% of common software solutions, that is, software development projects, can usually be completely specified by using only 20 percent of the language constructs. If that is true, then only the most commonly used constructs constitute the majority of software development efforts, and that 20 percent of the language should therefore define practical complexity. Moreover, if many of the constructs are rarely or ever used, it would not be necessary to learn the complete syntax of the language in order to develop the majority of systems. Of course field validation of these contentions beyond an experimental setting, and to develop more accurate metrics, will be necessary if this is to provide value to researchers, those revising the UML specification, and software development experts in general.

Conclusion

Our results indicate that theoretical complexity might not accurately predict practical complexity. The long-term objective of this research is to propose a set of metrics to estimate practical complexity of modeling methods. Although formulating practical complexity is difficult, and practical complexity depends on many circumstances (e.g., project domains, structured/semi-structured/unstructured), coming up with an estimation of practical complexity is possible and useful. For example, the function point analysis (Albrecht & Gaffney, 1983), constructive cost model (Boehm, 1981), and activity-based costing model (Cooper & Kaplan, 1988) are illustrations of the usefulness of estimation—even rough estimation.

In addition, UML 2.0 has been released and identifying a "kernel" of the language has already been set as a goal by a number of those involved in developing the new version. These results can also provide a possible future direction for researchers studying complexity in development methodologies, since theoretical or total complexity would become a less prominent factor (although still extremely important in determining limits) in dealing with human cognitive limitations involving systems development.

References

Albrecht, A. J., & Gaffney, J. E. (1983). Software function, source line of codes, and development effort prediction: A software science validation. *IEEE Transaction on Software Engineering*, *19*, November, 639-648.

Anderson, J. (1976). *Language, memory and thought*. Lawrence Erlbaum Associates.

Anderson, J. (1983). *The architecture of cognition*. Harvard University Press.

Anderson, J. (1993). *Rules of the mind*. Lawrence Erlbaum Associates.

Anderson, J., & Lebiere, C. (1998). *The atomic components of thought*. Lawrence Erlbaum Associates.

Boehm, B. W. (1981). *Software engineering economics*. Englewood Cliffs, NJ: Prentice-Hall.

Booch, G., Jacobson, I., & Rumbaugh, J. (1999). *The unified modeling language user guide*. Addison-Wesley.

Briand, L., Wüst, J., & Lounis, H. (1999). A comprehensive investigation of quality factors in object-oriented designs: An industrial case study. In *Proceedings of the 21ˢᵗ International Conference on Software Engineering*, Los Angeles, CA (pp. 345-354).

Cooper, R., & Kaplan, P. S. (1988, September/October). Measure costs right: Make the right decisions. *Harvard Business Review*, 96-103.

Dobing, B., & Parsons, J. (2000). Understanding the role of use cases in UML: A review and research agenda. *Journal of Database Management, 11*(4), 28-36.

Ericsson, K., & Kintsch, W. (1995). Long-term working memory. *Psychological Review, 102*(2), 211-245.

Kim, J., Hahn, J., & Hahn, H. (2000). How do we understand a system with (so) many diagrams? Cognitive processes in diagrammatic reasoning. *Information Systems Research, 11*, 384-303.

Kobryn, C. (2002). Will UML 2.0 be agile or awkward? *Communications of the ACM, 45*(1), 107-110.

Mcleod, G., & Roeleveld, D. (2002). Method evaluation in practice: UML/RUP vs. inspired method. In *Proceedings of the International Workshop on Evaluation of Modeling Methods in Systems Analysis and Design (EMMSAD'02)*.

Miller, G. (1956). The magical number seven, plus or minus two: Some limits on our capacity for processing information. *The Psychological Review, 63*(2), 81-97.

Rossi, M., & Brinkkemper, S. (1996). Complexity metrics for systems development methods and techniques. *Information Systems, 21*(2), 209-227.

Rumbaugh, J., Jacobson, I., & Booch, G. (1999). *The unified modeling language reference manual*. Addison-Wesley.

Siau, K. (1999). Information modeling and method engineering: A psychological perspective. *Journal of Database Management, 10* (4), 44-50.

Siau, K., & Cao, Q. (2001). Unified Modeling Language (UML)—A complexity analysis. *Journal of Database Management, 12*(1), 26-34.

Siau, K., & Loo, P. (2002). Difficulties in learning UML: A concept mapping analysis. *Seventh CAiSE/IFIP8.1 International Workshop on Evaluation of Modeling Methods in Systems Analysis and Design (EMMSAD'02)*, Toronto, Canada (pp. 102-108).

Siau, K., Wand, Y., & Benbasat, I. (1997). The relative importance of structural constraints and surface semantics in information modeling. *Information Systems*, 22(2&3), 155-170.

Siau, K. (2004). Informational and computational equivalence in comparing information modeling methods. *Journal of Database Management, 15*(1), 73-86.

Siau, K., Erickson, J., & Lee, L. (2002). Complexity of UML: Theoretical versus practical complexity. In *Proceedings of the 12th Workshop on Information Technology and Systems (WITS'02)*, Barcelona, Spain (pp. 13-18).

Siau, K., & Lee, L. (2004). Are use case and class diagrams complementary in requirements analysis? An experimental study on use case and class diagrams in UML. *Requirements Engineering, 9*(4), 229-237.

Vessey, I., & Conger, S. (1994). Requirements specification: Learning object, process, and data methodologies. *Communications of the ACM, 37*(5), 102-113.

Zendler, A., Pfeiffer, T., Eicks, M., & Lehner, F. (2001). Experimental comparison of coarse-grained concepts in UML, OML, and TOS. *Journal of systems and Software, 57*(1), 21-30.

Appendix A: UML Core Concepts and Constructs

Class Diagrams			
Object Types	**Property Types**	**Relationship Types**	**Role types**
Class	Class name	Association	Association
Interface	Class attribute	Aggregation	Aggregation
Package	Class operation	Composition	Composition
Subsystem	Association end	Generalization	Generalization
Object	Association name	Single inheritance	Single inheritance
Note	Association constraint	Multiple inheritance	Multiple inheritance
Constraint	Association qualifier	Qualified association	Qualified
Tagged value	Aggregate end	Instantiate	Instantiate object
Stereotype	Generalization constraint	Dependency-realization	Dependency part
	Interface name	Dependency-usage	Realization part
	Interface attribute		Usage part
	Interface operation		
	Package name		
	Subsystem name		
	Object name		
	Object attribute		
	Note comment		
	Constraint string		
	Stereotype string		
	Tagged value string		

Use Case Diagrams			
Object Types	**Property Types**	**Relationship Types**	**Role types**
Actor	Actor name	Association	Association
Use case	Use case name	Extend	Generalization
Package	Package name	Generalization	Base use case
Subsystem	Subsystem name	Dependency	Extended use case
Note	Note comment	Uses	Included use case
Constraint	Constraint string	Include	
Tagged value	Stereotype string		
Stereotype	Tagged value string		

Activity Diagrams			
Object Types	**Property Types**	**Relationship Types**	**Role types**
Activity state	Activity name	Transition	Guard condition name
Action state	Action name	Branch	
Object	Object name	Fork	
Swimlane	Swimlane name	Join	
Initial state	Note comment	Object flow	
Stop state	Constraint string		
Note	Stereotype string		
Constraint	Tagged value string		
Tagged value			
Stereotype			

Sequence Diagrams			
Object Types	**Property Types**	**Relationship Types**	**Role types**
Actor	Message name	Message	Create
Object	Actor name		Destroy
Lifeline	Object name		Call
Focus of control	Note comment		Return
Note	Constraint string		Send
Constraint	Stereotype string		
Tagged value	Tagged value string		
Stereotype			

Collaboration Diagrams			
Object Types	**Property Types**	**Relationship Types**	**Role types**
Object	Object name	Link	Local
Actor	Sequence number		Global
Note	Message name		Transient
Constraint	Actor name		Create
Tagged value	Path stereotype		Destroy
Stereotype	Note comment		
	Constraint string		
	Stereotype string		
	Tagged value string		

Object Diagrams			
Object Types	**Property Types**	**Relationship Types**	**Role types**
Object	Object name	Link	Local
Note	Class name		Global
Constraint	Object attribute		Transient
Tagged value	Note comment		
Stereotype	Constraint string		
	Stereotype string		
	Tagged value string		

Statechart Diagrams			
Object Types	**Property Types**	**Relationship Types**	**Role types**
State	Event name	Transition	Guard condition
Sub-state	State name	Branch	
Event	Action name	Fork	
Action state	Activity name	Join	
Activity state	Event trigger		
Initial state	Entry action		
Final state	Exit action		
Object	Internal transition		
Note	Deferred event		
Constraint	Note comment		
Tagged value	Constraint string		
Stereotype	Stereotype string		
	Tagged value string		

Component Diagrams			
Object Types	**Property Types**	**Relationship Types**	**Role types**
Deployment component	Component name	Generalization single inheritance	Generalization part
Work product component	Path name	Generalization multiple inheritance	Single inheritance part
Execution component	Package name	Association	Multiple inheritance part
Interface	Subsystem name	Aggregation	Association
Package	Interface name	Composition	Aggregation
Subsystem	Interface operation	Realization	Composition
Note	Interface attribute	Dependency	Dependency part
Constraint	Note comment	Dependency-usage	Usage part
Tagged value	Constraint string		Imports
Stereotype	Stereotype string		Exports
	Tagged value string		

Chapter IX

Data Quality:
An Assessment

Jeretta Horn Nord, Oklahoma State University, USA

G. Daryl Nord, Oklahoma State University, USA

Hongjiang Xu, Central Michigan University, USA

Elizabeth S. Myrin, Oklahoma State University, USA

Abstract

This chapter presents results from a large-scale survey of Australian CPA members regarding data quality. The research investigates and reports major stakeholders' opinions on the importance of critical success factors affecting data quality and the actual performance on each of those factors. The results reveal whether dissimilarly sized organizations differ in the way they measure the importance and performance of critical success factors for data quality in accounting information systems.

Introduction

Companies lose billions of dollars annually due to poor data quality (DQ). Regardless of the organization's size, data quality issues impact its information system. With the proliferation of data warehouses, communication and information technology managers have experienced an increase in their awareness of and need for high DQ (Lee, Strong, Beverly, & Wang, 2002). Dirty data can damage every aspect of a business (D'Agostino, 2004). Thus, DQ has been rated as a top concern to data consumers (Wang, 1996) and reported as one of the six categories commonly employed in management information systems research (Delone & McLean, 1992).

More and more electronically captured information requires processing, storage, and distribution through information systems (Siau, Lim, & Shen, 2001). Advances in information technology (IT) have dramatically increased the ability and capability to process accounting information. At the same time, however, it presents issues that traditional accounting systems have not experienced. Real-world practice suggests that DQ problems are becoming increasingly prevalent (Huang, Lee, & Wang, 1999; Redman, 1998; Wang & Wang, 1996). The traditional focus on the input and recording of data needs to be offset with recognition that the systems themselves may affect the quality of data (Fedorowicz & Lee, 1998). If DQ issues have not been addressed properly, IT advances can sometimes create problems rather than benefit the organization. Most organizations have experienced the adverse effects of decisions based on information of inferior quality (Huang et al., 1999). The number of errors in stored data and their consequent organizational impact are likely to increase in number (Klein, 1998). Inaccurate and incomplete data may adversely affect the organization's competitive success (Redman, 1992). Indeed, poor quality information can have a significant social and business impact. For example, NBC News reported that dead people still eat! Because of outdated information in U.S. government databases, food stamps continued to be sent to recipients long after they died. Fraud from food stamps costs U.S. taxpayers billions of dollars each year (Huang et al., 1999). Another example from a business perspective occurred when a financial company absorbed a huge net loss, totaling more than $250 million, when interest rates changed dramatically and the company was caught unaware due to poor data handling (Huang et al., 1999).

Examples of the consequences of poor DQ in AIS are also common. Errors in an inventory database may cause managers to make decisions that generate overstock or understock conditions (Bowen, 1993). One minor data entry error such as the unit of product/service price could go through an organization's AIS without appropriate DQ checks and cause financial losses and damage to the organization's reputation. Therefore, DQ has become crucial for the success of accounting information systems (AIS) in today's IT age.

The primary purpose of this research is to explore whether various sized organizations assess the factors influencing DQ in accounting information systems differently. There is a readily identifiable literature link to stakeholder groups relating to DQ. However, precise perceptions of the importance of critical factors from different stakeholder groups and organizational size are not explicit in the extant literature. This research allows for an investigation as to whether organizational size influences the critical success factors and whether it is possible to generate some common critical success factors for different sized organizations.

Therefore, the hypothesis of this study is:

H₁: *There is a significant difference between different-sized organizations in their perceptions of importance and performance of critical factors for accounting information systems' data quality.*

To provide insight, the research investigates major stakeholders' opinions on the importance of factors affecting DQ and the actual performance (achievement) on each of those factors. This knowledge will help assist organizations to increase the operating efficiency of their accounting information system and contribute to the effectiveness of the management decision-making process.

Background

Data quality (DQ) has become an increasingly critical concern of organizations (Lee et al., 2002; Lee, Pipino, Strong, & Wand, 2004; Redman, 1998; Wang & Wang, 1996). A survey conducted by PricewaterhouseCoopers across a broad mix of "Top 500" corporations confirmed that most corporations experience major impacts to their businesses as a result of poor data quality (*Wall Street and Technology*, 2004). The general definition of data quality is data that is fit for use by data consumers (Huang et al., 1999). Data quality dimensions refer to issues that are important to information consumers (people who use information). Many data quality dimensions have been identified that endeavor to set the framework for identifying quality issues relating to data. Strong, Lee, and Wang (1997) group the data quality dimensions into four categories that are widely acceptable in the literature (Lee et al., 2002): conceptual data quality, intrinsic data quality, accessibility data quality, and representation data quality. A recent report issued by the United States Government Accountability Office (2005) lists the following as key aspects of internal controls to ensure data quality.

- **Guidance:** Guidance should clearly and consistently define all data elements required for reporting and effectively communicate this information.

- **Data entry procedures and edit check software:** These can help ensure that data entering the designated reporting system is accurate and consistent. Written guides establishing who is responsible for each step in data creation and maintenance and how data is transferred from initial to final formats can ensure that data is consistently reported.

- **Monitoring:** Monitoring can ensure that reported data is accurate and complete. Common monitoring practices may include formal on-site reviews of individual case files and source documentation.

Although there are no uniform lists for data quality dimensions, we adopt one of the commonly identified data quality dimensions for purposes of this research:

- **Accuracy:** Which occurs when the recorded value is in conformity with the actual value

- **Timeliness:** Which occurs when the recorded value is not out-of-date

- **Completeness:** Which occurs when all values for a certain variable are recorded;

- **Consistency:** Which occurs when the representation of the data values is the same in all cases (Ballou & Pazer, 1982, 1985, 1987; Ballou, Wang, Pazer, & Tayi, 1993)

In the data quality and data warehouse fields, four stakeholder groups are responsible for creating, maintaining, using, and managing data that has been identified. They are data producers, data custodians, data consumers, and data managers (Shanks & Darke, 1998; Strong et al., 1997; Wang, Lee, Pipino, & Strong, 1998). In the accounting information systems area, auditors were recognized as fulfilling the role of monitoring how the accounting information systems work and the quality of the information that has been generated by the systems. A major job function of the internal auditor is to perform the internal policing of financial records and to help ensure quality within the organization.

Much of data quality research focuses on processing, while accounting management research focuses on results checking and monitoring of data. In addition, the quality management area underscores and focuses on the source from which raw data originates. As a result, the quality management literature reveals that suppliers' quality management has been highlighted as an important aspect of total quality management (Badri, Davis, & Davis, 1995; Saraph, Benson, & Schroeder, 1989). In accounting information systems, data suppliers also play a role in data quality management. Therefore, they are included in the framework.

Thus, in summary and concurring with the above mentioned research areas, the stakeholders in accounting information systems have been identified as follows:

- Information producers create or collect information for the AIS.
- Information custodians design, develop, and operate the AIS.
- Information users use the accounting information in their works.
- Information managers are responsible for managing the information quality in the AIS.
- Internal auditors monitor the AIS and its data quality and check internal controls in the AIS.
- Data suppliers provide the unorganized raw data to the AIS.

The critical success factors model of accounting information systems' data quality (represented in Figure 1) was developed based upon the AIS, data quality, quality management literature, and previous studies conducted by the authors (Xu, Koronios, & Brown, 2001, 2002). Several categories of factors were identified that, according to the theoretical and empirical literature, have the potential to influence data quality in AIS. These categories were AIS characteristics, data quality characteristics, stakeholders' related factors, organizational factors, and external factors.

Figure 1. Categories of factors impacting data quality in AIS (Source: Xu et al., 2001, 2002)

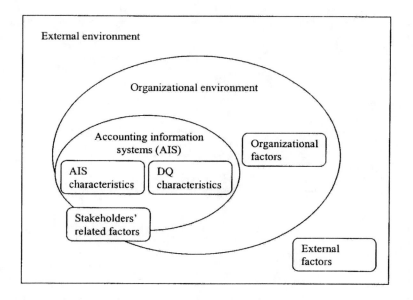

According to the relationships of those factors, they were organized into the research model shown in Figure 1, which contains five constructs at three levels. The first level is the external environment, which consists of external factors; the second level is the organizational environment, which consists of organizational factors; and the third level is the accounting information systems, which has AIS characteristics and data quality characteristics. Although there is only one factor, nature of the AIS under the category of AIS characteristics, this factor has many attributes, such as the number of the systems/packages, the number of staff, what kind of system it is, the age and maturity of the system, and the organizational structure of the system. Stakeholders of AIS could come from within the AIS, outside the AIS but within the organization, and outside the organization. For example, AIS could have both internal and external information suppliers and customers. Within each of those identified categories, a list of factors was grouped. Factors were identified by the comprehensive literature review and the empirical case studies (Xu, 2000).

The relationship among factors and categories is shown in Figure 2 and forms the model for factors influencing data quality in accounting information systems. There

Figure 2. The model for factors influencing data quality in accounting information systems (Source: Xu et al., 2001, 2002)

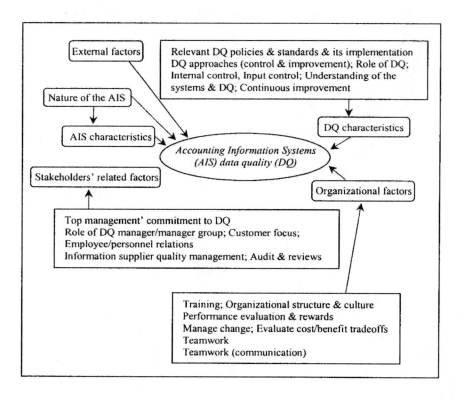

are seven factors listed under the category "data quality characteristics"; those factors are all related directly to the data quality itself. They are: appropriate DQ policies and standards and its implementation, DQ approaches (control and improvement), Role of DQ, internal control, input control, understanding of the systems and DQ, and continuous improvement of DQ.

The stakeholders could come from both inside and outside the AIS and the organization. Human-related factors have always been the focus of social science and IT research. The category of stakeholder-related factors in this research deals with the human-/people-related factors that influence DQ in accounting information systems. They include top management's commitment to DQ, the role of the DQ manager/manager group, customer focus, employee/personnel relations, information supplier quality management, and audits and reviews. There are seven factors at the organizational level: training, organizational structure, organizational culture, performance evaluation and rewards, management of change, evaluation of cost/benefit trade-offs, and teamwork (communication). External factors have been identified as factors outside the organization from the external environment over which the organization has little or no control.

This framework integrates several key themes concerning data quality management in accounting information systems. More specifically, this framework identifies five

Figure 3. Theoretical framework of this research

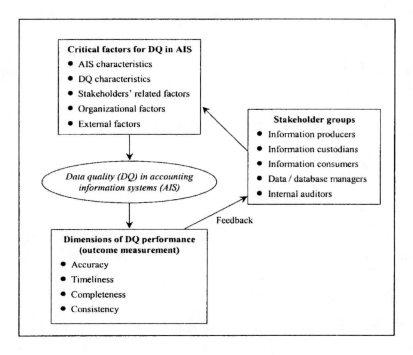

key categories for factors that impact data quality in AIS. Those categories are AIS characteristics, DQ characteristics, stakeholders' related factors, organizational factors, and external factors. In addition, five stakeholder groups for data quality in AIS also have been identified. The research framework shown in Figure 3 assimilates the groups into data quality management in AIS, the segment of the framework that relates to data quality outcome measurement; the Ballou et al. (1993) data quality dimensions were adopted.

Issues, Controversies, and Problems

The issues investigated included an assessment how different stakeholder groups in different industries consider the importance and performance of critical success factors for data quality in AIS. A nationwide Australian survey was conducted, which was supported and administered by the Australian Certified Practicing Accountants (CPA) Association. A total of 1,000 Australian CPA members were surveyed. Because the survey was administered by the Australian CPA and due to privacy policy restrictions on the disclosure of member information, it was not possible to identify the respondents who did reply to the first mailing (that is, the first letter and questionnaire) or the addresses of the undelivered surveys. The second letter, which was a combined thank you/reminder courtesy letter, was printed at the same time as the first letter and questionnaire. It was dated and sent out to all members one week after the first mailing. An estimated 15% of the surveyed members were deemed not eligible or not available to answer the questionnaire for various reasons, as detailed in the following. Several non-responding members of the sample gave the following reasons for non-response:

- Retired
- No longer or not working with the AIS
- Moved overseas
- Don't feel qualified to answer the questionnaire

From the estimated 850 eligible questionnaire recipients, we received 182 completed questionnaires. This makes the response rate approximately 21%.

The survey questions and design were developed based on the results of multiple case studies conducted by the authors in earlier stages of the research project. The questionnaire includes three key sections: 25 Critical Success Factors for AIS's data quality, the three most and least important factors, and demographic details about the respondents and their organizations. Most of the questions were closed-ended to elicit comparable and measurable responses. The respondents also were given the opportunity to add written comments at the end of the survey.

The primary analysis tool used for the research was SPSS. A one-way ANOVA was employed for the testing. Turkey Post Hoc within ANOVA was applied to determine the relationships between paired groups.

Demographic Information

The survey respondents were asked to provide some basic information about their roles in relation to data quality in their organizations and their evaluations of data quality in their current AIS. This section describes basic demographic information about the respondents.

Table 1 shows that 36% of the respondents were information producers who created or collected data for the AIS or managed those who created or collected data. Another 32.3% of respondents were information custodians. They were responsible for designing, developing, and operating their AIS or managing those who did that work. Only 0.5% of respondents were internal auditors who were auditing or reviewing data in AIS.

The respondents were asked to evaluate data quality in their current AIS. Figure 4 shows that more than half of the respondents (54.6%) considered their AIS's overall quality of data to be high. Another 13.1% of respondents rated it very high. Only 8.7% of respondents were not satisfied with the data quality in their systems.

Background information was collected about each of the respondents' organizations and themselves. The organization's industry, location, and size and the respondent's job levels are presented in Figure 5. Since the purpose of this study was to examine the extent to which organizational size influences data quality, only the revenue figures of the surveyed organizations are presented.

Table 1. Respondents' main role

Stakeholder	Main Role	Percent
Information Producer	Create or collect data for the AIS; Manage those who create or collect data for the AIS	36.0
Information Custodian	Design, develop, and operate the AIS; Manage those who design, develop, and operate the AIS	32.3
Information Manager	Manage data and/or data quality in AIS	17.5
Internal Auditor	Audit or Review data in AIS	0.5
Information User	Use accounting information in tasks	11.5

Figure 4. Respondents' evaluations of current data quality level

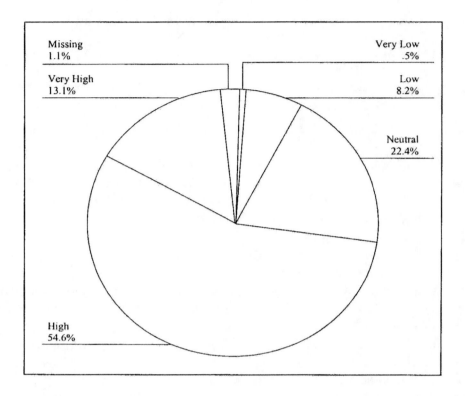

Figure 5 shows that 74 organizations' revenues were between $10 million and $99 million. Only 25 organizations' revenues were under $5 million. Two respondents indicated that they were not permitted to disclose their organizations' revenue.

Major Findings

An organization's annual revenue figures were used as the scale for organization size for the purpose of this study. The questionnaire was designed to identify an organization's size, based on annual revenue, as follows: under $5 million, $5 million to $9 million, $10 million to $99 million, and over $100 million. Two additional options were provided in the survey for those respondents who were either not sure or not permitted to disclose their organizations' annual revenue figures. Table 2 shows how the annual revenue figures represent the different sized organization. For the purpose of this research, the scale for organization size is categorized as very small organizations (under $5 million), small organizations ($5 million to

Figure 5. The annual revenue of the surveyed organizations

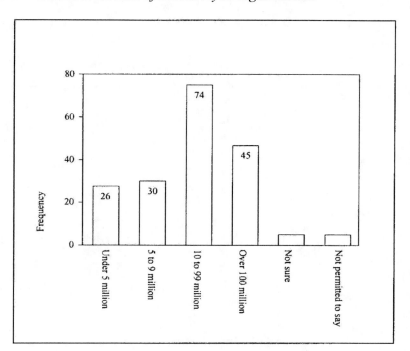

Table 2. Annual revenue represents the size of the organizations

Annual Revenue	Size of the Organization
Under $5 million	Very Small
$5 million to $9 million	Small
$10 million to $99 million	Medium
Over $100 million	Large

$9 million), medium-sized organizations ($10 million to $99 million), and large organizations (over $100 million).

ANOVA analysis was used to explore whether any significant differences exist between different sized organizations, regarding the importance of the critical factors for accounting information systems' data quality. The ANOVA was chosen because of the constructs of interest (dependent variables); importance of the factors was measured on the interval scale, and the organizational size was seen as the independent variable. Table 3 presents the ANOVA results for the different sized organizations' respondents' perceptions regarding the importance of the critical factors for data quality in AIS.

Table 3. Different sized organizations' responses on the importance and performance of critical factors

		Importance			Performance		
	Revenue	Mean	Std. Deviation	Sig.	Mean	Std. Deviation	Sig.
Top Management Commitment	Under $5 million	4.16	.688		3.44	1.044	
	$5 million to $9 million	4.07	.828		3.17	1.053	
	$10 million to $99 million	4.16	.703		3.22	1.216	
	Over $100 million	4.22	.823	.938	3.33	1.066	.500
	Not sure	4.00	.000		2.50	2.121	
	Not permitted to disclose	4.50	.707		4.50	.707	
	Total	4.16	.745		3.28	1.132	
Middle Management Commitment	Under $5 million	4.04	.735		3.48	.918	
	$5 million to $9 million	3.97	.809		3.07	.980	
	$10 million to $99 million	4.16	.683		3.07	1.058	
	Over $100 million	4.09	.821	.814	3.22	1.085	.199
	Not sure	4.00	.000		2.50	2.121	
	Not permitted to disclose	4.50	.707		4.50	.707	
	Total	4.10	.742		3.18	1.049	
Education and Training	Under $5 million	3.64	1.075		3.04	1.197	
	$5 million to $9 million	4.00	.910		2.63	1.033	
	$10 million to $99 million	4.08	.807		2.85	1.244	
	Over $100 million	3.91	.793	3.41	2.89	1.092	.792
	Not sure	4.00	.000		3.00	1.414	
	Not permitted to disclose	3.50	.707		3.50	.707	
	Total	3.96	.862		2.86	1.155	
Clear DQ Vision for Entire Organization	Under $5 million	3.72	1.100		2.92	1.222	
	$5 million to $9 million	3.70	.915		2.50	1.106	
	$10 million to $99 million	3.81	.822		2.67	1.202	
	Over $100 million	3.69	.900	.964	2.73	1.095	.724
	Not sure	4.00	.000		2.50	2.121	
	Not permitted to disclose	3.50	.707		3.50	.707	
	Total	3.75	.888		2.70	1.161	

continued on following page

Table 3. continued

	Revenue	Importance			Performance		
		Mean	Std. Devia- tion	Sig.	Mean	Std. Devia- tion	Sig.
Establish DQ Manager Posi- tion to Manage DQ	Under $5 million	3.00	1.041		3.60	1.780	
	$5 million to $9 million	2.93	1.163		3.48	1.724	
	$10 million to $99 mil- lion	3.31	1.227		3.26	1.764	
	Over $100 million	3.40	1.009	.472	3.38	1.403	.886
	Not sure	3.50	.707		2.50	2.121	
	Not permitted to disclose	3.50	2.121		4.00	2.828	
	Total	3.23	1.142		3.38	1.669	
Organizational Structure	Under $5 million	3.52	.963		3.36	1.319	
	$5 million to $9 million	3.52	.986		3.67	1.605	
	$10 million to $99 mil- lion	3.64	.837		2.88	1.322	
	Over $100 million	3.62	1.007	.966	3.18	1.267	.140
	Not sure	4.00	.000		2.50	2.121	
	Not permitted to disclose	3.50	.707		3.50	.707	
	Total	3.60	.912		3.16	1.377	
DQ Policies and Standards	Under $5 million	3.48	.872		3.16	1.313	
	$5 million to $9 million	3.53	.900		2.97	1.474	
	$10 million to $99 mil- lion	3.85	.886		2.84	1.054	
	Over $100 million	3.80	.815	.332	3.07	1.232	.786
	Not sure	4.00	.000		2.50	2.121	
	Not permitted to disclose	4.00	.000		3.50	.707	
	Total	3.74	.866		2.97	1.215	
Organizational Culture	Under $5 million	3.76	1.052		3.12	1.201	
	$5 million to $9 million	3.90	.845		3.00	1.365	
	$10 million to $99 mil- lion	3.95	.941		2.69	1.134	
	Over $100 million	3.91	.668	.970	2.98	1.055	.362
	Not sure	4.00	.000		2.50	2.121	
	Not permitted to disclose	4.00	.000		4.00	.000	
	Total	3.90	.864		2.89	1.173	

continued on following page

Table 3. continued

	Revenue	Importance			Performance		
		Mean	Std. Devia-tion	Sig.	Mean	Std. Devia-tion	Sig.
DQ Controls	Under $5 million	3.68	.627		2.84	1.106	
	$5 million to $9 million	3.80	.664		2.60	1.003	
	$10 million to $99 million	3.84	.898		2.75	1.160	
	Over $100 million	3.96	.673	.751	2.98	.941	.634
	Not sure	4.00	.000		2.50	2.121	
	Not permitted to disclose	3.50	.707		3.50	.707	
	Total	3.84	.762		2.80	1.074	
Input Controls	Under $5 million	4.28	.792		3.28	.936	
	$5 million to $9 million	4.37	.669		3.27	.944	
	$10 million to $99 million	4.31	.681		3.07	1.051	
	Over $100 million	4.49	.661	.640	3.31	.949	.615
	Not sure	4.00	.000		3.00	1.414	
	Not permitted to disclose	4.00	.000		4.00	.000	
	Total	4.35	.684		3.20	.988	
User Focus	Under $5 million	3.84	.624		3.00	1.118	
	$5 million to $9 million	4.20	.847		2.80	1.095	
	$10 million to $99 million	4.11	.732		2.85	1.178	
	Over $100 million	4.16	.767	.562	2.89	.885	.556
	Not sure	4.00	.000		2.00	1.414	
	Not permitted to disclose	4.00	.000		4.00	.000	
	Total	4.10	.742		2.88	1.082	
Nature of AIS	Under $5 million	4.24	.523		3.20	1.080	
	$5 million to $9 million	4.20	.761		2.97	1.217	
	$10 million to $99 million	4.27	.668		2.97	1.072	
	Over $100 million	4.29	.695	.677	3.29	.991	.446
	Not sure	4.00	.000		4.00	.000	
	Not permitted to disclose	3.50	.707		3.50	.707	
	Total	4.25	.669		3.10	1.074	

continued on following page

Table 3. continued

	Revenue	Importance			Performance		
		Mean	Std. Devia-tion	Sig.	Mean	Std. Devia-tion	Sig.
Employee Rela-tions	Under $5 million	4.32	.627		3.32	1.069	
	$5 million to $9 million	4.03	.850		2.83	1.085	
	$10 million to $99 mil-lion	4.14	.728		2.93	1.151	
	Over $100 million	3.93	.939	.276	2.93	1.031	.394
	Not sure	3.50	.707		2.00	.000	
	Not permitted to disclose	3.50	.707		3.50	.707	
	Total	4.08	.799		2.97	1.094	
Management of Changes	Under $5 million	3.88	.600		3.20	1.000	
	$5 million to $9 million	4.03	.556		2.93	.828	
	$10 million to $99 mil-lion	4.11	.653		3.08	1.044	
	Over $100 million	3.98	.812	.592	3.02	.988	.911
	Not sure	4.00	.000		3.00	.000	
	Not permitted to disclose	3.50	.707		3.50	.707	
	Total	4.02	.672		3.06	.975	
Measurement and Reporting	Under $5 million	3.60	1.000		3.24	1.234	
	$5 million to $9 million	3.87	.681		2.80	.925	
	$10 million to $99 mil-lion	3.84	.937		2.91	1.207	
	Over $100 million	3.87	.815	.600	2.69	1.164	.488
	Not sure	4.00	.000		3.50	.707	
	Not permitted to disclose	3.00	.000		3.00	.000	
	Total	3.81	.868		2.89	1.149	
Data Supplier Quality Man-agement	Under $5 million	3.28	.980		3.24	1.690	
	$5 million to $9 million	3.50	.861		2.73	1.112	
	$10 million to $99 mil-lion	3.53	.914		2.73	1.158	
	Over $100 million	3.76	.802	.434	3.02	1.196	.432
	Not sure	3.50	.707		2.50	.707	
	Not permitted to disclose	3.50	.707		3.50	.707	
	Total	3.55	.885		2.88	1.244	

continued on following page

Table 3. continued

	Revenue	Importance			Performance		
		Mean	**Std. Devia-tion**	**Sig.**	**Mean**	**Std. Devia-tion**	**Sig.**
Continuous Im-provement	Under $5 million	3.64	.860		2.80	1.190	
	$5 million to $9 million	3.83	.648		2.50	.938	
	$10 million to $99 million	3.82	.783		2.64	1.054	
	Over $100 million	3.91	.793	.501	2.82	.984	.603
	Not sure	4.00	.000		3.50	.707	
	Not permitted to disclose	3.00	.000		3.00	.000	
	Total	3.81	.770		2.70	1.030	
Teamwork (Communica-tion)	Under $5 million	3.92	1.115		3.24	1.268	
	$5 million to $9 million	4.13	.629		3.17	1.020	
	$10 million to $99 million	4.14	.581		2.97	.979	
	Over $100 million	4.11	.832	.316	3.00	1.022	.883
	Not sure	4.00	.000		3.00	.000	
	Not permitted to disclose	3.00	.000		3.00	.000	
	Total	4.08	.751		3.05	1.027	
Cost/Benefit Analysis	Under $5 million	3.56	1.158		2.96	1.172	
	$5 million to $9 million	3.53	.973		2.87	1.408	
	$10 million to $99 million	3.45	.830		2.68	1.376	
	Over $100 million	3.40	.889	.944	2.62	1.284	.822
	Not sure	3.50	.707		2.00	.000	
	Not permitted to disclose	3.00	.000		3.00	.000	
	Total	3.46	.909		2.73	1.313	
Understanding the Systems and DQ	Under $5 million	4.08	.640		3.29	.999	
	$5 million to $9 million	3.93	.583		2.97	.964	
	$10 million to $99 million	3.92	.736		2.82	1.012	
	Over $100 million	3.89	.714	.416	2.67	.826	.204
	Not sure	4.00	.000		3.00	.000	
	Not permitted to disclose	3.00	.000		3.00	.000	
	Total	3.93	.689		2.88	.957	

continued on following page

Table 3. continued

	Revenue	Importance			Performance		
		Mean	Std. Deviation	Sig.	Mean	Std. Deviation	Sig.
Risk Management	Under $5 million	3.96	1.020		3.16	1.179	
	$5 million to $9 million	3.87	.681		2.70	1.149	
	$10 million to $99 million	3.76	.824		2.51	1.230	
	Over $100 million	3.76	.830	.686	2.60	.939	.100
	Not sure	4.50	.707		1.50	.707	
	Not permitted to disclose	3.50	.707		3.50	.707	
	Total	3.81	.829		2.66	1.150	
Personnel Competency	Under $5 million	4.20	.957		3.28	1.208	
	$5 million to $9 million	4.27	.583		3.03	1.159	
	$10 million to $99 million	4.08	.717		2.86	.984	
	Over $100 million	4.07	.728	.642	3.14	.824	.314
	Not sure	4.00	.000		2.00	1.414	
	Not permitted to disclose	3.50	.707		3.00	.000	
	Total	4.12	.733		3.01	1.017	
Physical Environment	Under $5 million	3.96	.676		3.84	3.738	
	$5 million to $9 million	3.80	.847		3.13	1.196	
	$10 million to $99 million	3.68	.848		3.30	1.082	
	Over $100 million	3.73	.837	.706	3.38	.960	.746
	Not sure	3.50	.707		3.50	.707	
	Not permitted to disclose	3.50	.707		3.00	.000	
	Total	3.74	.817		3.37	1.700	
Audits and Reviews	Under $5 million	3.36	1.221		3.68	1.626	
	$5 million to $9 million	3.63	.890		2.50	1.280	
	$10 million to $99 million	3.68	.829		2.82	1.297	
	Over $100 million	3.93	.863	.159	3.09	1.041	.???*
	Not sure	4.00	.000		1.50	.707	
	Not permitted to disclose	3.00	.000		3.00	.000	
	Total	3.69	.916		2.94	1.318	

continued on following page

Table 3. continued

	Revenue	Importance			Performance		
		Mean	**Std. Deviation**	**Sig.**	**Mean**	**Std. Deviation**	**Sig.**
Internal Controls	Under $5 million	3.88	.833		3.20	1.118	
	$5 million to $9 million	4.03	.490		3.03	.928	
	$10 million to $99 million	4.20	.662		3.15	1.056	
	Over $100 million	4.20	.694	.044	3.16	.928	.991
	Not sure	4.50	.707		3.00	.000	
	Not permitted to disclose	3.00	.000		3.00	.000	
	Total	4.12	.683		3.13	.994	

*Indicates significant difference between groups.

As shown in Table 3, significant differences also are found regarding the importance of internal controls and the performance of audits and reviews between organizations that had different revenues. The Tukey Post Hoc analysis was also used to compare the pairs. The significant difference is found to exist only among the subgroups under the performance of audit and review factor. Table 4 summarizes the analysis of the Tukey test.

The Tukey tests showed that the means were significantly different between very small (annual revenue under $5 million), small ($5 million to $9 million), and medium ($10 to $99 million) organizations in the performance of audits and reviews factors with significant P, values of 0.011 and 0.049; and the mean differences were 1.18 and 0.86, respectively, which were the only two pairs that showed significant differences. Therefore, hypothesis H_1, that there is a significant difference between different-sized organizations in their perceptions of importance and performance of critical factors for accounting information systems' data quality, is supported for only one factor's performance, audits, and reviews, but not supported for other factors.

Table 4. Tukey post hoc test of paired difference between groups

Revenue	Revenue	Mean Difference	Sig.
Under $5 million	$5–$9 million	1.18	.011
Under $5 million	$10–$99 million	.86	.049

Dependent variable: The performance of audits and reviews.

Lack of significant differences among the different sized organizations may be explained on the basis of the proliferation of the awareness of information quality issues in accounting information systems across all surveyed organizations. It illustrated that the size of the respondents' organizations did not have a significant influence on their perceptions of the degree of importance and performance of critical factors for data quality.

Solutions and Recommendations

Data quality management and maintenance is crucial for successful implementation of accounting information systems. The level of importance and performance of critical success factors was similar in surveyed organizations, regardless of their size. Therefore, the possibility of generating a set of commonly applicable critical success factors for ensuring data quality in accounting information systems across different sized organizations is great. The research reported in this study has theoretical implications in the following key areas: the extension of theory to an area not previously addressed, the development of a research framework for critical success factors for data quality in AIS, and the identification of stakeholder groups for accounting information systems' data quality.

Future Trends

Data quality issues will continue to be increasingly critical concerns for organizations ranking among the top integration issues facing U.S. corporations. Future studies should consist of cross-country, cross-culture studies in order to address more issues in this field. Replication of this study in other countries, including both developed and developing countries, is needed to provide insights into international practices. Research on cross-country and cross-cultural comparison of critical factors that impact data quality will play a significant role in theory building as well as having practical implications.

In addition, the objective evaluation of data quality outcomes should be combined with stakeholders' perceptions in this study to build the linkage between people's subjective perceptions of importance with objective actual outcomes of data quality.

Conclusion

Only one critical success factor—audits and reviews performance—revealed statistical results showing that our research hypothesis, stating that different sized organizations consider the importance and performance of critical factors for data quality differently, was not supported. The study reveals some insights in data quality issues in AIS that have not been investigated before. The most significant findings are that the stakeholder groups in different sized organizations did not have significantly different evaluations regarding the importance and performance of most of the factors. Therefore, the study could help IT professionals and different sized organizations have a better understanding of critical success factors' impact on data quality in their specific AIS. It also provides a benchmark for organizations to evaluate their own data quality performance against other organizations.

References

Badri, M. A., Davis, D., & Davis, D. (1995). A study of measuring the critical factors of quality management. *International Journal of Quality and Reliability Management, 72*, 36-53.

Ballou, D. P., & Pazer, H. L. (1982). The impact of inspector fallibility on the inspection policy serial production system. *Management Science. 28*, 387-399.

Ballou, D. P., & Pazer, H. L. (1985). Modeling data and process quality in multi-input, multi-output information systems. *Management Science, 31*, 150-162.

Ballou, D. P., & Pazer, H. L. (1987). Cost/ quality tradeoffs of control procedures in information systems. *OMEGA: International Journal of Management Science, 15*, 509-521.

Ballou, D. P., Belardo, S., & Klein, B. (1987). Implication of data quality for spreadsheet analysis. *DataBase, 18*, 13-19.

Ballou, D. P., Wang, R. Y., Pazer, H. L., & Tayi, K. G. (1993). *Modeling data manufacturing systems to determine data product quality* (Total Data Quality Management Research Program No. TDQM-93-09). Cambridge, MA: MIT Sloan School of Management.

Bowen, P. (1993). *Managing data quality accounting information systems: A stochastic clearing system approach.* Unpublished doctoral dissertation, University of Tennessee.

D'Agostino, D. (2004). Data management: Getting clean. *CIO Insight, 1*(42).

Delone, W. H., & McLean, E. R. (1992). Information system success: The quest for the dependent variable. *Information Systems Research*, *3*, 60-95.

Fedorowicz, J., & Lee, Y. W. (1998). Accounting information quality: Reconciling hierarchical and dimensional contexts. In *Proceedings of 1998 Association of Information Systems (AIS) Conference*.

Huang, H.-T., Lee, Y. W., & Wang, R.Y. (1999). *Quality information and knowledge*. Prentice Hall PTR.

Klein, B. D. (1998). Data quality in the practice of consumer product management: Evidence from the field. *Data Quality*, *4*(1).

Lee, W. Y., Strong, D. M., Beverly, K., & Wang, R.Y. (2002). AIMQ: A methodology for information quality assessment. *Information & Management*, *40*, 133-146.

Lee, W., Pipino, L., Strong, D. M., & Wand, R.Y. (2004). Process-embedded data integrity. *Journal of Database Management*, *75*(1), 87-103.

Redman, T. C. (1992). *Data quality: Management and technology*. New York: Bantam Books.

Redman, T. C. (1998). The impact of poor data quality on the typical enterprise. *Communications of the ACM*, *41*.

Saraph, J. V., Benson, P. G., & Schroeder, R. G. (1989). An instrument for measuring the critical factors of quality management. *Decision Sciences*, *120*, 457-478.

Shanks, G., & Darke, P. (1998). Understanding data quality in data warehousing: A semiotic approach. In *Proceedings of the 1998 Conference on Information Quality*, Boston.

Siau, K., Lim, E., & Shen, Z. (2001). Mobile commerce: Promises, challenges, and research agenda. *Journal of Database Management*, *12*(3), 4-13.

Strong, D. M., Lee, Y. W., & Wang, R. Y. (1997). Data quality on context. *Communication of the ACM*, *40*, 103-110.

United States Government Accountability Office (2005, November). *Workforce investment act: Labor and states have taken actions to improve data quality, but additional steps are needed* (GAO-06082), Washington, DC.

Wall Street and Technology. (2004). *Leveraging data quality to manage risk and improve business performance*, 6-7.

Wang, Y., & Wang, R. Y. (1996). Anchoring data quality dimensions in ontological foundations. *Communications of the ACM*, *39*, 86-95.

Wang, R. Y., Lee, Y. W., Pipino, L. L., & Strong, D. M. (1998). Manage your information as a product. *Sloan Management Review*, *39*, 95-105.

Xu, H. (2000). Managing accounting information quality: An Australian study. In *Proceedings of the 21st International Conference on Information Systems (ICIS 2000)*, Brisbane, Australia.

Xu, H., Koronios, A., & Brown, N. (2001). A model for data quality in accounting information systems. *The Invited Session Data and Information Quality (DIQ), The 5ᵗʰ World Multiconference on Systemics, Cybernetics and Informatics (SCI 2001)*, Orlando, FL.

Xu, H., Koronios, A., & Brown, N. (2002). Managing data quality in accounting information systems. In L.A. Joia (Ed.), *IT-based management: Challenges and solutions*. Hershey, PA: Idea Group Publishing.

Chapter X

Cover Stories for Key Attributes:
Expanded Database Access Control

Nenad Jukic, Loyola University Chicago, USA

Svetlozar Nestorov, University of Chicago, USA

Susan V. Vrbsky, University of Alabama, USA

Allen Parrish, University of Alabama, USA

Abstract

In this chapter, we extend the multi-level secure (MLS) data model to include non-key related cover stories so that key attributes can have different values at different security levels. MLS data models require the classification of data and users into multiple security levels. In MLS systems, cover stories allow information provided to users at lower security levels to differ from information provided to users at higher security levels. Previous versions of the MLS model did not permit cover stories for key attributes because the key is used to relate the various cover stories for a particular entity. We present the necessary model changes and modifications to the relational algebra, which are required to implement cover stories for keys. We demonstrate the improvements made by these changes, illustrate the increased expressiveness of the model, and determine the soundness of a database, based on the described concepts.

Introduction

There is an increased urgency today to ensure the security and proper access control for databases that contain sensitive information (Baskerville & Portougal, 2003). Addressing security problems on an as needed basis is no longer an acceptable approach to dealing with database security issues. Instead, databases need to provide a security approach that is tightly integrated into the database to ensure the proper access control. Database access control ensures that, once a user enters a database environment, all accesses to database objects occur only according to the models and rules fixed by protection policies. In general, there are two approaches to enforcing access control policies: *discretionary* and *mandatory*.

Discretionary access control is based on granting and revoking privileges for the use of data objects. This approach requires privileges to be granted (or revoked) to every user separately, typically by the owner of the data object. Discretionary access control policies allow access rights to be propagated from one user to another. Discretionary access control is a standard feature of all contemporary relational database management system (RDBMS) software tools, and it is used as the primary access control measure for most commercial applications.

For mandatory access control, the users are grouped into clearances, and data are grouped by their classifications. Such an identity-based access control approach is useful in situations where the privileges assigned to users are stable (Park & Giordano, 2006). Mandatory access control is applicable in systems containing large amounts of extremely sensitive information with very strict access and security requirements. Examples of such systems are governmental agencies, the military, airlines, and so forth. In a mandatory access control policy, access to data is determined solely by the user's and data object's membership in security classes. The systems that implement mandatory access control policies are known as multilevel secure (MLS) systems.

In MLS relational databases, multiple records on various security levels can depict the same real-world entity. For such records, non-key attributes can have different values at different security levels. (Key attributes are used to uniquely identify each entity.) Providing information to users at lower security levels that is different from the information stored at higher security levels is called a *cover story*. Cover stories provide a mechanism to protect information that should only be known to users at higher security levels from users at lower levels. Until recently, every MLS model required the key attributes to have the same value at all security levels. This requirement excluded the possibility of users at different security levels from seeing different values for the key attributes. However, there are applications for which it may be necessary to provide a cover story for the key attributes, in order to mask the value of an object's identifier to users at lower security levels.

In a previous article (Jukic, Nestorov, & Vrbsky, 2003), we identified this shortcoming as "the cover story dependence on a user-defined key" (p. 15) and we proposed a conceptual approach for addressing this problem. In this chapter, we describe the working details of the actual solution. We present the model changes; the subsequent relational algebra modifications; and the new insert, delete, and update procedures, which are all required in order to facilitate the proposed improvements. In addition, we illustrate the increased expressive power of our data model compared to existing models and we demonstrate the security and soundness of such a database.

MLS Models

MLS models have been proposed by Denning (1988); Haigh, O'Brien, and Thomasen (1991); Jajodia and Sandhu (1992); Smith and Winslett (1992); Winslett, Smith, and Qian (1994); Sandhu and Chen (1995); Schaefer, Lyons, Martel, and Kanawati (1995); and Jukic, Vrbsky, Parrish, Dixon, and Jukic (1999). MLS models are based on the classification of the system elements, where classifications are expressed by security levels. Data objects have security levels and users have clearance levels. The security levels of objects are also known as security labels. A security label can contain one security level or a list of levels (Gong & Qian, 1995). As an example, we consider the three possible classifications: S—secret, C—classified, and U—unclassified, where S is a higher classification than C and U, and C is a higher classification than U. A security (or clearance) level l_1 *dominates* another level l_2 (stated as $l_1 \geq l_2$), if l_1 is higher than or on the same level as l_2 in the partial (or total) order of security levels. For example, $S \geq C \geq U$. According to the Bell-LaPadula simple property (Bell & LaPadula, 1974), a subject (user) can read a certain object (data) only if the subject's clearance level dominates the object's security level. In other words, a subject cannot read an object at a higher or incomparable security level than the subject. A second restriction on multilevel secure databases is the star-property (Bell & LaPadula, 1974), which states that all writes take place at the subject's security level or higher.

Early work in MLS relational database models focused on the semantics and the relational algebra for MLS models. The SeaView model (Denning, 1988; Denning & Lunt, 1987) was the first formal MLS secure relational database designed to provide mandatory security protection. The SeaView model extended the concept of a database relation to include the security labels. A relation that is extended with security classifications is called a multilevel relation. The Jajodia-Sandhu model (Jajodia & Sandhu, 1990; Jajodia & Sandhu, 1991) was derived from the SeaView model. It was shown by Jajodia and Sandhu (1990) that the SeaView model can result in the proliferation of tuples on updates and the Jajodia-Sandhu model addresses this shortcoming. The Smith-Winslett model (Smith & Winslett, 1992; Winslett,

Smith, & Qian, 1994) was the first model to extensively address the semantics of an MLS database. The MLR model (Sandhu & Chen, 1995; Sandhu & Chen, 1998) is substantially based on the Jajodia-Sandhu model, and also integrates the belief-based semantics of the Smith-Winslett model.

It was shown that all of the aforementioned models can present users with some information that is difficult to interpret (Lunt, 1992). Consequently, we developed the belief consistent MLS (BCMLS) model (Jukic et al., 1999), which addresses these concerns by including the semantics for an unambiguous interpretation of all data presented to the users. Within a table in the BCMLS model, each attribute is accompanied by an attribute classification. The attribute classification is a security label that contains one or more letters, with each letter representing a security level. Each security level in the label must dominate the level to its left. The first letter in the label indicates the security level on which the value of the attribute was created. Such a level is called the *primary level* of that attribute. Information is always believed to be true by the users whose clearance is equal to the primary level of the label. The letters that follow this first letter of the label are called secondary levels. They indicate the security levels for users who have a belief about labeled information, and this belief can be either true or false. Letters that are not preceded by the "-" symbol indicate the secondary levels, where the information is believed to be true. The letters following the "-" symbol indicate the secondary levels, where the information is believed to be false. When every attribute of a tuple is labeled as false on a certain level, a user from that level considers that tuple to be a *mirage tuple* (Jukic et al., 1999). In other words, they do not believe in the existence of such an entity.

In addition to labeling each attribute with a security label, the tuple, as a whole, has a tuple classification (TC) label. The tuple is visible on a certain level, only if the TC label contains that level. We note that not every part of the label is visible to every user. Only the parts of the label that depict the user's security clearance level or lower security levels are visible. To illustrate the main features of an MLS database, we will use the following example scenario, where the underlying MLS database is based on the BCMLS model.

Example 1

National Airline keeps track of its passengers in a relational MLS database. Figure 1 illustrates the MLS relation Flight 1234, which has a primary key of Passenger Name. The airline classifies its database users into three clearance categories: U, C, and S, which determine the sensitivity of information they are allowed to see. Every passenger of every flight must be accounted for, on every clearance level. However, the correct passenger's type and ticket pricing information may have to be hidden from some security levels. All the information about passengers Mike

Smith and Bob Johnson is available for all three clearance levels. However, the information about passenger Sue McCoy is more sensitive. The subjects on the S level correctly see both her ticket pricing information and the fact that she is an Air Marshal. The subjects on the C level see her correct ticket pricing information, but the fact that she is an Air Marshal is masked by a cover story indicating she is a Regular Passenger. The subjects on the U level are given a cover story for both her passenger type and ticket pricing information.

Figure 1. National airlines flight 1234 table

Passenger Name	Seat Assg.	Type	Ticket Pricing	TC
Mike Smith UCS	First UCS	Regular Passenger UCS	Paid Ticket UCS	UCS
Bob Johnson UCS	Coach UCS	Crew in Transfer UCS	No Charge UCS	UCS
Sue McCoy UCS	Coach UCS	Regular Passenger UC-S	Paid Ticket U-CS	U-CS
Sue McCoy UCS	Coach UCS	Regular Passenger UC-S	No Charge CS	C-S
Sue McCoy UCS	Coach UCS	Air Marshal S	No Charge CS	S

Figure 2. National Airlines Flight 1234 Table: U view, C view, & S view

Passenger Name	Seat Assg.	Type	Ticket Pricing
Mike Smith	First	Regular Passenger	Paid Ticket
Bob Johnson	Coach	Crew in Transfer	No Charge
Sue McCoy	Coach	Regular Passenger	Paid Ticket

(a) U View

Passenger Name	Seat Assg	Type	Ticket Pricing	TC
Mike Smith UC	First UC	Regular Passenger UC	Paid Ticket UC	UC
Bob Johnson UC	Coach UC	Crew in Transfer UC	No Charge UC	UC
Sue McCoy UC	Coach UC	Regular Passenger UC	Paid Ticket U-C	U-C
Sue McCoy UC	Coach UC	Regular Passenger UC	No Charge C	C

(b) C View

Passenger Name	Seat Assg.	Type	Ticket Pricing	TC
Mike Smith UCS	First UCS	Regular Passenger UCS	Paid Ticket UCS	UCS
Bob Johnson UCS	Coach UCS	Crew in Transfer UCS	No Charge UCS	UCS
Sue McCoy UCS	Coach UCS	Regular Passenger UC-S	Paid Ticket UCS	U-CS
Sue McCoy UCS	Coach UCS	Regular Passenger UC-S	No Charge CS	C-S
Sue McCoy UCS	Coach UCS	Air Marshal S	No Charge CS	S

(c) S View

Figure 2 illustrates how the information in the table in Figure 1 is displayed to the users at each of the three different clearance levels. Note that no security labels appear in the lowest level, U view. Even a security label of U could indicate to a U-level user that there may be higher levels containing secret information not available to the U-level user. This would violate security, as it would provide an indirect and unwanted flow of information (as will be discussed in the next section).

As was mentioned previously, in MLS relations, multiple tuples can exist at different security levels, representing contradictory information about the same entity. Assume a user is at security level c. If a lower level tuple with a TC< c, represents the same entity as some other higher level tuple, where TC = c, the lower level tuple is interpreted by a higher level user as a false tuple that represents a cover story (Garvey & Lunt, 1992; Sandhu & Jajodia, 1992) for the entity represented by the higher level tuple. Every user on the higher-level c has the following belief about the cover story lower-level tuple: "Some attribute values of this lower level tuple incorrectly represent a real-world entity." In the S-view in Figure 2(c), S level users see the third and fourth tuples as a cover story of the fifth tuple. Cover stories have been used in MLS models for non-key attributes only. None of the existing models have considered a cover story involving a key attribute. In the next section, we will show how the usage of cover stories can be expanded to involve key attributes.

Covert Channels and Polyinstantiation

The two aforementioned Bell-LaPadula properties prevent the direct flow of information from objects and/or subjects at a higher security clearance level to subjects at a lower level, and are the basis for all MLS models. However, a system may not be secure even if it always enforces the two Bell-LaPadula properties. There may exist a *covert channel*, which allows for an indirect flow of information from a higher level user to a lower level user. For example, suppose a lower level user wishes to insert a tuple that already exists in the database at a higher level of security. A user may want to insert a record "James Bond" into the Spy table on the U level, when there is already a record "James Bond" on the S level in the same table. If this insert is rejected by the system, the lower level user will know that there already exists the same tuple at a higher level. In other words, the user will learn there is a higher security-level spy James Bond.

One way to address this problem is to allow both James Bonds to exist in the system. However, this violates the key constraint of the relational model, in which two tuples must not exist in a relation with the same values for the primary key attribute. On the other hand, requiring the key constraint to hold would result in a covert channel, if the insert of James Bond at level U is rejected. In order to avoid covert channels in

MLS data models, subjects with different classifications are allowed to operate on the same relations through the use of polyinstantiation (Jajodia, Sandhu, & Blaustein, 1995; Lunt, 1992). The term polyinstantiation refers to the simultaneous existence of multiple tuples with the same primary key, where such tuples are distinguished by their classification levels (Lunt, 1992). Polyinstantiation is illustrated in Figure 1, where there are three tuples representing Sue McCoy.

There are two kinds of polyinstantiation that can occur within an MLS relation: attribute polyinstantiation and entity polyinstantiation. Attribute polyinstantiation occurs when two tuples representing the same entity have different values associated with the same attribute (e.g., two different ticket pricing entries for Sue McCoy). Cover stories utilize the concept of attribute polyinstantiation. They are often used to deceive lower level users about the nature of the sensitive information as illustrated by the example in Figure 1. Entity polyinstantiation occurs when two tuples have the same primary key and different classifications associated with the primary keys. In the James Bond example, the lower-level user would have to be allowed to insert a James Bond tuple into the table in order to prevent a covert channel. That would lead to entity polyinstantiation, due to the existence of two different James Bonds in the relation (e.g., James Bond U and James Bond S). Since a U-level user does not know about the existence of James Bond S, it is assumed that James Bond U is a different entity, unless an S-level user indicates differently.

The Key-Loophole and Non-Key Related Cover Stories

We now describe the problems that occur when MLS models do not allow the key attributes to have a cover story. The key attributes that identify the entities in the MLS model are called the *entity identifier*. In the BCMLS model, the entity identifier is composed of the primary key, K, and the primary level, pl, of its classification attribute, KC. In other words: $K + pl(KC)$. The entity identifier of the third tuple in Figure 1 is "Sue McCoy U," since $pl(UCS) = U$. Within MLS models, the link between a tuple and its corresponding lower-level cover story tuple is the matching value of their entity identifier. For example, Figure 1 shows that the third, fourth, and fifth tuples share the same entity identifier "Sue McCoy U." In this case, the entity identifier value identifies the third and fourth tuples as cover stories for the fifth tuple on the S level. The same entity identifier identifies the third tuple as the cover story of the fourth tuple on the C level.

Existing MLS models use a value-based approach for defining the entity identifier, which limits the scope of their usage. For example, the stored values "Sue McCoy U" were used to indicate that that the third, fourth, and fifth tuples refer to the same entity. As a result, while users at different security levels can have different beliefs about the values of non-key attributes, this is not true of the values of key attributes. In order to portray this limitation, we will slightly alter Example 1, introduced earlier in this chapter.

Example 1 (Altered)

As in the first version of this example, all the information about passengers Mike Smith and Bob Johnson is available for all three security/clearance levels. However, the information about passenger Sue McCoy is more sensitive. The subjects on the S level are allowed to correctly see her seat assignment, passenger type, ticket pricing, and name. The subjects on the C level are allowed to see her seat assignment and ticket pricing, but her passenger type and her name should be masked by a cover story for passenger type and a cover story for name. The subjects on the U level can see her correct seat assignment and should be given a cover story for her passenger type, ticket pricing and her name.

In this altered example, the value of the key attribute—the identity of the entity—is sensitive information and needs to be protected. For example, a U level user could be a ticket agent who can see that a particular seat is taken and the ticket for it is issued, simply by the fact that Sue McCoy has a ticket and a seat assignment. However, we should still protect Sue McCoy's identity (classified as S) from the U and C level users. Therefore, the Passenger Name, seen and believed by the U and C levels, is different from that at the S level. It is not possible to simply not give any passenger name for Sue McCoy to U and C level users. Because MLS is a relational model, users need to be able to access a tuple by an identifying key that is value-based. In addition to violating entity integrity, using a null value for the key would also compromise security. It could signal to the user that the identity of the object is sensitive information. For example, we cannot present a null value for the Passenger Name field for Sue McCoy to U and C level users, because these users can infer her existence. They can simply look at her occupied seat in the airplane or assist her with the check-in procedure and realize that an attempt is being made to protect her identity. Instead, because her name is sensitive information, U and C level users see and believe a different name than S users. The entity that U and C level users see as Jane Clark exists; it is just that S users should know that the actual name for that same passenger is Sue McCoy.

No existing MLS model is capable of properly handling this scenario. The reason for it is the cover story depends on a value-based key. Figure 3 illustrates the situation. The S level user would treat all records relating to Jane Clark as so-called mirage tuples, which represent a non-existing entity. The user on the S level would know that there is no passenger named Jane Clark, but has no way of knowing that Jane Clark is a cover story for Sue McCoy. This can cause problems in situations

Figure 3. National airlines flight 1234 table

Passenger Name	Seat Assg.	Type	Ticket Pricing	TC
Mike Smith UCS	First UCS	Regular Passenger UCS	Paid Ticket UCS	UCS
Bob Johnson UCS	Coach UCS	Crew in Transfer UCS	No Charge UCS	UCS
Jane Clark UC-S	Coach UC-S	Regular Passenger UC-S	Paid Ticket U-CS	U-CS
Jane Clark UC-S	Coach UC-S	Regular Passenger UC-S	No Charge C-S	C-S
Sue McCoy S	Coach S	Air Marshal S	No Charge S	S

when an S level user has to communicate with lower level users. For example, the S level user would be unaware that C level users are aware of the passenger Sue McCoy as Jane Clark.

The following is a definition of the problem illustrated by this example.

Definition: Key Loophole Problem

Suppose that tuple A represents an entity on a particular security level, while tuple B represents that same entity on a lower security level. This indicates that tuple B is a lower-level cover story for tuple A. The key loophole problem occurs when tuple A cannot be connected to the lower-level cover story tuple B, if tuple B has a different key attribute value.

In Jukic et al. (2003), we identified the key loophole problem and we introduced a change in the way the entity identifier is defined. We proposed a system defined entity identifier (SEID), whose value would remain hidden to all users on all security levels and would be used only internally by the MLS DBMS. Here, we illustrate how this new SEID would be used to properly handle the situation depicted in the Example 1. This is shown in Figure 4.

The SEID column contains the new system defined entity identifier. If an S level user requests all information about Sue McCoy, the fifth tuple along with the cover story third and fourth tuples, would be displayed. The S level user would now be aware

Figure 4. National airlines flight 1234 table

SEID	Passenger Name	Seat Assg.	Type	Ticket Pricing	TC
1111	Mike Smith UCS	First UCS	Regular Passenger UCS	Paid Ticket UCS	UCS
2222	Bob Johnson UCS	Coach UCS	Crew in Transfer UCS	No Charge UCS	UCS
3333	Jane Clark UC-S	Coach UCS	Regular Passenger UC-S	Paid Ticket U-CS	U-CS
3333	Jane Clark UC-S	Coach UCS	Regular Passenger UC-S	No Charge CS	C-S
3333	Sue McCoy S	Coach UCS	Air Marshal S	No Charge CS	S

Figure 5. National airlines flight 1234 table

Passenger Name	Seat Assg.	Type	Ticket Pricing	TC
Mike Smith UCS	First UCS	Regular Passenger UCS	Paid Ticket UCS	UCS
Bob Johnson UCS	Coach UCS	Crew in Transfer UCS	No Charge UCS	UCS
Jane Clark UC-S	Coach UCS	Regular Passenger UC-S	Paid Ticket U-CS	U-CS
Jane Clark UC-S	Coach UCS	Regular Passenger UC-S	No Charge CS	C-S
Sue McCoy S	Coach UCS	Air Marshal S	No Charge CS	S
Next Record	...	...	...	...
Its Cover Stories	...	...	...	...

of the fact that Jane Clark's records are cover stories about Sue McCoy, given to the lower level users. Using SEID still results in polyinstantiation. Users at different levels have different beliefs about attributes referring to the same entity. Hence, multiple tuples will exist for the same entity, with different values for attributes at different levels. SEID facilitates the concept of *non-key related cover stories*, which are cover-stories that are not related through matching values of key attributes.

Note that we cannot use SEID as a standard primary key because its value is not unique within a relation. For example, in Figure 4, three tuples share the same SEID value. Since the only use of SEID is to connect tuples that refer to the same entity, we omit the SEID from a user interface and simply bundle tuples that refer to the same entity, as shown in Figure 5. Such an interface to an MLS application can now connect each tuple with its related cover stories, even if the cover stories are not related via a key value.

ER Model Representation

We can also demonstrate the differences between the SEID enhanced BCMLS model and other MLS data models through the use of entity-relationship (ER) style diagrams. An ER diagram can illustrate how the entities, tuples, and elements of the tuples are related in MLS models. The basic assumption is that each entity has a key, each tuple has a tuple classification, and each element has a set of attributes and attribute classifications.

Figure 6 illustrates an ER diagram of the MLR data model and Figure 7 illustrates the ER diagram of the SEID enhanced BCMLS data model. As shown in Figure 6, each entity in the MLR data model has a unique key A_1 and key classification C_1. An entity consists of one or more tuples, each of which has a tuple classification, TC. Each tuple consists of one or more elements having attributes $A_i (2 \leq i \leq n)$ and their classifications $C_i (2 \leq i \leq n)$. As shown in Figure 7, an entity in the SEID enhanced BCMLS data model has a unique SEID and consists of one or more *iden-*

Figure 6. ER diagram of the MLR data model

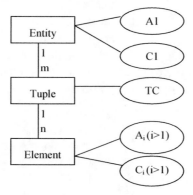

Figure 7. ER diagram of the BCMLS data model

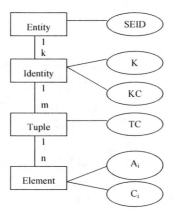

tities. Unlike the MLR model, the identity and not the entity has a key K and key classification KC. Each real-world entity can have multiple identities. An identity has one or more tuples associated with it, where each tuple has a tuple classification, TC. Each tuple consists of one or more elements, which have attributes $A_i (1 \leq i \leq n)$ and their classifications $C_i (1 \leq i \leq n)$. In the BCMLS model, we allow the identity of the entity to exist separately from the entity itself. The existence of identity as a separate component increases the expressive power of the SEID enhanced BCMLS model, by allowing for a cover story of the key attribute. As a result, this allows cover story tuples to be related by a non-key.

Model Changes: Properties

As we will show, the proposed solution to the key loophole problem of using an SEID requires considerable technical changes within MLS models, as well as within the associated relational algebra and update procedures. At the same time, the improvements gained in the robustness of the extended model have far reaching implications for its practical applicability, and therefore, warrant the effort required to make the changes.

We first describe how the introduction of the new entity identifier approach changes the properties of the BCMLS model. We are using the BCMLS model as a representative of MLS models, and the changes described here would not be significantly different for other contemporary MLS models. We presented the original properties of the BCMLS model in Jukic et al. (1999). We give an abbreviated version of these properties in Figure 8. We define the following notation used in the remainder of the chapter.

Notation:

R: multilevel relation

t: tuple

A_i: Attribute

KC: security classification label of K

FK: foreign key

SEID: system entity identifier

K: value-based key

TC: tuple security classification label

C_i: security classification label of attribute A_i

KK: one column of a value-based key

FKC: security classification label of FK

max-view$_c$(R): all tuples c-level user eligible to see

Functions:

bcl[l$_i$, l$_j$]: set of all possible belief consistent labels between security levels l$_i$ and l$_j$

lb[l$_i$, L]: indicates if belief is true or false in label L for security level l$_i$

pl[L]: primary (lowest) level of label L, indicates level where tuple created

Figure 8. Key properties of the belief-consistent MLS data model

LABELS: In the BCMLS model, bcl[L, H] indicates, for the set of totally-ordered security levels ranging from the lowest level security L to the highest level security H, a set of possible security labels (belief-consistent labels) available. For example, in the environment with two security levels, U and C, where C dominates U (U $\leq$ C), the set of possible security labels is bcl[U, C] = {U, UC, U-C, C}. Function pl(c), where c $\in$ bcl[L,H], extracts a primary level from the belief-consistent label c. For example, pl(UC)=U, pl(U)=U, and pl(C) = C.

RELATION SCHEME: A multilevel *relation scheme* is denoted by $R(K, KC, A_1, C_1,...,A_n, C_n, TC)$, where K is the data primary key attribute(s), KC is the classification attribute of K, each A_i is a non-key data attribute over domain D_i, each C_i is the classification attribute for corresponding A_i, and TC is the tuple classification attribute. The domain of KC, TC, and C_i is the set of possible belief-consistent labels $bcl[L,H]$.

RELATION INSTANCE: A relation instance, denoted by $r(K, KC, A_1, C_1,...,A_n, C_n, TC)$, is a set of distinct tuples of the form $(k, kc, a_1, c_1,...,a_n, c_n, tc)$, where each $k, a_i \in D_i$, and $kc, c_i \in bcl[L,H]$, and tc is a set of labels defined as follows: *for every security level l in the range [L,H]:*

a.   **if** there is a label kc or c_i *(for $1 \leq i \leq n$)* that does not contain *l*, then $l \notin tc$ (*l* is not included in *tc*);

b.   **else if** there is a label kc or c_i *(for $1 \leq i \leq n$)* in which *l* is false, then $-l \in tc$ (*l* is false in *tc*);

c.   **else** security level *l* is true in every label kc and c_i *(for $1 \leq i \leq n$)*, and $l \in tc$ (*l* is true in *tc*).

Entity Integrity Property: A multilevel relation R satisfies entity integrity iff, $\forall t \in R$:

1. $KK \in K \Rightarrow t[KK] \neq null,$

2. $\forall KK \in K, pl(KK) = c$

3. $t[KC] \neq null$

4. $\forall A_i \notin K \Rightarrow pl(t[C_i]) \geq pl(t[KC]),$ *for $1 \leq i \leq n$.*

Polyinstantiation Integrity Property: A multilevel relation R satisfies polyinstantiation integrity iff, $\forall t \in R$:

1. $K, pl(KC), pl(C_i) \rightarrow A_i$ *for $1 \leq i \leq n$*

2. $K, pl(KC), pl(TC) \rightarrow A_i, C_i$ *for $1 \leq i \leq n$*

Base Tuple Integrity Property: A multilevel relation R satisfies the base tuple property iff, $\forall t \in R$ there is a $t_b \in R$, such that:

1. $t[K] = t_b[K]$

2. $pl(t(KC]) = pl(t_b[KC])$

3. $pl(t_b[KC]) = pl(t_b[C_i]) = pl(t_b[TC])$ *for $1 \leq i \leq n$*

4. $t_b[A_i] \neq null$ *for $1 \leq i \leq n$*

continued on following page

Figure 8. continued

Referential Integrity Property: When *FK* is a foreign key of the referencing relation *R1*, with *FKC* as its classification, and *R2* is the referenced relation with a primary key *K*, instances *r1* of *R1* and *r2* of *R2* satisfy referential integrity iff, $\forall$ *t1* $\in$ *r1*, such that *t1[FK]* $\neq$ *null*, and there exists a *t2* $\in$ *r2* such that:

1. t1[FK] = t2[K]

2. pl(t1[FKC]) $\geq$ pl(t2[KC])

3. lb(pl(t1[TC]), t2[TC]) = pl(t1[TC]).

Foreign Key Integrity Property: If *FK* is a foreign key of the referencing multilevel relation *R*, relation *R* satisfies the foreign key property iff $\forall$ *t* $\in$ *R*:

1. *Either* $\forall$ A_i $\in$ *FK*, *t[A_i]* = *null*   *for 1 $\leq$ i $\leq$ n*

   or $\forall$ A_i $\in$ *FK*, *t[A_i]* $\neq$ *null*   *for 1 $\leq$ i $\leq$ n*

2. $\forall$ A_i, A_j $\in$ *FK*, *t[C_i]* = *t[C_j]*   *for 1 $\leq$ i $\leq$ n and 1 $\leq$ j $\leq$ n*

Belief Integrity Property: A multilevel relation *R* satisfies the belief property iff, $\forall$ *t* $\in$ *R*:

1. *if lb(c, t[TC])* $\neq$ $\varnothing$ *then lb(c, t_b[TC])* $\neq$ $\varnothing$, $\forall$ *t_b such that t_b[K]* = *t[K], t_b[pl(KC)]* = *t[pl(KC)] and t_b* $\in$ *max-view$_c$(R)*.

2. *if lb(c, t[TC])* = $\varnothing$ *then lb(c, t_b[TC])* = $\varnothing$, $\forall$ *t_b such that t_b[K]* = *t[K], t_b[pl(KC)]* = *t[pl(KC)] and t_b* $\in$ *max-view$_c$(R)*.

3. *if lb(c, t[TC])* = *c then lb(c, t_b[TC])* = *-c and lb(c, t_b[KC])* = *c, $\forall$ t_b such that t_b[K]* = *t[K], t_b[pl(KC)]* = *t[pl(KC)] and t_b* $\in$ *max-view$_c$(R)*.

4. *if lb(c, t[KC])* = *-c then lb(c, t_b[KC])* = *-c, $\forall$ t_b such that t_b[K]* = *t[K], t_b[pl(KC)]* = *t[pl(KC)] and t_b* $\in$ *max-view$_c$(R)*.

In the remainder of this section, we show how the original model properties are changed in order to accommodate the system defined entity identifier SEID.

Relation Schema and Relation Instance

The relation schema $R(K, KC, A_1, C_1,...,A_n, C_n, TC)$, shown in Figure 8, is now expanded to account for the new system defined entity identifier and it is denoted by $R(SEID, K, KC, A_1, C_1,...,A_n, C_n, TC)$. Consequently, a relation instance is now denoted by $r(SEID, K, KC, A_1, C_1,...,A_n, C_n, TC)$, and it represents a set of distinct tuples of the form *(seid, k, kc, a_1, c_1,...,a_n, c_n, tc)*.

Entity Integrity

The entity integrity property ensures that every tuple has a system entity identifier assigned to it.

Entity Integrity Property: *A multilevel relation R satisfies entity integrity iff,* $\forall$ *t* $\in$ *R*

1. $KK \in K \Rightarrow t[KK] \neq null$
2. $\forall KK \in K, pl(KK) = c$
3. $t[KC] \neq null$
4. $t[SEID] \neq null$

The first condition ensures that no key attribute column *KK* of tuple *t* can contain null values. The second condition ensures every key attribute column *KK* of tuple t is at the same primary classification level. The third condition ensures that no key classification *KC* of tuple *t* can contain null values. This property needs the addition of the fourth condition of no SEID of a tuple equal to null. We have also deleted the original third condition (see Figure 8), in which the primary level of a classification of the non-key attribute (denoted as $pl(t[C_i])$) must dominate the primary level of the classification of the key attribute (denoted as $pl(t[KC])$). This is because, with the addition of a cover story for the key, a non-key attribute may no longer dominate the classification of a key attribute if it is a cover story (e.g., last tuple in Figure 4).

Polyinstantiation Integrity

The polyinstantiation property defines the key of a multilevel relation. This constraint is necessary because there can be more than one tuple (and identity in the case of an SEID enhanced BCMLS) associated with the same entity.

Polyinstantiation Integrity Property: *A multilevel relation R satisfies polyinstantiation integrity iff,* $\forall$ *t* $\in$ *R*

1. $K, pl(KC), pl(C_i) \rightarrow A_i$ *for* $1 \leq i \leq n$
2. $K, pl(KC), pl(TC) \rightarrow A_i, C_i$ *for* $1 \leq i \leq n$
3. $SEID, pl(KC) \rightarrow K$

The first condition defines the primary key as the value *K* and the primary level of its key classification *KC*. The second condition indicates that there can be at most one tuple with the same key *K* and primary level of the key classification *KC* per security level. The last property has been added to accommodate a cover story for the key. It indicates that for any entity, there can be, at most, one cover story for a key *K* at any primary level of the key classification *KC*. In other words, there can be, at most, one identity of an entity per classification level.

Base Tuple Integrity Property

The base tuple integrity property ensures that there exists a tuple believed to be true at some security level, and this is typically the level at which the tuple was first created.

Base Tuple Integrity Property: *A multilevel relation R satisfies the base tuple property iff, $\forall t \in R$ there is a base tuple $t_b \in R$, such that:*

1. $t[SEID] = t_b[SEID]$
2. $pl(t_b[KC]) = pl(t_b[C_i]) = pl(t_b[TC])$ *for $1 \leq i \leq n$*
3. $t_b[A_i] \neq null$ *for $1 \leq i \leq n$*

The first condition of the base tuple integrity property establishes the entity identifier. This property replaces the first two properties in the original definition (Figure 8), which referred to the key attribute value and its classification as the entity identifier. This is replaced with a reference to the SEID instead, which ensures that all the tuples that are referring to the same entity share the same system entity identifier. The second and third conditions ensure that for every entity depicted in the relation, there will be a base tuple t_b with an equal primary level of the classification for each attribute and no null values for any attribute.

Belief Integrity Property

The belief property is unique to our belief-consistent model. There are three requirements to the belief property and they are defined by the three possible beliefs: true, false, and irrelevant.

In other words, a multilevel relation R satisfies the belief property iff, $\forall t \in R$:

1. *if $lb(c, t[TC]) \neq \varnothing$, then $lb(c, t_b[TC]) \neq \varnothing$, $\forall t_b$ such that $t_b[SEID] = t[SEID]$ and $t_b \in max\text{-}view_c(R)$.*
2. *if $lb(c, t[TC]) = \varnothing$, then $lb(c, t_b[TC]) = \varnothing$, $\forall t_b$ such that $t_b[SEID] = t[SEID]$ and $t_b \in max\text{-}view_c(R)$.*
3. *if $lb(c, t[TC]) = c$, then $lb(c, t_b[TC]) = -c$, $\forall t_b$ such that $t_b[SEID] = t[SEID]$ and $t_b \in max\text{-}view_c(R)$.*

The first requirement states that if a user has a belief about a tuple t, which represents a certain entity, the user must have a belief about all other tuples t_b that represent the same entity and are visible to the user. Consequently, the second requirement states that if a user does not have a belief about a visible tuple (that is, irrelevant tuple), the user has no belief about any other visible tuple with the same SEID. The third requirement states that if a user believes that a tuple t, which represents a certain entity is a true tuple, the user must believe that all other tuples t_b that represent the same entity and are visible to the user, are cover story tuples. Once a user has asserted a belief of true for tuple t, then attributes in any other visible lower level tuple t_b (that represents the same entity as t) with the same or different values must be true or false, respectively. Note that the fourth requirement from the original Belief Integrity Property (see Figure 8) is omitted. The original fourth requirement states that if a user believes that a tuple t, which represents a certain entity is a mirage tuple, the user must believe that all other tuples tx that represent the same entity and are visible to the user, are mirage tuples as well. This is still true, but the definition of the mirage tuple is now different. In the SEID enhanced BCMLS model, $lb(c, t[KC]) = -c$ no longer unambiguously indicates a mirage tuple (it could be a mirage tuple *OR* a non-key related cover story tuple). Therefore, the fourth property no longer holds. The way that the system would unambiguously recognize a mirage tuple is the following: *if $lb(c, t[TC]) = -c$ and $\forall t_b$ such that $t_b[SEID] = t[SEID]$, $lb(c, t_b[TC]) = -c$ and $t_b \in$ max-view$_c$(R), then t is a mirage tuple.* In other words, there is still a way to indicate a mirage tuple, but there is no longer a need to mandate in a belief integrity property how to directly assert a mirage tuple belief. Instead, the SEID determines in a simple way if a tuple is mirage or cover story: if false tuple's SEID is only connected to (that is, same as) nothing but false tuples, then the tuple is a mirage.

The above changes in the four integrity properties will not cause additional changes in the definitions of the Referential Integrity Property (which ensures that a foreign key on each security level references an existing value in another table that is true on the same security level), and the Foreign Key Property (which ensures that the security classifications of each part of the composite foreign key are the same.) These properties are listed in Figure 8.

Model Changes: Relational Algebra

In addition to the above described model property changes, the new definition of the entity identifier also requires changes in the relational algebra. We introduce the new concept of *query result entity equivalence* as a basis for the relational algebra of the SEID based model. This concept ensures that, for each record that satisfies the condition of the query, the result includes all other records that refer to the same entity, if they satisfy all parts of the query condition that do not involve the key value.

This concept is necessary in order to recognize and include Non-Key Related Cover Stories in the query results. For example, consider the select operation:

$$\sigma_\Phi(R),$$

where σ is the select operator, Φ is the select condition, and R is the MLS relation on which the select operation is being applied. The select condition Φ has the following form:

$$\Phi = clause\ (boolean\_op\ clause)^*,$$

where * means zero or more, *boolean_op* is AND, OR, and NOT, and

clause $:= E_i\ op\ E_j\ |\ E_i\ op\ a\ |\ E_i\ L\ b\ (boolean\_op\ L\ b)^* |\ TC\ L\ b\ (boolean\_op\ L\ b)^*,$

where E_i represents a value attribute (either key K or non-key) from R

op is one of the comparison operators ($<$, $=$, $>$, $\leq$, $\geq$, or $\neq$);
a is a constant;
L is a single label representing a security level (e.g., U, C, or S);
b is a belief held by that level (e.g., *true* or *false*);
TC is the tuple classification label.

As an example, suppose an S-level user issues the following select operation on the relation shown in Figure 1, to choose all tuples referring to the passenger Sue McCoy that show her correct ticket pricing:

$\sigma_{\text{Passenger Name ='Sue McCoy' AND Ticket Pricing S true}}$ (NATIONAL AIRLINES FLIGHT 1234 TABLE).

The result is:

Sue McCoy UCS	Coach UCS	Regular Passenger UC-S	No Charge CS	C-S
Sue McCoy UCS	Coach UCS	Air Marshal S	No Charge CS	S

The same query issued on a table where cover stories are not related through the value of the key (Figure 4) would result in:

Sue McCoy S	Coach UCS	Air Marshal S	No Charge CS	S

This result deprives S users of the information that C level users know this passenger under a different name, but are aware of the correct pricing for the requested passenger (see table in Figure 5).

In order to accommodate non-key related cover stories, we redefine the select operation as follows:

$$\sigma'_{\Phi} (R),$$

where Φ is the select condition that has the form $\Phi = clause\ (boolean\_op\ clause)*$, R is the MLS relation on which the select operation is being applied, and σ' is the newly defined select operator:

if   clause $= K\ op\ E_j \mid K\ op\ a,$

then $\sigma'_{clause}(R) = \sigma_{SEID\ in\ (\pi_{SEID}(\sigma_{clause}(R)))}(R),$

else /* for all other clauses */,

$$\sigma'_{clause}(R) = \sigma_{clause}(R),$$

where K represents the key value attribute from R,

E_j represents a value attribute (key or non-key) from R;

a is a constant;

π is the regular BCMLS relational algebra project operation;

σ is the regular BCMLS relational algebra select operation;

in is the set membership boolean operator.

This new definition of the select operation ensures entity equivalence in the query result. For example, the query Q1 executed on the table shown in Figure 4, using the new select statement, will select the records:

| Jane Clark   UC-S | Coach UCS | Regular Passenger UC-S | No Charge CS | C-S |
| Sue McCoy S | Coach UCS | Air Marshal   S | No Charge CS | S |

Even though the two tuples have different key attribute values, both tuples refer to the same entity and are entity equivalent. An interface, such as the one illustrated by Figure 5, would ensure that the user clearly recognizes entity equivalent records.

A SELECT statement is now defined as:

SELECT A_1 [, A_2] ...
FROM R_1 [, R_2] ...
[WHERE Φ],

where R_1, R_2 ... are MLS relation names, A_1, A_2, ... are attribute names in the tables R_1, R_2 ... and Φ is the select condition as defined above.

Model Changes: Insert, Delete, and Update Operations

In this section, we redefine the INSERT, DELETE, and UPDATE statements for the SEID based model.

Insert

The insert operation creates a new tuple that represents a new entity by itself and has the following form:

INSERT INTO R
VALUES $(k, a_1 , a_2 ... a_i, ... a_n)$,

where R is an MLS relation, k is the key value, and a_i are values from domains of attributes A_i for all n value attributes of the relation R.

Every tuple inserted by a user is a base level tuple on the user's level. The classifications KC, TC, and all C_i's have the same label containing simply the user's level. The only constraint on the INSERT command is the key constraint and it is similar to the key constraint of the traditional relational model.

Insert Constraint

If a user on security level L issues a command to insert a tuple t into a relation R, the insert will be accepted if and only if there is no $t' \in R$ such that $t'[K] = t[K]$, $pl(t'[KC]) = pl(t[KC]$ and $pl(t'[TC]) = pl(t[TC])$, and the resulting database state satisfies entity integrity, foreign key integrity, and referential integrity; otherwise, insert will be rejected.

In other words, there can be no two tuples within the MLS relation with the same K, pl(KC), and pl(TC). If the insert is accepted, it is regulated according to the following procedure:

Insert Procedure

If a user from the security level L issues a command that inserts a tuple t with values $(k, a_1 \dots a_n)$ into the relation $R(SEID, K, KC, A_1, C_1 \dots A_n, C_n, TC)$, the resulting tuple $t \in R$ is defined as follows:

1. $t[K] = k$
2. $t[A_i] = a_i$
3. $t[SEID] = $ *new seid value generated by system*
4. $t[KC] = t[C_1] = \dots = t[C_n] = t[TC] = L.$

The first two requirements of the insert procedure state that the value attributes of the new tuple will correspond to the values indicated in the insert command. The third requirement is the new SEID generated by the system. The fourth requirement states that all of the classifications of the newly inserted tuple will be simple labels, indicating the level of the user who inserted the tuple.

Delete

The delete operation eliminates a tuple from an MLS relation and has the following form:

> DELETE FROM   *R*
>
> WHERE   *P*

where *R* is an MLS relation and *P* is a select condition that identifies tuples to be deleted. The delete operation can delete one or more tuples. Deleting tuples is restricted by the following constraint.

Delete Constraint

If a user from security level L issues a command to delete a tuple t, $\forall \ t \in R$, DELETE t is accepted iff: pl(t[TC]) = L and referential integrity is satisfied.

In other words, a user can delete tuples only on his or her own level. Even with this restriction, there are several different cases during which a delete operation can occur. The delete operation is regulated according to the following procedure.

Delete Procedure

If a user on the security level L issues a command to delete from a relation R:
$\forall \ t \in R$, if t satisfies P and if pl(t[TC]) = L

1.   *t is deleted from R*
2.   *$\forall \ ta \in R$, if ta[SEID] = t[SEID], and pl(ta[KC]) = pl(t[KC]), and pl(ta[TC]) > L, then user on the pl(ta[TC]) chooses between*
      deleting ta
      or keep ta and delete L from KC and from appropriate $C_i \ (i \leq 1 \leq n)$

The first requirement states that every tuple that satisfies the where clause of the delete command and the delete constraint will be deleted. The second requirement states that if a lower level tuple is deleted, and if there is a higher level tuple with the same SEID, then the user from the higher level decides to either delete the higher level tuple or keep the higher level tuple. If the tuple is kept, the level L is deleted from KC and from the appropriate $C_i \ (i \leq 1 \leq n)$. As a result, this changes the primary level of the tuples to a higher security level and creates a base tuple at a higher level.

Update

The update operation is used to change the values of one or more attributes in a tuple (or tuples) of an MLS relation and has the following form:

UPDATE R
SET $\quad A_x = a_x$
WHERE P,

where R is an MLS relation, A_x is a value attribute or a key attribute K from R, a_x is a value from the domain of A_x, and P is a select condition that identifies tuples to be updated. In order to simplify the update definitions, updating of only one attribute at a time is assumed. These definitions can easily be expanded to handle the cases, when more than one attribute is updated at the same time. Updating tuples is restricted by the following constraint.

Update Constraint

If a user from the security level L issues an update command, $\forall\ t \in R$, UPDATE t is accepted iff lb(c, TC) ≠ -L and entity integrity, foreign key integrity, and referential integrity are satisfied.

With this constraint, updating a tuple that is verified false on a specific level by a user from that level is prohibited. Such a tuple is either a mirage tuple or a cover story tuple. A mirage tuple cannot be used as a base for a new true tuple on the user's level, since the user does not believe in the entity's existence. A cover story tuple means that there is another tuple with the same EID that is already believed by the user to correctly represent a real-world entity.

If the update is accepted, it is regulated according to the following procedure.

Update Procedure

If a user on the security level L issues a command to update a relation R:
$\forall\ t \in R$, *iff t satisfies P :*

1. if pl(t[TC]) = L, t will be updated.
2. if pl(t[TC]) < L and lb(c, t[TC]) = L, a new tuple tn based on t will be inserted on the L level, while the attribute values of tuple t will not change.

3.   if $pl(t[TC]) < L$, $lb(c, t[TC]) = \varnothing$, and $\rceil \exists\ t_i \in R$ such that $t_i[SEID] = t[SEID]$ and $pl(t_i[TC]) < L$, a new tuple tn based on t will be inserted on the L level, while the attribute values of t itself will not change.

4.   if $pl(t[TC]) < L$, $lb(c, t[TC]) = \varnothing$, and $\exists\ t_i \in R$ such that $t_i[SEID] = t[SEID]$ and $pl(t_i[TC]) < L$, the user will choose a tuple tu from among all t_i's (including t), and a new tuple tn based on tu will be inserted on the L level, while the attribute values of tu itself will not change.

The first requirement states that every tuple on the user level that satisfies the WHERE clause will be updated. The second requirement states that for every true lower level tuple that satisfies the WHERE clause, a new tuple with the same SEID will be inserted on the user level, due to the update command. The third requirement states that if there is a tuple on the lower level that satisfies the WHERE clause with no belief (true/false) asserted at level *L*, and there is no other lower level tuple with the same SEID, a new tuple with the same SEID will be inserted on the user level. The fourth requirement states that if there is a tuple on the lower that satisfies the WHERE clause level with no belief (true/false) asserted at level *L*, but there are other lower level tuples with the same SEID, a new tuple, based on the one of the lower level tuples with the same SEID, will be inserted on the user level.

Security

Security of an MLS model is determined by whether or not the MLS model satisfies the security requirements of no downward flow of information (Sandhu & Chen, 1998). Similar to Sandhu and Chen (1998), our proof of security is based on the concept of noninterference. We also do not consider timing covert channels, since, as noted in Sandhu and Chen (1998), the channels are implementation specific. We do consider the signaling channels that are inherent to a deterministic data model, and define the security requirement as follows:

Definition 1: *A secure data model is non-interfering if, given a security level L, deleting any input from a user with a security classification higher than L, does not affect the output to any user with a security classification lower than or equal to L.*

In other words, the BCMLS model is secure if changing data values at a higher security level: 1) does not affect the output (results) to a query posed by users at a lower security level, and 2) does not affect the database state at a lower security level.

Notation:

   Z: all users with a clearance level

   T: all tuples with a security level

For a given security level L,

   $Z_{\leq L}$: the set of users with clearance levels lower than or equal to L

   $Z_{>L}$: the set of users with clearance levels higher than L, it is equal to $Z - Z_{\leq L}$

   $T_{\leq L}$: the set of tuples with security levels lower than or equal to L

   $T_{>L}$: the set of tuples with security levels higher than L, it is equal to $T - T_{\leq L}$

For any security level L, $Z = Z_{\leq L} \cup Z_{>L}$ and $Z_{\leq L} \cap Z_{>L} = \varnothing$; similarly $T = T_{\leq L} \cup T_{>L}$ and $T_{\leq L} \cap T_{>L} = \varnothing$.

The input to the BCMLS data model is a series of operations, SELECT, INSERT, DELETE, UPDATE, from users at different security levels. The output is either a set of tuples returned from a SELECT statement or a success/failure from an INSERT, DELETE, or UPDATE command.

Theorem 1: The BCMLS model is secure.

We begin by proving the following two lemmas.

Lemma 1: *For any security level L, changing $T_{>L}$ does not affect the output to any user $s \in Z_{\leq L}$.*

Proof: When a SELECT statement is processed that is issued by an L' level user, where $L' \leq L$, no tuples in $T_{>L'}$ will be used in the calculation of the output, or placed into the returned tuple set. Since $L' \leq L$ implies $T_{>L'} \supseteq T_{>L}$, changing $T_{>L}$ does not affect the tuple set that is output to the user $s \in Z_{\leq L}$.

When an INSERT, DELETE, or UPDATE is given by any L' level user $s \in Z_{\leq L}$ ($L' \leq L$):

An INSERT statement is rejected iff:

1.   There is a duplicate tuple at the same level:

      t' $\in$ R such that pl(t' [TC]) = pl(t[TC]) and t' [SEID] = t[SEID];

2.   or it violates any of the integrity constraints described earlier.

A DELETE statement is rejected iff:

1.   the tuple satisfying the where condition of the delete statement is at a different security level:

$pl(t[TC]) \neq L$

2.   or it violates any of the integrity constraints described earlier.

An UPDATE statement is rejected iff:

1.   The tuple is a false tuple:

$lb(c, TC) = -L$

2.   or it violates any of the integrity constraints described earlier.

For INSERT, DELETE, or UPDATE, since $t, t' \notin T_{>L'} \supseteq T_{>L}$, changing $T_{>L}$ does not affect the success/failure output to $s \in Z_{\leq L}$. Therefore, changing $T_{>L}$ does not affect the tuple set that is output to the user $s \in Z_{\leq L}$.

Lemma 2: *For any security level L, deleting input from a user $s \in Z_{>L}$ does not change $T_{\leq L}$.*

Proof: We note that a user can change database states only by issuing an INSERT, DELETE, or UPDATE statement.

An INSERT statement issued by an L'-level user (L' > L) can only result in an L'-level tuple t'. Since L' > L, $t' \notin T_{\leq L}$.

A DELETE statement issued by an L'-level user (L' > L) can only:

1.   Delete L'-level tuples and propagate the changes to tuples at higher levels L"; or

2.   Delete or update referencing tuples at levels L", and propagate changes to higher levels L"'

Since L"' > L" > L' > L, the corresponding tuples t"', t", t' $\notin T_{\leq L}$.

An UPDATE statement issued by an L'-level user (L' > L) can either change an existing tuple at level L' or add a new L'-level tuple and propagate any changes to higher level tuples t" and t"' at levels L" and L"', respectively. Since L"' > L" > L' > L, the corresponding tuples t"', t", t' $\notin T_{\leq L}$.

We can see that deleting any input from user $s \in Z_{>L}$ does not change $T_{\leq L}$. We now prove Theorem 1.

Proof: [Theorem 1] From Lemma 1 and 2, for any security level L, since $Z = Z_{\leq L} \cup Z_{>L}$ and $Z_{\leq L} \cap Z_{>L} = \varnothing$, $T = T_{\leq L} \cup T_{>L}$ and $T_{\leq L} \cap T_{>L} = \varnothing$, deleting any input from user $s_1 \in Z_{>L}$ does not affect output to $s_2 \in Z_{\leq L}$.

Soundness

We now present a proof of the soundness of the BCMLS data model. Soundness is defined in Sandhu and Chen (1998) with the following two definitions:

Definition 2: *A legal database state is one in which all relation instances satisfy the integrity properties of the model.*

Definition 3: *A sound data model is one in which any sequence of provided operational statements will transform any legal database state to another legal database state.*

In order to demonstrate the soundness of our BCMLS data model, we must show that any sequence of operations will transform one legal database state into another legal database state. There are six integrity properties in the BCMLS model: Entity Integrity, Polyinstantiation Integrity, Base Tuple Integrity, Referential Integrity, Foreign Key Integrity, and Belief Integrity. All six of these properties must be satisfied for the database to be in a legal state.

Theorem 2: The BCMLS model is sound.

Proof: We prove that INSERT, DELETE, and UPDATE will transform a BCMLS database from one legal state to another legal state by showing that the six integrity properties are still satisfied after any of these operations. A legal database state is unchanged by the SELECT statement.

Insert

The semantics of the insert statement will enforce Entity Integrity, Foreign Key Integrity, and Referential Integrity. Assume we want to insert tuple t at security level c into relation **R**. Polyinstantiation Integrity, Base Tuple Integrity, and Belief Integrity are satisfied as follows:

1. Polyinstantiation Integrity is satisfied because:
    a. There is no tuple t' $\in$ **R** with t'[K] = t[K], pl(t'[KC]) = pl(t[KC]) = pl(t'[TC]) = c, since inserting the tuple t is permitted only if there is no t' $\in$ **R** such that t'[K] = t[K], pl(t'[KC]) = pl(t[KC]) and pl(t'[TC]) = c;
    b. There is no tuple t' $\in$ **R** with t'[K] = t[K], pl(t'[KC]) = pl(t[KC]) and pl(t'[TC]) > c, since the relation R satisfies base tuple integrity;
    c. There is no tuple t' $\in$ **R** with t'[K] = t[K], pl(t'[KC]) = pl(t[KC]) and pl(t'[TC]) < c, since the definition of a relation instance requires tc $\geq$ pl(t[kc]).
2. Base Tuple Integrity is satisfied, since there exists no t[A$_i$] $(1 \leq i \leq n)$ in t with pl(t[C$_i$]) < pl(t[TC]) because pl(t[C$_i$]) = pl(t[TC]) in a new tuple to insert.
3. Belief integrity is maintained because, by definition, the insertion of a new tuple at level c indicates a belief of true at that level.

Delete

Referential Integrity is enforced by the semantics of the delete operation. As a result, we must demonstrate that any database state after a delete statement satisfies Entity Integrity, Polyinstantiation Integrity, Base Tuple Integrity, Foreign Key Integrity, and Belief Integrity. We assume that all tuples t in R that satisfy the predicates in the delete statement at level c are to be deleted from R.

1. Entity Integrity is maintained because there is no tuple t' in R, that will have t'[SEID] or t'[K] changed as the result of the delete of t.
2. Polyinstantiation Integrity is maintained because:
    a. A new tuple is not added;
    b. Any tuple t' in R with t'[SEID] = t[SEID], pl(t'[KC]) = pl(t[KC]) and pl(t'[TC]) = c will be deleted;
    c. Any tuple t' in R with t'[SEID] = t[SEID], pl(t'[KC]) = pl(t[KC]) and pl(t'[TC]) > c will be either deleted or have c deleted from t'[KC] and t'[Ci] $(1 \leq i \leq n)$;
    d. By definition, there is no tuple t" $\in$ R with t"[SEID] = t[SEID], pl(t'[KC]) = pl(t[KC]), pl(t"[TC]) < c and pl[t"[C$_i$]) = c $(1 \leq i \leq n)$.

3. Base tuple integrity is maintained because all the tuples t' in relation R with t'[SEID] = t[SEID], pl(t'[KC]) = pl(t[KC]), pl(t'[TC]) > c, and pl(t'[Ci]) = c ($1 \leq i \leq n$) will be either deleted or belief level c deleted from t'[KC] and t'[Ci] ($1 \leq i \leq n$), resulting in a new base tuple.

4. Foreign Key Integrity is maintained because:

    a. All tuples t in the relation R originally satisfied the Foreign Key Integrity property;

    b. All tuples t' in the relation R with t'[SEID] = t[SEID], pl(t'[KC]) = pl(t[KC]), pl(t'[TC]) > c and pl(t'[C_{FK}]) = c will be deleted, or t'[A_{FK}] set to null or to a default value.

5. Belief integrity is maintained because upon deletion of a tuple, a user is prompted by the system to reassert his/her belief in all other tuples about the same entity.

Update

Entity Integrity, Foreign Key Integrity, and Referential Integrity are enforced by the semantics of the update operation. As a result, we must demonstrate that any database state after an update statement satisfies Polyinstantiation Integrity, Base Tuple Integrity, and Belief Integrity. We assume that all tuples t in R that satisfy the predicates in the update statement at level c are to be updated.

1. Polyinstantiation Integrity is maintained because:

    Update to non-key A_i:

    a. A tuple t with pl(t[TC]) = c will be updated. No changes are made to t[SEID], pl(t[KC]), pl(t[C_i]), or pl(t[TC]), and no new tuples are added.

    b. For any tuple t with pl(t[TC]) < c that is believed true at level c or is a mirage tuple, a new tuple t' based on t will be inserted on the c level.

        i.   Changes can be made to a t[C_i] in t, but no changes are made to a primary level pl(t[C_i]) ($1 \leq i \leq n$), or to pl(t[KC]), pl(t[TC]) or t[SEID];

        ii. In the new tuple t' the t'[SEID] = t[SEID], t'[K] = t[K], pl(t'[KC]) = pl(t[KC]) and pl(t'[TC]) = c. The appropriate t'[A_i] is updated and its corresponding t'[C_i]. There is no tuple t'' ∈ R with t''[SEID] = t'[SEID], t''[K] = t'[K], pl(t''[KC]) = pl(t'[KC]) and pl(t''[TC]) = c.

    Update to key K:

    a. A tuple t with pl(t[TC]) = c will be updated. The t[K] will be updated, while the attribute values of t[A_i]) $\leq$ c ($1 \leq i \leq n$) will not change. No changes are made to t[SEID], pl(t[KC]), pl(t[C_i]) ($1 \leq i \leq n$), or pl(t[TC]), and no new tuples are added.

b.　For any tuple t with pl(t[TC]) < c that is believed true at level c or is a mirage tuple, a new tuple t' based on t will be inserted on the c level. In the new tuple t', the t'[SEID] = t[SEID], t'[K] = new K, and pl(t'[TC]) = c. There is no tuple t" $\in$ R with t"[SEID] = t'[SEID], t"[K] = t'[K], pl(t"[KC]) = pl(t'[KC]), and pl(t"[TC]) = c.

2.　Base tuple integrity is maintained because:

Updates to non-key A_i:

a.　A tuple t with pl(t[TC]) = c will be updated. No changes are made to pl(t[C_i]) ($1 \leq i \leq n$), and there still exists a base tuple t" $\in$ R with t"[SEID] = t[SEID], pl(t"[KC]) , pl(t"[TC]) = pl(t"[C_i]) = c ($1 \leq i \leq n$).

b.　For any tuple t with pl(t[TC]) < c that is believed true at level c or is a mirage tuple, a new tuple t' based on t will be inserted on the c level. No changes are made to any pl(t[C_i]) ($1 \leq i \leq n$), and there still exists a base tuple t" $\in$ R with t"[SEID] = t[SEID] and pl(t"[KC]) = pl(t"[TC]) = pl(t"[C_i]) ($1 \leq i \leq n$).

Updates to key K:

a.　A tuple t with pl(t[TC]) = c will be updated. The t[K] will be updated, but no changes are made to t[SEID], pl(t[KC]), pl(t[C_i]), or pl(t[TC]), and no new tuples are added. There still exists a base tuple t" $\in$ R with t"[SEID] = t[SEID], pl(t"[KC]) = pl(t"[TC]) = pl(t"[C_i]) = c ($1 \leq i \leq n$).

b.　For any tuple t with pl(t[TC]) < c that is believed true at level c or is a mirage tuple, a new tuple t' based on t will be inserted on the c level. Again, since no changes are made to any pl(t[C_i]), there still exists a base tuple t" $\in$ R with t"[SEID] = t[SEID], pl(t"[TC]) = pl(t"[KC]) = pl(t"[C_i]) ($1 \leq i \leq n$).

3.　Belief Integrity is maintained because, as defined in the update operation constraints, a false tuple cannot be updated, only a true tuple. If a tuple to be updated is a mirage tuple, then a new tuple is inserted as described above.

Hence, we have demonstrated that any single operation INSERT, DELETE, UPDATE, and SELECT will transform any legal database state into another legal database state. Therefore, any sequence of these operations will transform any legal database state into another legal database state.

Conclusion

The inability to accommodate cover stories for key attributes (that is, the key-loop-hole) presents a major inefficiency of existing MLS models, which restricts their use in practical applications and limits the database access control. We presented a solution to this problem by developing a new MLS model that uses the concept of system-defined entity identifiers (SEID). In order to enable an implementation of the new model, based on the concept of system-defined entity identifiers, we made the necessary changes to the basic MLS properties and we developed the new relational algebra and update procedures. Theses changes can be implemented in a real system, without creating a performance overhead (Jukic, Nestorov, Vrbsky, & Parrish, 2005). Finally, we also demonstrated the soundness of the model and the increased expressive power of the SEID enhanced BCMLS model.

As was demonstrated by the examples, the solution presented here has great potential to make database access control methods more sophisticated, and therefore, more effective. As computer security in general, and database security in particular, continue to gain prominence in today's world, we hope that our proposed solution to a real security issue provides a useful addition to the arsenal of the security practitioners.

References

Baskerville, R., & Portougal, V. (2003). A possibility theory framework for security evaluation in national infrastructure protection. *Journal of Database Management, 14*(2), 1-13.

Bell, D. E., & LaPadula, L. J. (1974). *Secure computer systems: Mathematical foundations and model.* Technical report, MITRE Corporation.

Denning, D. E. (1988). The sea view security model. In *Proceedings of the IEEE Symposium on Security and Privacy*, Oakland, CA (pp. 218 -233).

Denning, D. E., & Lunt, T. F. (1987). A multilevel relational data model. In *Proceedings of the IEEE Symposium on Security and Privacy*, Oakland, CA (pp. 220-234).

Garvey, T. D., & Lunt, T. F. (1992). Cover stories for database security. In S. Jajodia & C. E. Landwehr (Eds.), *Database security V: Status and prospects*. North-Holland: Elsevier Science.

Gong, L., & Qian, X. (1995). Enriching the expressive power of security label. *IEEE Transactions on Knowledge and Data Engineering, 7*(5), 839-841.

Haigh, J. T., O'Brien, R. C., & Thomasen, D. J. (1991). The LDV secure relational DBMS model. In S. Jajodia & C. E. Landwehr (Eds.), *Database security V: Status and prospects* (pp. 265-279). North-Holland: Elsevier Science.

Jajodia, S., & Sandhu, R. (1990). Polyinstantiation integrity in multilevel relations. In *Proceedings of the IEEE Symposium on Security and Privacy*, Oakland, CA (pp. 104-115).

Jajodia, S., & Sandhu, R. (1991). Toward a multilevel secure relational data model. In *Proceedings of the ACM SIGMOD*, Denver, CO (pp. 50-59).

Jajodia, S., Sandhu, R., & Blaustein, B. T. (1995). Solutions to the polyinstantiation problem, essay 21 of information security. In M. Abrams, S. Jajodia, & H. Podell (Eds.), *An integrated collection of essays*. Los Alamitos, CA: IEEE Computer Security Press.

Jukic, N., Vrbsky, S., Parrish A., Dixon B., & Jukic, B. (1999). A belief-consistent multilevel secure relational data model. *Information Systems, 24*(5), 377-402.

Jukic, N., Nestorov, S., & Vrbsky, S. (2003). Closing the key-loophole in MLS databases. *ACM SIGMOD Record, 32*(2), 15-20.

Jukic, N., Nestorov, S., Vrbsky, S., & Parrish, A. (2005). Enhancing database access control by facilitating non-key related cover stories. *Journal of Database Management, 16*(3), 1-20.

Lunt, T. (1992). *Research directions in database security.* New York: Springler-Verlag.

Park, J. S., & Giordano, J. (2006). Access control requirements for preventing insider threats. *Intelligence and Security Informatics Conference* (pp. 529-534), San Diego, CA.

Sandhu, R., & Chen, F. (1995). The semantics and expressive power of the MLR data model. In *Proceedings of the IEEE Symposium on Security and Privacy*, Oakland, CA (pp. 128-143).

Sandhu, R., & Chen, F. (1998). The Multilevel Relational (MLR) data model. *Transactions on Information and System Security, 1*(1), 93-132.

Sandhu, R., & Jajodia, S. (1992). Polyinstantiation for cover stories. In *Proceedings of the European Symposium on Research in Computer Security*, Toulouse, France. Springer-Verlag.

Schaefer, M., Lyons, V. A., Martel, P. A., & Kanawati, A. (1995). TOP: A practical trusted ODMS. In *Proceedings of the 18th National Information Systems Security Conference*, Baltimore (pp. 50-62).

Smith, K., & Winslett, M. (1992). Entity modeling in the MLS relational model. In *Proceedings of the 18th VLDB Conference*, Vancouver, British Columbia (pp. 199-210).

Winslett, M., Smith, K., & Qian, X. (1994). Formal query languages for secure relational databases. *ACM Transactions on Database Systems*, *19*(4), 626-662.

About the Contributors

Keng Siau is the E.J. Faulkner professor of MIS at UNL. He is currently serving as the editor-in-chief of the *Journal of Database Management* and as the director of the UNL-IBM program. He received his PhD degree from the University of British Columbia (UBC), where he majored in MIS and minored in cognitive psychology. His master's and bachelor's degrees are in computer and information sciences from the National University of Singapore. Dr. Siau has over 200 academic publications. He has published more than 90 refereed journal articles, and these articles have appeared (or are forthcoming) in journals such as *Management Information Systems Quarterly*; *Communications of the ACM*; *IEEE Computer*; *Information Systems*; *ACM SIGMIS's Data Base*; *IEEE Transactions on Systems, Man, and Cybernetics*; *IEEE Transactions on Professional Communication*; *IEEE Transactions on Information Technology in Biomedicine*; *IEICE Transactions on Information and Systems*; *Data and Knowledge Engineering*; *Decision Support Systems*; *Journal of Information Technology*; *International Journal of Human-Computer Studies*; *International Journal of Human-Computer Interaction*; *Behaviour and Information Technology*; *Quarterly Journal of Electronic Commerce*; and others. In addition, he has published more than 100 refereed conference papers (including 10 ICIS papers), edited or co-edited more than 15 scholarly and research-oriented books, edited or coedited nine proceedings, and written more than 20 scholarly book chapters. He served as the organizing and program chair of the International Workshop on Evaluation of Modeling Methods in Systems Analysis and Design (EMMSAD, 1996-2005). He also served on the organizing committees of AMCIS 2005, ER 2006, and AMCIS 2007. For more information on Dr. Siau, please visit his Web site at http://www.ait.unl.edu/siau/.

* * *

Colleen Cunningham holds a master's degree in software engineering and a Master's in information science from the Pennsylvania State University (USA). She has worked as a systems analyst and a knowledge management analyst. She is currently a data warehouse manager and doctoral student in the College of Information Science and Technology at Drexel University (USA). As an adjunct faculty member in the College of Information Science and Technology at Drexel University, her teaching interests include database management systems and database administration. Her research interests include data warehousing to support customer relationship management (CRM), data mining, case-based reasoning (CBR), and knowledge management. Her work has appeared in the *Proceedings of the 7th ACM International Workshop on Data Warehousing* and *OLAP; Advances in Case-Based Reasoning*, *Lecture Notes in Artificial Intelligence*, *Information Technology and Organizations*, *Encyclopedia of Data Warehousing and Mining*, and the *Journal of Database Management*.

John Erickson is an assistant professor in the College of Business Administration at the University of Nebraska at Omaha (USA). His current research interests include the study of UML as an OO systems development tool, software engineering, and the impact of structural complexity upon the people and systems involved in the application development process. He has published in *Communications of the ACM*, the *Journal of Database Management*, several refereed conferences such as AMICIS, ICIS WITS, EMMSAD, and CAiSE, authored materials for a distance education course at the University of Nebraska-Lincoln, collaborated on a book chapter, and co-chaired minitracks at several AMCIS Conferences. He has served as a member of the program committee for EMMSAD and is on the editorial review board for the *Journal of Database Management*, and the *Decision Sciences Journal*.

Pedro Nuno San-Bento Furtado is an assistant professor of computer sciences at the University of Coimbra (Portugal), where he teaches both undergraduate and postgraduate curricula, mostly in data management related areas. He is also an active researcher in the Data Management group of the CISUC research laboratory. His research interests include data warehousing, approximate query answering, parallel and distributed database systems, with a focus on performance and scalability and data management in distributed data intensive systems. He received a PhD in computer science from the University of Coimbra (Portugal) (2000).

Patrick Heymans is a professor of software and information systems engineering at the PRECISE Research Centre at the University of Namur (Belgium). Dr. Heymans' research interests include information systems modeling, requirements engineering, and software product lines. He is the (co-) author of more than 30 refereed journal, conference, workshop papers, and book chapters. He is a member of the IEEE and the ERCIM working group on software evolution and serves regularly as a reviewer for premier international journals and on the program committees of renowned international conferences and workshops.

Nenad Jukic is an associate professor of information systems and the director of Graduate Certificate Program in Data Warehousing and Business Intelligence at Loyola University Chicago (USA) School of Business Administration. Dr. Jukic conducts active research in various information technology related areas, including data warehousing/business intelligence, database management, e-business, IT strategy, and data mining. His work was published in a number of management information systems and computer science journal and conference publications. Aside from academic work, his engagements include projects with U.S. military and government agencies, as well as consulting for corporations that vary from startups to Fortune 500 companies.

Lih Yunn Lee graduated with a master's degree from the University of Nebraska – Lincoln (USA). Her master thesis focuses on the use case and class diagrams in UML.

Mauri Leppänen is a lecturer at the Department of Computer Science and Information Systems at the University of Jyväskylä (Finland). He holds a PhD degree in Information Systems from the University of Jyväskylä. Leppänen is the author or co-author of about 30 publications in journals and conference proceedings on information systems development, metamodeling, method engineering, ontology engineering, and databases. He has served as a PC member of and a reviewer for several conferences such as ER, ICIS, EJC, and ECIS. He has participated in many national and international research projects, including the EU projects.

Sergio Luján-Mora is a lecturer at the Computer Science School at the University of Alicante (Spain). He received a BS in 1997, a master's degree in computer science in 1998, and a PhD in computer science from the University of Alicante (Spain) (2005). His research spans the fields of multidimensional databases, data warehouses,

OLAP techniques, database conceptual modeling and object oriented design, UML, Web engineering, and Web programming. He is author of several papers in national journals and international conferences, such as ER, UML, CAiSE, and DOLAP.

Raimundas Matulevičius received his PhD from the Norwegian University of Science and Technology (2005) in the area of computer and information science. Currently, he is a postdoctoral candidate at the PRECISE Research Centre at the University of Namur (Belgium). His research interests include goal-oriented modeling languages, enterprise modelling (EM), assessment of enterprise modeling languages (EMLs), requirements engineering (RE), requirements engineering tools (RE-tools), and process improvement in information systems.

Elizabeth S. Myrin is a PhD student in the Department of Marketing at Oklahoma State University (USA). She recently received her Bachelor of Science and Master of Business Administration degrees from Oklahoma State University. Myrin was honored as the top graduating senior in the Spears School of Business (2005).

Svetlozar Nestorov is an assistant professor of computer science at the University of Chicago (USA). Dr. Nestorov received his BS, MS, and PhD in computer science from Stanford University (USA). Dr. Nestorov is involved in active research in a spectrum of areas including artificial intelligence, computational science, bioinformatics, information integration, and Web technologies. He has advised and collaborated with a number of startups, including Google. His work was published in a number of journal and conference publications.

Mariska Netjes is a PhD candidate in business process management on faculty in the Technology Management Department at Eindhoven University of Technology (Netherlands). She holds a master's degree in industrial engineering and management. Her main research interests are business process redesign, business process management, and Petri nets.

G. Daryl Nord is professor of management information systems at Oklahoma State University (USA). He is currently managing director of the International Association for Computer Information Systems, editor of the *Journal of Computer Information Systems*, and serves on editorial boards for a number of professional journals. He has served on the National Publications Committee and Member Services Committee for the DSI. He has authored numerous conference proceedings and published articles in many journals, including *Expert Systems with Applications: An International Journal, Journal of Small Business Management, Journal of Information and Technology Management, Computerworld, Communications of* *the ACM, ACM Publications*, and others. Dr. Nord's research interests are in the areas of data quality, e-commerce systems, Internet monitoring, and systems project design and development.

Jeretta Horn Nord is a professor in the Department of Management Science and Information Systems and the Associate Dean for Undergraduate Programs at Oklahoma State University (USA). She recently served as a visiting scholar at the University of California-Los Angeles (USA) and as a visiting professor at the University of Southern Queensland (Australia). Jeretta is currently editor-in-chief of the *Journal of Computer Information Systems* and director of publications for the International Association for Computer Information Systems. She has authored numerous refereed articles and a textbook. Her current research interests are in the areas of data quality, global strategies for increasing the effectiveness of scholarly knowledge creation and transmission, and technological issues for entrepreneurs.

Andreas L. Opdahl is a professor of information systems development at the Department of Information Science and Media Studies at the University of Bergen (Norway). Dr. Opdahl is the author, co-author, or co-editor of more than fifty journal articles, book chapters, refereed archival conference papers and books on requirements engineering, multi-perspective enterprise and IS modeling, software performance engineering, and related areas. He is a member of IFIP WG8.1 on Design and Evaluation of Information Systems. He serves regularly as a reviewer for premier international journals and on the program committees of renowned international conferences and workshops.

Allen Parrish is a full professor in the Department of Computer Science and director of the CARE Research and Development Laboratory at the University of Alabama (USA). He received a PhD in computer and information science from the Ohio State University (USA). His research interests are in software testing, software deployment, data analysis and visualization, and highway safety information systems. His sponsors have included the National Science Foundation, the Federal Aviation Administration, the National Highway Transportation Safety Administration, the Federal Motor Carrier Safety Administration, the Department of Homeland Security, and a variety of other agencies.

Torben Bach Pedersen is an associate professor of computer science at Aalborg University (Denmark). His research interests include multidimensional databases, data streams, OLAP, data warehousing, federated databases, and location-based services. He received his PhD degree in computer science from Aalborg University. He is a member of the IEEE, the IEEE Computer Society, and the ACM.

Hajo A. Reijers is an assistant professor in business process management on faculty in the Department of Technology Management at Eindhoven University of Technology (Netherlands). He holds a PhD in computing science from the same university. In the past decade, he has worked for several management consultancy firms, most recently as a manager within the Deloitte and Touche consultancy practice. He has published in various scientific journals, such as the *Journal of Management Information Systems* and the *International Journal of Cooperative Information Systems*. His main research interests are business process management, workflow management systems, Petri nets, and simulation.

Il-Yeol Song is a professor in the College of Information Science and Technology at Drexel University (USA). He received his MS and PhD degrees from the Department of Computer Science, Louisiana State University (USA) (1984 and 1988, respectively). Dr. Song has won three teaching awards from Drexel University: Exemplary Teaching Award (1992), Teaching Excellence Award (2000), and the Lindback Distinguished Teaching Award (2001). Dr. Song has authored or co-authored more than 140 refereed technical articles in various journals, international conferences, and books. Dr. Song is a co-author of the ASIS Pratt_Severn Excellence in Writing Award at National ASIS meeting (1997) and the Best Paper Award in the 2004 IEEE CIBCB (2004). He is a co-editor-in-chief of the *Journal of System and Management Sciences*. He is also an associate editor for the *Journal of Database Management* and *International Journal of E-Business Research*. In addition, he was a guest editor for *Journal of Database Management, Data & Knowledge Engineering*, and *Decision Support Systems*.

Juan Trujillo is an associated professor at the Computer Science School at the University of Alicante (Spain). Trujillo received a PhD in computer science from the University of Alicante (Spain) (2001). His research interests include database modeling, data warehouses, conceptual design of data warehouses, multidimensional databases, data warehouse security and quality, mining data warehouses, OLAP, as well as object-oriented analysis and design with UML. He has published many papers in high quality international conferences such as ER, UML, ADBIS, CAiSE, WAIM and DAWAK. He has also published papers in highly cited international journals such as *IEEE Computer, Decision Support Systems* (DSS), *Data and Knowledge Engineering* (DKE), and *Information Systems* (IS). Dr. Trujillo has served as a Program Committee member of several workshops and conferences such as ER, DOLAP, DAWAK, DSS, JISBD. and SCI, and has also spent some time as a reviewer of several journals such as JDM, KAIS, ISOFT, and JODS. He has been Program Chair of DOLAP'05 and BP-UML'05, and Program Co-chair of DAWAK'05, DAWAK'06, and BP-UML'06. His e-mail is jtrujillo@dlsi.ua.es.

Wil M. P. van der Aalst is a full professor of information systems at the Technische Universiteit Eindhoven (TU/e) (Netherlands) and has a position in both the Department of Mathematics and Computer Science and the Department of Technology Management. Currently, he is also an adjunct professor at Queensland University of Technology (QUT) (Australia) working within the BPM group. His research interests include workflow management, process mining, Petri nets, business process management, process modeling, and process analysis.

Susan V. Vrbsky is an associate professor of computer science at the University of Alabama (USA). Dr. Vrbsky received her PhD in computer science from the University of Illinois, Urbana-Champaign (USA). She received an MS in computer science from Southern Illinois University, Carbondale, IL (USA) and a BA from Northwestern University in Evanston, IL (USA). Her research interests include real-time database systems, uncertainty and approximations, data grids and mobile data management. Dr. Vrbsky's work has been published in a number of journal and conference publications in the fields of computer science and information systems.

Hongjiang Xu is an assistant professor with the Business Information Systems Department at Central Michigan University (USA). Her PhD dissertation, titled *"Critical Success Factors for Accounting Information Systems Data Quality,"* was completed at the University of Southern Queensland (Australia). She has a Master of Commerce in information systems from the University of Queensland (Australia) and a graduate certificate in information systems from Griffith University (Australia). Prior to her academic career, she was a supervisor accountant for years. She holds CPA (Australia) status and several other accounting qualifications. She is also a member of AIS, IRMA, IACIS, and DSI. Her research interests are in the areas of data and information quality, accounting information systems, ERP systems, and electronic commerce.

Xuepeng Yin is currently a PhD student in computer science at Aalborg University (Denmark). His research interests include data streams, online analytical processing (OLAP), and online data integration. He is or has been working on data integration of OLAP systems and XML data and integration of current and historical stream data. He received his Master of Science degree in Computer Science from Aalborg University, and his Bachelor of Science degree from University of Shanghai for Science and Technology, (PRC). His PhD fellowship is funded by Danish Research Council for Technology and Production under grant no. 26-02-0277.

Index

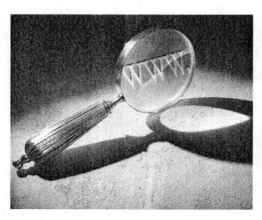